ENERGY POLICIES OF THE WORLD

ENERGY POLICIES OF THE WORLD VOLUME I

Canada, China, Arab States of the Persian Gulf, Venezuela, Iran

Edited by Gerard J. Mangone

Contributing Authors
Lawson A. W. Hunter
Choon-ho Park
Thomas C. Barger
Aníbal R. Martínez
Jahangir Amuzegar

See pages 375 and 376 for biographical information about the Editor and Contributing Authors

Volume I
ENERGY POLICIES OF THE WORLD

Canada, China,
Arab States of the Persian Gulf,
Venezuela, Iran

Edited by
GERARD J. MANGONE
Director, The Center for the Study of Marine Policy

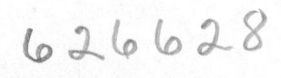

ELSEVIER
New York/Oxford/Amsterdam

American Elsevier Publishing Company, Inc.
52 Vanderbilt Avenue, New York, New York 10017

Elsevier Scientific Publishing Company
335 Jan Van Galenstraat, P.O. Box 211
Amsterdam, The Netherlands

Copyright © 1976 by The Center for the Study of Marine Policy
Published by American Elsevier Publishing Company, Inc.

Library of Congress Cataloging in Publication Data
Main entry under title:
Energy policies of the world.
Includes bibliographical references and index.
CONTENTS: v. 1. Canada, China, Arab States of the
Persian Gulf, Venezuela, Iran.
1. Energy policy—Collected works. 2. Power
resources—Collected works. I. Mangone, Gerard J.
HD9502.A1E538   333.8'2   76-18973
ISBN 0-444-00196-4

Manufactured in the United States of America

To Seymour Orlofsky
—a business executive with a love for learning

Contents

FOREWORD ix
INTRODUCTION xi

CANADA 1
by Lawson A. W. Hunter

The World Energy Crisis and Canada, 3. Governmental and Legal Framework, 5. Supply and Demand, 17. Factors Affecting A Canadian Energy Policy, 38. Conclusion, 53. Notes, 56.

CHINA 61
by Choon-ho Park

Introduction to China's Energy Situation, 63. Historical Background, 67. Oil Reserves, 75. Oil Production, 79. Major Production Centers, 84. Demand and Supply of Energy, 92. Oil Refining Capacity, 99. Imports and Exports of Oil, 104. Observations, 108. Selected Bibliography, 116.

ARAB STATES OF THE PERSIAN GULF 121
by Thomas C. Barger

Introduction, 123. Background of the Arab States on the Gulf, 124. Oil Industry: Pricing, Production, and Participation, 135. The Arab Oil Embargo of 1973, 151. Offshore Oil and Natural Gas, 159. Considerations in Making Energy Policy, 167. Policies of the Seven Gulf Countries, 177. Conclusion, 198. Bibliographical Note, 204.

VENEZUELA 205
by Anibal R. Martinez

Critical Contemporary Issues, 207. Historical Development of Energy Uses, 213. The Energy Resources of Venezuela, 218. The Production and Consumption of

Energy in Venezuela, *243*. Means and Ends in Formulating Policy, *258*. Recommendations for a Venezuelan Energy Policy, *274*. Observations and Conclusions, *287*. Selected References, *294*.

IRAN 295
by Jahangir Amuzegar

Introduction, *297*. The Development of Individual Fuel Policies, *299*. National Energy Policy: The 1970's and Beyond, *350*. Institutional Arrangements, *361*. The Future Energy Policy of Iran, *369*. Notes, *371*.

BIOGRAPHICAL INFORMATION	375
LISTING OF MAPS AND CHARTS	377
INDEX	379

Foreword

In 1975 the United States and the world faced a highly publicized energy crisis largely due to the rising demand for petroleum products and their escalting prices. Although many studies of the dynamic issues of energy supply, demand, prices, allocations, and conservation focused upon the American scene, few gave a systematic overview of the energy policies of foreign countries whose resources, trade, and political objectives impinged upon the U.S. economy.

The Center for the Study of Marine Policy in the graduate professional College of Marine Studies at the University of Delaware has been engaged in research on the legal, political, and economic aspects of the oceans, the seabed, and the coastal zone since its creation in January 1974. Among the interests of the Center, the exploitation of mineral resources from the sea floor and its subsoil was one of the major energy resource developments in this century. It suggested the importance of a series of studies that might enlighten scholars, public officials, businessmen, and public interest groups about the energy policies of foreign governments and their relation to the United States.

Five distinguished authors agreed to contribute their respective analyses and insights to a unique study of the country with which each had extraordinary experience. Thus Lawton A. W. Hunter is an eminently qualified observer of Canadian government and politics, having served in both the Department of Justice and the Department of Consumer and Corporate Affairs in Ottawa, with both legal training and post-doctoral work in marine studies. Choon-ho Park brings to his study of China's energy policy a knowledge of Korean, Japanese, and Chinese, years of study in the Orient, and first-hand experience with law of the sea matters, including concessionary claims and rights to the seabed for offshore exploitation. For the Arab Persian Gulf countries, few Americans in history have spent so much time in the region and have learned as much Arabic as Thomas C. Barger. One of the first mining engineers to arrive in Saudi Arabia in 1937 and one who helped the fantastic development of its petroleum resources, Barger grew to know the oil business better than almost anyone, rising in rank through the Arabian-American Oil Company to become its President in 1959. At the time of commissioning the study of Venezuela, Caracas was in the throes of nationalizing all the foreign oil properties. No one could have prepared a better analysis of his country's energy policy than Aníbal R. Martínez. He had long experience with the affiliate of the (Exxon) Standard Oil Company of New Jersey, Creole Petroleum, and was the chief of the enforcement and information departments of the Organization of Petroleum Exporting Countries. Later he served as executive director of the National Front for the Defense of Venezuelan Petroleum and was a member of the executive board of the Venezuelan State Oil Company, not to mention his authorship of several petroleum studies, notably the *Historia Petrolera Venezolana en 20 Jornadas*. To close this series, Ambassador Jahangir Amuzegar, an outstanding authority on economic policy, foreign technical assistance, planning, and development in Iran kindly found time to write a penetrating study. Among other ministerial posts, he was Chairman of the High Council of the National Iranian Oil Company and has headed the Iranian Economic Mission in Washington while writing for *Foreign Affairs* and other journals as well as co-authoring *Iran: Economic Development under Dualistic Conditions*.

The purpose of this volume is to illuminate the background, conditions, and influences upon the energy policies of key foreign countries around the world, and to examine some of the options available to the government and interested public for policies that can contribute to national development, international trade, and world peace. These studies in Volume One will be followed by other studies of Indonesia, the North Sea, and other countries with significant energy resources or uses in Volume Two.

The Center for the Study of Marine Policy wishes to thank the Columbia Gas System for its generous support of this series. Each study, however, is the responsibility of the individual authors and their opinions should not be attributed in any way to the Columbia Gas System or to the Center for the Study of Marine Policy. Among others who have helped in the production of this volume, Roslyn Foner deserves special credit for copy editing, Pamela Duncan for typesetting, and my own secretary, Gloria Cresswell, for her constant and cheerful assistance.

GERARD J. MANGONE
Director

Introduction

By 1850 the price of tallow candles in the United States had risen to fifteen cents a pound. Only six candles made a pound. The sperm oil of whales, by far the best source of illumination for the ordinary household of Boston, New York, or Philadelphia, had averaged about 80¢ a gallon until 1845, but its price soared in the next ten years to about $1.80 a gallon. Something better had to be found to meet the rising demand for lighting and to match the escalating prices of candles and whale oil. This was "rock oil" or petroleum, known to be a burnable substance for more than a thousand years, but never refined in the United States until 1850 and never drawn from the earth in large quantities by drilling until 1859.

In the subsequent one hundred years the use of petroleum revolutionized world society, first as oil was refined to light lamps and then burned for heat to be transformed into power to drive, lift, pull, thrust, and drill. And the price of petroleum has been cheap. From 1859 onward more and more pools of petroleum or reservoirs of gas were discovered, sucked from the porous underlying rocks, and refined at comparatively decreasing costs to propel ships, trains, and automobiles; to generate electricity; and to heat, cook, and cool.

Petroleum ousted whale oil for lighting in a single year in the United States; the burning of wood for fire was gradually reduced to ornamentation; and decade after decade, in both the United States and industrial Europe, coal, although not eliminated, yielded to oil and gas as the more convenient fuel. The chief cause of the shift of the industrialized nations to an ever-greater use of petroleum was its availability from seemingly limitless sources, first locally and then in developing countries at a low price.

During the nineteenth and early twentieth centuries the United States opened a whole spectacular series of wells that gushed forward with profligacy. Russia too spouted with oil finds, as did Roumania. Exploitation thereafter moved to Iran, Iraq, Indonesia, Mexico, Venezuela, and other countries. Fifty years ago most geologists believed there was no oil under Bahrain, Kuwait, or Saudi Arabia, only to discover the greatest of all petroleum reservoirs known on earth to date. Finally, following World War II, engineers pricked the seabed itself, locating and recovering more and more oil from submerged lands, in the Gulf of Mexico, the Persian Gulf, and the North Sea, moving offshore in many places to ever greater depths. But the comparative price of petroleum had begun to rise.

In the industrialized countries, like the United States, the costs for oil and gas started to go up in a society that required greater mining safety, more protection against environmental damage, better wages, and higher taxes under public price regulations. Moreover, the old wells began to decline in productivity while new wells were more costly to locate and exploit.

In the developing countries the changing scale of world power brought new governments into control of their resources. No longer ignorant of their wealth in petroleum and the shortages of the industrialized societies, and no longer intimidated by western European or American military intervention, these governments first demanded higher prices from the foreign operating companies and then took control of the operations by joint ventures, total nationalization, and other devices elaborated in the studies in this volume.

Thus, at the beginning of the 1970's, with the world-wide demand for petroleum and its products rising constantly and the costs of this energy source reversing its historical trend, a political crisis was in the making for the industrialized states. Not only had Japan, western Europe, and America become generally dependent upon a singularly cheap, convenient energy source, but millions of automobiles, the indispensable item of the 20th century modern society, were virtually helpless without gasoline. When the petroleum exporting countries threatened to cut off supplies abruptly unless the industrialized countries paid higher prices and adjusted their foreign policy, particularly with respect to Israel, international tension mounted. Under these circumstances, every country, whether industrialized or developing, has been forced to reconsider its energy policies for the remaining quarter of the twentieth century. Price increases for fuels will affect the economics of the poorer countries not endowed with coal or petroleum deposits more than the richer countries. And even those governments made fortunate by geology during the last century need to examine the limits of their finite mineral resources at present rates of exploitation as well as their own domestic needs in the future.

In this volume the energy policies of Canada, China, the Arab states of the Persian Gulf, Venezuela, and Iran are examined. All the countries studied have been or could be major petroleum product exporters, yet each of them has been giving serious reconsideration to both the diversification of its various energy uses at home and the international trade balances that must be maintained for economic growth and political peace.

In the case of Canada, for example, which has a complex governmental framework for the implementation of its energy policy, the 1973 oil crisis for the neighboring United States brought a fresh appraisal of Canadian resources, including their potential and prices, their ownership and management, and their conservation. Conscious of the anomaly of a country with a surplus of resources in its west being exported while the industrialized populous east required foreign imports, Ottawa had to take into account both a unique trading relationship with the United States and the political ramifications of protecting its resources at a good price for the Canadian people. Lawson A. W. Hunter has very skillfully drawn the dynamics of this fortunate though often perplexed country in reaching its energy policy decisions.

China is another matter. With almost 800,000,000 people and occupying 3,691,543 square miles of land, China is a giant state of the world. And it is no longer a sleeping giant, but one aroused by a revolutionary zeal. It is sternly bent upon industrial progress under conditions of national independence and a socialist economy guided by the Communist party.

For nearly all its history the chief source of energy for China was the muscle of its toiling masses, yet Marco Polo noted the widespread use of "burning black stones" by the Chinese in the thirteenth century. Moreover, China is alleged to have drilled the first oil well in the world in 1521. No one has ever doubted the ingenuity and stamina of the highly intelligent and resourceful Chinese people. Yet in the nineteenth century, weakened by internal strife, with a decaying shell of government under the minority Manchu dynasty, stiffly isolated from the rest of the world and technological progress, burdened by a rapidly increasing and impoverished population, and penetrated by superior forces from America, western Europe, Russia, and Japan, ancient China finally collapsed. The leadership of Chiang Kai-shek, heir to Sun Yat-sen, crumbled under the onslaughts of the Japanese army from without and then the attacks of the Communist partisans from within. Unable to recover the support of the people, especially the agrarian masses, by any mixture of force and persuasion, the Nationalist government gave way to the new People's Republic of China in 1949.

The last twenty-five years of Chinese history have not been easy. Whatever the costs to traditional culture and customs, to private property and enterprise, to the freedoms of press and speech, the government of China has been determined to pursue a policy of national self-efficiency, secure against any threat from the Soviet Union or the United States, while promoting an egalitarian society in which food, shelter, education, health care, and other social services, no matter how small or simple, will be shared by everyone.

By any western or Japanese standard, China is still a very poor country. Choon-ho Park, has, of course, emphasized that all figures about the Chinese economy must be examined carefully, but for the past ten years or so the gross national product of China seems to have grown at an average rate of four or five percent annually. Most of that growth has occurred in heavy industry and in consumer products, again bearing in mind that the initial base for these calculations was extremely low. Some 30% to 40% of the gross national product in 1975 will probably come from industry—and any further expansion, which may cause problems for agriculture, will surely require more use of energy.

Little more than ten percent of China's energy requirements has been met by oil. Even a developing country like India has six times as many automobiles per capita as China. The break with the Soviet Union beginning in 1960 with its effect upon technical assistance and supplies to China through the discovery and the development of both onshore and offshore production and the export of Chinese oil are traced in this volume, revealing that Chinese oil prices have soared and that distant transport will be expensive so long as no port in China can accommodate more than a 50,000-ton tanker. Finally Dr. Park examines the implications of Chinese energy policy for the Soviet Union, the United States, Japan, and other countries in the light of international relations and the political motivations of Peking.

The Middle East has had both old and new experiences with oil and gas, playing a star role upon the stage of world politics. As early as the thirteenth century Marco Polo had described with wonder the quantities of oil scooped up by crowds with vessels near present-day Baku to be used for healing, greasing, and burning. The modern boom of the Caspian oil industry, with its steam-powered drills, came in the 1870's. Thereafter entrepreneurs and exploiters turned to nearby Persia, and on 26 May 1908 oil was struck at Masjid-a-i-Sulaiman at 1200 feet underground. Within a year the Anglo-Persian Oil Company was formed, essentially at the behest of the British government, to exploit both this field and the rest of the William Knox D'Arcy concession, which dated from 1901.

Yet even greater finds of oil and gas were to come from Iraq and the western shores of the Persian Gulf, which were inhabited by Arabs. An increasing flood of petroleum from this region continued to revolutionize the world-wide use of energy and bring profound political-economic adjustments to the international system. In 1927 a well in Baba Gurgur near Kirkuk, Iraq gushed with oil—and American companies, for the first time, gained an interest (25%) in a Middle East concession. Two years earlier a New Zealander had obtained a concession to the island of Bahrain only twenty miles from the Saudi Arabian shore, but he sold an option to the Gulf Oil Company, which sold it in turn to Standard Oil of California (Socal). The first well on Bahrain was brought in by Bahrain on 14 October 1933. Then Kuwait, exploited jointly by Anglo-Persian and Gulf, produced oil in 1938. Finally on 1 May 1939, just four months before Germany invaded Poland and launched World War II, King Ibn Saud turned with his own giant hand the valve that opened the first well to commercial production in Saudi Arabia, under a concession to the California Arabian Standard Oil Company—Socal and the Texas Oil Company. Not a single U.S. government representative was present on that momentous occasion, because none was yet accredited to the King.

World War II slowed development in the Middle East, but since 1945 millions of tons of oil and billions of dollars have been exchanged between the Arab states of the Persian Gulf and the rest of the world. Ancient civilizations of date palms and shell fisheries, with tribal wars and desert wastes, have been swept pell-mell into western technologies and modern ways. With sudden and fantastic wealth these Arab states have gained extraordinary weight on the scales of international power. They have radically changed their relations with foreign oil companies and they have obtained universal public attention for the leverage they can exert in foreign policy through their valuable energy resources.

Yet wealth and power have brought their own problems to these countries. Thomas C. Barger gives a succinct but clear overview of the land and peoples of the Arab states of the Persian Gulf in this volume, and presents a detailed analysis of the production and pricing policies of oil, with valuable information on the Organization of Petroleum Exporting Countries and the oil embargoes. Most interesting are the conclusions about the future of energy policy in this region and their effect upon the United States and world political-economic relations.

Venezuelan energy policies captured news headlines even as the studies in this volume were being completed. On 29 August 1975 President Carlos Andrés Pérez signed into law a bill approved by the Venezuelan Chamber of Deputies and the Senate ordering the nationalization of the country's oil industry. Complete control over some 21 private companies, most of them subsidiaries of American corporations, like Exxon, Gulf, Mobil, Sun Oil, Texaco, Chevron, and Arco, took effect in January 1976. Although questions of compensation for the private companies and operations of the new national holding company through joint or cooperative ventures with foreign firms were still under discussion, the event of nationalization was dramatic in the development of Venezuela as a modern state. The nationalization act ended once and forever a remarkable period of more than half a century in which foreign oil companies first dominated the exploitation of Venezuelan petroleum resources, then gradually and grudgingly yielded more and more of their profits to the Caracas government with ever-diminishing returns upon their capital, and finally faced expropriation.

Throughout its history Venezuela had depended almost entirely upon agriculture for its economy until the twentieth century. Probably no more than two and a half million people lived in the country in 1900, mostly outside the cities, and the cultivation of crops was neither intensive nor highly productive, although before World War I, Venezuela was the second largest coffee exporter—after Brazil.

Oil stains on the seas and beaches were well-known in Venezuelan history, but modern production began in 1878 when the owner of a hacienda near Rubia, Manuel Antonio Pulido, found petroleum deposits, obtained a concession from the government, and, using a homemade still, processed kerosene for lighting fuel from the thick liquid that was pumped by hand from a shallow well into wooden barrels.

Nevertheless, the exploitation of Venezuela's petroleum resources languished. Without an assurance of title, enterprise was hardly attracted to make drilling investments. In 1904 the mining laws were amended to provide that the actual discovery of a mineral resource was no longer required in order to obtain a concession from the government. In the same year a 25-year contract for 1,214 hectares (almost 3,000 acres) was granted to Andrés Espina in the Perijá and Maracaibo districts of Zulia. Other such contracts covering very large areas were made—all to Venezuelan citizens—with the exception of contracts for the exploitation of asphalt. In the very years that witnessed the development of the automobile and the shift of ship propulsion from coal to oil, the exploitation of Venezuelan petroleum still lagged behind the rest of the world.

In 1912, Dr. Ralph Valladares, a Venezuelan lawyer, obtained a concession for an American group, the Caribbean Petroleum Company, and by 1914 two wells had been successfully drilled by the company. The British, through Dutch Shell, had established two local companies and brought in a few wells between 1914 to 1918. But total production in the country was only a couple of hundred thousand barrels. At this point Dr. Gumersindo Torres, a friend of the wily dictator Gómez, who completely dominated the country with a fearful iron rule until 1935, devised a new Petroleum Law (1920) that granted to the landowner the right to obtain a permit for exploration and the subsequent right to obtain a concession to exploit the area covered by his property. Not only would concessions be given to all who asked for them, but the concessions could be transferred to third parties, even foreigners. Within a short time millions of acres of the country's surface were covered by concessions and sold in the New York and London markets to a large number of petroleum companies, some of which greatly succeeded in Venezuela, but most of which failed after a few years.

The surge in the production of petroleum in Venezuela thereafter was fantastic. In 1920 about 500,000 barrels were produced; in 1930, about 135,000,000 barrels; in 1940, 186,000,000 barrels; and in 1950, 546,800,000; and as Aníbal Martínez shows, well over a billion barrels a year in the 1960's and '70's.

Petroleum is not the only source of energy for Venezuela, despite its immediate and vital importance to the economy, particularly in maintaining the export earnings of the country. Dr. Martínez carefully analyzes in his study not only production and reserve figures for petroleum, taking into account problems of increasing domestic consumption and the depletion of non-renewable resources, but he also examines the potential of natural gas, hydraulic power installations, coal, nuclear fission resources, and the sun as adjuncts to or substitutes for petroleum in formulating a coherent energy policy for the future of Venezuela. The institutional framework through which Venezuela has been attempting to achieve sound planning and the execution of its energy policy is also described. Keeping in mind the variety of resources available while taking account of domestic pressures and international constraints, these are very important years in the history of Venezuela as one of the greatest oil producing and oil exporting nations in the world.

The fifth and final part of this volume deals with the fabulous rise of Iran from poverty to wealth on a tide of black gold. At the turn of the twentieth century, Persia—or, as the state is now styled, Iran—was one of the most backward countries in the world. Some nine million people, 95% illiterate, lived mostly in villages or as nomads. Only four roads totaling eight hundred miles were suitable for wheeled transport, the rest being little more than mule tracks, and only eight miles of railroad had been built. On the Persian Gulf, about 88% of all ship tonnage calling at Iranian ports was British, and on the Caspian sea all cargo vessels touching Iranian ports were Russian. Only one electricity plant existed in the country—to supply power for the capital, Tehran. Those householders who could afford it usually burned wood or coal brought into town from the mines by pack animals, or kerosene imported from Russia.

Ninety percent of the Iranian population in 1900 was engaged in agriculture or related activities. Modern factories employing steam or water power were virtually unknown, although cottage industries, notably Persian carpets, existed in towns and villages. The production from primitive mines, mainly turquoise and copper, iron, lead, coal, salt, or marble, hardly amounted to half the value of the hand-worked carpet industry. No modern budget or statement of accounts was available from the government, but probably three-quarters of all the state's revenues, derived from taxes on land and animals, customs duties, lease of state monopolies, and revenue from Crown lands, as well as requisitions, fines, and confiscations went to an incompetent military force and "pensions."

Since 1908, when the first wells of Masjed-Sulaiman brought up substantial quantities of marketable oil, and particularly in the last fifteen years, the economy of Iran has been rapidly changing and has become almost a miracle of modernization. The rise in government revenues from oil alone soared from $285 million in 1960 to about $20 billion in 1974. A considerable amount of planning has gone into the economic development of Iran, and a major concern of the government is to utilize its depletable wealth in oil as wisely as possible for balanced growth in the future.

Jahangir Amuzegar describes the development of Iran's petroleum resources from the end of the nineteenth century to the mid-twentieth century—with the famous D'Arcy concession, the formation of the Anglo-Iranian Oil Company, and the bitter struggles between the government and British interests that led to the nationalization of the Company in 1951. In this drama the author also relates the pressures of the Russians upon Tehran as well as the abortive effort of the Iranians to attract American investment. He then analyzes the acrid negotiation from 1951 to 1954 culminating in the formation of a consortium of oil companies to develop and market the petroleum resources under the National Iranian Oil Company (NIOC), and the ways in which the government moved over the next decade to give NIOC in 1973 full and absolute control over the industry.

Dr. Amuzegar also deals with supply and price policy, production, export policy, and the financial arrangements of the Iranian oil industry as well as with electric power, natural gas, and the development of alternative energy sources, notably nuclear fuels. There is an outline of the institutional arrangements through which the government is managing Iranian energy policy and above all a valuable prospective view of the national energy policy of the country in the 1970's and beyond.

In sum, the energy policies of many states of the world have become inextricably linked to each other and the welfare of their peoples. Few issues will be so important to world politics in the future as the national use of energy resources and the international exchange of fuels to power the industry and commerce of modern society at fair prices. Without facts and figures and lacking the perspectives of all governments with stakes in energy resource development, a modern policy maker may be at a loss or worse, in peril of wrong decisions. The studies that follow are designed to illuminate the issues and to suggest problems that both business and government need to resolve in peaceful and equitable ways.

Canada
Lawson A.W. Hunter

THE WORLD ENERGY CRISIS AND CANADA

The so-called energy crisis precipitated by the rapid increase in the price in recent years of exportable oil and gas from the major surplus-producing countries of the world and aggravated by the embargoes and constraints on production introduced by OPEC countries in 1973 had less impact on Canada than on any other major industrial nation of the world. This was the case primarily because, on paper, Canada is a net exporter of energy resources. This is not to say that Canada was unaffected by the actions of OPEC, for although Canada is a net exporter of energy resources, the existing transportation and distribution system is not adequate for Canadian energy sources to reach all Canadians; consequently Canada imports about 45% of her crude oil requirements while exporting about 50% of her crude oil production.

In the last half of 1973 and the first half of 1974, the greatest governmental activity and public interest in energy questions ever seen in Canada occurred. Part of this activity was a direct response to the general international situation, with the government taking short-term measures to protect Canadians. For example, the federal Department of Supply and Services, in anticipation of shortages in fuel oil in eastern Canada in the winter of 1973-74, purchased Eastern European fuel oil at prices close to $20.00 a barrel. Severe shortages never developed, in part due to the mild winter of 1973-74 in that region of Canada. The federal government also shipped western Canadian oil through the Panama Canal and the St. Lawrence Seaway in late 1973 to supply eastern Canada, which was totally reliant on imported oil. But by far the greatest response to the crisis was the acceleration of development and debate on a long-term national energy policy for Canada.

The question of a national energy policy touched on several public issues. Even though Canada was not severely affected by the crisis of 1973, the shortages suffered in other countries brought home the present reality of the finite nature of hydrocarbon fuel resources. Canada needed a policy for the future to assure the development of her own energy resources if the country was to experience continued prosperity and economic growth. The problems of how to develop Canada's remaining oil and gas potential, at what cost and at what price to the ultimate consumer, had to be confronted. The question of restraint of energy use and demand in the future was also raised.

On the domestic political front the crisis resulted in the conflict between the three energy-producing provinces and the non-producing provinces and the federal government. Alberta, Saskatchewan, and British Columbia contribute almost all of Canada's production in oil and gas. Alberta in 1972 produced 84% of Canada's petroleum and 90% of her natural gas. In addition, the greatest amount of coal produced in Canada comes from Alberta and British Columbia. The conflict between the federal government and these producing provinces had serious constitutional dimensions as well.

Discussion of a national energy policy also had international ramifications. This was primarily true with respect to Canada's relations with her largest trading partner, the United States, both in terms of short-run measures to deal with the crisis, and in the long run, in connection with the development of energy resources. The politically sensitive question of a continental energy plan was raised once more.

To understand the policy options open to Canada with regard to energy in the future, it may be helpful to set out, first, the basic structure of the energy sector of the Canadian economy as well as the governmental role in energy policies. In considering the government's role in future energy policies, the constitutional situation will be discussed as well as the regulatory aspects of government activity, both federally and provincially. The sources of energy available to Canada will then be presented in an attempt to understand the supply side of the equation, as well as the projected demand for energy in Canada to the turn of the century and the implications of various prices and policies on demand.

After setting the physical, structural, and administrative framework, the various factors which combine to make up a national energy policy can be examined and various policy options available to Canada considered. Finally an effort will be made to place Canada's energy policies in a larger global framework.

The uncertainties involved in elaborating the shape of the future in an area as complex as energy are surely known to all. There are no simple solutions and no simplistic analysis will be presented. Rather this will be an attempt to establish briefly the situation in which Canada must develop her energy policies and then to consider the economic, political and legal factors which will bear on the selection of particular policies.

GOVERNMENTAL AND LEGAL FRAMEWORK

Canada is a federal state comprising ten provinces and two territories, the Yukon and the Northwest Territories. The federal government is primarily responsible for the government of the two Arctic territories but shares governmental responsibility with the ten provinces. The division of jurisdiction is determined by the British North America Act, an Act of the Imperial Parliament in London passed in 1867. This legislation of the British Parliament is Canada's written constitution, and Sections 91 and 92 of the Act set out the division of jurisdiction between the federal and provincial governments.[1] The interactions between Sections 91 and 92 bearing on the energy situation in Canada and the judicial interpretation of those sections are too complex to consider in detail. However, the principal areas of uncertainty and conflict can be summarized as follows: S.92(13) and S.109 give the provinces the ownership of most natural resources located in the provinces, including those resources situated underground. The exceptions to the Provinces' control of natural resources include some aspects of the fisheries [S.91 (12)] and offshore submarine resources. However, despite a Supreme Court decision by way of reference in favor of the federal government concerning the ownership of offshore resources, negotiations are still continuing between the coastal provinces and the federal government over their exploration, ownership, royalties, etc. As landlords of the resources used in energy generation, the producing provinces have a substantial impact on national energy policies, for they control production and determine fiscal matters important to the energy industry through royalty and taxation policies.

The federal government derives its jurisdiction over and interest in the energy field from several heads of Section 91. First, the "peace, order and good government" clause of Section 91 gives the federal government pre-emptive authority to act in matters of general national concern, although one should be careful not to construe the general power too broadly, for the courts have generally restricted its application to real emergency situations. Recent decisions have seen some liberalization of this strict interpretation.[2] However, it would be preferable, politically speaking, for the federal government to derive its jurisdiction for energy matters from a more specific and functional head of S. 91.

The federal government can also rely on the trade and commerce power for its jurisdiction. Even so, the Courts have interpreted the trade and commerce power rather restrictively, holding that it gives the federal government authority over international and interprovincial trade, but not over intraprovincial trade solely within one province.[3] Control over international and interprovincial trade, of course, is a very substantial power, for it allows the federal government to control the maximum amount of production in the country. However, the producing provinces control the minimum levels of production and presumably could through such control cut off export trade. Related to the trade and commerce power of the federal government is S.121 of the BNA Act which prohibits restrictions on the free flow of trade between the provinces.[4] Since the producing provinces are eager to maximize their revenues, the federal trade and commerce power, coupled with S.121, gives the federal government substantial authority over the natural energy resources of the country.

Finally the federal government, through its taxing power, has substantial fiscal levers. The corporate tax system is a principal, federal, fiscal control over the energy sector. Its primary effect is on the climate for exploration and development of new resources. The power to control exports also gives the federal government a fiscal lever through the imposition of export surcharges.

In the final analysis it is clear that neither the federal government nor the producing provinces have unfettered control over the production and supply of domestic energy resources in Canada. What often strikes outsiders, and particularly Americans, as difficult to understand, is the seeming inability of the federal government in Canada to determine national economic and hence energy policy. But in construing Canada's constitution, the courts in England and Canada have been rather more provincial-rights oriented than the Supreme Court of the United States has been on the question of states rights. This has been particularly true with respect to the interpretation of the trade and commerce power. Hence in Canada today it is not a simple matter for the federal government to determine production levels, prices, and the distribution of revenue and profits with respect to natural energy resources located in the provinces.

The division of jurisdiction between the federal and provincial governments gives rise to two levels of regulatory activity with respect to the energy sector in Canada, each pertaining to the particular jurisdictional competence.

◀ Federal Agencies

Prior to 1973, three administrative centres of activity operated by the federal government affected the energy industry. The first and most important of these was the National Energy Board, established in 1959.[5] The ambit of the Board's responsibilities is cast rather broadly, but it has been primarily concerned with hydrocarbon and electricity sectors.

Within its authority the Board has performed four main functions. First, the Board has provided the federal government with information and advice based on research it conducts and data it collects. From this data it has prepared forecasts on production and reserve figures. Hence the Board has monitored particular energy sectors and provided the government with basic information about those sectors.

The second function of the Board has been the operation of the National Oil Policy. This policy was brought into effect in 1960 after the report of the Royal Commission of Enquiry on Energy chaired by Henry Borden. The consequence of the National Oil Policy was the division of the country into two markets separated by the Ottawa Valley (Borden) Line. The western market, which included most of Ontario and the four western provinces, was supplied by Alberta oil. By guaranteeing a market for western Canada oil, the policy assured the development of the Canadian petroleum industry which was suffering from chronic overcapacity in 1960 with resultant uncompetitive prices for their product.

The eastern half of the country, including Montreal, Quebec and the four Atlantic provinces, continued to be supplied by cheaper imported oil from Venezuela and the Middle East. The policy was adopted after negotiations with the United States resulting in the opening of the midwest United States market to western Canadian crude. The American-owned Alberta producers are said to have arranged this tradeoff.[6] In exchange it was also agreed that the Montreal market would be served by a pipeline built mainly across United States territory from Portland, Maine to just east of Montreal.

The National Energy Board continued to administer this policy until the federal government announced during the 1973 crisis that it planned to extend the pipeline system from western Canada to Montreal. The announcement of the abolition of the

Ottawa Valley Line was made in the House of Commons by Prime Minister P. E. Trudeau on December 6, 1973.

The third function performed by the National Energy Board since its establishment has been the control and licensing of exports and imports of natural gas and electricity. This control was not applied to oil until the 1973 crisis, when the government announced control would extend to liquid hydrocarbons as well. The Board's control over gas exports is designed to ensure that only gas which is "surplus" to Canadian needs is exported. S.83(a), Part VI, Exports and Imports, of the National Energy Board Act requires that before issuing a licence for the export of gas, the Board must be satisfied that:

> The quantity of gas . . . to be exported does not exceed the surplus remaining after due allowance has been made for the reasonably foreseeable requirements for use in Canada having regard to the trends in the discovery of gas in Canada.

Further, S.83(b), Part VI of the Act requires that the Board be satisfied that:

> The price to be charged by an applicant for gas . . . exported by him is just and reasonable in relation to the public interest, before issuing a licence.

This "just and reasonable" test was intended to act as a counterpart to the U.S. Federal Power Commission's test that a "fair" price be charged for imports. As part of its authority to licence exports, the Board in part controls the price of exports since it can set tariffs and tolls on pipelines.

The fourth function which the Board has performed has been the power to grant a "certificate of public convenience and necessity," primarily for the construction of pipelines. In deciding to grant a certificate, the Board looks at (a) availability of the commodity; (b) the economic aspects of the project; (c) the financial feasibility of the project; (d) the market situation; and (e) the public interest.

Through these four functions, the National Energy Board has exercised a considerable influence on the Canadian energy picture. However, it should be noted that all decisions or orders of the Board are subject to disapproval by the Governor in Council. The Governor in Council (which means the federal Cabinet) cannot initiate orders but it can disapprove any order made by the Board. This power of disapproval allows the Cabinet to exercise very considerable influence and this influence has been growing in recent years. It would be impossible for a major project, such as the Mackenzie Valley pipeline, to go forward without government concurrence. The involvement of the political structure in energy decision-making began in the early 1970's when a more active stance was taken by the Department of Energy, Mines and Resources. The trend increased during the crisis situation and has considerably lessened the power and influence of the National Energy Board as well as making it a less independent body. This turn of events is all the more interesting since one of the primary reasons for the establishment of the Board in 1959 was the wish to remove sensitive energy decisions from the political area; a bit of wishful thinking on the part of the government of the day which, of course, could not survive events such as those which occurred in the fall of 1973.

The other two federal agencies with regulatory power affecting the energy industry prior to the energy crisis were the Department of Energy, Mines and Resources and the Department of Indian Affairs and Northern Development. Both Departments exercise regulatory powers because of their responsibility as landlords over particular frontier areas of land.

The Department of Indian Affairs administers the Territorial Lands Act[7] and thereby controls the use of land north of the 60° parallel. The Department also has general responsibility for the native people living north of the 60° parallel and for the development of the northern territories.

The Department of Energy, Mines and Resources has responsibility over offshore mineral rights. Hence, it has responsibility for the granting or licensing of exploratory drilling operations off Canada's east coast and in the offshore Arctic islands as well. It also has responsibility for negotiating with the provinces with respect to offshore mineral rights.

◄ *Provincial Agencies*

The provincial agencies prior to the 1973 crisis which had an impact on Canada's national energy policy were primarily those associated with the production of petroleum hydrocarbons in western Canada. And of these the agencies established in Alberta were by far the most important and developed.

Forms of energy other than hydrocarbons have been regulated by the provinces mainly through provincial-owned utilities concerned with the supply of electricity. These provincial agencies have also been responsibile for the development of nuclear electric generating plants. However, they have been heavily reliant on the Federal Atomic Energy Control Commission for expertise in nuclear power.

With regard to the agencies in hydrocarbon-producing provinces, there were two administrative agencies operating in Alberta prior to 1973 with regulatory authority. First was the Alberta Energy Resources Conservation Board, established in 1938, under the Oil and Conservation Act. This Board is the primary means of controlling production in Alberta. It sets production levels and promulgates standards designed to prevent wastage. It also establishes minimum spacing rules as a control on production. The Board collects its own royalties from operators in Alberta and hence is quite independent of the government. It is the only example of a truly independently financed administrative board in Canada. The Board also uses a "pro-rationing" system to establish monthly production quotas and divides up the quota among all operators. The Board also determines the amount of gas which may be exported from Alberta using a surplus system similar to that used by the National Energy Board.

The second agency operating in Alberta was the Public Utilities Board, under the Public Utilities Act of 1970, which is also the Board responsible for the Gas Utilities Act of the same year. Under the Gas Utilities Act all provincial gas utilities are regulated and the price of gas determined. Similar legislation exists in most other provinces for the regulation of public utilities supplying energy.

In summation, before the 1973 crisis the regulatory structure in Canada was relatively straightforward. The provincial bodies in consuming provinces were primarily concerned with the regulation of public utilities as natural monopolies. In producing provinces, there were agencies to conserve resources and control production levels. The federal agencies had regulatory authority in areas where the federal government owned property. The federal government also regulated the international and interprovincial movement of electricity and gas in the national interest.

Changes in the regulatory system, federally and provincially, occurred as a result of the so-called energy crisis. These changes incorporated both non-legislative fundamental changes in policy as well as proposed or enacted legislative changes.

◀ *Federal Agencies*

The National Energy Board has been affected by the energy crisis primarily through changes in government policy. The National Oil Policy was abandoned, requiring the Board to administer the transportation of petroleum products east of the Ottawa Valley line. Western crude moving into the Montreal and eastern market has required readjustments and diversions from the U.S. export market. The announcement by the government of a Sarnia to Montreal pipeline has meant that the Board will have to conduct a hearing and studies on the proposal to determine whether it should grant a certificate of convenience and necessity. The decision of the government to alter its pricing policy, at least for exports of oil and gas, saw the Board studying and proposing changes in basic pricing policy on export oil and gas. The government had announced its intention to levy an export tax equal to the difference between the frozen domestic price and the export price (which was to be the international price) as determined by the Board. Also it was clear that western Canadian gas was underpriced in the context of current U.S. prices and the value of substitutable fuel resources. The Minister of Energy, Mines and Resources announced the government's intention to raise gas prices to the U.S. dramatically on September 20th, 1974. The Board has also considered the implications for domestic prices of such export price changes. Finally the "self-sufficiency" aspect of the Government's policy has meant that the Board must proceed expeditiously with its processing of the application by Canadian Arctic Gas to build the Mackenzie Valley Pipeline, among other projects, and hearings were scheduled in 1974, with the expectation that they would continue for two years.

During the crisis, the federal government also proposed the creation of three new bodies. First, an Energy Supplies Allocation Board was established by legislation and was given the authority "to conserve the supplies of petroleum products within Canada during periods of national emergency caused by shortages or market disturbances affecting the national security and welfare and the economic stability of Canada . . ."[8] The Board could exercise its authority only after the Governor in Council (the Cabinet) had declared that a national emergency existed requiring the mandatory allocation of supplies, and it could ration supplies only after a further order by the Governor in Council stating the short supply was so serious as to require consumer rationing. Hence the Board has no real function in times of ample supply other than to monitor the situation and to prepare contingency plans for the implementation of an allocation and rationing program.

The government's intention was to have the Board administer and disperse the export tax on crude oil it had imposed, but legislation to that effect never passed the legislature before its dissolution for the July 8th, 1974 general election. The proposed legislation was entitled the Petroleum Administration Act, under which the National Energy Board would collect the tax, but the Energy Supplies Allocation Board would administer a Petroleum Import Cost Compensation program to subsidize importers of crude oil in non-producing provinces. The government announced its intention to reintroduce the legislation in the next session of Parliament, for it is vital to the negotiations between the federal government and the provinces.

The second agency which the government proposed to create as a result of the crisis was a national petroleum company to be called Petro-Can. The legislation to create the crown corporation died in Parliament in the spring of 1974, but the government was strongly committed to reintroduce it at an early date. The legislation would give the corporation the authority to engage in a broad-ranging set of activities. However, the government's stated intention was to use the corporation primarily in exploratory and research fields at the beginning. It could also be used as a public vehicle for purchasing world oil supplies in times of shortage to ensure Canadian supply and reduce reliance on multinational oil firms. In the longer run, the corporation could get into downstream marketing and distribution activities.

The third federal government agency resulting from the energy crisis was the creation of an office of Energy Conservation within the Department of Energy, Mines and Resources. The office has received little publicity and has had little impact to date. It primary functions will be to provide policy advice on energy conservation techniques, to conduct a limited research program and to publicize the means of and need for energy conservation. The first year budget of the office was about $500,000.

The federal government, of course, took many non-regulatory actions in response to the energy crisis, primarily of a fiscal nature, the long-run implications of which will be examined later.

◄ **Provincial Agencies**

From an administrative viewpoint, the most dramatic response by the provinces, following the energy crisis of 1973, was the establishment of a means to control prices in some provinces and additionally, in some cases, to allocate supply. The producing provinces, for example, adjusted royalty and tax rates to ensure they received a larger share of the return on petroleum production. The schemes by and large regulated the petroleum distributing industry much as a public utility would be regulated, that is, with broad, general tests applied by a quasi-judicial administrative board. The scheme which received the most publicity and has had the greatest impact was established by Nova Scotia. That province, using the basic framework of the previously existing Nova Scotia Gasoline Licensing Act,[9] gave the Public Utilities Board the power to set prices, and empowered the Board to require all wholesalers and retailers of gasoline products to file information with the Board respecting costs and prices. Further, no wholesaler may increase the price of gasoline or fuel oil without simultaneously filing a statement with the Board "setting forth the amount of the increase and the reasons for such increase." The Board may then hold a hearing requiring the wholesaler to justify the increase. If the Board has not been satisfied that the increase is "justified," it:

> . . . may by order determine the price or prices at which the wholesaler shall sell gasoline or fuel oil to retailers, consumers or classes of consumers in all or any part of the Province for use in the Province.

The tests applied by the Board to determine what is a "justified" price increase have not been specified in the Act. The amendment to the legislation before the Nova Scotia legislature would charge the Board to determine if prices were "just and reasonable" to both consumers and distributors, but this test does not seem any more specific than the "justified" test. It also conjures up notions of a just price used in medieval days, although it has a history of use in other Canadian legislation. The legislation in effect granted the Public Utilities Board the power to set prices with no specific legal standards. However, the Board has not shirked its duty and has ordered the rollback of prices by several oil firms including Imperial Oil Limited, Exxon's subsidiary in Canada and the largest oil company in Canada. The Board's authority has been somewhat hampered by the fact that it could only inquire into price increases after they had come into effect. The government of Nova Scotia, however, intends to amend the Act to give the Board prospective as well as retrospective authority.

The arbitrariness of the Nova Scotia legislation is unusual in Canadian law; yet the effectiveness and public acceptance of the measure is unquestioned. Premier Regan of Nova Scotia won re-election in June, 1974, largely on the basis of his tough stand during the energy crisis. Other provinces have been looking at the type of legislation enacted by Nova Scotia as a model. Provincial legislation enacted in response to the energy crisis to control price, except for Alberta, has also been short on standards and tests, giving great discretionary power to administrative tribunals.

British Columbia has also passed very arbitrary legislation. The Energy Act[10] passed by that province created a British Columbia Energy Commission with very broad powers, including the power to regulate the petroleum industry in British Columbia. Among these provisions was a prohibition of practices by any person engaged in the petroleum industry in British Columbia which "in the judgment of the Commission, *unduly*" increased the price of petroleum products to the consumer. The unamended version of the Act had used the word *clearly* rather than unduly, making it an offence to "clearly increase" the price of petroleum products. It is uncertain just what a clear increase in price would or would not have been. The Act also gave the Commission power to fix prices by an interim price order prior to a hearing and to require approval of price increases before they were imposed. Only increases which in the opinion of the Commission are "just and reasonable" are allowed. The sections giving the Commission power to fix prices had not yet been proclaimed in force at the end of 1974.

The Nova Scotia and British Columbia price-setting legislation were similar in many respects. On the other hand, the two major producing provinces adopted a somewhat different approach. Saskatchewan has given the Minister of Mineral Resources the power to set the price of crude petroleum and the wholesale price of refined petroleum products sold or delivered in Saskatchewan.[11] This is substantially different from the Nova Scotia legislation where a quasi-independent commission has the power to set prices. In Saskatchewan the Minister, a political figure, is directly responsible. In Alberta, the Public Utilities Board has the power to fix the just and reasonable price paid for natural gas used, consumed or retained within Alberta. Also, many gas purchase contracts have provided for the redetermination of the price of gas subject to the contract at some time during the life of the contract. Often the redetermined price has been established by arbitration. Since the Alberta government wished to increase the price of natural gas, the Alberta Arbitration Act set out the method to be used in redetermining prices by an arbitration board.[12] The method to be used is much more specific than that set out in any other legislation affecting price currently enforced in Canada. The basic field value of gas is its commodity value, less just and reasonable transportation and delivery costs. The "commodity value" means the aggregate of (1) "the thermal value of gas determined by reference to the volume-weighted average prices of substitutable energy sources competing with gas for the various end uses of gas in the consuming markets served . . . by the buyer of gas," and (2) "the premium value of gas determined by reference to its inherent special qualities when compared with competing energy sources." Hence, the legislation has tried to equate different energy sources and to establish a price based on the equivalent value of these competing energy resources. Its intent was quite different from that of the Nova Scotia or British Columbia legislation, which was designed to keep prices as low as possible.

Several provinces have passed legislation creating crown corporations to enter the petroleum business. The British Columbia government passed the Petroleum Corporation Act, creating the British Columbia Petroleum Corporation as an agent of the Crown in right of the Province.[13] The B. C. Corporation has the power to buy, sell, and deal in petroleum and natural gas; to purchase or build pipelines, gathering systems, and storage facilities; to explore for, develop and produce petroleum and natural gas, and to own and develop lands containing petroleum or natural gas. The Act does not appear to limit the powers of the corporation to land and property located in British Columbia. Presumably the company could own and develop land elsewhere in Canada and perhaps become an owner of Panarctic, the corporation controlled by the federal government. Soquip, the provincially-owned petroleum corporation in the province of Quebec, announced it wished to purchase shares in Panarctic, but the federal government's response was somewhat cool.

Alberta has created a separate crown corporation called the

Chart No. 1   ENERGY SUPPLY (Production, Including Exports, plus Imports) by Energy Source 1960-1970*

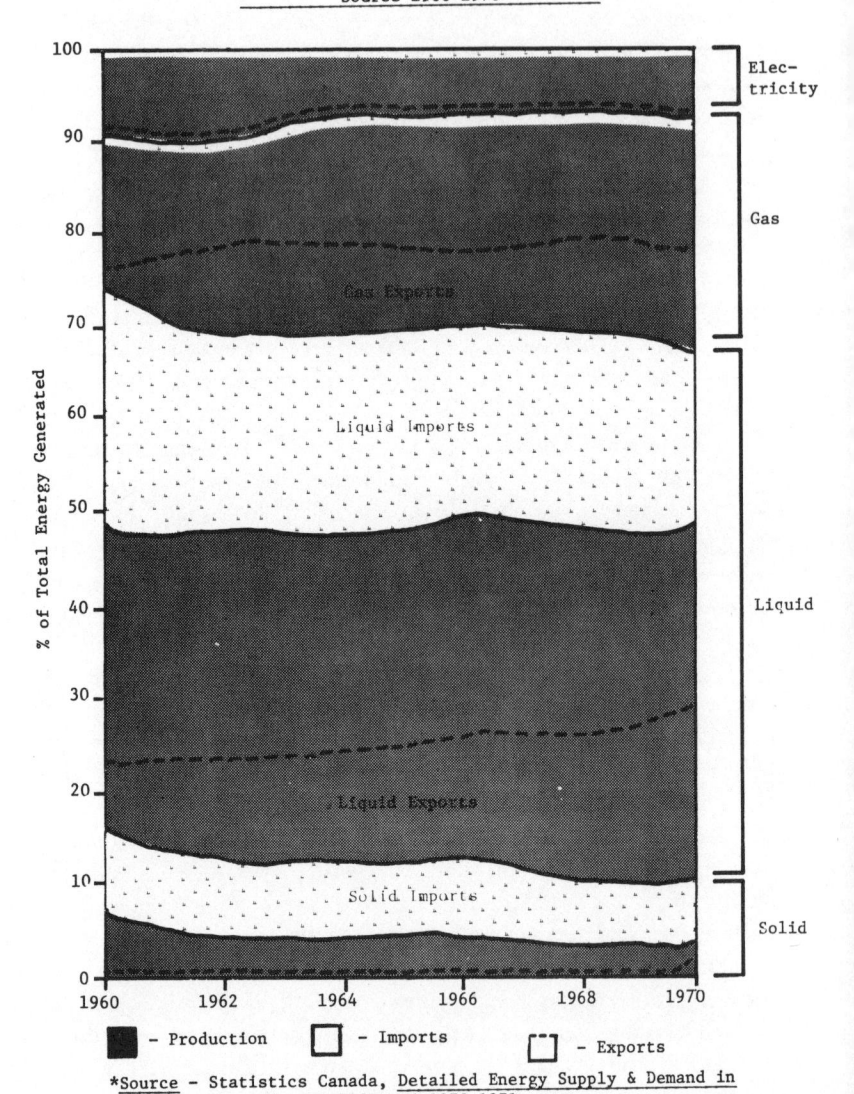

*Source - Statistics Canada, Detailed Energy Supply & Demand in Canada, 1958-1969 and 1970-1971.

Alberta Petroleum Marketing Commission.[14] It has powers very similar to the British Columbia Corporation, including the power to acquire, sell, or exchange petroleum in Alberta, and to own and operate pipelines and storage facilities in Alberta. It should be noted that the Alberta Corporation's activities have been restricted to the province of Alberta, contrary to the British Columbia example mentioned above. However, since Alberta owns the bulk of proved petroleum reserves in Canada, it has had less need to look outside the province to assure supply. Quebec had already created Soquip and, finally, Ontario announced that it intended to create a provincial energy company for the exploration and development of energy resources and to assure supplies in Ontario. As mentioned earlier, provincially-owned or -run corporations or departments already exist in the electricity field.

The number of provincial regulatory agencies, therefore, affecting the energy industry in Canada is not inconsiderable. Also the situation brought on by the Arab embargo hastened the direct intervention by all levels of government in the oil industry. The degree of intervention varies from jurisdiction to jurisdiction, but the lesson which can be learned from the response by governments to the crisis is that never again will the energy industry be allowed to be self-regulating to a large degree. Public expectations and the inability of the government to allow as vital an industry as energy to escape acting in the public interest ensure a changed relationship between the private energy industry and the public sector.

SUPPLY AND DEMAND

The primary concerns of the western world over energy are economic ones since energy is such a vital commodity in industrial society. Perhaps the most essential characteristic of energy from an economic perspective is *price*. It is the price of energy that serves as a means of rationing in normal situations of adequate supply and free competitive markets. But it is precisely an abnormal situation which precipitated the energy crisis of 1973. The Arab embargo made petroleum a short commodity with resultant effects on price. In addition the cartel of producing countries prevented the free market from operating, allowing those countries to exploit their monopoly situation. To ensure that they would not be continually held to ransom, the consuming countries sought ways to increase supply and reduce demand so that shortages might be

Chart No. 2   ENERGY SUPPLY (Total Energy Generated
by Production, Including Exports,
plus Imports) by Region
1960–1970**

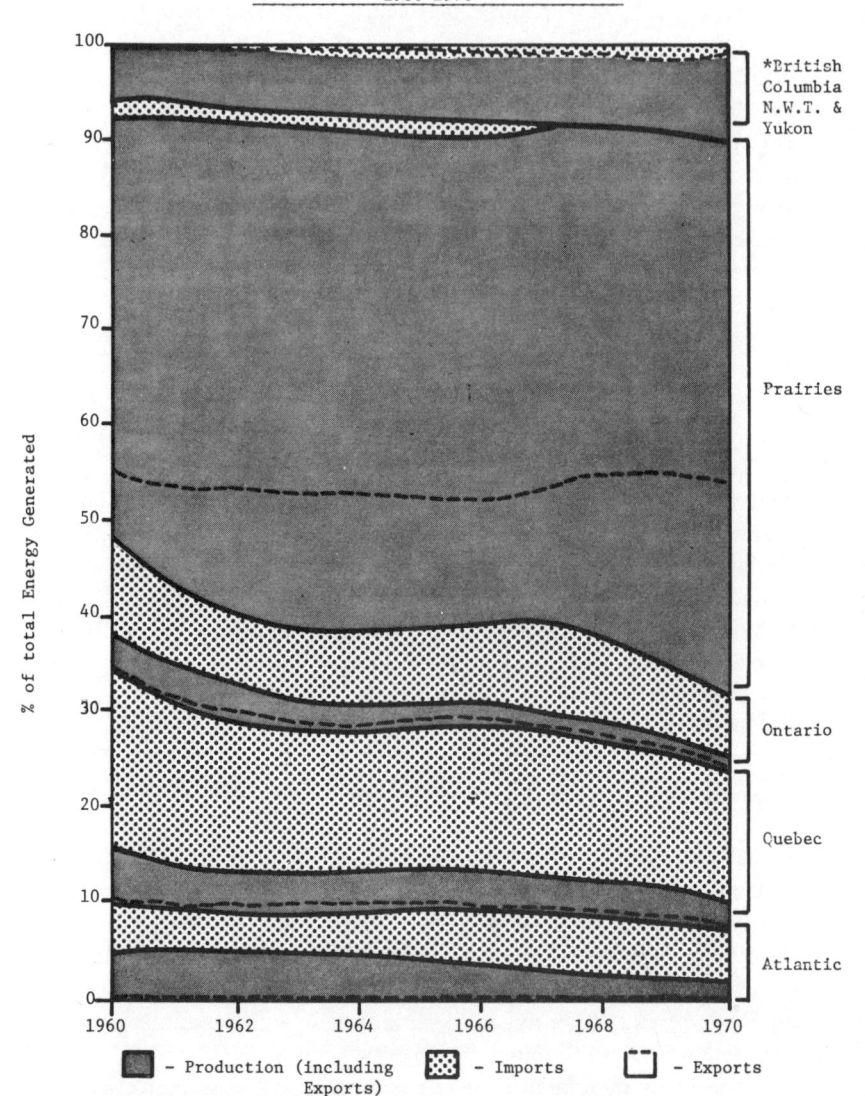

% of total Energy Generated

*British Columbia N.W.T. & Yukon

Prairies

Ontario

Quebec

Atlantic

■ – Production (including Exports)   ▨ – Imports   ⌷ – Exports

* In this region nearly all production was exported
** <u>Source</u> – Statistics Canada

prevented. Thus, whether in normal or abnormal circumstances, the supply and demand of energy resources and the factors affecting supply and demand are an essential element of any country's energy policy.

◄ *Energy Consumption and Supply Patterns*

In order to show the projected demand for energy in the future, it may be helpful to look at the past patterns of energy supply, demand, and consumption and to understand those patterns by energy source, geographical variations, and end-use consumption. This section will analyze the patterns of Canadian supply and consumption for the years 1960 through 1970, the last year for which accurate figures are available. During those years the average annual growth rate in demand for gas energy sources was 11.28%; for liquid energy sources it was 5.75%, and for solid energy sources, 3.7%.[15]

Chart Number 1 shows the total Canadian energy market from 1960 to 1970. The term energy used here means primary energy. That is, it is the gross energy available. It is a summation of the amount of energy available to the final consumer (or secondary energy) and the quantities consumed by the energy supply industries themselves, plus wastage and conversion losses. Conversion losses mean, for example, losses in processing refined petroleum, or losses due to thermal or mechanical inefficiencies in converting from one energy form to another. Such efficiency factors vary depending on the processes involved.

Each fuel source shows the amount produced, exported and imported as a percentage of the total market. It should be borne in mind that the chart shows the relative changes in percentage terms of the various energy sources considered. This should be considered against the general background of the absolute growth or decline in production and consumption of that energy source in the decade being considered.

The chart shows that solid fuels have declined in terms of market share primarily on the domestic production side. However, at the end of the decade there was a sharp increase in the percentage of domestic production entering the international market. This stems chiefly from the exportation of coal from Alberta and British Columbia to Japan. Exports of western Canadian coal are still increasing in quantity. Liquid exports, almost entirely to the United States, have risen at a faster rate than production growth. Increased exports resulted primarily from the overland exemption grants to Canada under the U. S. mandatory import quota system established by President Eisenhower in 1959, and the inability to prevent overage in the quotas granted Canada when Canadian crude was in great demand in the late 1960's. Liquid imports also declined slightly in relative terms over the decade, with the result that Canada was a net exporter of liquid energy in 1970.

Perhaps the most important feature of the chart is the increased percentage of the market taken by gas. Imports of gas are of minimal significance but exports of gas are very significant. Over 40% of Canada's gas production is exported to the United States on long-term supply contracts, usually of 25 years duration. Finally, electricity's share of the total market has declined, due primarily to the increasing use of gas as a competing energy source.

Chart Number 2 shows total primary energy generated by region for the decade 1960-1970. For purposes of inter-energy source comparisons, natural units have been converted to common B.T.U.'s (British Thermal Units). In this chart all energy sources are treated as part of total energy supply and the chart breaks down into domestic production, including exports plus imports. The value of the chart is that it shows the extreme dichotomy between the eastern industrial provinces and the producing western provinces. The chart does not show inter-regional movements of energy. In relative terms, it shows a fairly stable import market in the eastern regions and a rapidly expanding export market for western energy.

Map Number 1 shows the supply and disposition of crude oil, liquid natural gas and products for the year 1973, based on industry information, since official government figures were not available. The map shows not only imports and exports into and out of the country, but also inter-provincial movement of liquid products. It shows the heavy reliance of the eastern provinces on imported crude and the equally striking volumes of western liquid products being exported to various regions of the United States.

Map Number 2 shows the similar supply and disposition of Canadian natural gas in 1972, again based upon industry information. Since imports of natural gas into Canada are almost nil, the map shows the exports of natural gas plus the inter-provincial movements of natural gas. The map also shows that regions of Canada east of Toronto consume very little natural gas.

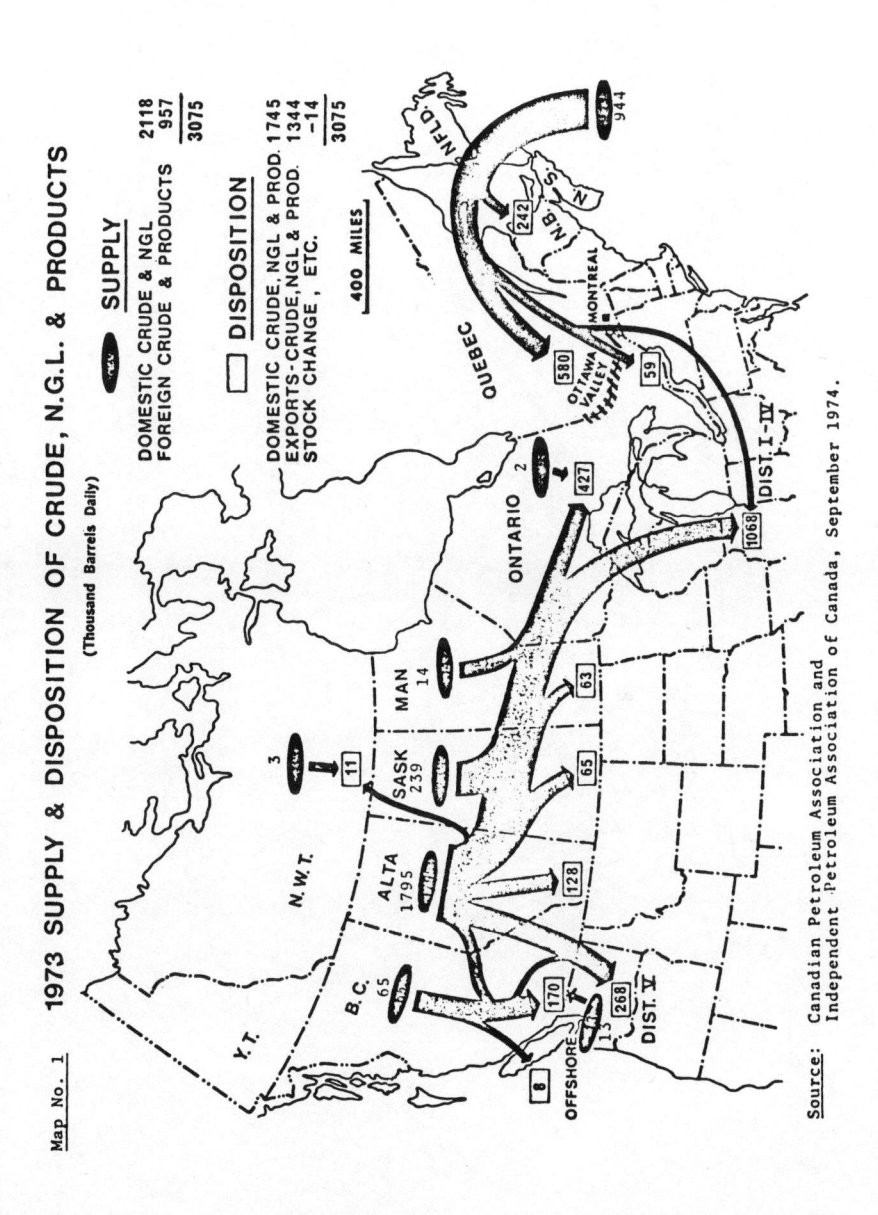

Map No. 1 1973 SUPPLY & DISPOSITION OF CRUDE, N.G.L. & PRODUCTS

(Thousand Barrels Daily)

SUPPLY
- DOMESTIC CRUDE & NGL — 2118
- FOREIGN CRUDE & PRODUCTS — 957
- Total — 3075

DISPOSITION
- DOMESTIC CRUDE, NGL & PROD. — 1745
- EXPORTS - CRUDE, NGL & PROD. — 1344
- STOCK CHANGE, ETC. — -14
- Total — 3075

Source: Canadian Petroleum Association and Independent Petroleum Association of Canada, September 1974.

Map No. 2

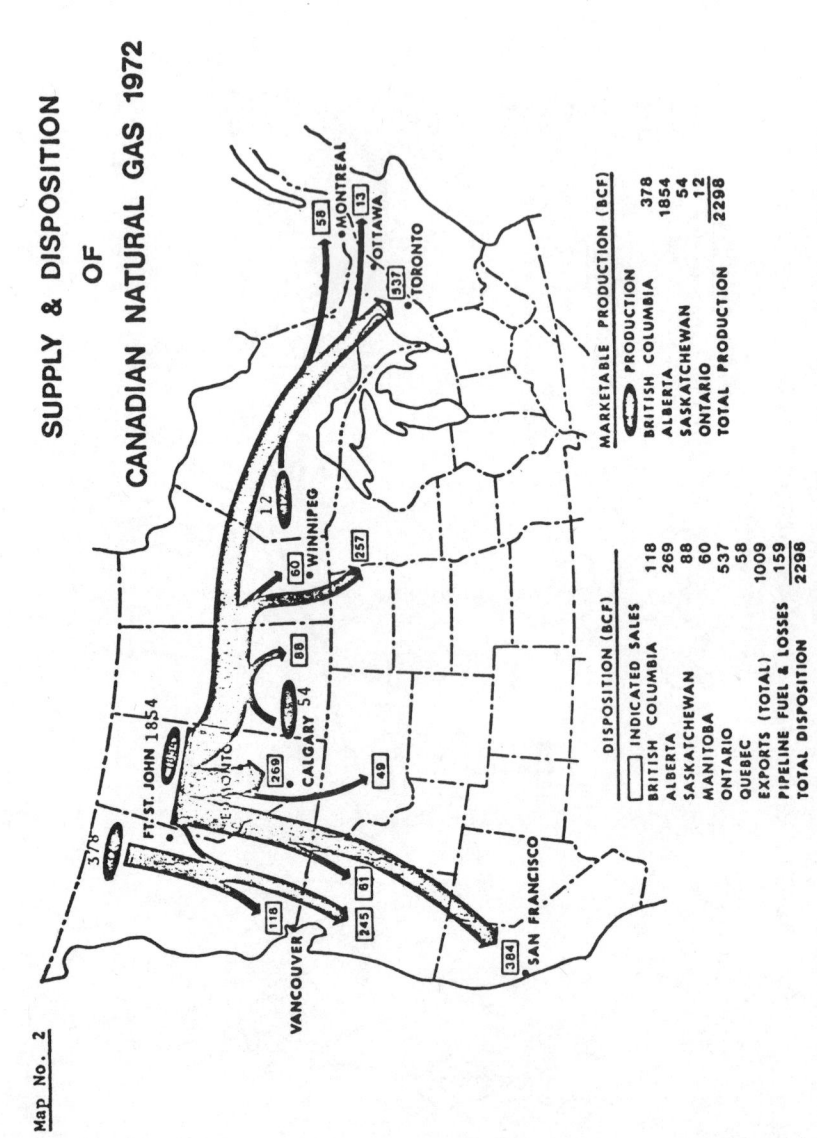

SUPPLY & DISPOSITION OF CANADIAN NATURAL GAS 1972

DISPOSITION (BCF)	
INDICATED SALES	
BRITISH COLUMBIA	118
ALBERTA	269
SASKATCHEWAN	88
MANITOBA	60
ONTARIO	537
QUEBEC	58
EXPORTS (TOTAL)	1009
PIPELINE FUEL & LOSSES	159
TOTAL DISPOSITION	2298

MARKETABLE PRODUCTION (BCF)	
BRITISH COLUMBIA	378
ALBERTA	1854
SASKATCHEWAN	54
ONTARIO	12
TOTAL PRODUCTION	2298

Source: Canadian Petroleum Association and Independent Petroleum Association of Canada, September 1974.

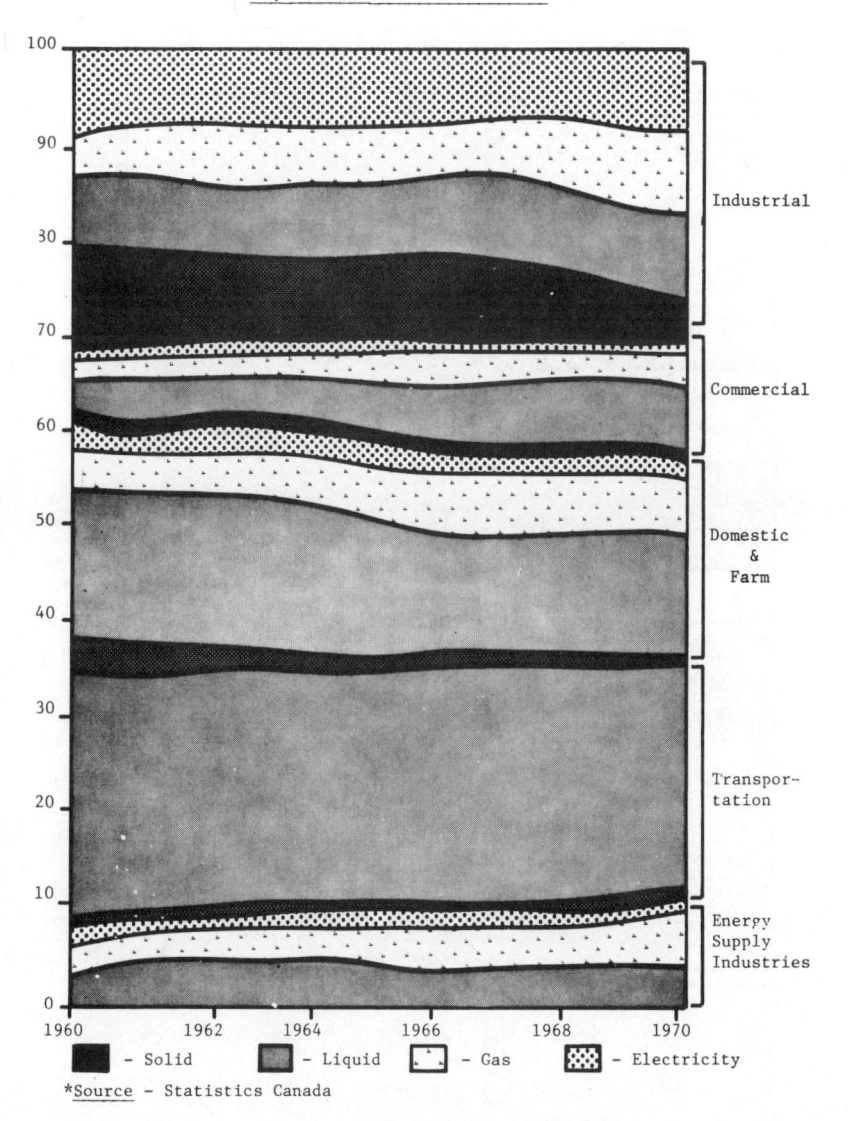

Chart No. 3 CONSUMPTION (Supply Allocation of Production & Imports-Exports) by Source and Use 1960-1970*

- Solid
- Liquid
- Gas
- Electricity

*Source - Statistics Canada

Chart No. 4   CONSUMPTION (Supply Allocation of
              Production & Imports-Exports)
              by Use and Region 1960-1970*

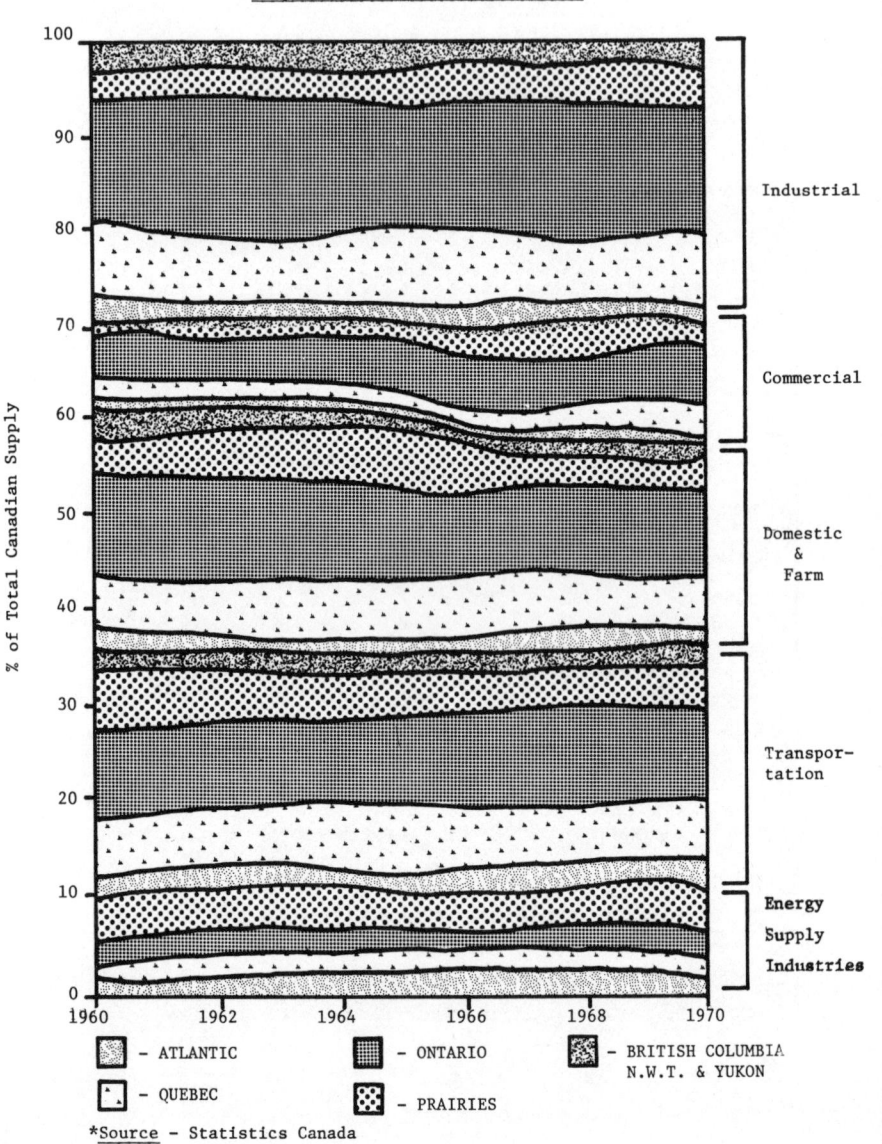

% of Total Canadian Supply

Industrial

Commercial

Domestic & Farm

Transportation

Energy Supply Industries

- ATLANTIC
- QUEBEC
- ONTARIO
- PRAIRIES
- BRITISH COLUMBIA N.W.T. & YUKON

*Source - Statistics Canada

Chart Number 3 moves from the supply of energy to the allocation of supplies according to energy source and end-use for the years 1960-1970. It deals only with the domestic Canadian market, hence it excludes exports of Canadian production. It does include imports. The chart is fairly complicated but its main feature shows a significant increase by all end-use sectors in their preference for gas over other energy sources. This is most pronounced in the industrial sector and the energy supply industries. The increase in gas usage in the industrial sectors is accompanied by a dramatic decline in the use of solid fuels by that sector, showing a swing away from coal.

The other main feature of the chart is the increasing share of the total market taken by the commercial and energy supply industries sectors, primarily at the expense of the domestic and farm sector. The growth in the commercial sector was related to the growth in the service sector, which now accounts for 60% of the labour force. The importance of the energy supply industries sector will likely be of continuing significance. For example, it is estimated that 19% of natural gas production in the Mackenzie Valley will be used for process shrinkage and compressor fuel for pipeline transportation. It is also unlikely that there will be significant advances in refining efficiencies or in cutting electricity losses during transmission. However, the fact that natural gas has been underpriced in a commodity value sense partly explains the rapid increase in natural gas consumption during the 1960's. Chart Number 3 also indicates that the industrial and transportation sectors remained relatively stable in their overall market shares.

Chart Number 4 shows the consumption of energy during the decade 1960-1970 by region and end-use. Except for the Energy Supply Industries, Ontario and Quebec dominate all end-use energy sectors. This should not be unexpected since they account for about two-thirds of the country's population and are the most highly industrialized regions in Canada. Perhaps the surprising feature of the chart is the decline and relatively small share of the domestic and farm sector taken by the prairie region. This is presumably accounted for by the increased rationalization and efficiency of the farm industry on the prairies as well as a relatively static population.

In conclusion, this section has graphically described the historical patterns of the Canadian energy market by energy source, regional consumption, and end-use sectors and hopefully indicated the main trends in the Canadian energy market, showing as well the regional differences and characteristics of the country.

◄ *Canadian Energy Resources*

Having set out the pattern of supply and consumption in Canada over a ten-year period, it may be useful to consider the remaining reserves of various energy sources in Canada. In discussing the question of reserves, an effort will be made to assess the likelihood of future success in discovering and utilizing new energy reserves.

Table Number 1 sets out the proved and potentially recoverable reserves in Canada by region and source. *Proved reserves* means the volume of liquid and gas fuels that can be demonstrated by geological and engineering data to be recoverable with reasonable certainty under existing economic and operating conditions. *Potential reserves* means the quantities of liquid, solid, and gas fuels postulated to be present in sedimentary rocks that are potentially available through intensive exploration and development. The Athabasca Tar Sands and Alberta Heavy Oil are treated as potential reserves here, even though parts of them may presently be recovered through expensive thermal or open-mining techniques. The various sources are expressed in natural units as well as their equivalent B.T.U. values to aid inter-energy source comparison. There is considerable certainty and confidence about the proved reserve figures, reflected here to March 1973, primarily because of the intensive development of the western Canadian fields where most of the proved reserves are situated. However, there is much less certainty about the potential reserves figures.

Looking at the reserves by energy type, the table shows that solid fuels are concentrated (98%) in the three western provinces. At 1973 production rates of 205 million tons, Canada has proved solid-fuels reserves sufficient to last 500 years, and potential reserves with a life index in the thousands of years. The major division of allocation of current coal production is between electric-generating facilities on the prairies and the Japanese export market. Transportation costs to Ontario are prohibitive of a major west-east market for coal currently. Thermal electric generation and the steel industries are the main users of coal in Ontario and that market is now supplied by closer American areas, but American energy policies of self-sufficiency may reduce this source for Ontario users in coming years. Solid fuels in this study exclude uranium

Table No. 1 PROVED & POTENTIAL RESERVES REMAINING (1973)[1]

a) SOLID

Region		Thousands of Short tons	Billions[2] of B.T.U.s
Nova Scotia	– Proved	126,000	2,683,800
	– Potential	115,000	2,385,000
New Brunswick	– Proved	10,000	213,000
	– Potential	–	–
Ontario	– Proved	240,000	5,112,000
	– Potential	–	–
Saskatoon	– Proved	291,500	6,208,950
	– Potential	11,722,400	249,687,120
Alberta	– Proved	2,203,900	46,943,070
	– Potential	45,036,300	959,273,190
British Columbia	– Proved	7,328,600	156,099,180
	– Potential	52,128,400	110,334,920
TOTAL	– Proved	10,200,000	217,260,000
	– Potential	109,002,100	1,321,680,230

b) LIQUID

		Billions of Barrels	Billions of B.T.U.s
Artic Islands & N.W.T	– Proved	.1	500,000
	– Potential	28.0	140,000,000
Western Canada (Provinces)	– Proved	9.7	48,500,000
	– Potential	5.0	25,000,000
Alberta Oil Sands & Heavy Oil[3]	– Proved	–	–
	– Potential	331.0	1,655,000,000
Eastern Canada (Provinces)	– Proved	.1	500,000
	– Potential	–	–
East Coast (offshore)	– Proved	–	–
	– Potential	50.0	250,000,000
TOTAL	– Proved	9.9	49,500,000
	– Potential	414.0	2,070,000,000

GAS

Region		Trillions of Cubic Feet	Billions of B.T.U.s
Western Canada (Provinces)	– Proved	51.4	51,400,000
	– Potential	44.0	44,000,000
Eastern Canada (Provinces)	– Proved	.3	300,000
	– Potential	–	–
East Coast (offshore)	– Proved	–	–
	– Potential	326.0	326,000,000
Arctic Islands & N.W.T.	– Proved	1.3	1,300,000
	– Potential	342.0	342,000,000
TOTAL	– Proved	53.0	53,000,000
	– Potential	712.0	712,000,000

TOTAL REMAINING RESERVES OF
SOLID, LIQUID, & GAS (Billions of B.T.U.s)

– Proved   319,760,000
– Potential 5,103,744,730

1– Source– Canadian Petroleum Association (Dec/72), Geological Survey of Canada, (Mar/73),

2– Conversion Factors – Solid=21.3, Liquids=5,000,000 Gas=1,000,000

3– Approx. 65 Billion Bbl's are recoverable through unconventional technology from the Athabasca Tar Sands reserves. They only include coal, coke, and coke oven gas. Reasonably assured reserves of uranium (U_3O_8) at the 1972 production rate result in a complete depletion in about 50 years, but the potential for additional resources is quite high. However, the expected growth in nuclear power also makes the 1972 base rate rather unrealistic.

The table shows that the substantial potential reserves of liquid energy sources are located in frontier regions of the country or in the unconventional Alberta Tar Sands and Alberta Heavy Oil deposits. The Alberta Tar Sands are contained mainly in major deposits at Athabasca, Wabasca and Peace River. They consist of a highly viscous bitumen-like crude oil mixed with sand. The deposits range from surface outcrops to over-burden depths of up to 2,000 feet. Normally the oil is tar-like and does not flow. To recover it requires unconventional mining techniques such as heat injection or solvents to reduce its viscosity and induce flow. The Alberta Heavy Oils are a transitional substance between the heavier oil-sand type bitumen deposits and conventional crude oil. They are highly viscous and either do not flow or flow at very low rates under normal conditions. They also require heat or solvents to induce normal flow.

With respect to the tar sands, one facility with a 50,000 barrel per day capacity has already been operating in the Athabasca deposit, and four more were announced or are planned. There is no question as to the potential reserves contained in the tar sands and heavy oil deposits. The three primary parameters in bringing this resource on line are technology, capital, and price, the first two limiting the third. If the great potential of these deposits is to be realized, new *in-situ* technology must be developed to allow access to the deeper lying deposits. Current and planned operations use an open-pit mining method. It is estimated that 30-40 billion barrels of crude can be recovered by this method. Also huge amounts of capital will be required. It has been estimated that each plant with a 100,000 barrel-per-day capacity will cost $2 billion.[16] Finally, a price of over $10.00 per barrel on a world price scale is necessary to make such operations viable. In 1974 the Canadian government froze the price of crude oil produced in Canada at just over $6.00 per barrel.

The tar sands do present a fairly large reserve for Canada with existing technology and world prices. However, a major breakthrough in technology is required before the real potential of these deposits can be realized. Also, producers must be assured a market at a price range that makes the huge investment required justifiable. The current frozen price of Canadian crude is too low to achieve this result.

Lastly, the table shows that the situation with gas is similar to that for liquid reserves. At current rates of production, proved reserve gas will last for another 23 years. Proved reserves are primarily located in western Canada. The potential reserves of gas are primarily located in frontier regions of the country, either offshore or in the high Arctic.

Since the frontier regions of the country will be the regions where future conventional reserves are likely to be found, it may be useful to examine the exploration work that has been going on in those areas and the results to date. Map Number 3 shows the location of the major sedimentary basins in Canada broken down into particular areas.

◀ East Coast

More than sixty wells have been drilled in the East-Coast offshore since exploratory drilling began. The offshore East Coast includes the Scotian Basin, the Avalon Uplift and Flemish Cap, the East Newfoundland Basin, the Labrador Shelf and Slope, the Baffin Island Shelf and Slope, and the St. Lawrence Platform. There have been a few encouraging finds to date, but virtually no commercial volumes of oil and gas encountered so far. However, the number of wells drilled so far is insufficient to reach any conclusions about the potential productivity of the region, although the lack of success has certainly been disappointing. It should be remembered, however, that there were 400 wells drilled in the North Sea to find six commercial gas fields and ten exploitable oil fields. Total exploration work obligations represented by offshore permits issued thus far for East-Coast exploration approach $1 billion.

Exploration to date indicates that the Scotian Basin of the south coast of Nova Scotia may eventually yield above-average quantities of gas relative to oil. However, the finds may be contained in many small pools with relatively few very large accumulations.

The Avalon Uplift and Flemish Cap, which covers the Grand Banks, is unlikely to contain commercially viable oil and gas reserves, according to reconnaissance seismic data.

Although no drilling has yet begun on the East Newfoundland Basin, it appears to have "the basic criteria for a major hydrocarbon province" with "above average source-bed potential."

Below-average yields are expected from the huge Labrador and Baffin Island Shelf and Slope. However, a recently announced find off Labrador makes this region look somewhat more promising. The Hudson Platform in Hudson's Bay, a huge sedimentary mass, is expected to have low commercial potential due to a lack of geological "traps" of hydrocarbon sources.

Exploration is currently underway in the St. Lawrence Platform at the mouth of the St. Lawrence River, but early results are very uncertain. Finally, a low commercial petroleum potential is expected from the Maritime Basins, owing to highly faulted sediments.[17]

In conclusion, it would appear that considerably more exploratory work will be necessary to ascertain the real potential of the East-Coast offshore area. Results to date have been rather disappointing, with the one recent exception mentioned above. The West Coast basins have been even less encouraging and it would be unrealistic to expect more than a token potential from them. Added to this have been major problems of data base development for analysis, and gaps in industry and government management and planning of offshore exploratory activity.

◄ The Arctic

Some major future gas fields are expected to be found in the Canadian Arctic. The Arctic region includes the Sverdrup Basin, the Arctic Fold Belt, the Arctic Stable platform, the Arctic Coastal Plain (North), the Beaufort-Mackenzie Delta Region and the Mainland North West Territories.

The Sverdrup Basin is considered to have good hydrocarbon potential, and much gas and some oil have been found. Giant fields and a number of different oil and gas systems have been anticipated, though most have not yet been evaluated by drilling. Although no significant hydrocarbon accumulations have been found to date in the Arctic Fold Belt, geologists have claimed that the area holds the possibility of the discovery of giant fields. The Arctic Stable Platform is expected to contain many shallow basins of oil but these are likely to occur only in small pools.

The Arctic Coastal Plain (North) remains something of a mystery due to lack of geological data. The data available is en-

Map No. 3

CANADA'S PETROLEUM BASINS

1. Sverdrup Basin
2. Arctic Fold Belt
3. Arctic Stable Platform
4. Arctic Coastal Plain (North)
5. Beaufort - MacKenzie
6. Mainland N.W.T.
7. Alta., Sask., Man.
8. Tar Sands & Heavy Oils
9. Scotian Basin (Inc. Sydney Basin)
10. Avalon Uplift & Flemish Cap
11. East Newfoundland Basin
12. Labrador Shelf & Slope
13. Baffin Island Shelf & Slope
14. Hudson Platform
15. St. Lawrence Platform

Source: Canadian Petroleum Association and Department of Energy, Mines and Resources.

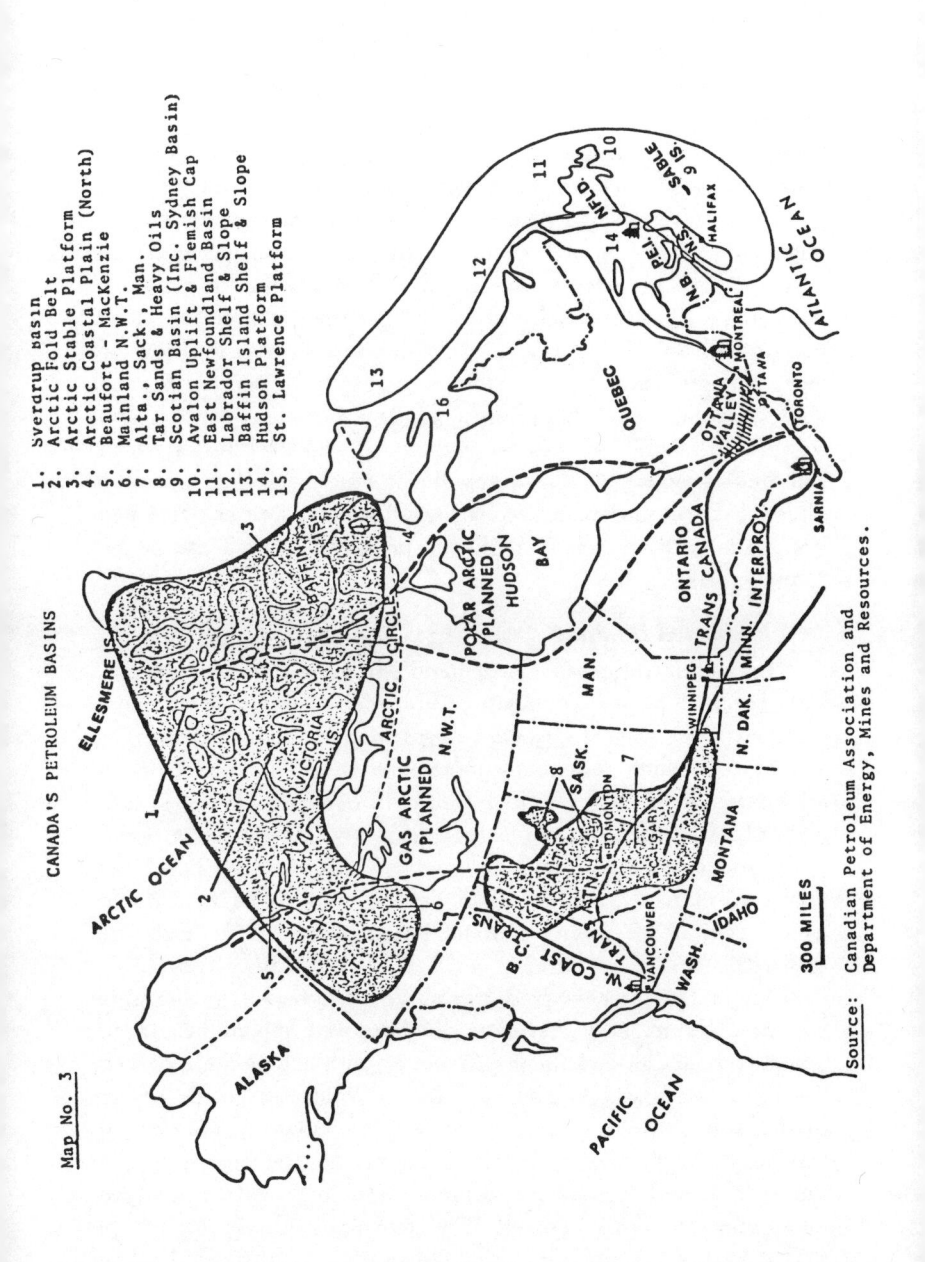

couraging and indicates a structure somewhat similar to the Beaufort Sea-Mackenzie Delta region which has been the most successful to date. Although actual proved gas reserves in the area are uncertain, it is believed that at least 15-20 trillion cubic feet has been discovered. As yet only small quantities of petroleum have been discovered, but further exploration offshore may yet yield oil.

While investors and developers have been placing their bets in huge sums on the Arctic's potential, the whole question of Arctic development still poses many unanswered questions; for example, the cost of a gas pipeline from the Mackenzie Delta region alone may exceed $5 billion. The need for engineering modifications to overcome problems of low temperature, shifting permafrost and waste disposal, as well as pressure for environmental controls and concern for native peoples all add up to severe obstacles which will undoubtedly slow the development and marketing of Arctic oil and gas. Yet the frontier regions just discussed must be developed if Canada is to rely on domestically produced oil and gas in the coming years.

◄ Projected Demand

Estimating future energy demand is a very uncertain exercise. Variables such as price, population, supply elasticity, price elasticity, technological advances, growth in gross national product, environmental constraints, and many more, are all legitimate factors in attempting to project into the future. Because of this great uncertainty, it is difficult to make forecasts, but they can be useful if the foundations and assumptions on which they are based are explained clearly. Then they can describe the events that would likely occur if the assumptions used in making the forecasts are realized.

There are three ways of forecasting future energy demand. The simplest method would be to divide proved reserves by current annual production and thereby come up with a time-life index on the remaining reserves. This type of projection was made earlier in this study with respect to certain energy sources. The second way would be to look at historical energy demand over a certain time period and thereby try to understand the trends in demand for particular energy sources. This technique is also limited in that it cannot account for major discontinuities affecting demand which may occure in the future. It does, however, aggregate underlying reasons for the development of trends during the time period in question. It is this sort of projection that will be used in the following pages and it is designed to show what demand might be if historic energy supply and demand patterns continue to the end of this century, with all other variables remaining unchanged.

The third approach would be to attempt to make educated guesses as to trends and patterns that will occur in the future and then take these factors into account in making projections, but it is questionable whether "educated" guesses are any more reliable than historical trends. In fact the basic conclusions reached when using the second and third methods in the Canadian situation seem to be quite similar.

The most important factor affecting demand is undoubtedly price.[18] However, this variable is perhaps the one which is the most uncertain. Also price is important, of course, only if the commodity in question is price-elastic. There is a fair amount of evidence to indicate that energy supplies are price-elastic and that certain pricing techniques result in considerable energy source substitution. It would seem, however, that the commodity pricing technique being currently proposed would only ensure that all price changes will be relative price changes, thus tending to dampen substitution consequent on price differential between energy sources. In considering projected demand, it should be borne in mind that a rapid change in price as experienced in 1973 is virtually unpredictable.

Using a linear projection of historical energy consumption patterns for the years 1960-1970, projections of energy demand by energy source to the year 2000 can be plotted. Chart Number 5 shows projected energy demand for solid fuels to 2000 A.D., broken down by end-use sector. It should be pointed out that the charts plot Canadian domestic demand only. They do not include exports of Canadian production. As mentioned earlier in this paper, there are substantial reserves of coal remaining in Canada. There would be some change if exports, primarily to Japan, were included. However, even so, the chart would show sufficient reserves remaining to the end of the century. Two other factors that would affect the chart are the development of coal gasification schemes and an increased market for western Canadian coal in Ontario and eastern Canada.

Chart Number 6 shows projected energy demand for liquid fuels to 2000 A.D. by end-use sector. The chart shows Canada's proved liquid reserves running out before the end of the century.

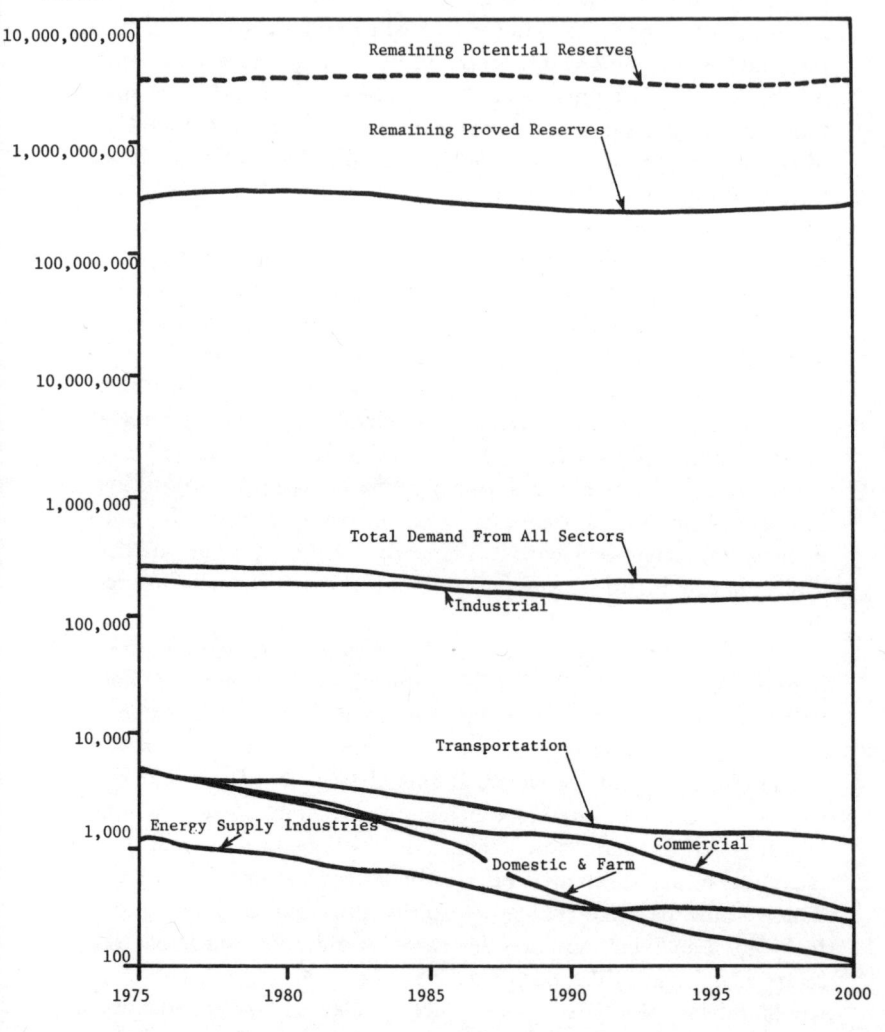

Chart No. 5 Projected Energy Demand For Solid Fuels   1975-2000

Billions of BTU's

Chart No. 6   Projected Demand For Liquid Fuels   1975-2000

Billions of BTU'S

* Includes ≈ 325,000,000 Billion BTU's recoverable from Athabasca Tar Sands through unconventional technology.

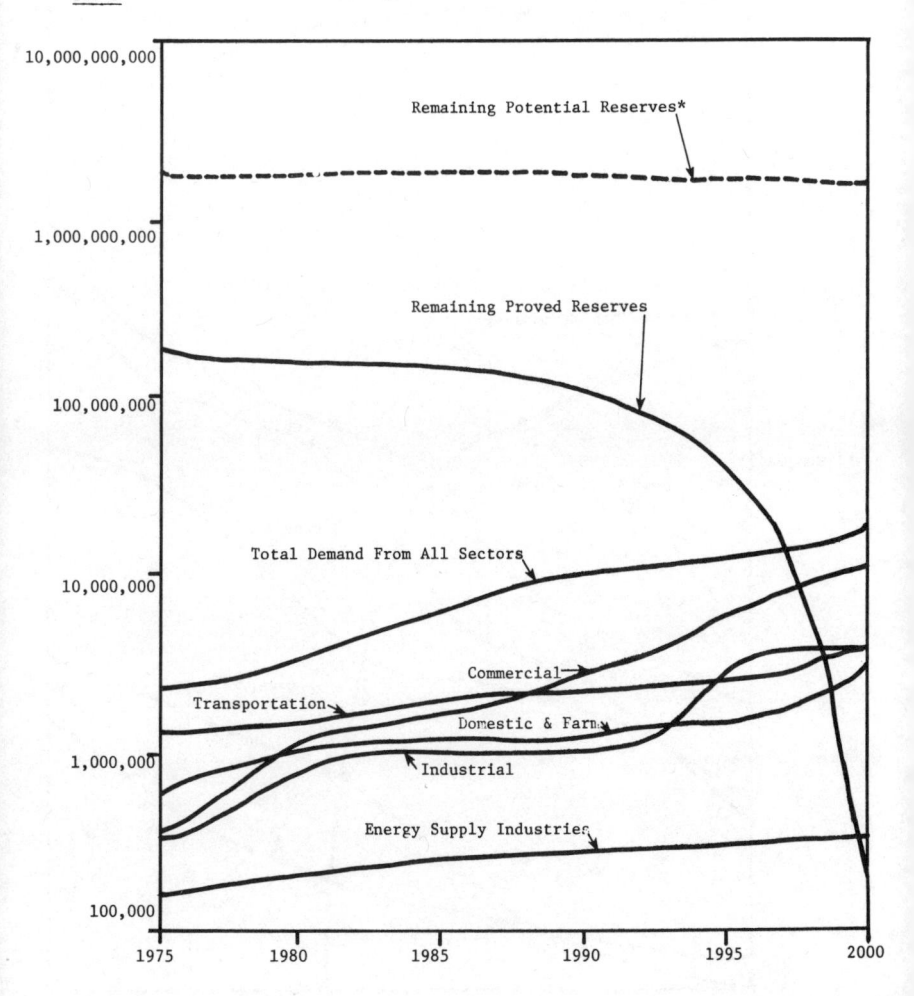

- Remaining Potential Reserves*
- Remaining Proved Reserves
- Total Demand From All Sectors
- Commercial
- Transportation
- Domestic & Farm
- Industrial
- Energy Supply Industries

Chart No. 7   Projection Demand For Gas Fuels   1975-2000

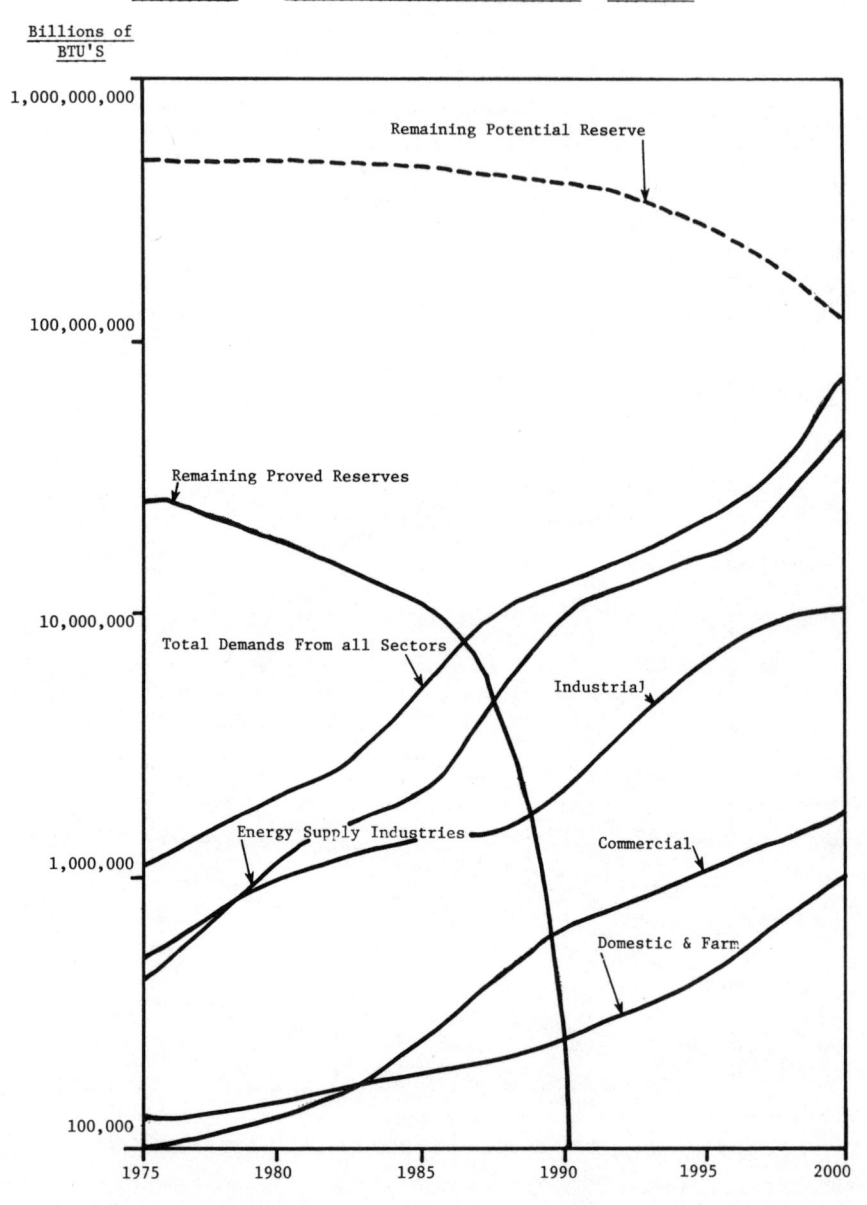

Billions of BTU'S

If exports to the United States continue, even at current rates, Canada's petroleum reserves would run out before 1990. The situation presented by the chart illustrates the need for intensive exploratory and development work to bring the potential reserves on line. This situation is further exacerbated by the fact that absolute reserves of liquid fuel have been declining in recent years. It should be recalled that the Athabasca Tar Sands have not been included as part of proved reserves. But the capital and technological problems inherent in developing the tar sands means that a total capacity of 500,000 barrels per day by 1985 would be optimistic, and to reach that figure a price range of over $10 per barrel would be required.

Chart Number 7 shows projected energy demand for gas fuels to 2000 A.D. This chart presents a most startling picture. It projects remaining proved reserves of gas fuels running out around 1990. And if U.S. exports continue at current rates, the date would be closer to 1985. The other startling feature of the chart is the sharp drop in remaining potential reserves, which is projected to occur after 1995.

Factors which would change the scenario are a decline in the rate of growth of the gas fuel sector from the 11.28% per year experienced in the sixties and an increase in the price of gas to make it comparable, on a commodity value basis, to liquid fuel. The demand for gas by the Energy Supply Industries sector is the most dramatic. The continued rate of growth of this sector at a 20% annual rate seems unlikely.

The final fuel source to be considered is electricity. It is difficult to chart future demand for electricity realistically from historical patterns. The rapid expansion of nuclear power-generating facilities is a major break with current patterns of electricity supply in Canada, where hydroelectric power accounts for nearly two-thirds of total supply. It has been estimated that nuclear-generated power will account for 10% of total energy by 1990 and 18% by the end of the century. It has also been estimated that capital expenditures of $50 billion will be required to meet this goal.

In conclusion, it would appear that Canada's proved reserves of gas and oil are going to run out by the turn of the century *without* considering future exports. There is, however, good potential for further petroleum discoveries in frontier and offshore regions. But these potential reserves must be discovered, explored and developed if Canada is to rely on petroleum as an energy source into the 21st century and if exports at a meaningful rate are to continue until the turn of the century. The success to date in discovering and exploiting new reserves in frontier regions suggests that major changes are likely in the nature and operation of the energy industries in Canada over the next few years.

FACTORS AFFECTING A CANADIAN ENERGY POLICY

The previous sections of this study have outlined the basic legal and institutional framework affecting energy policy in Canada as well as the supply and reserve aspects of energy resources. These factors do not constitute the complete spectrum of Canada's national energy situation, even if they do give indications of trends in energy development and likely bargaining postures. Hopefully, they do provide a framework by which to understand more perceptively the complex factors which are part of developing a national energy policy for Canada. This section will turn to a consideration of the factors, primarily of an economic and legal nature, which are additional and essential elements in a national energy policy.

These factors do not vary greatly from those found in many industrial countries, particularly those countries with substantial domestic energy production and reserves. For instance, the factors involved in energy policy in Canada and the United States are very similar. Nevertheless, the weight given to each factor and the precise decision-making context is never the same for any two countries.

It can be argued, of course, that Canada already has a national energy policy. That policy was given its most definitive and comprehensive parameters by the Prime Minister in his speech to the House of Commons on December 6, 1973.[19] The points called for in Mr. Trudeau's speech were:
  (1) the establishment of the Energy Supplies Allocation Board with power to allocate and ration petroleum products in times of shortage;
  (2) the abolishment of the "Ottawa Valley Line" to ensure an outlet for increased western oil production and to assure supply to the eastern provinces;
  (3) the establishment by the government of pricing policies to ensure sufficient incentives for the development of domestic oil resources, including frontier oil resources

such as the Arctic potential and non-conventional tar sands reserves;
(4) the government's intention not to "cut off exports" to the United States and not to "reduce imports from reliable suppliers";
(5) government measures to ensure that windfall returns and revenues from higher prices are used in a manner conducive to security of supply and self-sufficiency;
(6) the creation of a publicly-owned petroleum company primarily to expedite exploration and development;
(7) the building of a pipeline to serve Montreal and more easterly points and to assure supply;
(8) increased support for oil sands technology research to permit their full and rapid development;
(9) measures to maintain the price of heating oil during the then current heating season (the winter of 1973-74);
(10) the continuation of an export tax on oil equal to the difference between an agreed-upon domestic price and the export price as determined by the National Energy Board; and
(11) a sharing of the proceeds of the export tax with the producing provinces on an agreed-upon formula.

The speech was designed to assure and inform consumers, producer provinces, the United States, and private oil companies of the federal government's reasonable intentions. Although the principal thrusts of the policy have remained the same, it would be well to go behind some of the factors in the Prime Minister's speech in more detail in order to understand their full implications in the Canadian context.

The factors which will be considered cover a wide range of perspectives including economic, political, legal and social viewpoints. They do not present discrete problems by any means, but of all the factors the economic ones deserve the most important consideration.

Price. The price of energy to the ultimate consumer, whether householder or industrialist, is perhaps the most important, if subtle, factor affecting the energy industry. In a relatively competitive and open market, price serves an allocation or rationing function, albeit without much regard for distributive questions. It also acts as a regulator on demand, hence affecting the supply situation.

There is considerable discussion about the price elasticity of certain energy sources. Some authors argue that petroleum products are very price-responsive, while others argue that energy is such a vital commodity that the responsiveness to price is marginal at best. The truth, as usual, probably lies somewhere in the middle.

Price may also be used by the energy industry as a decision indicator of where to invest, after taking fiscal government measures into account. Consequently, price plays an important role in the guarantee of assurance of future supply. The method of pricing different energy sources also serves to regulate the substitution of one fuel source for another. In sum, price and pricing policies are a vital factor in any national energy policy. Granted that the action of cartels such as OPEC, and that political questions beyond national control may displace major policy options available to consuming countries, nevertheless, the pricing stance of consuming countries is an important factor in bargaining with the producing countries, as well as vitally affecting the interests of its own nationals. In countries such as Canada, which enjoy a large domestic production capacity, pricing policy is of even more importance.

However important it may be, price is still a very elusive factor. In essence it provides only a snapshot of the present. It is this elusive characteristic of price as intermediary between the past and future which complicates policies toward price. In 1973 when the international price of imported petroleum shot rapidly upward, the Canadian government froze the price of oil products in Canada below the new international price to protect Canadian consumers from the full impact of the new prices. However, the embargo imposed by the Arabs served as a notice of the fragility of supply resources and hastened a move toward self-sufficiency by the Canadian government. But the best incentive to private industry to explore for new petroleum in Canada was a guarantee of a higher price for newly discovered products in years to come. Thus, it has been possible for the Canadian government to cushion Canada's consumers from the full impact of international oil prices since the fall of 1973, but it has also been necessary to consider the price at which the government was willing to let new domestic energy production be sold in order to ensure that new supplies were forthcoming.

Although the federal government froze the price of crude oil in September, 1973, the price has since risen to $6.50 per barrel following a joint agreement of the federal government and the provinces at an energy conference of first ministers in February, 1974. However, this price was still about $5.00 per barrel lower than the 1974 international prices for oil. To offset the higher price of imported oil flowing into the five eastern provinces, the federal government has subsidized those imports by paying a consumer subsidy equal to the differential between the world price and the frozen domestic price. The cost of this subsidy program has been enormous: about $2 billion per annum. To raise this revenue, the federal government by legislation imposed an export tax on all oil exported from the country.[20] The United States is actually the only export customer for Canadian crude oil from western Canada. The tax was equivalent to the difference between the posted domestic price and the international price in the Chicago market. Since Canada in 1974 exported slightly more oil than it imported, the ledger showed a slight surplus as a result of this action.

It is likely that the price of oil in Canada will continue to rise, probably in stages to cushion the impact of the increases. It can be argued that if the price of Canadian oil does not rise and international prices remain at or near current levels, intense pressure will be applied to Canada to increase the price to remove the non-tariff trade advantage given to Canadian industry through lower fuel costs. The evidence of the real impact of energy costs on Canada's trade practices is still unclear, for most of Canada's major export industries such as pulp and paper and mining are not energy cost intensive. Another factor influencing a move toward an increased price is the likelihood that the import-export ledger, now tilted slightly toward exports, will shift within the next five years. Hence to continue the consumer subsidy, when imports exceed exports, would be very costly and have an adverse effect on the country's balance of payments position. Therefore, a staged increase in price is the most likely pricing policy for Canada.

A problem which has not yet been solved with respect to pricing policy, however, is the method of pricing different sources of energy. It was noted previously that the use of natural gas has increased much more rapidly than other fuel sources in recent years. A primary reason for the rapid increase in natural gas consumption has been the cost approach to pricing adopted in the past.[21] This approach is largely due to the same method of pricing adopted until fairly recently by the Federal Power Commission in the United States. However, the twenty-five year contracts usually written for gas also kept prices low. So also did the dominating position of the Trans-Canada Pipeline Company in the movement of western gas to eastern Canada. As a result, natural gas is a cheaper source of energy per common energy unit than coal or liquid petroleum products. For example, as indicated earlier, there has been a fantastic increase in gas consumption in the energy supply industries, indicating a switch to gas in the electricity-generating business. The Alberta government in 1972 realized the danger of this pricing approach and has since, through its program of "guided arbitration" attempted to renegotiate long-term contracts, using the "commodity value" approach, explained previously, as the method of pricing. It would appear that to preserve the efficient use of all energy source fuels, the federal government will also have to adopt a "commodity value" system. However, the rationality of that system will depend somewhat on the reliance upon, and expected supply of, foreign oil. Taking such factors into account, it has been suggested that the proper approach is to determine "the price to which foreign oil could or would rise if alternative energy supplies were not forthcoming."[22] Such factors may indeed have to be considered in setting prices, at least to the point of setting the price necessary to the development of new energy sources.

Another consideration in energy pricing is the distinction between "old" sources and "new" sources. The question is whether pricing policies should take into account the fact that existing energy sources are already viable at uninflated prices. Hence should "new" sources be priced differently and at a higher rate than "old" sources to encourage the development of more expensive new energy sources? This factor will be of declining importance in Canada as conventional proved reserves are depleted. But it is of some importance now, if only for political reasons, to ensure that windfall profits do not accrue to the energy industry. Over a period of time, however, this differential may be phased out.

The complex nature of pricing policies can be seen from the above analysis. This study has assumed that national pricing policy is being established determinatively by governments rather than by the market process, an assumption that seems viable for the foreseeable future. As already shown, some provinces have passed price control legislation. However, it would appear at this time that the federal government has taken the upper hand in pricing policies. Although there is still an important constitutional question as to whether the federal government has the authority to determine price, the federal government has announced its intention to give itself the legislative authority, on a standby basis, to set prices for both petroleum and natural gas. Such power would be obtained through passage of the Petroleum Administration Act. "Determining price" means setting prices directly by order, rather than affecting prices indirectly through taxation measures. It is possible, but rather unlikely that the Supreme Court would strike down federal legislation on a subject of such national dimensions.

Thus, the role of the private sector and its relationship to the government has been altered considerably as a result of the energy crisis.

Fiscal Measures. Another important factor affecting the establishment of a national energy policy is the set of fiscal measures adopted by the federal and provincial governments. In fact, it has been the level and method of taxation and the splitting of the revenues generated by such taxation which have caused the most difficult negotiating problems between the federal and provincial governments and the private sector in recent years.

The energy industry argues that it must have a share of any higher revenues generated by taxes and royalties if it is to be able to generate funds and undertake the massive expenditures necessary to develop Canada's tar sands and the frontier regions.[23] Without increased revenues, the industry argues, the level of exploration and development in Canada will drop sharply. In 1974, there were already some indications of a shift of exploratory drilling activities out of Canada. Higher royalties in the producing areas and the federal export tax have prevented much higher revenues for the industry since the energy crisis. As a result the increases in oil company profits in Canada have not been as excessive as those which have occurred elsewhere.

The producing provinces lay claim to the increased revenue arising from taxes, using the argument that they own the resources; therefore any economic rent generated from the resources should belong to them. The primary means of collecting such rent used by the provinces are royalties and licensing fees.

The federal government also lays claim to the increased revenue, contending it must act in the national interest to ensure that all Canadians are equally treated. To allow Alberta to recoup all the higher revenue from increased prices would put the rest of the country in an untenable position. Hence the federal government has used its cross-subsidization program: paying a consumer subsidy in eastern Canada and charging tax on western oil that is exported, to ensure an equal price for petroleum products across the country.

The federal government also argues that it needs the revenue because it is tied into a program of equalization payments with all provincial governments whereby federally-generated revenue is paid to the poorer provincial governments to allow them to maintain governmental services at a level near the national average. The equalization payments question is important, for if the producing provinces' revenues were to rise dramatically, it would require the federal government to make larger payments to the poor provinces, since the system is based on the amount of revenue generated in all provinces. The corporate income tax structure would be the chief means used by the federal government to collect this extra revenue.

The federal and provincial governments have been negotiating on a joint proposal to settle these fiscal matters. By 1974 no firm agreement had been reached, although the provinces had recognized the federal government's claim to part of the increased revenue. The federal government was already splitting the proceeds of the export tax on a 50/50 basis with the producing provinces. However, the major question to be settled by the two levels of government is the disposition of the economic rent that will be generated in future years from energy resources. In particular, agreement must be reached on what portion of that rent, if any, will go to the energy industry as a means of encouraging future exploration and development. Although the negotiations now concern the energy sector, they overflow into other natural resource areas, since the vital issue at stake is the control of natural resources in the country.

Self-Sufficiency and Security of Supply. A fundamental part of the federal government's energy policy has been the adoption of measures to ensure Canada's future self-sufficiency in energy resources as well as to ensure a security of energy supply for all Canadians. Although, as pointed out previously, Canada technically is self-sufficient at the present time, transportation and distribution difficulties have meant that the eastern half of the country still relies on imported oil. The recent policy of the government in dividing the country into two regions along the Ottawa River has prevented the movement, technically as well as legally, of western Canadian petroleum into eastern Canada. But even the technical self-sufficiency of Canada may not be long-lived. Current estimates show that by the end of this decade imports will exceed exports if present trends of the declining export curve continue.

The achievement of self-sufficiency depends to a large degree upon the price and fiscal stance in the country, which has been considered previously. Looking at the problem from a physical and technical point of view, what measures must the government take to ensure that the actual level of production of domestic resources and the distribution system to deliver those resources are adequate to meet all the country's needs? There are several dimensions to this problem.

First, an effort must be made to discover and develop new resources in the frontier regions of the Arctic and offshore East Coast. As one means of promoting exploration, the government has established a crown corporation, Petro-Can, to undertake such exploratory work. The government also wishes to ensure a rate of return on such work sufficiently attractive to encourage exploratory work by the private sector, but the industry contends that fiscal measures taken to date by the federal and provincial governments have had the opposite effect. The level of success in exploratory work thus far in the frontier areas has not been particularly encouraging, although it is extremely difficult to predict the success of such efforts.

It has been the government's strategy to rely in the medium run on the vast Alberta Tar Sands as the primary new source of petroleum. If this is to be so, new technology must be developed to exploit the tar sands. Strip mining can recover a portion of the potential reserves of these deposits. Perhaps 30-40 billion barrels may be recoverable by these techniques. But *in situ* methods of exploitation will be necessary to extract the deep-placed sands. The federal government as well as the government of Alberta have been funding research in new technology for exploiting the tar sands. However, it is likely that even if such technologies were developed, they would be viable only at prices exceeding $12 per barrel. In 1974 it seemed that the government's strategy with respect to the tar sands was unlikely to be realized. In any case, exploration, research, and technological development will be a vital part of ensuring a self-sufficient supply of energy in years to come, not only from the tar sands, but from frontier regions as well.

Another approach to ensuring self-sufficiency is to reduce future demand and production. One means of controlling demand would be the promotion of conservation. Although the federal government has established an office of energy conservation, the level of funding for the program has not suggested a concerted effort toward conservation on the government's part. Needless to say, it is difficult to enforce conservation measures when the government's two-price system for petroleum, under which domestic prices are lower than world prices, encourages inefficient energy utilization. The domestic consumption of natural gas was expected to increase by over 10% in 1974, almost the 10-year average for 1960-70, while petroleum consumption was expected to increase by 5.4%, again almost the 10-year average.[24] A second method of controlling demand and production would be to reduce export volumes. It is expected that exports to the United States will decline during this decade as western conventional reserves are reduced. If other means could be found to supply eastern Canada at reasonable prices, the development of an excess capacity in western Canadian reserves would serve as a means of ensuring self-sufficiency.

So far the self-sufficiency question has been discussed from a balance-sheet perspective only. However, in addition to a technical self-sufficiency, a distribution system for domestic production must be developed if all of the country is to be supplied by Canadian reserves. The distribution question goes chiefly to the security-of-supply problem. As a means to ensure security of supply to eastern Canada, the federal government has announced its intention to extend the inter-provincial crude pipeline system to Montreal and possibly beyond. If such a pipeline were built, export capacity in western Canada could be diverted to eastern Canada in times of shortage. Although the project, when announced, was to receive top priority, construction haa not even begun by the end of 1974.

It is questionable whether a pipeline to Montreal is really a good buy for Canadians. During the embargo by OPEC in 1973, the government was able to supply eastern Canada via shipments through the Great Lakes and the Panama Canal. And if increased storage capacity were available in eastern Canada, the situation might be further protected. In the final analysis, the cost-benefit calculations will depend on the assessment made of the likelihood of future embargo actions by the producing countries which will affect Canada. If the domestic price of Canadian oil is held at

$6.50/bbl. for some time and international prices remain at the $10-$11/bbl. range, when imports start to exceed exports, the cost of keeping the Canadian price at $6.50/bbl. will become increasingly onerous. Also if the pipeline were reversible, which it easily could be, it might be used in the future to transport offshore east-coast oil to central Canada as well as imported oil. Given the situation in 1974, however, and the other means available to ensure supply to eastern Canada, the $160 million investment does not seem sensible.

A different approach to the security-of-supply question might be to take steps to increase the consumption, actual or potential, of natural gas in eastern Canada by an expanded pipeline system for gas. Western gas already is available in the Montreal area, but consumption of natural gas has been very low in that region compared to the western provinces. It is likely that the quantity of gas available from western Canada and the Arctic will, in the long run, exceed the oil supplies available from those areas. Also, the prospects for gas finds off the East Coast look more promising than do oil discoveries. Hence to encourage consumption of gas, which is a more efficient and cleaner source of fuel than oil, might be a preferable step to building an oil pipeline to Montreal.

Before leaving the self-sufficiency problem, it would be well to consider the timing of such a policy. Should the government be aiming for self-sufficiency in the short run or the long run? Or should self-sufficiency be in the form of a viable contingency supply plan to be used in cases of emergency only? Very likely little would be gained by rushing to a self-sufficiency status, which would only deplete domestic non-renewal resources when there is ample world supply of oil and when the threat of future shortages is fairly low. Self-sufficiency is an emotive political slogan that often does not incorporate rational arguments as to the best course to pursue. However, the subjective judgments of the probability of future shortages or embargoes ultimately will likely be the determining factor, and they are political judgments.

Micro-economic Issues. A very important element of national energy policy relates to the micro-economic questions of industry structure, competition, and pricing mechanisms.[25] Perhaps the most important point that can be made respecting these issues is that the relationship between government and the energy industry has been irrevocably changed as a result of the 1973 crisis. This changed relationship will be brought to light most vividly in the micro-economic aspects of the energy industry.

The structure of the energy industry in Canada has been very similar to that of the United States. The seven "majors" of the world oil industry all have had a significant presence in Canada with Imperial Oil Ltd., Exxon's subsidiary in Canada, by far the largest.[26] Most have had fully integrated operations in Canada, covering the whole range of production, refining, and distribution. The exploration industry in Canada would appear to be somewhat more competitive that its U.S. counterpart, having a fairly large number of independents. Government regulation of the industry has been steadily increasing, as we have seen, evidenced by the great number of federal and provincial bodies involved in some aspect of regulation. In addition, the anti-combines laws also have been applicable to the industry.[27] Perhaps an indication that the government has been unsatisfied with the level of competition in the industry is the fact that it established Petro-Can with very broad powers, including the power to enter the distribution and retailing business. The government stated that initially Petro-Can would be involved only in exploration work and the purchase of imported petroleum on the government's behalf. However, the threat that it might become involved in down-stream operations could provide some discipline to the market. In addition there is always the possibility that the government would use Petro-Can to buy out an existing operation such as Gulf Oil Canada, Ltd. The government should encourage the development of a vigorous, efficient energy industry through its long-run competition policies, and a great potential exists to use micro-economic policies to promote a national energy plan. It only requires the political will to do so.

A final topic touching on micro-economic issues is the whole question of the information-disclosure requirements of the energy industry. The lack of information in the government's hands, both in Canada and elsewhere in 1973, was a frightening example of the power of the world's major oil companies. As a consequence, it was these companies who allocated supply across the high seas during the crisis. It is unlikely this will ever be allowed to occur again. As one commentator has predicted, the operations of the oil companies will become more "transparent."[28] One method of achieving such transparency would be to ensure that the energy industry provides full disclosure of costs, production levels, exploration results, distribution systems, reserve capacity, and other data to the government on a continuing basis.

It is unclear from the legislation that has been passed to date in Canada whether this information has been made available to the government in a manner conducive to furthering the public interest. But there should be no hesitancy on the part of the government to require the full and complete disclosure of all aspects of the energy industry in Canada to ensure that public policy reflects the actual situation and conditions existing in that industry.

Macro-economic Questions. In a time of chronic inflation, a consideration of the macro-economic implications of any energy policy initiatives is essential. This is particularly important because of the huge sums of capital which will be required to develop frontier petroleum reserves and an adequate nuclear-generation capacity. Even prior to the energy crisis of 1973, estimates of capital requirements for energy developments in this decade alone amounted to as much as $68 billion. Much of the capital that will be required in Canada during the coming years will be raised on international money markets with resultant effects on Canada's balance of payments and exchange rate. Also, the oil industry is highly capital intensive with the result that little employment is created for the amount of capital expended.[29] The government will have to understand and manipulate its macro fiscal levers very astutely to protect Canadians from higher prices and an appreciated exchange rate. Also the taxation and royalty system of the federal and provincial governments will have to be coordinated into an overall macro-economic policy.

Environmental Issues. The development of new energy resources could have serious effects on the Canadian environment. The environment of the Arctic region is extraordinarily fragile. It is an important area of the world from a climatic and meteorologic point of view. The technology that will be required to develop and deliver Arctic energy resources to the consumer has not been tested. Technological problems also exist with respect to certain eastern offshore regions located in centres of iceberg activity. And in addition to the technical difficulties of exploiting frontier reserves, there is also the question of the consequences of industrial development and a rapidly increasing population in hitherto relatively unspoiled lands.

Canada has been a prime mover in the development of international environmental law in recent years, particularly with respect to the oceans. The fear of oil pollution in the Arctic led to the passage of the Arctic Waters Pollution Prevention Act in 1970, while Canada has also taken the lead in establishing compensation funds for oil pollution from ships.[30] The concern for pollution has been a contentious point between Canada and the United States with respect to the transportation of Alaskan oil from Port Valdez to the continental United States off Canada's west coast. This commitment to the environment and particularly to the virgin frontier regions of the country will surely be taken into account when policy decisions are being made on the development of these regions. It is important that the true cost of the development of these regions be considered before commitments to exploit are made.

Foreign Ownership. For some time Canadians have been concerned about the level of foreign ownership of Canadian industry. This concern led to a federal government report in 1970 on foreign direct investment in Canada, which was the impetus for the passage of the Foreign Investment Review Act, 1973. It provided a screening mechanism for takeovers by foreigners of Canadian industry. The oil industry has had the highest percentage of foreign ownership of any industry sector in Canada. In 1973, foreign-controlled firms owned 91% of Canada's petroleum industry and accounted for 95% of the sales in the industry. Foreign control of the fully-integrated oil companies was 100%.

Foreign ownership has also been a significant factor in the coal (73.2% foreign controlled), petroleum transportation (18.7% foreign controlled), and uranium (22.5% foreign controlled) industries. The high concentration of foreign ownership has exacerbated Canadian efforts to increase competition in the industry. The management decisions made abroad on the level of exploration and research undertaken by the majors in Canada have also been of vital concern to Canadian policy makers. In 1974, a bill before Parliament to amend the Combines Investigation Act included provisions aimed at ensuring that directives of foreign companies to subsidiaries in Canada reflect Canadian economic policy and interests.

The establishment of Petro-Can by the federal government and the various provincial energy corporations will have, of course, some impact on the level of foreign ownership of Canada's energy industries. However, those corporations are likely to be restricted to exploration activities, due to lack of managerial expertise, for the next few years, although this situation could be changed if a crown corporation bought out an operating petroleum company. The Foreign Investment Review Act of 1973 will also control increased investment, if that is possible, by foreigners in Canada's energy industries. In conclusion, it is likely that the question of foreign ownership will continue to be a concern of Canadian governments for the foreseeable future in their efforts to devise a national energy policy.

International Cooperation and Relations. There have been two principal aspects of Canada's energy policy affecting international relations. The first is the matter of a coordinated bargaining front by the consumer countries with a contingency supply plan. The second is the policy Canada should adopt with respect to developing an export capacity for Canadian energy resources. A coordinated approach by consumer countries to energy problems is already well underway. Canada was and is an active participant in the Energy Coordinating Committee established by the Wasnington Energy Conference of February 1974. What is Canada's national interest in such a coordinating group?

In 1974, the Energy Coordinating Group was nearing the end of negotiations and it appeared that the main elements of the proposed agreement would be a sharing arrangement among the consumer countries in the event embargoes or other circumstances produced shortages in the future. The agreement would probably also call for compulsory measures to restrain demand in times of shortage. Another provision of the agreement would be the compulsory disclosure of information by energy companies in the future, with such information shared by all countries party to the agreement.

It could be argued that since Canada is technically self-sufficient in energy, there is no incentive for Canada to join such an agreement. However, there are several difficulties with this argument. First Canada's self-sufficiency is likely to be short-lived, certainly not lasting beyond 1980. Hence Canada may indeed be vulnerable to shortages in world energy which may arise in the relatively near future. Second, since Canada faces problems of domestic supply over the next 10-20 years, it is to her advantage to be able to rely on foreign imports during that period. From a bargaining perspective, a united front by the consumer countries would seem an important deterrent to arbitrary action in the future by the producer countries. Third, since Canada's medium- and long-run objectives are likely to be a domestic price for energy close to the world price, a collective effort by consumers is likely to ensure more reasonable prices than would unilateral negotiations.

The information aspect of the agreement may well prove to be its most important feature. As mentioned above, it is vitally important that governments have available to them all the relevant information when making decisions on energy matters. The compulsory disclosure of cost, price, and reserve figures by energy conglomerates is a very important measure. The sharing of this information by all the major consumer nations adds another important dimension in dealing with information problems and it would certainly add to the "transparency" of multinational oil firms operations.

In conclusion, there would appear to be distinct advantages to Canada's participation in a coordinated approach to energy problems by the consumer countries, particularly in the short run. And the importance of the disclosure provision may, in the long run, far outweigh even the short-run advantages of the scheme.

The second part of the international-relations side of Canada's energy policy is the question of developing an export capacity for Canada's energy resources. The argument in favour of Canada exporting her energy resources is that only truly competitive international trade in energy will assure the most efficient use of those resources. Canada now exports a large percentage of her domestic production of oil and natural gas. An export capacity also exists in the coal and electricity sectors. However, it is unlikely that exports of oil and gas at current levels will be able to be maintained in the short run because of the declining reserves of conventional resources. Thus the question of an export capacity in these fuels must refer to the longer-term development of new reserves rather than the potential of the next decade or so.

Another fact which should be recognized in considering Canada's position on exports is the reality that the United States is the only likely customer for Canada's energy resources. Japan imports Canadian coal and will continue to do so, but an overseas market for Canadian oil and gas does not seem probable given the close proximity of the huge American market which is already served by Canada. If the American goal of self-sufficiency is not realized by the end of the decade, Canada, which in 1973 provided approximately 6% of U.S. oil needs and 4% of U.S. natural gas consumption, may be under extreme pressure to export energy to the United States.

It seems likely that Canada's export position will develop along the following lines: because of declining conventional reserves of oil and gas, Canada will start reducing exports of these commodities in 1974-75, and this process of phasing out will continue until the early 1980's; at that point all further exports of proved conventional gas and oil will cease. Exports will only recommence when new reserves of oil and gas have been found and exploited. Indeed, because of the huge amount of capital required to exploit frontier resources, the guarantee of American markets may be essential to the development of these resources.[31] The question then becomes the timing for developing frontier resources, and this will be a crucial element in Canada's policy. It is conceivable that the tar sands would provide an export capacity of crude oil in the 1980's. However, the difficulties encountered in developing the tar sands would seem to indicate that the probability of excess capacity from the sands for export is unlikely. Should the government encourage the speedy exploration for and development of its yet undiscovered frontier petroleum resources? Or would a more sensible course be a steady but not intensive effort to bring new reserves on line? Given the availability of import oil at reasonable prices for the foreseeable future, Canada is likely to opt for a "middle growth" approach. With respect to coal, Canada will likely continue to export western coal in significant but not overly large amounts. Electricity may be a more likely area for exports if Canada develops her hydroelectric capacity and nuclear-generating capacity.

Finally, the next few years will be very important in determining the amount of energy Canada will be able to export. The most likely export curve would see a decline in exports throughout the remainder of this decade and into the early 1980's. At that point the curve will likely have reached its lowest point. Whether and when the curve begins to rise will depend on the availability of frontier reserves.

CONCLUSION

This brief study has set out the legal and regulatory framework of the energy industry in Canada as well as the matters of supply and demand. It has also considered various factors, primarily economic and political, which affect Canada's national energy policy. Certain conclusions have been suggested. First, it is necessary for the government to develop policies to ensure an adequate supply of energy resources for the Canadian people at reasonable prices. This entails taking measures aimed at the development of Canada's vast energy potential. To encourage exploration and the exploitation of hydrocarbon resources, the government must guarantee a reasonable rate of return for companies involved in the industry. At the same time it must take steps to ensure a healthy competitive structure for the energy industry. The National Petroleum Company, as well as provincial petroleum companies, may provide a competitive stimulus to the industry.

The government should also take measures to conserve energy resources and ensure that the most efficient use is being made of existing and future energy sources. A reduction in the rate of growth in demand is perhaps the most effective way of ensuring supply. So far, there is no indication that any level of government in Canada is paying serious attention to the question of conservation. In fact, the 1974 domestic price of crude oil in Canada was over $5.00 per barrel under the international price and hence encouraged the inefficient use of this scarce resource. For this reason any approach to conservation must go hand in hand with the price question.

The pricing structure of competing energy sources should be such as to encourage the most efficient utilization of these resources. As regards the price of oil and natural gas, in relation to international prices, an increase in stages would seem the most desirable approach. However, pressures to increase exploration and rising consumption may force a more rapid rate of increase of the domestic Canadian price in relation to the prevailing international selling price.

On the question of security of supply, the Montreal pipeline for liquid petroleum seems unnecessary. Only if substantial resources of oil were found on the Atlantic shelf would a reversible pipeline to Montreal seem desirable. In the short run, to ensure supply to eastern Canada, the best approach would seem to be an improvement in the ability to move oil via the Panama Canal and the St. Lawrence Seaway to Montreal, as well as an increase in storage capacity in eastern Canada. Canada's participation in an international agreement among consuming countries should also work to assure supply in times of shortage.

On the political front, federal and provincial conflicts over jurisdiction must at least reach a point of equilibrium. It is more desirable that the various governments represented reach a compromise position rather than engage in a constitutional battle before the courts. It is crucial that a national energy policy be developed and operating in the short run. Litigation would only increase the uncertainty and harm the country in the long run. Out of federal-provincial negotiations there must also be developed a rational administrative structure over energy questions. The bewildering array of boards and tribunals with various powers and interests on the federal and provincial fronts at the present time only serves to increase uncertainty and inefficiency in the energy industries.

With respect to the relations between governments and the energy industry, more public disclosure of information by the industry is essential. The paucity of information available to the government in the fall of 1973 should not be allowed to continue. Such information is critical not only to the financial position of the energy industry, but also to the question of potential supply and reserves. Moreover, the government's understanding of the operations of the energy industry must be improved.

Finally, on the question of adequate environmental safeguards during the exploration and exploitation of energy sources, Canada should continue its progressive attitude toward the protection of the environment, particularly in fragile regions such as Arctic and submarine areas.

Canada weathered the 1973 embargoes and production cuts introduced by the OPEC countries with little short-run hardship. But the actions of the oil-producing countries brought home the finite nature of hydrocarbon reserves and the necessity for a coordinated and rational national energy policy. Only through decisive leadership and a coordinated approach to policies that involves all levels of government and industry can the long-run energy situation in Canada be secure. Through wise management Canadians should be able to avoid severe energy shortages in the foreseeable future and, in fact, enjoy a reasonable rate of growth in their consumption of energy.

NOTES

1. Section 91 reads: "It shall be lawful for the Queen, by and with the Advice and Consent of the Senate and House of Commons, to make Laws for the Peace, Order, and good Government of Canada, in relation to all Matters not coming within the Classes of Subjects by this Act assigned exclusively to the Legislatures of the Provinces; and for greater Certainty, but not so as to restrict the Generality of the foregoing Terms of this Section, it is hereby declared that (notwithstanding anything in this Act) the exclusive Legislative Authority of the Parliament of Canada extends to all Matters coming within the Classes of Subjects next herein-after enumerated; that is to say,

    1. The amendment from time to time of the Constitution of Canada, except as regards matters coming within the classes of subjects by this Act assigned exclusively to the Legislatures of the provinces, or as regards rights or privileges by this or any other Constitutional Act granted or secured to the Legislature or the Government of a province, or to any class of persons with respect to schools or as regards the use of the English or the French language or as regards the requirements that there shall be a session of the Parliament of Canada at least once each year, and that no House of Commons shall continue for more than five years from the day of the return of the Writs for choosing the House: provided, however, that a House of Commons may in time of real or apprehended war, invasion or insurrection be continued by the Parliament of Canada if such continuation is not opposed by the votes of more than one-third of the members of such House.

    1A. The Public Debt and Property.
    2. The Regulation of Trade and Commerce.
    2A. Unemployment insurance.
    3. The raising of Money by any Mode or System of Taxation.
    4. The borrowing of Money on the Public Credit.
    5. Postal Service.
    6. The Census and Statistics.
    7. Militia, Military and Naval Service, and Defence.
    8. The fixing of and providing for the Salaries and Allowances of Civil and other Officers of the Government of Canada.
    9. Beacons, Buoys, Lighthouses, and Sable Island.
    10. Navigation and Shipping.
    11. Quarantine and the Establishment and Maintenance of Marine Hospitals.
    12. Sea Coast and Inland Fisheries.
    13. Ferries between a Province and any British or Foreign Country or between Two Provinces.
    14. Currency and Coinage.
    15. Banking, Incorporation of Banks, and the Issue of Paper Money.
    16. Savings Banks.
    17. Weights and Measures.
    18. Bills of Exchange and Promissory Notes.

19. Interest.
20. Legal Tender.
21. Bankruptcy and Insolvency.
22. Patents of Invention and Discovery.
23. Copyrights.
24. Indians, and Lands reserved for the Indians.
25. Naturalization and Aliens.
26. Marriage and Divorce.
27. The Criminal Law, except the Constitution of Courts of Criminal Jurisdiction, but including the Procedure in Criminal Matters.
28. The Establishment, Maintenance, and Management of Penitentiaries.
29. Such Classes of Subjects as are expressly excepted in the Enumeration of the Classes of Subjects by this Act assigned exclusively to the Legislatures of the Provinces.

And any Matter coming within any of the Classes of Subjects enumerated in this Section shall not be deemed to come within the Class of Matters of a local or private Nature comprised in the Enumeration of the Classes of Subjects by this Act assigned exclusively to the Legislatures of the Provinces."

Section 92 reads: "In each Province the Legislature may exclusively make Laws in relation to Matters coming within the Classes of Subject next herein-after enumerated; that is to say,

1. The Amendment from Time to Time, notwithstanding anything in this Act, of the Constitution of the Province, except as regards the Office of Lieutenant Governor.
2. Direct Taxation with the Province in order to the raising of a Revenue for Provincial Purposes.
3. The borrowing of Money on the sole Credit of the Province.
4. The Establishment and Tenure of Provincial Offices and the Appointment and Payment of Provincial Officers.
5. The Management and Sale of the Public Lands belonging to the Province and of the Timber and Wood thereon.
6. The Establishment, Maintenance, and Management of Public and Reformatory Prisons in and for the Province.
7. The Establishment, Maintenance, and Management of Hospitals, Asylums, Charities, and Eleemosynary Institutions in and for the Province, other than Marine Hospitals.
8. Municipal Institutions in the Province.
9. Shop, Saloon, Tavern, Auctioneer, and other Licenses in order to the raising of a Revenue for Provincial, Local, or Municipal Purposes.
10. Local Works and Undertakings other than such as are of the following Classes:
    (a) Lines of Steam or other Ships, Railways, Canals, Telegraphs, and other Works and Undertakings connecting the Province with any other or others of the Provinces, or extending beyond the Limits of the Province;

(b) Lines of Steam Ships between the Province and any British or Foreign Country;
(c) Such Works as, although wholly situate within the Province, are before or after their Execution declared by the Parliament of Canada to be for the general Advantage of Canada or for the Advantage of Two or more of the Provinces.
11. The Incorporation of Companies with Provincial Objects.
12. The Solemnization of Marriage in the Province.
13. Property and Civil Rights in the Province.
14. The Administration of Justice in the Province, including the Constitution, Maintenance, and Organization of Provincial Courts, both of Civil and of Criminal Jurisdiction including Procedure in Civil Matters in those Courts.
15. The Imposition of Punishment by Fine, Penalty, or Imprisonment for enforcing any Law of the Province made in relation to any Matter coming within any of the Classes of Subjects enumerated in this Section.
16. Generally all Matters of a merely local or private Nature in the Province."

2. See *Munro* v. *National Capital Commission,* [1966] S.C.R. 663.
3. For a general discussion of the trade and commerce sections of the Canadian and U.S. Constitution, see A. Smith, *The Commerce Power in Canada and the United States* (1963). See also *Citizens Insurance Company* v. *Parsons* (1881), 7.A.C.96.
4. S.121 reads as follows: "All Articles of the Growth, Produce, or Manufacture of any one of the Provinces shall, from and after the Union, be admitted free into each of the other Provinces."
5. National Energy Board Act, 1970 R.S.C., c.N-6. For the Board's authority, see Roger Carter, *The National Energy Board Act* (1969), 34 Sask. L.R. 104, and for a brief discussion of some aspects of the Board's activities, see Anthony Scott and Peter H. Pearse, "The Political Economy of Energy Development in Canada," in *The Mackenzie Pipeline,* ed. by Peter H. Pearse (1974), pp. 23-26.
6. See Scott and Pearse, *op. cit.* p. 23; and J. M. DeBanné, "Oil and Canadian Policy," in Erickson and Wavermann, *The Energy Question,* vol. 2 (1974), p. 133.
7. *Territorial Lands Act,* 1970 R.S.C., c.T-6; other statutes bearing on Arctic development are the *Oil and Gas Production and Conservation Act,* 1970 R.S.C., c.O-4; the *Arctic Waters Pollution Prevention Act,* 1970 R.S.C., 1st supp., c.2; the *Canada Water Act,* 1970 R.S.C., 1st supp., c.5; and the *Northern Inland Waters Act,* 1970 R.S.C., 1st supp., c.28.
8. *Energy Supplies Allocation Act,* Stats. Can. 1973-74, c.52.
9. See *Nova Scotia Gasoline Licensing Act,* 1967 R.S.N.S., c.117 as amended by 1969, c.47 and 1972, c.35 and *An Act to Amend Chapter 117 of R.S., 1967, The Gasoline Licensing Act,* 1973, S.N.S., c.2 assented to December 12, 1973. A further amendment to the Act entitled *An Act to Amend Chapter 117 of R.S. 1967, The Gasoline and*

No. 278 (1973), Harvard Institute of Economic Research, for sources of various assertions in this section.

19. For a complete copy of the statement, see Hansard, Dec. 6, 1973, pp. 8478-84.

20. *Oil Export Tax Act*, S.C. 1974, c.53. S.22.2(1) sets the amount of the tax. Part II, S.4(2) sets a 50-50 split of the revenue generated between the federal government and the producing provinces.

21. See Hamilton, "Natural Gas and Canadian Policy," in Erickson and Wavermann, *op. cit.*, p. 149.

22. W. J. Levy, "World Oil Cooperation or International Chaos" (1974), 52 Foreign Affairs 690, p. 699.

23. For a statement of the industry position see *The Petroleum Industry and Canada*, prepared by the Canadian Petroleum Association and the Independent Petroleum Association of Canada (1974).

24. See *Oilweek*, Oct. 14, 1974, pp. 15 and 26, and Oct. 28, 1974, p. 20.

25. For an excellent discussion of the micro-economic issue, see M.A. Adelman, *Oil in the World Economy* (1970).

26. J. Laxer, *Canada's Energy Crisis* (1974), pp. 65-71.

27. See Combines Investigation Act, R.S.C. 1970, c.314. An inquiry under this Act was underway in 1974 with respect to the oil industry. Because of the confidentiality requirements of the Act, details are not available.

28. Hamilton, in Erickson and Wavermann, *op. cit.*, p. 695.

29. For an analysis of the national exchange rate problem and economic impact of Arctic development, see Helliwell, in Peter H. Pearse, ed., *op. cit.*, pp. 143-183. See also Science Council of Canada, *op. cit.*, pp. 217-222.

30. See R.S.C., 1970, 1st Supp., c.2 and Canada Shipping Act, S.C. 1971, c.27, SS. 743 and 757.

31. See Gray, "Why Canada Needs the Arctic Gas Pipeline," in Peter H. Pearse, ed., *op. cit.*, pp. 33-47.

Fuel Oil Licensing Act, 1974, Bill 46 received a second reading on June 18, 1974.

Other provinces which had some possible form of price or allocation control on their legislative books were Saskatchewan, *The Oil and Gas Conservation, Stabilization and Development Act,* 1973, Bill 42 of the 2nd Session, assented to December 19, 1973; British Columbia, *Energy Act,* 1973 S.B.C., c.29, Parts I, IV, and V as amended by *Energy Amendment Act,* 1974, all assented to and proclaimed except for SS. 68-71 inclusive on August 22nd, 1974; and Alberta, *The Petroleum Marketing Act,* 1973 S.A., c.96; *The Arbitration Act,* 1970, R.S.A., c.96 as amended by *The Arbitration Amendment Act, 1973,* 1973 S.A., c.88; *The Gas Utilities Act,* 1970 R.S.A., c.158, amended by 1971 S.A., c.30 and *The Gas Utilities Amendment Act, 1973,* 1973 S.A., c.91.

10. *Energy Act,* 1973 S.B.C., c.29, amended by the *Energy Amendment Act, 1974,* assented to and proclaimed on August 22nd, 1974, with the exception of SS. 68-71.

11. *The Oil and Gas Conservation, Stabilization and Development Act,* 1973, Bill 42 of the 2nd Session, 1973, assented to December 19, 1973.

12. See *The Gas Utilities Act,* 1970 R.S.A., c.158 amended by 1971 S.A., c.158 amended by 1971 S.A., c.30 and the *Gas Utilities Amendment Act,* 1973, S.A., c.91, and *The Arbitration Act,* 1970, R.S.A., c.21 amended by *The Arbitration Amendment Act, 1973,* 1973 S.A., c.88. The Act does not apply to the activities of gas utilities which are subject to the Public Utilities Board.

13. *Petroleum Corporation Act,* 1973 S.B.C., c.140 (2nd Session).

14. *The Petroleum Marketing Act,* 1973 S.A., c.96, S.2(1).

15. Historical data on production, imports, exports and demand have been derived exclusively from *Detailed Energy Supply and Demand in Canada 1958-1969,* and *Detailed Energy Supply and Demand in Canada 1970-71,* Statistics Canada. See also, MacNabb and Winter, *Energy Supply and Demand in Canada, 1970-2000,* presented to the 9th World Energy Conference, Detroit, Michigan, September 23-27, 1974.

16. G. D. Quirin, *Non-Conventional Energy Sources,* in Erickson and Wavermann, *op. cit.,* p. 326. See also MacNabb and Winter, *op. cit.,* p. 15.

17. Details on exploration and drilling on the East Coast region and the Arctic region that follows have been taken from Science Council of Canada, *Background Study No. 30: A Technology Assessment System, A Case Study of East Coast Offshore Petroleum Exploration,* March, 1974, p. 65, and Department of Energy, Mines and Resources, *An Energy Policy for Canada, Phase I,* Volume II, (1973), pp. 42-51.

18. See E. R. Berndt, "Forecasting North American Energy Demand," in Pearse, *op. cit.,* no. 5, p. 71; H. S. Houthakker, "The Energy Problem," in Erickson and Wavermann, *op. cit.,* no. 6, p. 239; and Marc J. Roberts, *Economic Consequences of Energy Costs,* Discussion Paper

Fuel Oil Licensing Act, 1974, Bill 46 received a second reading on June 18, 1974.

Other provinces which had some possible form of price or allocation control on their legislative books were Saskatchewan, *The Oil and Gas Conservation, Stabilization and Development Act,* 1973, Bill 42 of the 2nd Session, assented to December 19, 1973; British Columbia, *Energy Act,* 1973 S.B.C., c.29, Parts I, IV, and V as amended by *Energy Amendment Act,* 1974, all assented to and proclaimed except for SS. 68-71 inclusive on August 22nd, 1974; and Alberta, *The Petroleum Marketing Act,* 1973 S.A., c.96; *The Arbitration Act,* 1970, R.S.A., c.96 as amended by *The Arbitration Amendment Act, 1973,* 1973 S.A., c.88; *The Gas Utilities Act,* 1970 R.S.A., c.158, amended by 1971 S.A., c.30 and *The Gas Utilities Amendment Act, 1973,* 1973 S.A., c.91.

10. *Energy Act,* 1973 S.B.C., c.29, amended by the *Energy Amendment Act, 1974,* assented to and proclaimed on August 22nd, 1974, with the exception of SS. 68-71.

11. *The Oil and Gas Conservation, Stabilization and Development Act,* 1973, Bill 42 of the 2nd Session, 1973, assented to December 19, 1973.

12. See *The Gas Utilities Act,* 1970 R.S.A., c.158 amended by 1971 S.A., c.158 amended by 1971 S.A., c.30 and the *Gas Utilities Amendment Act,* 1973, S.A., c.91, and *The Arbitration Act,* 1970, R.S.A., c.21 amended by *The Arbitration Amendment Act, 1973,* 1973 S.A., c.88. The Act does not apply to the activities of gas utilities which are subject to the Public Utilities Board.

13. *Petroleum Corporation Act,* 1973 S.B.C., c.140 (2nd Session).

14. *The Petroleum Marketing Act,* 1973 S.A., c.96, S.2(1).

15. Historical data on production, imports, exports and demand have been derived exclusively from *Detailed Energy Supply and Demand in Canada 1958-1969,* and *Detailed Energy Supply and Demand in Canada 1970-71,* Statistics Canada. See also, MacNabb and Winter, *Energy Supply and Demand in Canada, 1970-2000,* presented to the 9th World Energy Conference, Detroit, Michigan, September 23-27, 1974.

16. G. D. Quirin, *Non-Conventional Energy Sources,* in Erickson and Wavermann, *op. cit.,* p. 326. See also MacNabb and Winter, *op. cit.,* p. 15.

17. Details on exploration and drilling on the East Coast region and the Arctic region that follows have been taken from Science Council of Canada, *Background Study No. 30: A Technology Assessment System, A Case Study of East Coast Offshore Petroleum Exploration,* March, 1974, p. 65, and Department of Energy, Mines and Resources, *An Energy Policy for Canada, Phase I,* Volume II, (1973), pp. 42-51.

18. See E. R. Berndt, "Forecasting North American Energy Demand," in Pearse, *op. cit.,* no. 5, p. 71; H. S. Houthakker, "The Energy Problem," in Erickson and Wavermann, *op. cit.,* no. 6, p. 239; and Marc J. Roberts, *Economic Consequences of Energy Costs,* Discussion Paper

China
Choon-ho Park

Introduction to China's Energy Situation

In East Asia few countries have been richly blessed with energy resources in general and oil in particular. This scarcity has always been a debilitating factor in the economy of the region as a whole. But it was not until late 1973 when the world-wide energy crisis occurred that the chronic poverty of oil began to have a painful impact upon almost all the countries of the region. Because the People's Republic of China has become "basically self-sufficient in oil" since 1963, it is in an enviable position compared to most of its neighbors, who are encountering the economic difficulties attributed to oil.

This study is an attempt to analyze the energy policy of the People's Republic of China with particular reference to oil. Other major sources of energy, such as coal, electricity and natural gas, have also been referred to insofar as deemed necessary in order to place the role of oil in the general perspective of China's energy consumption pattern.

Up to the mid-1960's, China was dependent on imported oil mainly from the Soviet Union, and on a smaller and sporadic scale, from Roumania and a few countries of Eastern Europe and the Middle East. During the latter part of the 1960's, it was reported that China had begun to supply limited amounts of oil to North Korea and North Vietnam, either in the form of foreign aid or commercial export. In 1974 China was exporting oil to Australia, Hong Kong, Japan, North Korea, North Vietnam, the Philippines, and Thailand, although the total amount was rather modest. Oil in China has been attracting considerable interest from the outside world. This has not been due merely to China's shift from being an importer of oil to an exporter, but is rather the result of the serious impact which the current oil crisis has had on the economies of many countries. It can also be said that such interest has not been prompted so much by the amount of oil China actually produces as by the great potential it is believed to have, especially with the growing promise of offshore deposits in addition to onshore reserves. Different sources now forecast China's oil production on the order of 200 to 400 million tons a year by 1980, which is four to eight times the 1973 production. Such figures must be viewed with caution; indeed skepticism must be exercised toward all future projections unless the Chinese publish certain data that have been unavailable.

As a general background it may be helpful to note some particular characteristics of oil. In its crude form, oil plays a dual role, both as a multi-purpose raw material and as a rare source of energy. In both roles, it is decisively superior to other natural resources in convenience and efficiency, and therefore it is not easily replaceable. Modern economies have become extremely sensitive and vulnerable to irregular supplies of oil, even on a limited scale. By virtue of these characteristics, rarely found in other resources, the intrinsic value of oil has long since acquired a political and strategic dimension. This can be seen from the fact that the world has more than once witnessed wars fought and economies developed or disrupted because of oil. The threat of war or economic disruption over oil supplies persists. In the wake of the current oil crisis, the community of nations has again become intensely conscious of the importance of natural resources and the unique position of oil. The distribution of oil is geographically irregular and the means to develop it disparate from one country to another. Only a handful of countries have been both fortunate in having this particular resource in abundance and capable of exploiting it by their own means. In times of energy shortages, therefore, the economic potential of a country can be measured to a large degree in terms of its self-sufficiency in or access to oil or equally useful resources.

A natural resource of such military-economic importance is bound to be an effective political lever, used by those who have it upon those who need it, especially if it is in the hands of a great emerging power like China. Until very recently China was singularly regarded as "poor in oil." This is no longer true. But it is important to examine a few points of particular relevance to an understanding of China's oil-development intentions and long-range energy policy.

● *First*, the economy of China as a national unit is immense in size. This fact alone makes it more difficult to interpret its economic behavior than that of any other country at similar stages of economic development. Further difficulties of interpretation arise from the fact that the Chinese economy is a planned one and operates under a principle of its own, commonly known as "self-reliance." Of necessity, a country of the size of China has to be largely self-dependent in order to be economically viable. A country with 800 million people to care for can not depend very much on others for survival and China's own experiences in history have demonstrated the importance of relying on its own resources and talents. Thus, analysis of China's economic behavior can not be divorced from its unique environment and it is often profoundly misleading to look at a particular economic issue of China simply in the context of what would happen under similar circumstances elsewhere.

● *Second*, the Chinese oil industry has to be seen within the framework of its natural resources development policy. The basic point of that policy is to prevent "long-range damage to production" by not aiming at "quick results." China was believed to have met over 80% of its energy demand with coal and slightly over 10% with oil in 1973. Its coal reserves were known to be comparable with those of the United States or the Soviet Union; in fact, these three countries alone held nearly 80% of the world's total deposits of coal. From these simple statistics it may be seen that the agricultural economy of China was under no pressure to hasten oil development beyond what its own national development scheme required. For these reasons it is also misleading to look at China's oil prospects in terms of its export potential or in terms of its investment potential.

● *Third*, a common problem which arises in the study of the Chinese economy is the difficulty in obtaining basic data, especially those which involve statistics. Since 1960 China has virtually ceased to publish information relating to its economy, and the very meager amount of data fragmentarily released has been given in relative terms only. Foreign observers have not only been baffled by this "information black-out" but also confused by the plausibilities to which it leads for want of actual data.

At times, however, some Chinese leaders have offered fragmentary but meaningful indications of China's oil production to visitors. Since the middle of 1974, moreover, some important oil centers in China have been shown to foreign diplomats and reporters. The meager amount of information thus made available has then been exhaustively scrutinized, often resulting in gross exaggeration or underestimation. In the wake of such scrutiny there has developed a habitual mistrust of Chinese statistics. To make matters more confusing to foreign observers, China's own response to such distortions has invariably been non-committal, a response which has been typical of the Chinese government. The oil crisis of 1973 showed many earlier forecasts on oil to have been to speculative, if not simply wrong; it has become clear that it takes much prudence to interpret the oil figures of China and that any predictions will be difficult.

Historical Background

China prides itself on the fact that it was among the first nations to use petroleum, since its record of use of oil dates back to the first century before Christ. However, according to certain Chinese records, the word *Shih-you*, literally meaning "stone oil," was not in use until the eleventh century when petroleum was so named by Shen Kuo (1031-1095), a Sung dynasty scholar. According to a book on the physical chemistry of Chinese petroleum (Chang et al., Peking, 1962), China was also the first nation to have an oil well, which was drilled in the present Szechwan Province of southwest China in 1521, allegedly preceding the first drilled well in the United States — by 339 years. Nevertheless, for almost four centuries following the drilling of the 1521 well, there was no significant oil development in China.

The petroleum industry in China in modern times began with the drilling in 1907 of the first Yenchang well in Shensi Province in central China. During the subsequent forty-two years to 1948 other oil centers were expanded or developed in Yumen, Tushantzu, Tsaidam, Karamai and Chwanchung (central Szechwan), reaching a total of at least forty oil and gas wells. Production by each of them was on such a limited scale that the total output of crude oil was only 2.78 million tons during the entire period of forty-two years. Following the peak year of 1943 when the output reached 319,000 tons, production gradually decreased to 122,000 tons in 1949, due to war with the Japanese and then to protracted civil war. (On the average, a ton of crude oil is 7.3 barrels or 1.17 kiloliters; the latter unit is used in Japan.) In terms of meeting the national demand for oil, therefore, indigenous production could meet only a bare share — for example, only 3% in 1947.

With the beginning of the communist regime in Peking in 1949, the oil industry in China entered a new stage of development. The new government was very conscious of the importance of this particular field of industry and placed great emphasis on it in economic planning. In April 1950 the Ministry of Fuel Industry convened a national conference on the oil industry and decided to restore oil production facilities within three years and to conduct surveys in order to develop the crude deposits in the northwest and the shale deposits in the northeast. This initial endeavor was so successful that by 1952, which was the target year of a three-year economic restoration plan, major oil production facilities had been restored and crude oil production had increased beyond the record level of 1943.

Following the three-year period of economic restoration, the first five-year economic development plan was put into effect for the years 1953-1957. The basic policy set up for the management of the oil industry was (1) to develop liquid and non-liquid oil resources concurrently; (2) to promote large, medium, and small units of the oil industry concurrently; and (3) to combine native and foreign methods of development. In March 1954 a national conference on oil exploration was held to evaluate the achievements of exploration during the preceding four years. This conference was followed by another one in October of the same year when further plans were adopted.

The emphasis of the government on oil development may also be seen in the fact that during the first five-year plan, almost two-thirds of the entire budget for the energy industry was earmarked specifically for oil. Moreover, the Ministry of Fuel Industry was reorganized into three full-fledged ministries of petroleum, coal, and electric industries in July l955. (The official names of these ministries, as reported at the time of the Fourth National People's Congress in January 1975, are the Ministries of Petroleum and Chemical Industry, Coal, and Water Conservancy and Power.) In spite of these extraordinary efforts by the government, the achievements of the first five-year plan as evaluated at the end of its target year of 1957 were not particularly satisfactory, due to various factors such as the lack of basic facilities and specialized personnel as well as the long lead-time for production which the oil industry usually requires. Consequently the crude production of 1.46 million tons in 1957 was only 72.5% of the target, but this was enough to meet roughly a third of the national demand for oil.

During the second five-year plan for the years 1958-1962 an event took place which marked the beginning of another era in the chronicle of oil development in China. In September 1959 a new oil field was discovered in Heilungchiang Province of northeast China, which, known as the Taching oil field, has become one of the major oil centers of China to date. China has other important oil centers comparable to Taching in their present and prospective output, but this discovery during the "great leap forward" movement period of 1958-1960 deserves to be noted because of its political and economic effects on China.

In 1955 the Chinese had begun a geophysical survey in the Sungliao Basin of northeast China with Russian cooperation rendered under the terms of a Sino-Soviet technical cooperation agreement. After three years of intensive exploration, it was determined with some certainty in 1957 that the areas surveyed held good prospects for oil development. At the end of 1958 a field conference was convened in Changchun to discuss the stratigraphy of the areas; and three Russian scientists were invited to attend this meeting. Taching was finally discovered in September 1959, shortly before the 10th anniversary of the communist regime's founding on October 1, 1949, whereupon the name "Taching" which means "great celebration" was subsequently applied. During the following years the Chinese guarded the location of the discovery so effectively that it took a rather amusing combination of "bird-watching" and "archeological patch-work" for the outside world to acquire what is still scanty knowledge of the discovery and its development. It was not until April 20, 1964, that Taching as the name of the oil field was first mentioned in the *People's Daily*. It is interesting to note that a map carried in the prestigious *Oil and Gas Journal* in the United States as recently as September 1970 seems to place Taching some 500 miles southwest of where it actually lies. The *Talu Wenti Chuanti Yenchiu* of Taiwan ascribed a similar placement of Taching to some Japanese observers.

Large-scale drilling at Taching began in 1960 and the Chinese government exerted considerable effort to develop the area. The construction of a refinery was begun in 1962. When production of crude oil began on a large scale after 1963, further efforts were exerted to make Taching not only the largest oil and petrochemical center of China, but also a huge industrial complex that would be a model for the effective combination of a variety of urban-rural and industrial-agricultural production systems. In fact, the experience of Taching was so highly valued in China that in 1964 Chairman Mao issued a call to the people which has since become a motto in developing industry: "In industry, learn from Taching." In an effort to make Taching also a training center for the oil industry, the Peking Petroleum College was moved there in 1966. China prides itself on the achievements of the Taching drilling teams, two of which drilled 100,000 meters each in 1966, thereby breaking a Russian record of 40,816 meters in 1965 and an American record of 90,325 meters slightly earlier. One of the Taching teams finally broke the world record by drilling 127,000 meters in 1971. It was also estimated in 1971 that Taching had 1,690 oil wells, from which 6.9 million tons of crude oil were produced. The current output of Taching is not known, although some foreign estimates have placed it between 15 to 20 million tons a year, which would approximate 40% of China's total production in 1973. Taching has been hailed as "the red banner on China's industrial front."

The Taching discovery was extremely important also in light of the developments that took place in the relations between China and the Soviet Union after 1958. The symptoms of rift between these two socialist allies began to be felt in September 1958 when the Soviet Union expressed its disagreement with the people's commune system in China, and again in September 1959 when the Soviets expressed their regret over the Sino-Indian border clashes that occurred in August. By July 1960 all the Russian technicians in China had been withdrawn. In 1961 China's import of crude and other oil products from the Soviet Union began to decrease sharply, dropping to virtually nothing in 1965. In brief, it can be said that but for the Taching discovery the Sino-Soviet rift might have brought China to an oil-supply crisis a decade before such shortages were felt elsewhere in the world. On 4 January 1974 Radio Peking explained the circumstances as follows:

> The battle for opening the Taching oil field was waged under very difficult conditions. Natural disasters had created temporary difficulties in China's national economy and investment and equipment were not adequate. When China faced such economic difficulties (1959-1961), imperialism and modern revisionism tore up its contracts, withdrew its experts and restricted its oil exports as pressure to bring China under its baton. At this time, China's oil workers, technicians and cadres launched a big battle for oil by adhering to the principle of "maintaining independence and keeping the initiative in our own hands and relying on our own efforts" as set forth by Chairman Mao and the party central committee.

Another point of interest about the Taching discovery and its development is its relationship to the "great leap forward" movement of 1958-1960, which is usually said to have had adverse effects on the Chinese economy as a whole and to have caused failures to fulfill production targets in many fields. Contrary to some views, originating mainly in Taiwan, oil seems to have been an exception. This may be seen from a report that the estimated crude oil production of 5.5 million tons in 1960 met the target set for oil production for the second five-year plan period of 1958-1962 two years ahead of schedule. This is supported by what was achieved in 1959 when there began a shift of emphasis from exploration to exploitation, and as a result, the output of crude oil was said to have increased by more than 50% in that year.

The above-mentioned second five-year plan was followed by a three-year period of economic adjustment (1963-1965) during which other events took place in addition to those noted in connection with Taching. First, at the time of the Fourth Session of Second People's Congress held in November-December 1963, it was reported that "our country which formerly depended on imported oil has now become basically self-sufficient in oil." This was a turning point in China's oil industry. But it is necessary to allow the meaning of the word "basically" in the statement above some flexibility because even after the statement of "complete self-sufficiency" three years later, there have been indications that China has continued to import oil as recently as August 1974, although on a sporadic and modest scale. Second, the export of oil by China to North Korea was reported to have begun in 1964 and to North Vietnam in 1965. More details on these activities will be given below, but it should be noted here that China's export or import of oil is not dictated by domestic demand or supply alone. Third, it was during this period that construction began (in 1964) at the Shengli oil field in Shantung Province in east China and that prospecting for oil began (also in 1964) at what has come to be known as the Takang oil field south of Tienchin. Situated on the coasts of Pohai Bay, both oil fields have grown rapidly and have been reported comparable to Taching in terms of future prospects. Strategically they are superior to Taching because of their remoteness from the Sino-Soviet borders.

The third five-year plan — for 1966-1970 — marked the

awakening of China's active interest in the exploration of its offshore areas for possible deposits of oil. It was reported in Japan in the mid-1960's that, in its own way, China had begun to prepare itself to develop oil from the sea, which shows that China's interest in seabed oil preceded that of the other coastal states of the region by at least four years. At the end of the 1960's the Bangkok-based UN Economic Commission for Asia and the Far East (ECAFE)* published a joint survey report, quoted in part below, hinting at the promise of oil in some areas of the Yellow and East China Seas; as a result, Japan, South Korea and Taiwan began a frantic race to grab as much offshore area as possible. Although their claims overlapped at many points, contracts were awarded to Western oil interests for the exploration and exploitation of oil in the areas. In the face of what appeared to be a complicated legal problem of sorting out the territorial rights of the various countries, the three coastal states planned a joint development scheme "freezing" the sea boundary issue. In December 1970 China strongly protested the plan. The dispute is still unsettled and remains one of the world's serious and complicated seabed controversies. No oil has been recovered yet from this seabed region.

While effectively preventing other coastal states from obtaining oil from the seabed pending agreement on the boundaries in the region, China made further progress in developing its own onshore deposits. In 1970 in the vicinity of the Shengli oil field in east China, another very promising discovery was reported in an area around the city of Itu. Also in 1970 active exploration was reported to have begun in what has come to be known as the Chiling oil field (Chiling means "seven zero" from "1970"). The exact location of this new field is not known, but Taiwanese oil experts have said

*ECAFE was retitled Economic and Social Commission for Asia and the Pacific (ESCAP) in 1974.

that the photographed landscape of the place suggests the estuary of the Pearl river system of Kwangtung Province in the south. Thus production of oil in 1970, the final year of the third five-year plan, was reported to have reached 20 million tons, an oft-quoted figure purportedly mentioned to Edgar Snow by Premier Chou En-lai. If true, production was running two years ahead of the schedule targeted for 1968. The first year of the third plan, 1966, marked the beginning of the "cultural revolution," which is generally believed to have caused disruptions in the Chinese economy as a whole, as did the "great leap forward" movement of 1958-1960. However, oil development does not seem to have been seriously affected.

The fourth five-year plan — for 1971-1975 — has seen a number of important developments which characterize the period as a take-off stage for what may be called a new version of the "great leap forward" movement in China's oil industry. First, largely due to the rapid expansion of Taching, Takang, and Shengli oil fields, the oil industry has begun to shift its center from west, northwest, and central China to east and northeast China. Convenience of transportation has probably been one of the major factors responsible for this shift. Important as Taching may be, a further shift seems to be taking place in favor of Takang and Shengli, which have definite advantages over Taching from the standpoint of transportation and strategic location. Second, with oil production increasing rapidly, there seems to have arisen a pressing need to improve transportation and port facilities. This was reportedly among the high priority projects in the fourth plan. Third, since the extraction of oil requires advanced technology, oil development machinery is being imported in great quantities from the West and Japan. Fourth and last but not least, oil has begun to play an important role in relations between China and those countries which seek to supply their domestic demand with imports from China. This may be seen particularly in the relations between China and Japan.

In sum, the history of the oil industry in the People's Republic of China began virtually from scratch in 1950. Within a quarter of a century the traditional impression of China being "poor in oil" has been erased. In fact, China has shifted from being a substantial importer of oil to the status of an exporter, although only in nominal amounts as of 1974.

Oil Reserves

China has emerged as a potential source of oil in the future, but there is a great deal of uncertainty about how much oil China may possess. Because new oil fields have been found one after another in China, it is possible that China itself has not been able to determine the exact amount of oil that lies under its territory. Even in other parts of the world where the most advanced technology is employed, the oil reserves actually ascertained often belie the predictions. Serious doubts, moreover, arise about the various foreign estimates of China's oil reserves, for with the exception of the Russian oil scientists who were in China up to the time of the Sino-Soviet rift in 1960, few oil geologists of the West have ever had the opportunity to probe beneath the Chinese soil in search of oil.

All the new oil fields in China were found by the Chinese themselves after the departure of the Russians, although some clues left by the latter may have been utilized. This probably means that the Russians themselves with the technology of the time did not know China's oil potential, unless it can be assumed they withheld their findings from the Chinese. In any event, since 1960 the Chinese have tended not to give any credit to the Russians for their cooperation in the development of oil in China, whereas in

1953 the text of an atlas, *Chunghua Jemin Kunghokuo Fensheng Titu*, "the Sino-Soviet joint-stock oil company [was earlier regarded as] greatly significant for the industrial development of our country as well as for Sino-Soviet economic cooperation."

Foreign estimates of China's oil reserves vary from 2.7 billion tons of proved reserves to 70 billion tons of possibly recoverable reserves. The latter figure includes possible offshore deposits. Plausible as such estimates may sound, it is essentially futile to speculate in numerical terms about what China itself chooses not to disclose in the interest of national security and/or due to technological difficulties in ascertaining its own reserves. From a number of circumstantial indications noted below, however, it is possible to form a well-founded conjecture that the volume of China's liquid and non-liquid reserves, including those lying offshore, is large enough to enable China to become a major producer of oil in the future, if not a substantial exporter, as some observers anticipate.

Onshore. Depending on the source of information, estimates of China's crude reserves onshore have varied from 2.7 to 20 billion tons. According to one estimate (Chen and Au, 1972), the areas with different degrees of oil prospects in China, including the eight major oil centers described in Part 5 of this study, amounted to nearly four million square kilometers, or roughly 40% of the total continental land mass of China. Until all the areas have been fully explored, it will not be possible to assess the reserves, much less to categorize them as proved or possibly recoverable. This in turn indicates that it is meaningless to try to cite a definite figure as the ultimate volume of reserves at any particular time. Under the circumstances of a burgeoning oil industry, therefore, it seems fair to say that with regard to onshore reserves alone, the rapidly increasing output at existing oil fields and the growing number of new fields strongly confirm China's future as a large-scale producer of oil.

Oil Shale. China is known to have very rich deposits of oil shale as well as oil-bearing coal and sand. Production of oil from these non-liquid sources is believed to have exceeded 10% of total production of oil (see Table 2 in Part 4 below). Although oil is being extracted from non-liquid sources on an extensive scale, this production is supplementary to the production of oil from liquid sources. The oil content of the shale found in the fourteen major shale-bearing regions in the north, northeast, northwest, and south, is said to range from 4% to 27% with an average of 6%.

In August 1959 Deputy Minister of Petroleum Industry Li Jen-chun was said to have reported that the amount of shale deposits in 21 provinces alone reached as much as 360 billion tons and that, with an average of 6% oil content, over 20 billion tons of oil might be extracted from it. Some observers, however, have regarded statistics on natural resources released during the "great leap forward" period as open to question because they were often compiled by people enthusiastic about growth, but lacking the expertise for assesment. Nevertheless, it has become reasonably certain since 1959 that deposits of oil shale and other non-liquid sources are large enough in China to supplement natural crude oil or even to substitute for it in the event of its depletion. While in some countries it has been difficult to extract oil from shale due to economic and environmental reasons, this would not be the case in China where the cost of labor does not matter and the environmental problems of extraction have been regarded differently.

Offshore. China has not given any estimate of its offshore oil deposits, nor has any other country that shares the Yellow and East China Seas with China. The only official prediction to date is the report of a geophysical survey conducted by ECAFE in 1968-1969, which reads in part:

A high probability exists that the continental shelf between Taiwan and Japan may be one of the most profilic oil reservoirs in the world. It is also one of the few large continental shelves of the world that has remained untested by the drill, owing to military and political factors, as well as to a lack of even reconnaissance geological information such as provided by this short report.

A second favorable area for oil and gas is beneath the Yellow Sea where three broad basins are present. These basins are interconnected, but the center of one is near Korea and the centers of the other two are near the mainland of China. The basins contain a thickness of nearly 1.5 km [kilometers] of sediment. . .and the sediments probably have a higher content of organic matter. . . .

The seabed topography of the South China Sea is almost completely different from that of the other two seas, and only a narrow belt of shallow continental shelf lies along the coasts of China and Vietnam.

Very little has been reported on exploration along the coasts of China and the prospects for oil. In September 1973 Radio Peking reported that China had made some progress in surveying offshore petroleum, but at the current state of exploration, it would be premature to expect even a very loose estimate of China's offshore deposits. Prospects of oil in the Pohai Bay deserve attention for the Bay, which is generally regarded as China's internal sea, is the only offshore area where China is reported to have been actively engaged in exploration. Except at its mouth the depth of the Bay does not exceed 35 meters and its periphery is lined with a shallow belt only 18 meters deep. It is probable that the deposits of Shengli and Takang oil fields sitting on the coasts are continuous with the area beneath the Bay. In a report on Shengli broadcast on 30 September 1974, Radio Peking said that ". . .continuous heavy rain hit part of the oil field this autumn and caused a sudden rise of sea tides. Battling in waist-deep water, the workers saved the oil wells and ensured a steady rise in crude oil output."

There are technological and politico-legal reasons to believe that it will not be possible for China to determine the amount of its offshore oil reserves in the near future. Comprehensive exploration would have to be preceded by the settlement of the sea-boundary issues with Japan and Korea as well as the territorial disputes over the ownership of the Tiaoyutai (Senkaku) Islands with Japan and the Paracel-Spratly Islands with other coastal states of the South China Sea. At least, from what is known of the geological structure of the shelf, the chances of China developing offshore oil seem promising.

Oil Production

Although official statistics may be lacking, the amount of oil that China actually produces is a matter of great interest to the rest of the world. If China does not know how much oil it has, it certainly knows how much it produces. Since 1960 when it ceased to publish statistics, oil production figures seem to have been casually discussed with foreign visitors by Premier Chou En-lai on two occasions: first with Edgar Snow in 1971, to the effect that the output in 1970 was 20 million tons; and second, with Japanese Foreign Minister Ohira in 1974, indicating that the output in 1973 was 50 million tons. On both occasions the figures were received with surprise and with skepticism by most foreign observers, based upon their habitual mistrust of Chinese economic statistics as well as doubts about the extent of production from non-liquid sources, such as oil shale and oil-bearing coal and sand.

A year later, however, experts had fewer reservations about China's oil production. Some Japanese importers of Chinese oil expected China's production to reach 70 million tons in 1974 and 100 million tons in 1976. Other Japanese sources anticipated Chinese production on the order of 400 million tons in 1980. By contrast, the Central Intelligence Agency of the United States, in a dispatch of the New York Times on 13 December 1974, expected China to "produce four million barrels a day by 1980, with one million available for export." Four million barrels a day amounts to 200 million tons a year.

Strictly speaking, it is not fair to say that China does not publish any statistics. But it publishes figures in relative terms only. To quote a few examples as given by Radio Peking on 5 September 1973, reporting on China's oil industry: "China's crude oil output in 1972 was four times the amount of 1965. . . . On the average, it rose 22 percent a year during this period. . . . Today China has a surplus of petroleum. . . . There was an average annual increase of 28 percent in crude oil output during the 1969-1972 period. . . . Six refineries doubled their output in 1970 after a technical transformation. . . . In 1971, 66 percent of all the new oil-refining capacity added was tapped this way." Another significant recent example may be seen in Premier Chou En-lai's report to the First Session of the Fourth National People's Congress of January 1975 that "petroleum output in 1974 increased 7½ times that of 1964."

With the base figures unavailable, such percentage terms are not very helpful. On the basis of percentages gleaned from various sources and the above figures which Chou En-lai quoted for 1970 and 1973, a great deal of effort has been exerted by expert observers to fill in the gap between 1959 (the last year for which official statistics were published by China) and 1970, and between 1970 and 1973. Different observers have arrived at different approximations which conflict with one another. The cause of the confusion has been attributable in part to the fact that the growth rates given in some Chinese sources have not always been consistent with other sources. Widely different estimates of the rate of growth of China's oil production have been made: Table 1 shows the approximations of different analysts.

It is interesting to note in this table that estimates by the ROC (Taiwan) tend invariably to be lower than the others, two conspicuous examples being the figures for 1970 and 1973. For the latter year, Taiwan's estimate is only 25 million tons. There has been a proliferation of China oil studies in both Taiwan and Japan, but their findings, especially those relating to production, differ considerably, with Japan's tending toward overestimation and Taiwan's tending toward underestimation.

Analysts of oil production in China must not only listen to the "drum." but also look at the "drummer." In their studies, specialists in both Japan and Taiwan occasionally have relied on data which originated in the West. These data have been sent back and forth over the Pacific and the Atlantic between Tokyo, Taipei and Hong Kong on the one side and North America and Western Europe on the other. Undeniably this tends to affect the authenticity or reliability of the findings by Japan and Taiwan, both of which, because of their proximity to China and their immediate interest in Chinese oil, might be expected to be more careful with their figures.

By any standard, however, production has been increasing at an extraordinary rate during the past 25 years, as may be seen from the table below. In global terms, China's output of 45 million tons (taking the highest estimate in the table) in 1972 would still be less than 2% of the world's total output in that year. This compares very modestly with production by the world's major producers: the United States' 530 million tons, the Soviet Union's 350 m/t, Kuwait's 152 m/t, and Libya's 105 m/t in 1972. On the assumption that China will continue to increase its output in the future, the exact rate will ultimately depend on three important factors. First, China has preferred not to develop its under-

TABLE 1
Estimates of China's Oil Production
(in 1,000 tons)

	PRC[1]	ROC[1]	USA	USSR	JAPAN-a[2]	JAPAN-b	JAPAN-c	JAPAN-d	JAPAN-e	UN
1949	121	x	x	x	x	x	x	x	x	x
1950	200	x	x	x	x	x	x	x	x	x
1951	305	x	x	x	x	x	x	x	x	x
1952	436	x	x	x	x	x	x	x	x	x
1953	622	x	x	x	x	x	x	x	x	x
1954	789	x	x	x	x	x	x	x	x	x
1955	966	x	x	x	x	x	x	x	x	x
1956	1,163	x	x	x	x	x	x	x	x	x
1957	1,458	1,458	1,458	1,500	1,458	x	x	x	x	x
1958	2,264	2,264	2,300	x	2,264	x	x	x	x	x
1959	3,700	3,700	3,700	3,700	3,680	x	x	x	x	x
1960	x	5,200	4,600	x	5,200	x	x	x	x	5,500
1961	x	5,400	4,500	x	5,000	x	x	x	x	6,200
1962	x	6,000	5,000	5,800	6,250	x	x	x	x	6,800
1963	x	7,000	5,500	x	7,000	x	x	x	x	7,500
1964	x	8,500	6,900	x	8,400	x	x	x	x	8,500
1965	x	9,500	8,000	x	10,000	x	12,500	10,500	x	10,000
1966	x	11,000	10,000	12,000	12,000	x	x	x	x	13,000

Year											
1967	x	8,500	10,000	10,000	10,000	x	x	x	x	11,000
1968	x	9,500	11,000	x	12,000	x	x	18,340	x	15,000
1969	x	11,000	14,000	x	14,500	x	x	21,610	x	20,000
1970	20,000	14,500	18,000	20,000	18,200	x	25,000	28,650	x	24,000
1971	25,440	18,500	23,000	25,000	22,000	36,700	31,800	36,420	39,350	x
1972	29,500	21,500	26,700	29,000	25,000	42,570	36,900	42,250	45,650	x
1973	50,000	25,000	x	x	x	50,000	x	50,000	54,000	x
1974	x	x	x	x	x	61,000	x	x	x	x
1975	x	x	x	x	x	80,600	x	x	x	x
1976	x	x	x	x	x	103,000	x	x	x	x
1977	x	x	x	x	x	134,000	x	x	x	x
1978	x	x	x	x	x	158,000	x	x	x	x
1979	x	x	x	x	x	168,000	x	x	x	x

1. PRC = The People's Republic of China; ROC = the Republic of China.
   Source: Chang Chun, "Peiping's [Peking's] Petroleum Industry: Growth and Future Development," *Issues and Studies*, 1974.
2. JAPAN-a by K. Takagi is from Chang above; JAPAN-b by Takahashi Shogoro, in *Nitchu Keizai Kaiho* (China-Japan economic report), Dec. 1973; and JAPAN-c by Ohno Hideo, "Tenkankio Mukaeta Chugokuno Sekyu" (China's oil at a turning point), *Chugoku Keizai Tsushin* (China economy report) a Japanese language monthly, Feb. 1973; and JAPAN-d and -e by Takabatake Ariyoshi, "Seyku," (oil) 1974.

ground resources in ways "which would produce quick results, but would do long-range damage to production," according to Radio Peking, on 8 January 1973. This policy will also affect the volume of oil reserves in China. Second, it will probably be some time before China's oil technology and its transportation system will reach a level comparable to that of the West. Each of these factors will require several years for development and improvement. Third, since China has shown little desire to meet its domestic demand for refined products with imports, the refining capacity of the country will have to be expanded to keep up with crude production and domestic oil needs.

Major Production Centers

It has been extremely difficult to keep up-to-date with China's discoveries of new oil fields because, first, China has apparently made it a rule not to report a new field until its development has reached an advanced stage and second, the names given to new oil fields have not necessarily been the geographical names of the places where oil has been found. In the four examples given earlier, Taching meant "great celebration," Takang, "great harbor," Shengli, "victory," and Chiling, "seven-zero." As a result, the exact location of Chiling, first reported by Peking in March 1966, is not yet known, which may indicate that other newly discovered fields are being developed unknown to the outside world.

The following profile of major natural and artificial crude oil production centers is based mainly on Chinese and Japanese language sources published during the past few years. The estimates of current production at each center, which have been taken mostly from Chien Yuan-heng's study in 1974, appear to be very conservative.

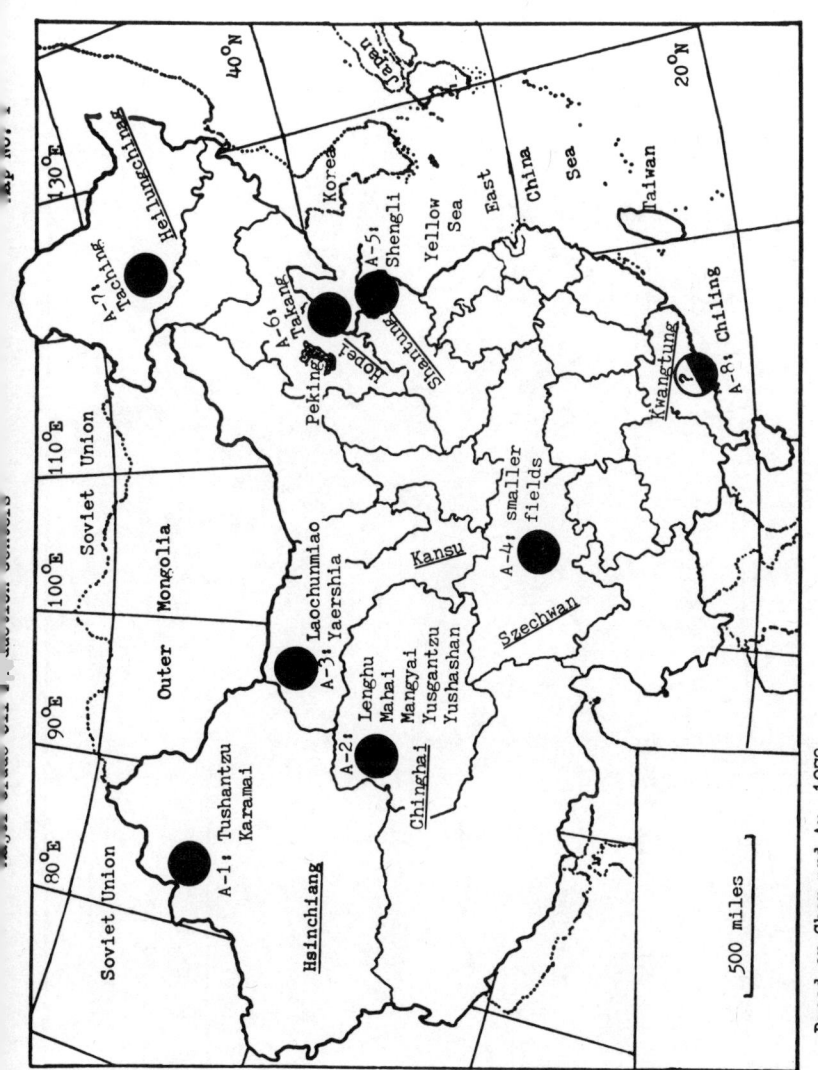

Based on Chen and Au, 1972

Map No. 2

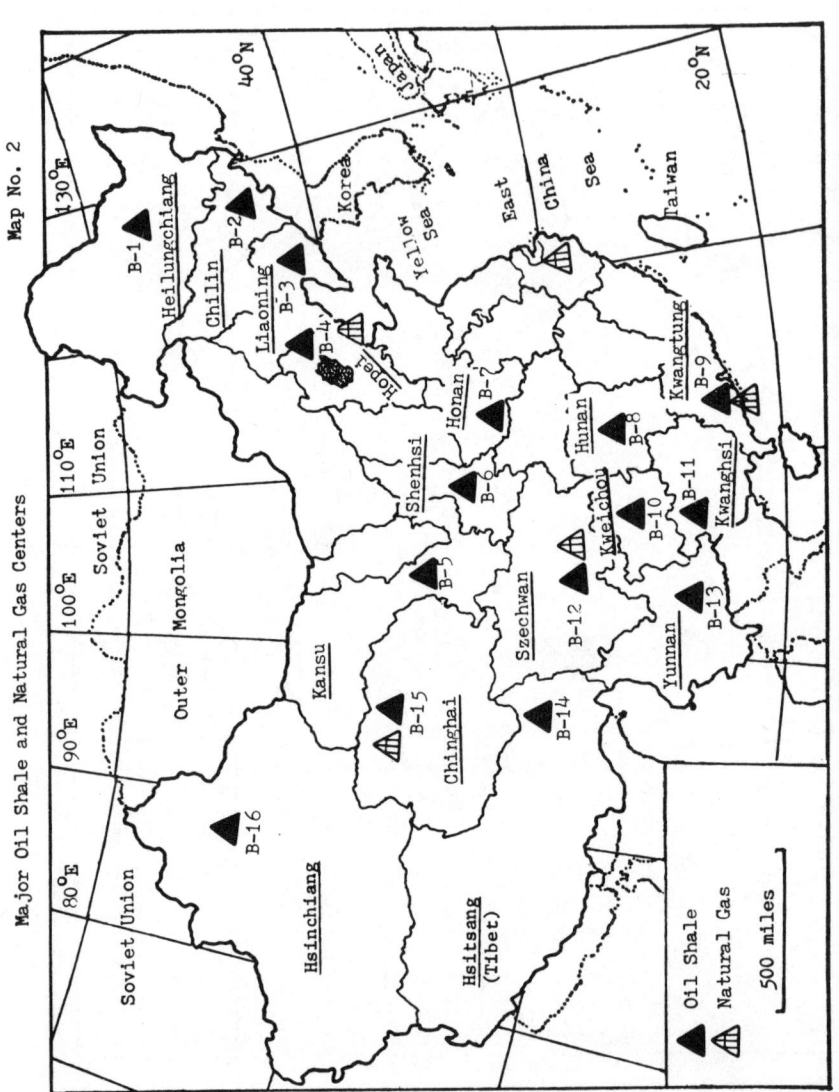

Major Oil Shale and Natural Gas Centers

Based on Chen and Au, 1972; and Studies on Mainland Economy Series No. 5, Taipei, 1967

A-1: Dzungarian Basin, Sinkiang, northwest China.
Tushantzu and Karamai (black oil in Uighurs) are the two major centers in this region, about 140 kilometers apart, and are connected with a pipeline built in 1959. There are now refining and other petrochemical facilities here. In October 1950, a Sino-Soviet partnership company was formed at Tushantzu to manage the field jointly, but was dissolved in 1956. The output at Karamai alone has been about 4 million tons a year.

A-2: Tsaidam Basin, Chinghai Province, west China.
The major fields here are Lenghu, Nahai, Mangyai and Yuchuantzu. The oil-bearing formations are so shallow that oil once gushed out from one of the wells at a depth of only 300 meters. This center also has refining and other petrochemical facilities and is one of the five natural gas-producing areas — the other four being Szechwan (A-4 below); Kwangchou, Kwangtung Province; Juian, Ningpo, and Hangchou of Chechiang Province; and Takang (A-6 below).

A-3: Yumen Oil Fields, Kansu Province, west China.
The major centers are Laochunmiao and Yaershia. A pipeline connects the Yumen railway station with Yaershia and other fields. A refinery has been built here, but surplus crude from this area is shipped to Lanchou for refining by means of an 882-kilometer pipeline, the longest one in China to date. A longer line from Taching to Chinghuangtao has been completed (see A-7, below). Output in 1973 was about 3 million tons.

A-4: Szechwan Basin, Szechwan Province, central China.
The major centers consist of relatively small fields which were developed after 1957 at the suggestion of Russian experts. Refineries of small size

have been built here. With more than 200 gas structures, this is also one of the two major natural gas centers in China, the other one being Takang (A-6 below). The 1974 output was about 2 million tons.

A-5: Shengli Oil Fields, Shantung Province, east China. One of the three largest oil fields in China is situated at the estuary of the Huang Ho River. The deposits here are believed to be continuous into the Pohai Bay. Some observers regard this center as "North" Shengli, with another field — "South" Shengli — situated further south in Anhwei Province. Another large field was reported in November 1973 (*Ming Pao*, Hong Kong) to have been found in Itu west of Shengli. Output in 1973 was about 5 million tons.

A-6: Takang Oil Fields, Hopei Province, east China.
This field was first mentioned by Peking briefly in January 1974 and again in more detail in May 1974. It was shown for the first time to visitors from a non-communist country, a Japanese oil mission, in August 1974. The Japanese visitors reported that there were two Takangs — South and North — both situated about 60 kilometers southeast of Tienchin along the coast of the Pohai Bay, and that the one they were shown was North Takang. Among the foreign correspondents in China, the Japanese were the first to be shown this field in November 1974. This is also one of the two major natural gas centers in China, the other one being Szechwan (A-4 above). The current output is not known, but in terms of future prospects, this oil field is thought to be one of the three largest in China.

A-7: Sungliao Basin, Heilungchiang Province, northeast

China. The famous Taching oil field which consists of five sections (north, south, east, west and central) is representative of this area, and the area as a whole is one of the three largest oil centers of China. In July 1973 further finds were reported to have been made to the north of the main field. In one section of the field each well produced on the average 47 tons of crude a day. The pipeline completed in 1974 between Taching and Chinghuangtao was 1,152 kilometers long. A large part of the installation at Taching is reported to be underground. Production in 1973 amounted to about 13 million tons.

A-8: Chiling Oil Field, exact location unknown.

This field was first reported by Peking in November 1972 and is now thought to have prospective resources comparable to each of the other three largest oil centers above. From fragmentary reports available, it is believed that this field is situated somewhere at the estuary of the Pearl River in Kwangtung Province, south China. Output in 1973 was believed to exceed one million tons.

According to a study done in Taiwan in the Ministry of Economic Affairs in June 1967, there were fourteen major oil shale production and refining centers throughout China, each producing an unknown amount of crude oil. Their locations were given as follows:

B-1: Nenchiang, Heilungchiang Province, northeast China.
B-2: Huatien, Chilin Province, northeast China.
B-3: Fushun, Liaoning Province, northeast China.
This is known to be China's oldest oil shale-producing area, where the Japanese built production

facilities in 1928.
B-4: Chengte, Hopei Province, northeast China.
B-5: Yingdeng, Kansu Province, central north China.
B-6: Ordos Plateau-Northern Shenhsi, Shenhsi Province, central north China.
B-7: Tungpai-Wucheng, Honan Province, east China.
B-8: Shaoyang-Hsianghsiang-Linfeng-Shihmen, Hunan Province, south China.
B-9: Mouming, Kwangtung Province, south China.
B-10: Fuchuan, Kweichou Province, south China.
B-11: Paishe, Kwanghsi Autonomous Region, south China.
B-12: Loshan, Szechwan Province, central China.
B-13: Menghua, Yunnan Province, southwest China.
B-14: Changtu, Hsitsang (Tibet), west China.
B-15: Menyuan, Chinghai Province, west China.
B-16: Mt. Poketa, Hsinchiang Autonomous Region, west China.

Of these sixteen centers, the first three are believed to be the most important in terms of current production and prospective output. According to the above-mentioned study, actual production of oil from such non-liquid sources as oil shale and oil-bearing coal and sand was being carried on at fifteen artificial oil plants, eleven of them located in northeast China, as well as at numerous other minor production facilities which are located throughout the country.

TABLE 2
Estimate of Shale Oil Production (1,000 tons)

	Shale Oil	Ratio with Natural Crude
1949	51	42.1%
1957	591	40.9
1965	1,950	22.5
1969	2,000	13.8
1970	2,000	10.0
1971	2,000	7.8

Source: *Kokusai Boeki* (International Trade), May, 1974

Demand and Supply of Energy

A planned economy adjusts its demand and supply of staples on the basis of planned priorities. Oil management in China is no exception to this rule. In addition to the problem of obtaining economic data, the factor of economic planning makes it far more difficult to analyze China's demand and supply of oil than to assess its reserves or production. Since it has not been possible to ascertain the growth rate of demand and supply in the past, it is hardly possible to make concrete forecasts for the future. All that can be done, perhaps, is to give some examples of past oil consumption patterns in China from which future trends may be deduced.

Oil consumption in China has always been very low. The primary reason for this is that the country still has a basically agricultural economy where the main energy requirements can be met with coal, a resource that China is known to have in abundance. In any analysis of the Chinese economy, the overriding importance of agriculture cannot be overlooked. The economic policy of the People's Republic of China has been to develop industry, not at the expense of, but as a supplement to the agricultural base. This is made emphatically clear by the maxim, "Take agriculture as the foundation and industry as the leading factor." This principle of Chinese development derives its rationale from the fact that so vast an economy as China's provides heavy industry with an important market, because, according to Red Flag, quoted by Radio Peking on 17 December 1973, "gradual progress in the technical improvement and modernization of agriculture calls for further development of machinery, fertilizer, water conservation and electric power projects and transport facilities for the farms, as well as fuel and building materials for the rural communes."

During the 1950's China's demand for oil was met for the most part with imports from the Soviet Union. The scarcity of oil during the early 1950's was evidenced by the tight controls the government placed on oil consumption. For example, in compliance with a directive issued in central and south China on 15 September 1951, persons or facilities in these regions in possession of oil in excess of 53 gallons were required to register with municipal authorities, and households in need of oil products were obliged to apply for ration tickets. During the mid-1950's the oil situation remained virtually unchanged due to the rising demand. Finding that over 90% of gasoline suppled was consumed by automobiles, the central government decided in February 1956 to lower the per-vehicle consumption by five to ten percent of the 1955 level by means of a monthly allocation system.

During the 1960's the domestic production of oil reached a level of self-sufficiency. Nevertheless the demand for oil in almost every sector continued to increase. By 1970 military demand alone was believed to consume almost 32% of the entire oil supply, the breakdown being 7.36% for the army, 8.64% for the navy, and 16% for the air force. Although direct comparison is not easy due to a difficult system of classification, the differences in the oil consumption patterns between China and selected other countries may be seen in Table 3.

On the assumption that the figures in the above table are reasonably accurate, it should be noted that gasoline represents 18.5% of China's oil consumption, and that 80% of the gasoline is consumed by motor vehicles. If the production of oil in 1970 were placed at 20 million tons and exports were ignored because they represented an insignificant amount, the share of consumption by motor vehicles would barely reach 15% of the total amount of oil products consumed. Unless there were vehicles using other fuels, this precentage appears very low in comparison with other countries, a phenomenon in keeping with an *Economist* report of 22 September 1973 that in 1970 there were only

TABLE 3

Demand by Products

	China	US	Japan	W/Germany	
Gasoline	18.5%	48.6%	20.0%	23.9%	Gasoline
Kerosene	40.0	30.9	21.1	51.9	Intermediary
Diesel	19.5	20.5	58.9	24.2	Diesel
Lubricant	12.0				
Misc.	10.0				
	100.0	100.0	100.0	100.0	

(China: c. 1970; U.S., Japan, and W/Germany: 1972)

Consumption by Use

China (c. 1970)

Gasoline . . . . 80% by motor vehicles
10% by aircraft
10% by misc.

Kerosene . . . . 70% by shipping craft
30% by power generation

Diesel . . . . 30-40% by tractors
16% by oil drilling, etc.
2-3% by power stations
10-30% by military
20% by drainage and irrigation

U.S., Japan, W/Germany (1970)

	U.S.	Japan	W/Germany
Domestic	34%	21%	33%
Industrial	31	59	42
Transportation	22	13	12
Power Gen.	13	7	13
	100	100	100

Sources:
1. *Arshih Nienlai Feichu Shihyou Kungyueh Yenbien* (The Progressive Changes of Petroleum Industry in Recent 20 years in Mainland China), Studies in Mainland China Economy, Series No. 42, Ministry of Economic Affairs, Taipei, May 1971, pp. 102-3.
2. *Sekyu Mondaino Sogo Kaisetsu* (Comprehensive Analysis of Oil Problems), Nihon Keizai Shinbunsha, Tokyo, Feb. 1974, pp. 119-20.

130,000 passenger cars in China, or one car for every 5,711 Chinese in contrast to India's ratio of 1 to 902 or Thailand's 1 to 175.

The demand for kerosene and diesel oil has been conspicuously high in China, as in Japan. But Japan's high demand for diesel oil has mainly been from industry, while China's kerosene and diesel oil demand has been from agriculture and the various means of transportation by road, inland rivers, canals and coastal waters. However, such a comparison of demand and supply patterns with respect to oil alone is hardly meaningful unless it is placed in the perspective of the energy consumption pattern as a whole. Hence it is necessary to compare the use of oil with that of other major sources of energy, such as coal, natural gas, and hydroelectric power.

In terms of the energy supply structure, coal is the most important product in China, meeting 86.7% of the total demand for energy. The share of oil was known to be 10.5% in 1973, with natural gas and hydroelectric power meeting the remaining fraction. With its coal reserves amounting to 1,044,000 million tons, China is known to rank third in the world, surpassed only by the United States' 1,420,000 m/t and the Soviet Union's 1,199,800 m/t. These three giants alone have almost 80% of the world's total reserves. Some Japanese estimates have placed China's reserves even higher — about 1,500,000 m/t — or more than the United States. The coal reserves and energy supply structure of China and other countries are compared in Table 4.

The importance of coal in China's energy supply situation does not require further comment, but the background of the coal industry is relevant to China's energy policy. Until very recently coal was produced mainly north of the Yangtze River, and south China was generally regarded as "poor in coal." Today China prides itself on the fact that since the Cultural Revolution coal mines have been found in the south,

TABLE 4

Coal Reserves[1] (million tons)

	Reserves	% of world total
China	1,011,400	21.8%
United States	1,420,000	30.6
Soviet Union	1,199,800	25.9
Japan	10,000	0.2

Energy Supply Structure[2]

	China	U.S.	Japan	W/Germany
Coal	86.7%	20.1%	17.9%	39.1%
Oil	10.5	44.3	73.5	52.7
Nat. Gas		31.6	1.3	4.8
Hydro.	2.8	3.4	6.7	0.5
	100.0	100.0	100.0	100.0

(China, U.S., and W/Germany: 1970; Japan: 1971)

Sources: 1. *Shigen Mondaino Tembo* (Outlook on Natural Resources Problems), Ministry of International Trade and Industry, Tokyo, 1971, p. 390.
2. Chen Cheng-siang and Au Kam-nin, "The Petroleum Industry of China," *Die Erde*, Heft 3/4, 1972, p. 318.
I. Kamada, *Nihonno Enerugi Kiki* (The Energy Crisis of Japan), Tokyo, 1973, p. 157.
Kokusai Boeki (International Trade; Japanese Weekly, Tokyo), 1 May 1973.

so the traditional flow of the "northern coal to the south" is not likely to continue. Before 1949 there seem to have been only eight major coal mines throughout the country, but that number had climbed to fifty-five by 1974. The foremost among these mines are the so-called seven majors: Chihsi, Fuhsin, Fushun, Hokang, Huainan, Kailan, and Tatung, most of which are in north and northeast China. The total number of coal mines of various sizes is said to be about 800, of which 700 have been developed since the "great leap forward" movement of 1958-1960. Among the new centers of the coal industry are Fengyi, Meitien, Pingtingshan, Shihchushan and Hsishan. The rate of growth in coal production since 1949, moreover, is as impressive as that in oil production, although there seems to have been more fluctuation in the growth rate (see Table 5).

TABLE 5

Coal Production (1,000 tons)

1949	32.4	1961	180.0 - 250.0
1950	42.9	1962	180.0 - 250.0
1951	53.1	1963	190.0 - 270.0
1952	66.5	1964	200.0 - 290.0
1953	69.7	1965	210.0 - 300.0
1954	83.7	1966	240.0 - 325.0
1955	98.3	1967	150.0 - 225.0
1956	110.4	1968	200.0 - 300.0
1957	130.7	1969	220.0 - 330.0
1958	270.7	1970	200.0 - 360.0
1959	347.8	1971	240.0 - 350.0
1960	400.0 - 425.0	1972	310.0

Sources: Heinz Harnisch and Hans G. Gloria, *Die Energiewirtschaft der Volksrepublik China, Rohstoffwirtschaft* International, Bd. 1, Essen, 1973, p. 47, and *Kokusai Boeki* (International Trade); Japanese Weekly, Tokyo, 1 May 1973.

Only a small fraction of China's energy requirements are met by natural gas and electric power, which together are believed to supply 2.8% of the total demand for energy in the country. The ratio of gas to electric power use is not known. There are only three reported gas fields in China: Szechwan, Shanghai, and Tsaidam. Szechwan is known to be both the largest and the oldest well. It was not until the latter part of the 1950's that the gas fields were actively developed or expanded. Production has increased very rapidly, as shown in Table 6.

TABLE 6

Natural Gas Production (million cubic meters)

1949	50
1953	98
1957	740
1961	4,000
1965	12,100
1971	34,000

Source: Chen and Au, 1972, p. 319

With respect to China's electric power industry, in 1955 when the total output was 12.28 billion kilowatt/hours, the ratio between hydro and thermal generation was said to be 47% to 48%. In an effort to modernize agriculture after the "great leap forward" movement, numerous medium and small power stations were built throughout the country in addition to existing large ones. By 1971 the total electric power output in China was known to have reached 84 billion KWH's. The total number of small power stations, which had been built for the specific purpose of meeting the demand in small communities of the rural areas, was reported in 1974 to exceed 350,000. The output of such stations supplies over 16% of hydroelectric power in China.

From the foregoing analysis, it appears that, in the pattern of energy consumption, coal meets the largest share of the demand in China. However, the trend is changing in favor of oil. Given the rather short history of the oil industry, the rate of change has been very rapid, as may be seen in Table 7.

The proportion of natural gas and electric power has remained virtually unchanged while coal has decreased in relation to oil. Aside from the change in the ratio between different sources of energy, it is certain that the demand for oil will increase in China as in other countries. Ultimately the point is not whether China's oil demand will increase, but how rapidly it will be allowed to increase, especially in the process of modernizing agriculture and industry. The policy choice will in turn depend on the priorities as set out in the forthcoming 5th five-year economic development plan for 1976-1980.

TABLE 7

Supply Pattern by Products

	Oil	Coal	Nat. Gas/Hydro, etc.
1960	4.1%	93.8%	2.1%
1965	5.6	92.4	2.1
1968	9.9	87.1	2.8
1970	10.5	86.7	2.8

Source: *Sekyuto Sekyu Kagaku* (Oil and Petrochemistry), Vol. 17, No. 1, as quoted in *Kokusai Boeki* (International Trade), Tokyo, 1 May, 1973.

Oil Refining Capacity

China's oil refining capacity seems to have increased almost at the same rate as its production rate. In September 1973 Peking reported that its refining capacity had reached 3.7 times that of 1965; but there is no way to ascertain the amount refined in 1965. Opinions differ widely with respect to China's current refining capacity. The following figures are cited just to show the differences in the amount of crude oil which some observers estimate China has refined in recent years:

1970: from 10 to 37.93 million tons
1971: from 30 to 44.03 million tons
1972: from 28 to 44.03 million tons

Sources: Ohno as quoted in Takabatake, 1974, p. 306; Chen and Au, 1972, p. 329; and others as quoted in Chang, 1974, p. 47.

Some arbitrary conjectures have been made that, since China was not able to refine as much oil as it produced, the marginal excess has been exported. But the truth seems to be simply that China has planned its oil production to complement its refining capacity.

Major refineries are located in Lanchou, Peking, Shanghai, and Taching, each with a capacity to refine over 3 m/t a year. Taching is said to be the largest of those built in oil-producing centers. Some of the crude produced here is sent to Fushun, Peking, Shanghai, Talien, and Tangku for refining. Lanchou, located in central China and nearer to other producing areas such as Yumen and Tsaidam to the northwest and Szechwan to the south, is rightly thought to be one of the largest and most important in China and draws crude from other oil fields. Lanchou has thus become not only an oil-refining center but also a petrochemical industrial complex. According to Radio Peking on 5 September 1973, "the variety of its products has increased from 16 in its early days to the present 160," and the workers in the petrochemical industry in China "have also succeeded in using refinery tail gas and aromatic hydrocarbon to produce synthetic rubber, fiber, and plastics, giving impetus to the growth of China's petrochemical industry."

A second group of at least six refineries is known to be in operation in Fushun, Karamai, Mouming, Nanchung, Tangku, and Tushantzu, each with a refining capacity of about 2 m/t a year. A third group of nine refineries with a capacity of less than a million tons has also been reported. In addition, there seem to be numerous smaller refineries throughout the country, especially in northeast China, as may be seen from their names, for example, Northeast Plant No. 1 through No. 10.

China is the only developing country in the world that has created an oil industry of its own without relying heavily on foreign countries for investment or technology. Because

Major Refining Centers   Map No. 3

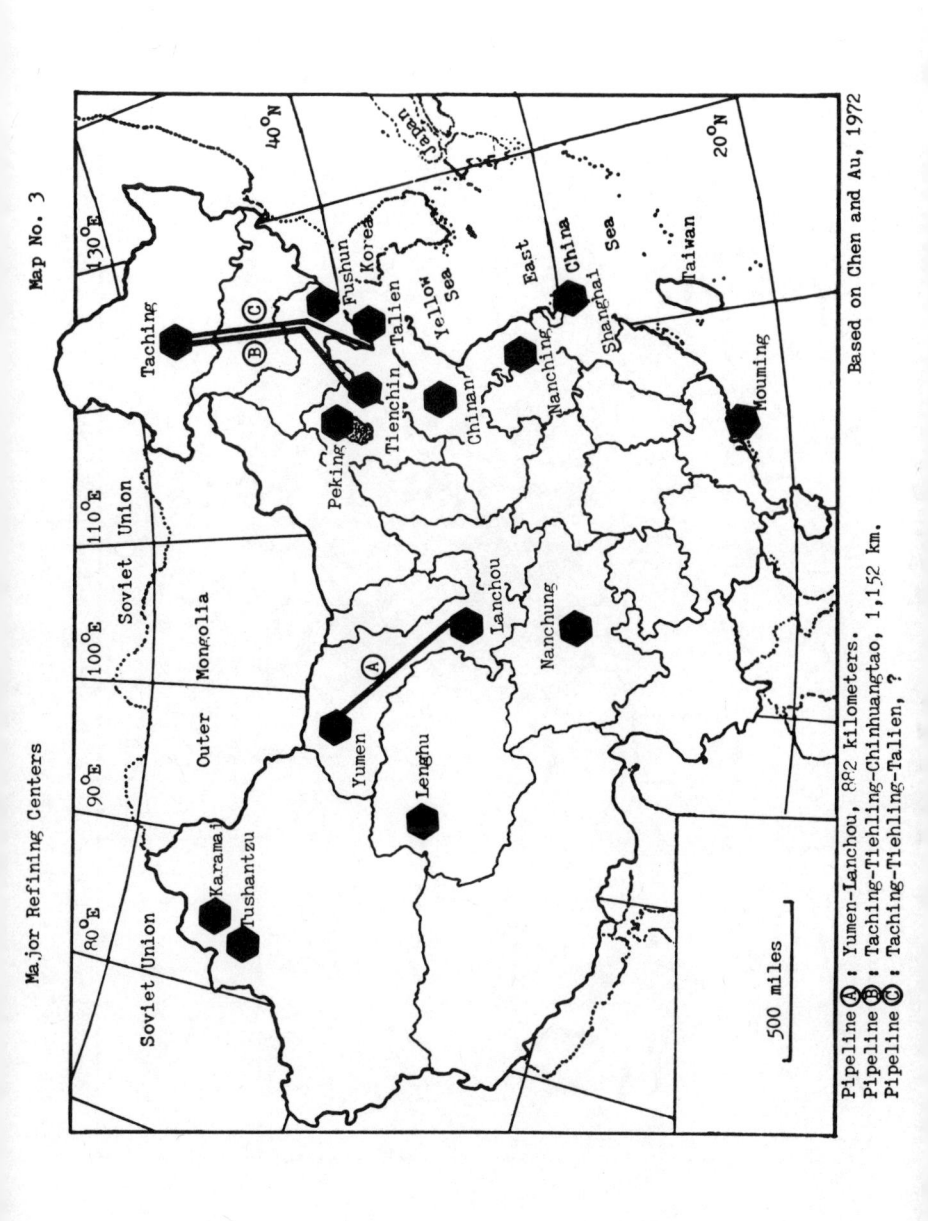

Pipeline Ⓐ : Yumen-Lanchou, 882 kilometers.
Pipeline Ⓑ : Taching-Tiehling-Chinhuangtao, 1,152 km.
Pipeline Ⓒ : Taching-Tiehling-Talien, ?

Based on Chen and Au, 1972

Areas with Coal Deposits   Map No. 4

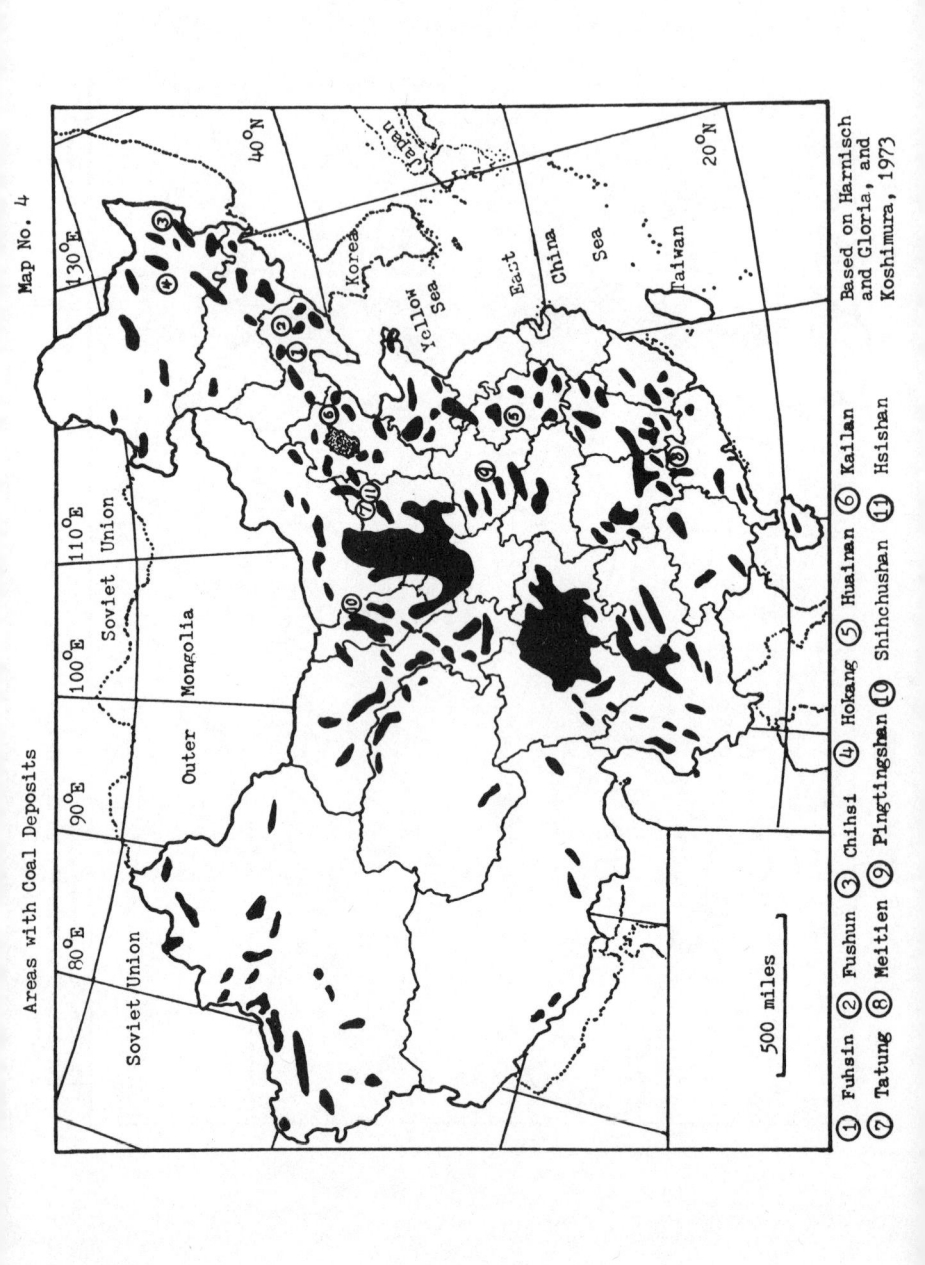

① Fuhsin ② Fushun ③ Chihsi ④ Hokang ⑤ Huainan ⑥ Kailan
⑦ Tatung ⑧ Meitien ⑨ Pingtingshan ⑩ Shihchushan ⑪ Hsishan

Based on Harnisch and Gloria, and Koshimura, 1973

of the confidence and experience that it has acquired this way, the Chinese government will not allow its limited oil-refining capacity to stand in the way of promoting the oil industry as a whole, and the lag in technology will very likely be reduced or eliminated in the next decade. In recent years, China has noticeably increased its imports of oil and petrochemical machinery, including equipment for the development of offshore oil. In fact, seven of the nineteen major contracts which China signed with Western firms during the first seven months of 1974 were reportedly for the expansion of its oil and petrochemical industries. Table 8 shows some outstanding examples of these imports:

TABLE 8
Imports of Oil Development Facilities

	From	Cost	Date
1. 2 support vessels for drilling	Japan	Y26.15 billion	Sept. 1972
2. Petrochemical plant	France	400 mil. francs	May 1973
3. Oil refinery equipment	France	US$300 mil.	Sept. 1973
4. Boring equipment	Sweden	16 mil. Krona	Jan. 1974
5. 8 support vessels for drilling	Denmark	US$20 mil.	Feb. 1974
6. Petrochemical plant	France	US$200 mil.	Feb. 1974
7. Well pressure control	U. S. A.	US$2 mil.	Feb. 1974
8. Coal mining equipment	W/Germany	DM20 mil.	Mar. 1974
9. 23 mining hoists	W/Germany	DM20 mil.	Apr. 1974
10. Oil drilling equipment	U. S. A.	US$20 mil.	Apr. 1974

Sources: 1, 2, 3, and 7 are from Chang, "Peiping's Petroleum Industry," *Issues and Studies*, 1974; and 4, 5, 6, 8, 9, and 10 are from *Kokusai Boeki* (International Trade), 1974.

Imports and Exports of Oil

China's export of oil is known to have begun in 1964 when a modest amount was shipped to North Korea. In 1965 North Vietnam became the second on the list of states receiving Chinese oil, a list that now includes Hong Kong, Japan, the Philippines, and Thailand.

The amount of oil exported by China to North Korea and North Vietnam is not known, nor is it clear whether they have been getting the oil purely on a commercial purchase basis or in the form of mutual help. The initial amounts of oil exported to the Philippines and Thailand, however, have been so meager that the exports in 1974 were more symbolic of friendship between the countries, fostered partly by the oil crisis, than substantive in terms of their total demand for oil. In relative terms, the oil exports of China to Japan have been the largest: one million tons in 1973 and 4.9 million tons in 1974. In August 1974 it was reported in Japan that some Japanese importers of Chinese oil expected the amount to reach 13 to 14 m/t in 1975. However, upon its return from China in early December 1974, a Japanese oil mission reported that 8 m/t was more likely to be the amount expected in 1975. In terms of Japan's demand for oil, which was over 230 m/t in 1973, the 8 m/t from China would be only a small fraction of the total, but Japan is greatly interested in the potential of China as an exporter of oil in the future.

Despite the appearance of China as an oil exporter, Peking was still reported to have been importing oil up to 1974; for example, the *Taihu*, a Chinese tanker built in Norway, arrived at Chanchiang, Kwangtung Province, with 60,000 tons of oil, apparently from Kuwait, on 23 August 1974. Until 1963 the Soviet Union was by far the largest supplier of oil to China, with occasional supplements coming from Albania, Iran, Iraq and Roumania. From 1964 onward other countries contributed proportionately more to Chinese oil imports, and it was reported that in 1970 some 400,000 tons of oil were shipped from countries in the Middle East to ports in China.

Table 9 shows the gradual decrease in China's oil imports.

Since the mid-1960's China has claimed self-sufficiency in oil, yet has imported oil as recently as August 1974. The explanation for this apparent contradiction may be found in China's foreign trade policy, on the assumption that its oil trade has also been conducted within the framework of its general foreign trade policy.

In 1974, three important articles on China's foreign trade policy appeared in the Chinese media: "New Developments in China's Foreign Trade" by Minister of Foreign Trade Li Chiang in *China's Foreign Trade*, No. 1, July 1974; "China's Foreign Trade" by Wang Yao-ting, Chairman, China Council for the Promotion of International Trade, in *Peking Review*, No. 41, 11 October 1974; and "Develop Foreign Trade by Maintaining Independence and Keeping the Initiative in Our Own Hands and Relying on Our Own Efforts" by Pu Hsuan in the *People's Daily*, 15 October 1974.

The philosophy embodied in each of the papers echoed what Chinese Vice-Premier Teng Hsiao-ping had said at the Sixth Special Session of the United Nations on Raw Materials and Development in April, 1974. Among the common points which the authors emphasized as basically important in promoting China's foreign trade were self-reliance, non-separation of politics and trade, and mutual benefit between partners. The third point — mutual benefit — was intended to mean that in foreign trade it is important to meet each other's needs, instead of either party's needs only. This interpretation may be extended to mean that in the name of friendship either partner may at times be required to import what it does not need, by way of meeting the other's need to export it. A deal thus made would then have little to do with the importer's actual demand and supply of the product. In the article above, Pu Hsuan says: "We have procured some of their products which were difficult to sell." Mutual benefit as it relates to China's foreign trade policy is not new; at least on one occasion during the late 1950's, Japan had rice in excess, but imported more from China because otherwise China would have refused to buy Japanese fertilizer.

The amount of oil which China is known to have imported from the Middle East in recent years has not been large enough to render implausible China's claim to self-sufficiency in oil. It appears small enough to be within the bounds of a "friendship trade." There have been allegations that the oil China exported to Thailand and other countries was of Middle East origin. Whatever the motive of the alleged re-export, it should not be difficult to ascertain the origin of the oil, because Chinese and Middle East crudes have different sulphur contents: China's crude is known to have less than one-tenth of one precent of sulphur, in contrast to the Middle East crude's eight-tenths to four and one-half percent.

In the final analysis, there is no reason to expect China to import oil in substantial quantities in the future. As regards its potential as a prospective exporter of oil, certain factors will encourage expanded shipments abroad. Oil is unusually effective as a political and economic instrument in foreign policy. Moreover, few other resources compare with oil as a source of "quick money," which China is going to need in increasing amounts in the future. On 13 December 1974, for example, it was reported in the *Nihon Keizai Shinbun* (Economic Daily of Japan), that negotiations in Peking over the export of Japanese fertilizer to China had had to be postponed due to a disagreement on the terms of a deferred payment. China was reported to have sought a longer term for payments on the grounds of a foreign currency shortage.

There are also factors that weigh against the increase of Chinese oil exports. First, China's own demand for oil is bound to increase, so that an increased output would not

TABLE 9

China's Imports of Oil (1,000 tons)

From the Soviet Union

Year	Crude	Kerosene	Diesel	Lubricant	Misc.	Total
1955	378	264	233	72	2	571
1956	397	240	377	74	2	693
1957	380	373	380	95	1	1,422
1958	672	333	663	199	1	1,836
1959	636	380	557	211	9	2,413
1960	568	386	709	212	11	2,373
1961	--	512	841	218	6	2,902
1962	--	488	378	210	6	1,847
1963	--	476	333	137	6	1,407
1964	--	139	80	15	1	505
1965	--	2	4	--	--	38

From Other Countries

Year	Rumania & Albania	Iran	Other Countries	Total
1955	--	0	276	1,219
1958	--	0	752	3,217
1960	--	199	728	3,847
1961	--	199	279	3,360
1962	462	199	576	3,021
1963	335	199	1,055	2,989
1964	238	199	1,356	2,264
1965	237	199	531	1,005
1966	235	199	--	474
1967	--	--	--	7
1968	--	--	--	1
1970	--	--	400	400

Sources: *Vneshnya Torgovlia* (Foreign Trade), Moscow, 1966-, as digested in Chen and Au, 1972, p. 332; and various sources as quoted in Chang, 1974, p. 53.

necessarily mean increased exports. The production of Chinese oil cannot be regarded solely from the standpoint of a prospective importer, and while some observers expect China to sell about 10% of its oil production, this ratio seems purely arbitrary. Second, China would not easily comprise its clearly-stated natural resource development policy, especially the principle of self-reliance. Third, the balance of payments position of China is not so unfavorable that any increase in price would call forth a large export of oil. Foreign observers place China's overall trade deficit for 1974 between $200 to $1,300 million. But, on the basis of $12.60 per barrel of crude (the price Japan paid to China in 1974), China could overcome even the higher 1974 deficit estimate by the sale of only fifteen million tons of crude, which is less than a quarter of what China produced in 1974.

Observations

China has based its economic policy on the principle of "self-reliance," a principle which has evolved from its unique experiences and circumstances. The development of its oil resources cannot be an exception to this principle, as may be seen, for example, from the statement made by Foreign Trade Minister Li Chiang in the article on "New Developments in China's Foreign Trade": "Socialist China will never try to attract foreign capital or exploit domestic or foreign natural resources in conjunction with other countries. . . . She will never go in for joint-management with foreign countries, much less grovel for foreign loans. . . ." On the other hand, it has been made clear by Minister Li and others in the leadership of the government that self-reliance is not synonymous with self-seclusion. What matters, therefore, is how flexibly China will apply the principle of self-reliance in the face of ever-growing opportunities for trade relations with the outside world.

The overall planning and decision-making process within the Chinese government as it relates to the national energy policy is hardly known to foreign observers. From various indications, however, it may be inferred that the system is a highly centralized one. For example, economic statistics, even in comparative terms, have usually been released not by the individual agencies but by the highest authorities in the government. This can be seen clearly in Premier Chou En-lai's report to the Fourth National People's Congress in January 1975.

The organization of the government's Cabinet, which consists of a premier, 12 vice-premiers, and 29 ministers, suggests that primary responsibility for energy affairs rests with the three energy ministries: Coal; Petroleum and Chemical; and Water Conservancy and Power; with the State Planning Commission coordinating them and the numerous other ministries, such as the seven machine-building ministries and the ministries of foreign affairs, foreign trade, and economic relations with foreign countries. The National Oil and Gas Exploration Cooperative would seem to be functional rather than part of the decision-making process through the ministries and the Cabinet.

China's oil development policy is bound to be of special interest to Japan, Korea, the Soviet Union, and the United States for the following reasons:

● *First*, although China's relations with Japan cannot be considered separately from its relations with the other three countries, it is important not to overlook an outstanding feature. Given Japan's vulnerability and China's abundant supply of oil, the former would no doubt lavish its capital and technology in return for whatever energy resources might be offered by the latter. However, it is doubtful whether China would ever hasten the pace of oil development solely in the interest of an important neighbor — Japan.

● *Second*, the prospects for the development of their seabed oil by Japan and Korea are to a great extent at the mercy of the Chinese principle of self-reliance. China has shown little enthusiasm for the desire of Japan and Korea either to seek agreement on the continental shelf boundaries in the Yellow and East China Seas or to develop the seabed oil through joint efforts. With the Third UN Conference on the Law of the Sea struggling to reach agreement on the law of ocean and shelf-boundary demarcation in 1975, and with the East China Sea full of insoluble legal issues, China seems to believe it preferable to seek offshore oil alone in areas not open to contest by the other coastal states, rather than to argue in vain over what is not likely to be settled as a purely legal issue. Unlike Japan and Korea, China is under no pressure to obtain oil from the sea, especially if to do so would compromise its principles or affect its other priorities adversely. In this connection, it may be noted that the Japanese-Korean joint development agreement of January 1974 relating to the overlapping areas of the East China Sea continental shelf might eventually prove abortive due to China's protest and Japan's calculated reluctance to ratify the agreement. As one of the three coastal states of the enclosed sea, China regards the agreement as outright collusion between Japan and Korea to carve up the resources for themselves only. On the part of Japan, it would appear that it has agreed to share with Korea what would eventually fall under its jurisdiction anyway by virtue of the possible international agreement on a 200-mile economic zone for coastal states, which seems to have gained consensus at the UN Law of the Sea Conference. It is conceivable that Japan failed not only to foresee the prospect of the economic zone, giving exclusive rights to the coastal state, but also did not appreciate the degree of China's sensitivity to this issue. Should the hard-wrought arrangements of the bilateral agree-

Seabed Areas with Oil Prospects   Map No. 5

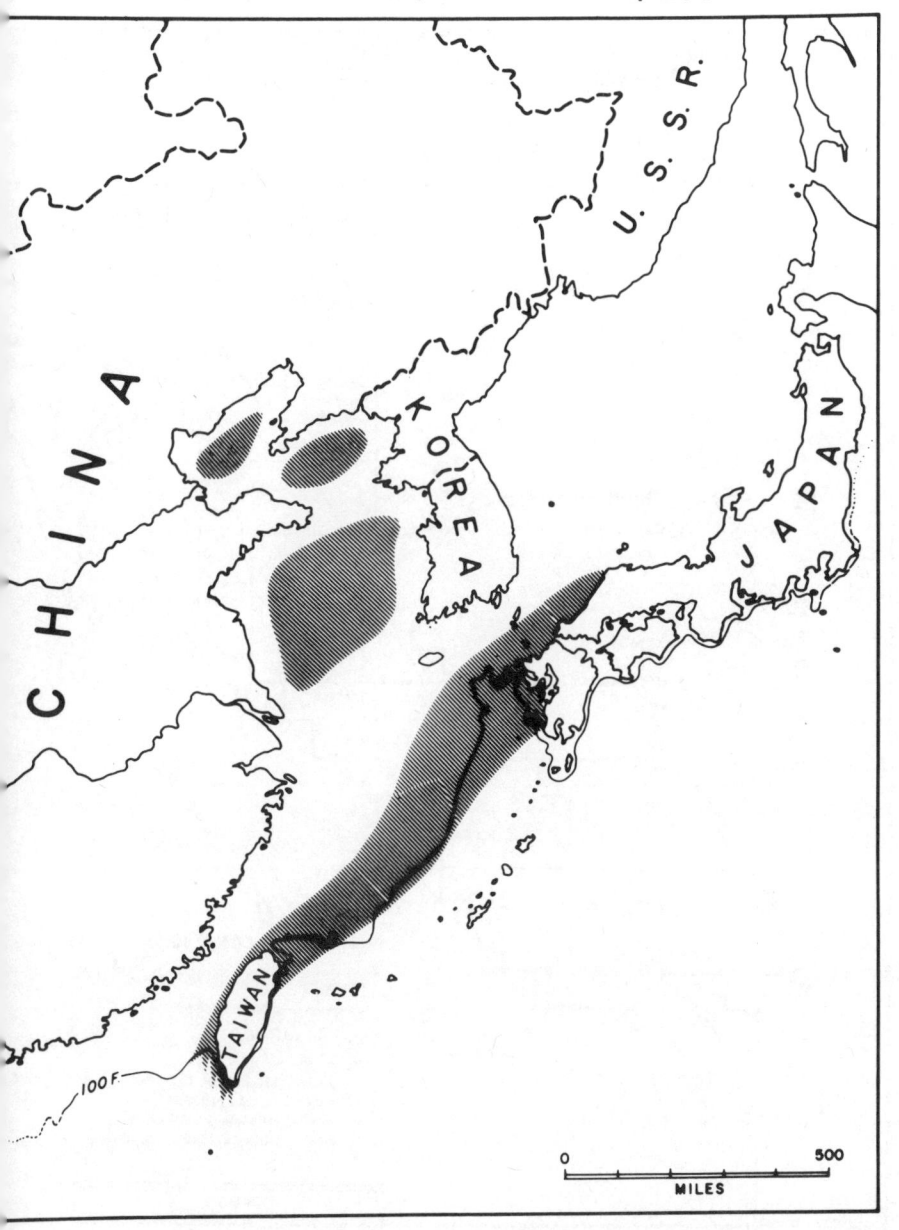

Based on ECAFE Tech. Bull., Vol. I, 1969

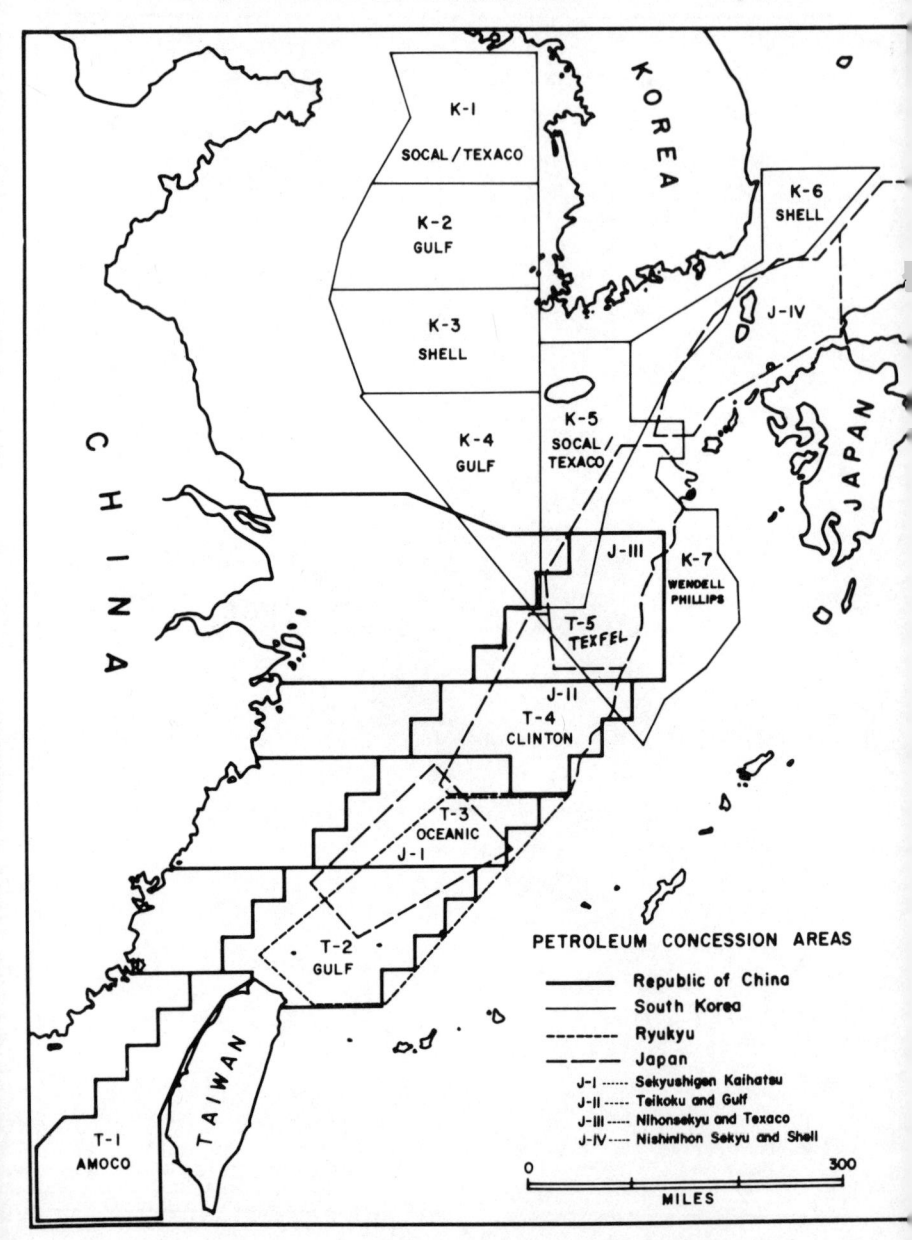

Unilateral Claims and Concession Areas   Map No. 6

Based on U. S. State Dept. Map 261 7-71

ment meet a "procedural death," even before their merits are tested, Korea would be left with no choice but to push forward with its original unilateral claims.

However, a sharpening of the oil controversy will not occur until oil is actually found in an area of overlapping claims. From the standpoint of the coastal states as well as the foreign oil interests holding oil development contracts with them, the reaction of China will be a matter of serious concern. Under present circumstances, the only way to test this crucial point is just to "risk and see." For example, Premier Chou En-lai's views on one of the overlapping areas were shown in January 1973 to a group of overseas Chinese students on a visit to China when he remarked, "Exploration for oil in the offshore waters of the Tiaoyutai (Senkaku) Islands may be tolerated, but not exploitation."

● *Third*, the oil strategies of China, Japan, and the Soviet Union are dominated by the sober reality that, as a resource-poor big power, Japan has to walk a tightrope between two resource-rich big powers that are fatally hostile to each other. Japan is irresistibly tempted by the natural resources of Russian Siberia on the one hand, but seriously concerned about China's objection to the exploitation and export of these resources by the Russians. Of five projects in the area — the development of Tyumen oil, Yakut natural gas, Sakhalin seabed oil, South Yakut coking coal, and Siberian timber — general agreements between Japan and the Soviet Union have been signed for starting only the last three, to which China is less sensitive. This slow progress can also be ascribed to lack of enthusiasm on the part of the United States as a prospective potentially stabilizing investor, and to Japan's own security considerations. Considering the strategic value of oil, Japan, as a major consumer, cannot depend too heavily upon any single source. Aside from Japan's traditional distrust of the Soviet Union, there would be a threat to Japan's security posed by the deployment of the Russian military in nearby

Siberia in connection with resource development.

If, in the circumstances, China's objection to Siberian resource development is "a stick" to Japan, the prospect of China's increased crude export to Japan is "a carrot." Although the 1974 Chinese export of about 4.9 million tons represents only a fraction of Japan's 230 million-ton annual demand, Tokyo realizes what it would mean to Japan should China relax its basic principle of self-reliance and expand its oil development and exports. As noted, many Japanese, rightly or wrongly, look forward to Chinese oil in the range of 50 million tons a year by 1980.

● *Fourth*, in international arenas, China seeks to advance its policies by emphasizing the principle of self-reliance. This was repeatedly manifested at the Special Session of the United Nations on Raw Materials and Development in April 1974 and at the Caracas Law of the Sea conference in the summer of 1974. The oil crisis had greatly enhanced the belief among the developing countries that natural resources, even in their crude state, represent tremendous assets regardless of indigenous means to develop them. As a result, an impetus was given to the desire of some developing countries to convene an international forum in order to debate specifically the problems of natural resources. Hence the U.N. Special Session in New York. These feelings spilled over into the Caracas conference and even into the Bucharest international conference on population in 1974. China is conscious of the fact that in the coming years developing countries, especially those with natural resources, will tend to be susceptible to such rhetoric as "self-reliance." Vice-Premier Teng Shiao-ping's speech delivered at the U.N. Special Session for Raw Materials and Development on 10 April 1974 greatly appealed to the sentiments of those countries.

Among its East Asian neighbors, China sees in Japan a good example of the impact of oil on the fate of a nation. Poverty in oil had led Japan to wage a world war and to lose it during the 1940's; an ample supply of cheap oil enabled it to create from the devastation of the war an economic miracle during the 1950's and 1960's; and with the end of cheap oil in the 1970's, its economy has been exposed to the threat of serious depression again.

China's own experience with oil, especially after the withdrawal of the Russian technicians at the end of the 1950's, has not been forgotten. The Sino-Soviet rift may very well have been a blessing in disguise for China's development of oil, for it provided an urgent and vital incentive to expand its resources. China was undoubtedly the least affected of the major powers by the 1972-74 oil crisis and has probably gained new assurance about both the reserves and production of its oil resources. Recognizing the value of oil to its own future economy as well as its utility as a political instrument, China may not be so easily tempted to earn "quick money" by exports at a quadrupled crude price as some observers have predicted.

In the final analysis, China is not likely to depart very far, if ever, from its self-reliance policy in developing its oil and other natural resources. Therefore it is reasonable to conclude that there is no immediate prospect for the participation of foreign commercial interests in the oil or any of the other industries of China. Having railed against multinational corporations and joint ventures, China cannot afford any inconsistency between what it says and what it does before the eyes and ears of the developing countries of the world. In the unlikely event of foreign commercial participation, policy and management will remain entirely in the hands of the Chinese. How flexible China will be in applying its self-reliance policy will ultimately depend, domestically, on the pace at which the Peking government plans to modernize its agriculture and industry and, in its foreign relations, on the strategic and trade relations with Japan, the Soviet Union, and the United States.

Selected Bibliography

Arshih Nienlai Feichu Shihyou Kungyueh Yenbien (The progressive changes in the petroleum industry in the last 20 years in Mainland China), Studies on Mainland China Economy, Series No. 42, Ministry of Economic Affairs, Taipei, 1971.

Chang Chun, "How China Developed Her Oil Industry," *China Reconstructs*, Vol. XXIII, No. 10, Oct. 1974, pp. 2-14.

———, "Peiping's Petroleum Industry: Growth and Future Development," *Issues and Studies*, Vol. X, No. 8, May 1974, pp. 41-56.

Chang Ming-nan, Chen Ju-hsi, Hsu Wen-chun, and Yang Chin-wu, *Chungkuo Shihyou Chingliofen ti Tzucheng* (Physical chemistry of Chinese petroleum), Peking, 1962.

Chen Cheng-siang, *Chungkuo Shihyou Ssuyuan chi Chikaifa* (Petroleum resources and their development in China), Research Report No. 5, Geographical Research Centre, Graduate School, Chinese University of Hong Kong, 1968.

Chen Cheng-siang and Au Kam-nin, "The Petroleum Industry of China," *Die Erde*, Heft 3/4, 1974, S. 316-333.

Chen Cheng-siang, *Chungkuo ti Kungyueh Chienshe* (Industrial development in China), Research Report No. 51, Geographical Research Centre, Graduate School, Chinese University of Hong Kong, 1972.

Chiang Li, "New Developments in China's Foreign Trade," *China's Foreign Trade*, No. 1, July 1974, pp. 2-5.

Chien Yuan-heng, "Chungkung Taching Youtien" (Taching Oil Field), *Feiching Yenchiu* (Studies on Chinese Communism), Vol. 1, No. 2, 1967, pp. 54-64.

———, "China's Minerals and Metals," *U. S. China Business Review*, Vol. 1, No. 6, November-December 1974, pp. 39-53.

———, "Kungfei Shihyou Kungyueh Kaikan chi Chisuche Tiwei Pingku" (Communist bandits' petroleum industry and its position in the world), *Talu Ching-chi Yenchiu* (Studies on the economy of the Continent), Vol. 6, No. 1, 1974, pp. 17-26.

———, "A Periscopic View on the Role of the Chinese Petroleum Industry in the World Energy Crisis," *Studies on Chinese Communism*, Vol. 8, No. 5, 1974, pp. 57-69; English version also available.

Chugoku Soran 1975 (China cyclopedia), Ajiya Chosakai, Tokyo, 1974.

Chunghua Jenmin Kunghokuo Fensheng Titu (Atlases of the provinces of the People's Republic of China), Peking 1953.

Fujiwara Hajime, *Sekyu Kikito Nihonno Unmei* (Oil crisis and the fate of Japan), Tokyo, 1973.

Harnisch, Heinz, and Gloria, Hans G., *Die Energiewirtschaft der Volksrepublik China*, Essen, 1973.

Hsieh Chiao-min, *Atlas of China*, McGraw-Hill, 1973.

Kamada Isao and Takagaki Setsuo, Nihonno Enerugi Kiki (Energy crisis in Japan), Tokyo, 1973.

Kambara Tatsu, "The Petroleum Industry in China," *The China Quarterly*, No. 60, December 1974, pp. 699-719.

Keizai Hyoron (Economic review, monthly), Tokyo, July 1973.

Keizai Orai (Economic transactions, monthly), Tokyo, June 1974.

Kokusai Boeki (International trade, weekly), Tokyo, 1974.

Koshimura Eiichi, *Chugoku Sangyo Daichizu* (Industrial atlas of China), Tokyo, 1973.

Li Tao-kuei, "Shihche Shihyou Weichi yu Kungfei Keneng Panyen ti Chishe" (World oil crisis and communist bandits' capabilities), *Talu Chingchi Yenchiu* (Studies on the economy of the Continent), Vol. 5, No. 4, Oct. 1973, pp. 1-18.

Ludlow, N., "China's Oil," *U. S. China Business Review*, Vol. 1, No. 1, January-February 1974, pp. 21-28.

Meyerhoff, A. A., "Developments in Mainland China," American Assn. of Petroleum Geologists Bull., Vol. 54, No. 8 (Aug. 1970), pp. 1567-1580.

Nanajunendaino okeru Shigengaiko (Natural resources diplomacy in the 1970's), Ministry of Foreign Affairs, Tokyo, 1972.

Nihonno Enerugi Mondai (The energy problems of Japan), Ministry of International Trade and Industry, Tokyo, 1973.

Ohno Hideo, "Tenkankio Mukaeta Chugokuno Sekyu" (China's oil at a turning point), *Chugoku Keizai Tsushin* (China economy report), a Japanese language monthly, Feb. 1973.

Oil and Asian Rivals: Sino-Soviet Conflict; Japan and Oil Crisis, Hearings, Subcomm. on Asian and Pacific Affairs, Comm. on Foreign Affairs, U. S. House of Representatives, 93rd Cong., First and Second Sess., Sept. 1974.

Park Choon-ho, *Continental Shelf Issues in the Yellow Sea and the East China Sea*, Occasional Paper No. 15, Law of the Sea Institute, University of Rhode Island, Sept. 1973.

―――, "Oil Under Troubled Waters: The Northeast Asia Sea-Bed Controversy," *Harvard International Law Journal*, Vol. 14, No. 2, 1974, pp. 212-260.

―――, "The Sino-Japanese-Korean Sea-Bed Resources Controversy and the Hypothesis of the 200-Mile Economic Zone," *Harvard International Law Journal*, Vol. 16, No. 1, 1975, pp. 27-46.

People's Republic of China: Atlas, U. S. Central Intelligence Agency, 1971.

Sangyo Kozono Choki Bijon (Long-range view of the structure of industries), Sangyokozo Shingikai (Council on Industrial structure), Tokyo, 1974.

Sekyukaihatsu Shiryo (Materials on oil development), Sekyu Tsushinsha (Oil press co.), Tokyo, 1973.

Sekyu Mondaino Sogo Kaisetsu (Comprehensive analysis of oil problems), Nihinkeizai Shinbun, Tokyo, 1974.

Shigen Mondaino Tembo (Outlook on problems of natural resources), Ministry of International Trade and Industry, Tokyo, 1971.

Shin Chugoku Nenkan (New China Yearbook), 1970-, Chugoku Kenkyusho, Tokyo.

Takabatake Ariyoshi, "Sekyu" (Petroleum), in a study done at Institute of Energy Economics, Tokyo, 1974.

Takahashi Shogoo, in *Nitchu Keizai Kaiho* (China-Japan economic report), Dec. 1973.

Talu Kungfei Shihyou Kungyueh che Yenchiu (Study on the petroleum industry of the communist bandits on the Continent), Ministry of Economic Affairs, Taipei, 1972.

Talu Shihyou Kungyueh Gailan (Summary of the petroleum industry of the Mainland), Studies on Mainland Economy Series No. 5, Ministry of Economic Affairs, Taipei, 1967.

Talu Wenti Chuanti Yenchiu Vol. 45, No. 5, Taiwan, 1967.

Weintraub, P., "China's Oil Production and Consumption," *U. S. China Business Review*, Vol. 1, No. 1, January-February 1974, pp. 29-31.

Arab States of the Persian Gulf
Thomas C. Barger

INTRODUCTION

In the Arab States touching upon the Persian* Gulf lie half the known oil reserves of the world. Another ten percent lies across the Gulf in non-Arab Iran. A quarter of the world's reserves lies within one country, the Kingdom of Saudi Arabia. These Arab states produce more than half the oil in the world's export trade. Their income from oil in 1974 was approximately $50 billion. Their energy policies are concerned with only the hydrocarbons — oil and gas.

This study attempts to trace very briefly the historical and social factors that affect the policies of the Arab states on the Gulf, especially with respect to the oil industry. It analyzes in some detail pricing, production, and participation in that industry in the Gulf region, the formation of the organization of Oil Producing and Exporting Countries (OPEC), and the Arab embargo of 1973. By examining, then, both the general policies of these countries and their individual needs and goals, an objective observer may be able to evaluate the future timing and tenor of energy policy in this region, which is bound to have a profound effect upon the industry and development of many countries in the world.

*Since the early sixties the Arab states have substituted "Arabian" for "Persian." The usage has not been commonly adopted in English. "Gulf" will be used in this paper, as Arabs do when talking to Iranians, unless the adjective is required to prevent ambiguity.

BACKGROUND OF THE ARAB STATES ON THE GULF

There are seven Arab producing countries contiguous to the Persian Gulf. From north to south they are: Iraq at the head of the Gulf, Kuwait, Saudi Arabia, Bahrain, Qatar, the United Arab Emirates, and Oman. The United Arab Emirates, a rather loose federation, has three oil-producing members: Abu Dhabi, Dubai, and Sharjah. Oman qualifies as "contiguous to" the Gulf only by reason of its possession of the point of land that comprises the southern shore of the Straits of Hormuz, where the Gulf opens to the Arabian Sea and the Indian Ocean. The vital statistics of these countries are shown in Table I. In brief, they occupy an area about equal to that of the United States east of the Mississippi, with a total population about equal to that of New York State. Collectively, in 1974, they produced nearly twice as much oil as the United States.

➤ *People, Land, and Religion*

Iraq's heterogeneous population is larger than all the other six countries combined. About a fifth of the inhabitants of Iraq are not Arabs. The largest single minority, the Kurds, even though non-Arab, are Muslims. The other minorities are Persian and Turkish Muslims and various small Christian sects. The once considerable Jewish population of Baghdad, some 125,000, has been reduced by emigration to Israel to a few thousand at most. The other states were almost wholly Arab and exclusively Muslim until recent years. The influx of foreigners as a result of the development of the oil industry has been very large, especially in the smaller countries. At least half of Kuwait's population is foreign. Some 20,000 foreigners make up a third of Bahrain's labor force. In Qatar, Abu Dhabi, Dubai, and Sharjah, the bulk of the labor force is foreign, largely Iranian, Pakistani and Indian. In much smaller numbers, "other Arabs" – principally Palestinians, Jordanians, Egyptians and Iraqis – as well as Europeans and Americans are present in technical, administrative, and managerial capacities. Foreigners are also numerous in Saudi Arabia, but they make up a much smaller proportion of the total population. Oman's relatively small and stable oil production, combined with a strict exclusionist policy, until recently has not required an inflow of foreign labor on a scale comparable with its neighbors.

Not only does Iraq have the largest population among the Arab countries about the Gulf, but it is unique in possessing natural resources other than oil. Two of the great rivers of the Middle East traverse its length. It has mountains in the north and east, and high plains capable of rainfall agriculture. The lower plains are irrigated by the Tigris and Euphrates. In fact, it is believed from tax records of the seventh and eighth centuries after the Muslim conquests that the land supported more people 1500 years ago than it does today.

In contrast to Iraq, there are no perennial rivers emptying into the Gulf below the Iraq-Kuwait boundary. The other states are largely sand and rock deserts. Even in the hinterlands of Saudi Arabia and Oman with their mountains and above-

TABLE I

	Population Thousands	Area Thousand Square Miles	1/1/75 Oil Reserves Millions Barrels	1974 Oil Production Thousand Barrels/Day
Iraq	10,000	168	35,000	1,900
Kuwait	900	7.8	72,750	2,550
Saudi Arabia	5,000-6,000	873	104,000	8,520
Bahrain*	230	0.26	336	68
Qatar	120	4.3	6,000	520
Total of United Arab Emirates	185	30	33,900	1,730
(Abu Dhabi)	50	26	30,000	1,430
(Dubai)	60	1.5	2,400	240
(Sharjah)	32	1.0	1,500	60
(Ajman)	4	0.1	--	--
(Fujairah)	10	0.4	--	--
(Ras Al Khaimah)	25	0.75	--	--
(Umm Al Qaiwayn)	4	0.3	--	--
Oman	700	82	6,000	290
Total	±17,500	1,165	258,000	±15,500

*Bahrain receives 1/2 the proceeds of the Abu Sa' afah field in Saudi Arabia producing 110,000 B/D, reserves 6.5 MMB. Figures for reserves have been taken from *Oil and Gas Journal*, December 30, 1974, except Kuwait and Saudi Arabia, from Arabian American Oil Co. publications.

average rainfall, life has been hard and nature has been stingy. The maritime states, like Bahrain, lived largely by their entrepot trade, or by their seaborne trade with primitive vessels and smuggling, as did Kuwait and the "Trucial States," now the United Arab Emirates.

As noted above, Iraq has minorities making up some twenty percent of its population. In addition, the two great divisions of Islam, the Sunnis and the Shi'ites, are almost equally represented. In a very rough way, these differences may be compared to the Catholic and Protestant divisions of Christendom. The Sunnis have usually been the governing class, but it is believed that the Shi'ites have been numerically greater. They are closely related to their fellow religionists in Iran where the majority of the Persians have always been Shi'ite.

The original people in the rest of these Arab states on the shores of the Gulf were Sunnis, except for the people of Bahrain and the coastal oases of Saudi Arabia among whom the Shi'ites predominated in number. In modern times the Sunnis have been in political ascendancy, notably in Saudi Arabia which, except for the eastern coast, is overwhelmingly attached to the Sunni sect of Islam.

➤ Governments

Iraq was formed as a British mandate after the First World War. Following a plebiscite, it became a kingdom under Faisal I, a prince from the family of the rulers of Mecca in what is now Saudi Arabia. It became an "independent" country in 1932. The monarchy was retained at least in name despite a series of coups d'etat by the military. In 1958 the monarchy was ended in a military takeover and Iraq has since been ruled by military governments with claims to an ideological foundation. The present regime is "Ba'athist," an ostensibly strongly nationalistic Arab socialist movement related to, but very much at loggerheads with, the "Ba'athist" government in Syria.

The rest of these Gulf states are ruled by regimes along traditional Arab tribal lines. Kuwait has a constitution and an elected assembly, but the Sabah family is still the effective ruler of the State. In Saudi Arabia, the Sa'ud family have been rulers of Central Arabia, with certain periods of eclipse, since before the American Revolution. The King, though very powerful, is not absolute; he rules as a monarch under the strictures of Islamic law, responsible to the citizenry. The deposition of King Faisal's brother, Saud, who had brought the State to the verge of ruin and bankruptcy by his inept performance was carried out in 1964 without participation by Faisal, but in accordance with traditional custom and Islamic law. Then on 25 March 1975 King Faisal was assassinated by a young, American-educated member of the royal family and succeeded by King Khalid. In other states, the families who ruled their respective territories long before the discovery of oil are still ruling, with varying degrees of modification of power and procedure to meet the demands of the world of the 20th century.

► The Economy and Oil

By reason of its natural resources Iraq's economy was the most thriving of the seven states. But even Iraq was very poor before the development of oil. It is said never to have recovered from the destruction of the irrigation canals and the decimation of population by the Mongols in the 13th century. It suffered for a long time from the harshness of its Turkish governors and only began to advance into the modern world after World War I. The overthrow of the monarchy in 1958 did not immediately promote economic advancement, and for a time it became a grain-importing country rather than a grain-exporting country.

All the other states of this group subsisted on fishing, pearling, and oasis agriculture before the discovery of oil. Pearling, which had been very important to Bahrain, Qatar, Kuwait, Abu Dhabi and eastern Saudi Arabia, came upon very hard times indeed in the nineteen-thirties with the simultaneous blows of the great depression and the development of cultured pearls in Japan. Even the annual influx of pilgrims to Mecca in Saudi Arabia contributed little to alleviate the poverty of this vast desert country: by way of example, during World War II the income of the Saudi Government for the year 1943 was estimated by the Middle East Supply Center at only $10 million.

The greatest single event in the history of this region since the advent of Islam in 622 was the discovery of oil in southern Persia in 1908. No further important discoveries were made in other countries of the Middle East until the great Kirkuk field was found in 1927 in northern Iraq. Five hundred miles from the Mediterranean, Kirkuk oil goes by pipeline to terminals on the eastern Mediterranean in Lebanon and Syria (and to Haifa before the creation of Israel in 1948). But the production from Rumailah and other fields discovered in southern Iraq since 1953, which now equals Kirkuk, is shipped from ports on the Gulf.

Bahrain's field, discovered in 1932, although one of the relatively minor fields of the region, was of great importance to the development of oil in the Gulf. All the fields previously discovered in Persia and Iraq had been in rocks younger than those exposed on the surface of Bahrain. Consequently, geologists acquainted with the Middle Eastern fields tended to downgrade the probability of oil being found in any geologic structures in rocks older than those in the fields of Persia and Iraq. The Bahrain discovery, by demonstrating that oil existed in such rocks, led to the concessions and subsequent discoveries in Saudi Arabia, Kuwait, Qatar, and the states of the Lower Gulf.

The dates of the original successful concessions, discoveries, and initial production are shown in Table II. It should be noted that the Iraq dates are for the Kirkuk field. A field on the Persian border which had been developed earlier only supplied the internal demand in Iraq.

The Saudi Arabia-Kuwait Neutral Zone is frequently misunderstood. It was formed as a result of an attempt in 1922 to delineate the boundary between Saudi Arabia and Kuwait. At a conference on this matter, it proved impossible to reach agreement on the boundaries of the grazing lands claimed by the tribes of the two governments, so a Neutral Zone was formed, in which tribes of both nations would have the right to graze. It was further agreed that each country would have an undivided one-half interest in any natural resources that might be discovered within the zone.

TABLE II

	Concession Date	Initial Oil Discovery Date	Initial Commercial Production
Iraq	1925	1927	1934
Kuwait	1934	1938	1946
Saudi Arabia	1933	1938	1939
Saudi-Kuwait Neutral Zone	1948	1953	1954
Bahrain	1930	1932	1934
Qatar	1935	1939	1949
United Arab Emirates			
Abu Dhabi	1939	1959	1962
Dubai	1952	1966	1969
Sharjah	1969	1972	1974
Oman	1937	1963	1967

In time the American Independent Oil Company obtained the onshore concession from Kuwait. Almost simultaneously, the Getty Oil Company obtained the Saudi rights in the zone. When the area offshore from the zone was let, the Arabian Oil Company (formed by a group of Japanese companies) obtained separate concessions from the two governments. Though the economic interest of the two governments are still "undivided," the zone itself has been divided for police and customs purposes, since the administration of an undivided zone by two bureaucracies operating side by side had proved impractical. This barren area, without any permanent habitation in 1922, now has proved oil reserves equal to about half of all those of the United States. However, no oil has been discovered in a similar neutral zone between Saudi Arabia and Iraq.

► *The Concessions*

The history of the oil concessions in the Middle East is very complicated. Here is a short outline of the essential aspects. The first concession that led to the actual production of commercial oil was granted to William Knox D'Arcy by the Shah of Persia on 28 May 1901. The next of importance was given by Iraq to the Turkish Petroleum Company in March 1925. The Turkish Petroleum Company eventually evolved into the Iraq Petroleum Company which, by 1938, had obtained rights to develop oil in the whole of Iraq. As in Iraq, the subsequent concessions by other countries before World War II, beginning with Saudi Arabia in 1933, usually covered either the whole of the country granting the concession or that part underlain by sedimentary rocks likely to contain oil.

The concessions given between the late twenties and World War II were remarkably alike in their general terms. The company obtaining the concession usually was required to make some kind of down payment or loan (recoverable only out of future production); to pay a "rent" on the area designated; to pay a royalty of four gold shillings (or its approximate equivalent) per ton on oil produced and sold; and sometimes to pay various other minor types of fees or government costs. The companies were exempt from all other taxes or imposts. In return, the agreements usually specified the annual payment of some minimum amount to the government whether in rents or royalty. The concessions were of very long duration, sixty to seventy-five years initially, though subsequent extensions to some lengthened the term to as much as ninety-nine years.

Subsequent to World War II the terms of new concessions changed markedly. Their duration was shorter. Royalties were more likely to be expressed in a percentage of the oil produced, which at government option, could be either sold to a third party or had to be taken by the concessionaire. Moreover, the government was given an option to purchase a share in the enterprise or was given a share outright. Provision was made for the payment of income tax on profits. Usually the concessionaire was required to relinquish to the state undeveloped portions of the concession after the passage of a specified period. By the late fifties, new concessions in the Gulf usually provided for a 50 percent ownership by the government after the discovery of oil, with or without some mechanism for repaying the concessionaire for the exploration and development costs. Eventually the concession came to be an agreement whereby the oil company became, in effect, a kind of contractor for the government, a contractor who bore the risks of the cost of finding oil and who was repaid in oil if his efforts were successful.

The idea of state participation in operations and profits raised by Saudi Arabia in the mid-sixties was not new. The original D'Arcy concession provided for Persian government participation in 16 percent of the "net profits." After oil was found, the Anglo-Persian Oil Company eventually became a company that not only produced oil in Persia, but also transported, refined, and marketed Persian oil in many countries. The determination of "net profits" in a business so integrated from oil well to final customer gave rise to interminable disputes between the company and the government as to how much profit should be attributed to the Persian operations. After a serious dispute between them in 1932, brought on by a sharp drop in government revenues, the percentage of profits was replaced by a fixed royalty of four shillings gold per ton in a new agreement in April 1933.

The pattern for oil royalties had been established in Iraq by the agreement signed in April 1925 with the Turkish Petroleum Company. To give some idea of what this payment meant at the time, four shillings gold per ton in 1925 was equivalent to about $0.13 per barrel of oil. In Oklahoma, oil of similar quality was selling at that time for about $1.74 per barrel. But by the time the Anglo-Persian agreement of 1933 was concluded, the price of Oklahoma crude oil had dropped to $0.40 per barrel. After devaluation of the dollar by the United States on 31 January 1934, the value of those four gold shillings rose to nearly $0.22 per barrel; and the Oklahoma crude was then valued at about $0.95 per barrel. Such comparisons are far from exact, as crude oils vary significantly in value. However, the Oklahoma oil was in the very midst of its market. To get the Kirkuk oil to market required the laying of the longest pipeline in the world at that time across the inhospitable desert before the oil could be loaded on a tank ship to proceed to its distributors in Europe. Nevertheless, as a rough measure, the payments to governments in those years were from 10 percent to 30 percent of the value of an equivalent oil produced in the United States for the biggest domestic market in the world.

After World War II both the demand for oil and its price

increased rapidly. The Oklahoma crude sold for about $2.50 per barrel, but the Oklahoma price in these examples had no direct part in setting prices in the world market. It is used here simply to indicate the general level of the price of oil at that time.* Although prices and profits rose abroad, the returns to the governments remained fixed at the four shillings gold per ton.

In the late nineteen-forties, the companies and the Venezuelan government came to an agreement that amounted to a 50/50 sharing of the proceeds from the export of Venezuelan oil. This general principle first appeared in the Gulf in an agreement between the Saudi Arabian Government and the Arabian American Oil Company (Aramco) that came to be known as the "50/50 Agreement." It provided, essentially, that the government would receive 50 percent of the proceeds from the sale of its oil, first through the payment of the royalty of four shillings gold per ton and the balance through a tax on income. This general formula in a short time was extended to the rest of the pre-war concessions in the Arab states. Partly in a dispute over the application of this formula, but largely for other reasons, Iran nationalized the Anglo-Persian Oil Company in 1951. Iran, unable to sell its oil in world markets, came to an agreement with the new "Consortium" of international oil companies (including Anglo-Persian, renamed British Petroleum) in 1954. Though Iran nominally owned all the oil at the wellhead, the Consortium was given such terms of operation that the financial effect for the government and the companies was the same as the 50/50 agreement in the "old" concessions in the Arab states.

*The American Petroleum Institute's "Petroleum Facts and Figures," 1974, contains prices for "Mid-Continent 36° API Gravity Crude Oil" by months from 1913 to 1969, a very convenient 56-year series.

OIL INDUSTRY: PRICING, PRODUCTION, AND PARTICIPATION

So long as revenues from oil depended upon fixed fees per ton of barrel produced and marketed, the governments had no interest in either prices or costs; but when the payments were derived to a large and growing extent from a percentage of profits, the governments immediately had a vital interest in both prices and costs as well as quantities of oil produced. So, to put the new arrangements into effect in a way that would be both understandable and acceptable to the governments, the companies had to establish a system of pricing.

➤ *Pricing*

Up until this time most of the oil produced had been taken by subsidiaries of the companies holding the concessions. Sales to third parties had been negotiated privately so that there was no readily available and public yardstick for prices in the Gulf. In the United States "posted prices" had long been in use as publicly advertised prices at which a refinery would buy crude oil from a producer. This term was adopted in the Gulf. But "posted price" there meant that price at which any buyer could purchase crude oil in tanker lots at the point of export. And "posted prices" became the basis on which profits were calculated for the payment of taxes.

The posting of prices raised many new issues. Foremost, perhaps, was the question of the relationship between the posted prices and the "transfer prices" of oil used by the concession holders in passing the ownership of the oil to their various affiliates. Heretofore the transfer prices were of no concern to the governments and could be arranged at whatever level suited the needs of the offtaking companies and their affiliates. On implementation of the 50/50 agreement, Aramco reported the transfer prices that had been previously used for selling oil to the Aramco shareholders as the basis for computing the revenues due the Saudi Government. This led to a most acrimonious dispute, since these prices were some 18 percent less than the posted prices at which oil would be sold to a third party in tanker lots. Eventually, the disagreement was settled by a make-up payment to the Saudi Government and an agreement on discounts from posted prices.

It seemed only reasonable that subsidiaries of the shareholders in the ventures should enjoy some preference since they marketed the bulk of the oil and were steady customers. So marketing discounts to concessionaire subsidiaries came into being. The extent of these discounts and the definition of the subsidiaries entitled to them were the subject of continued negotiations in the years that followed. Substantial discounts to third-party customers who were willing to enter into long-term contracts for large quantities of oil were also a practice of long standing. Not only were the costs of the transactions less, but the development of new facilities was also much more efficient since the level of future sales and capital investments for increased production could be more confidently estimated. In Saudi Arabia, for example, such sales were reported on the basis of actual realizations by the offtaker (i.e., the shareholder who actually took the oil and paid for it) for the payment of taxes to the Saudi Government. For the calculation of taxes these sales were only reported to Aramco* in lump sum, by the individual offtakers, so it was not unnatural that the Saudi Government should question the reporting. To assure compliance with the rules laid down for the definition of a "third party," and the determination of actual "realizations," a system was devised whereby these sales were reported to a firm of public accountants by the offtakers. This firm verified the reports, assembled them and reported them to the Saudi Government in detail but to Aramco only *in toto* so that the taxes due could be paid. A curious result was that while some Saudi officials were complaining they were insufficiently informed on the "real" price of oil, another branch of the bureaucracy had far more information than Aramco had on prices and, quite likely, more than was possessed by any individual offtaker.

As the years went on and producing capacity caught up with demand, and as the number of "third parties" proliferated, the tendency was to eliminate the "third party discounts." Put another way, the governments tended to disallow sales at anything less than the posted price for the purpose of calculating taxes. The Venezuelans, more forthrightly, called the prices on which taxes were calculated "tax reference values." There were still many exceptions: for example, the pricing of Liquefied Petroleum Gas (LPG) — butane and pro-

---

*Aramco, owned by four major American oil companies, was precluded from selling to anyone but its shareholders except for domestic sales in Saudi Arabia. Had it done so, the shareholders would have been in violation of American antitrust laws as conspiring through Aramco to fix prices. Nor could Aramco be permitted to know the individual discounts granted by any shareholder as it would be presumed such would become the common knowledge of all.

pane. This product required special facilities of very high capital cost, special tankers for transport and special terminals for unloading, and an assured market arrangement to guarantee continuous purchase for a long enough period to amortize the investment in producing and transport facilities. And there was no market-determined posted price for LPG.

The question of how to handle refined products presented more complications. One could put the crude oil into the refinery at posted prices and pay the government a refining fee on the basis of crude oil charged to the refinery. At the other end of the scale, the government could ask for an accounting for the refinery based on posted prices of the products actually produced and sold. Neither system invariably yielded the maximum return to the government at different times and under different market conditions.

Then there was the question of how to handle surplus products. One of the characteristics of a refinery is that beyond certain limits of tankage *all* the products must be disposed of. If the accumulation of one product exceeds the limit of storage available for that particular product, the refinery must shut down. There is a limit to the flexibility of any given refinery in producing more or less of one product from a given supply of crude oil. For example, this phenomenon accounted for the anomaly of an abundance of gasoline in the United States in December 1974 when the government was urging conservation and the oil companies were both supporting conservation efforts and trying to promote gasoline sales. The companies overestimated the consumption of gasoline in the preceding months and had to get rid of the stored gasoline in order to provide for the fuel oils likely to be needed in the winter ahead.

That phenomenon is seen more clearly in a refinery far from its markets. The Qatif oil field (near the refinery) was used by Aramco at one time to store excess fuel oil and later to store excess naptha (raw gasoline), both of which, years later, were taken from the field to meet changes in the demands of the market. Similar situations prevailed in other countries in the Gulf.

What caused more controversy between the governments and the companies was the debate on the rationale, or basis, of the posted prices themselves. Before World War II the world petroleum trade was largely in products, not in crude oil. Thereafter, a number of factors converged to increase greatly the building of refineries in consuming rather than in producing centers. Among these factors was the desire by the consumers to save foreign exchange and to obtain greater flexibility in sources of supply. The rapid growth in the size of tankers, moreover, lowered the cost of transporting fuel which would only be burned in the refining of the crude oil. Of even greater importance in the building of refineries in the consuming countries was the decline in exports from the United States.

In 1948 the United States became a net importer of crude oil. Before World War II the United States and Venezuela had both been the major and marginal suppliers of crude oil and refined products for the European market. The upsurge in demand after the war, however, could only be met by oil from the Middle East. It was both quicker and cheaper to build refineries in Europe than in countries with a paucity of skilled labor thousands of miles away from the sources of the materials required for their construction.

The magnitude of these shifts in the oil industry may be better appreciated through a few simple statistics. In 1948 the United States was a net exporter of crude oil and refined products by 5 million barrels. But by 1958, the year in which mandatory import controls were established, it imported 520 million barrels net of exports. In the same period world production doubled, Middle East production alone quadrupled and rose from 10 percent to nearly 25 percent of the world total. The size of the tankers began to change drastically. In

1949 vessels of less than 17,000 dead weight tons (d.w.t.) comprised 53 percent of world carrying capacity and 96 percent was in vessels smaller than 30,000 d.w.t. By 1959 vessels smaller than 17,000 had dropped to 36 percent of fleet capacity and those over 30,000 had risen to 28 percent. By 1973 some 75 percent of the world fleet was composed of vessels over 45,000 d.w.t. with 45 percent over 125,000 d.w.t.

Before World War II, the price of oil products in Europe had been largely determined by the cost of the supply of oil from the Caribbean. The American domestic market established a price at Gulf of Mexico ports to which freight costs to the European delivery point were added. These prices were extended practically around the entire world. But during the war the British and American governments objected to applying this system to oil originating in the Middle East and supplied to Allied forces operating in that area. By the end of the war these "local" supplies were priced at a level roughly equivalent to prices of comparable oils f.o.b. U. S. ports on the Gulf of Mexico. These were not publicly announced prices. Most of the oil exports from the Middle East at the time went to affiliates of the concessionaire companies, so that the prices of transfers were intra-company transactions until such time as the products were sold to independent distributors or consumers. Other transactions, generally, were negotiated long-term contracts.

After the war more independent refineries and marketers came into being, especially in Europe, and during the fifties companies that had not been engaged in foreign operations, largely American, began to develop production capacity outside their home country. The American companies obviously hoped to produce oil for import into the United States to supplement their domestic production, which was both decreasing and becoming more costly. But the imposition of mandatory quotas on imports by the United States left some of these companies with heavy obligations to meet, a producing capacity beyond their U. S. import allocations and no refining or marketing capabilities abroad. Such companies were forced to sell oil for whatever price they could get for it.

The explanations produced both by the companies and by independent observers in response to the governments' questioning of posted prices assumed that the two great sources of oil for the European market were the Caribbean and the Middle East. For the Caribbean area the American domestic economy and domestic oil production provided the market forces to set a competitively determined price. It was then assumed that the c.i.f. price of oil must be equal at some point between the two sources, American ports on the Gulf of Mexico and the Persian Gulf ports. The only question was to determine where this point should be. If it were London, for example, then the f.o.b. price to be posted in the Persian Gulf ought to be the c.i.f. cost of Gulf of Mexico oil delivered to London less the cost of transport of the oil from the Persian Gulf to London. If the point of equal prices were to be New York, the Persian Gulf price would obviously be lower and government revenues less by the greater cost of transport to New York instead of London. The discussion was, of course, complicated not only by the change in the status of the United States from a net exporter to a net importer, but also by the abandonment of the free market in the United States in 1958 to support domestic prices by import quotas. Lastly, as time went on, the European demand grew beyond the capacity of the Caribbean to meet further increases. In any formula based on the foregoing rationale, a disadvantage to a Middle Eastern produciing country was an advantage to the European consumer.

All through the nineteen-fifties much discussion and thought was given to the question of how prices should be determined. Though the relating of this history may be academic at the moment, there might come a time when the experience of that decade could become highly relevant. A great many formulae were proposed, including a system that would have constructed a floating dividing point somewhere in the Atlantic, depending upon fluctuations in shipping costs. As J. E. Hartshorn pointed out in 1962, the oil companies were helpful in why explanations and proposals for "rational" systems were wrong or would not work. But they didn't contribute much toward formulating a rational system.

Applying hindsight, it seems evident there could be no rational pricing system for this complex international industry. The positions of the companies engaged in the selling of oil from the Middle East, that is, the companies who were the offtakers, not the actual producers, were all different. Some were short of crude oil for their refineries and marketing outlets. Some had crude oil in excess of their own requirements. Their marketing areas were different: some had only American markets, others had marketing organizations well distributed throughout the world. And above all, not only did the cost of transport vary from company to company at any given moment depending upon the tanker market, the character of the fleet owned or chartered, and the degree of reliance on spot charters, but the growth in tanker size was steadily lowering the cost of transport.

The search for a nice neat formula for determination of posted prices was futile. It was inevitably a compromise to the gain of some and the loss of others. The factors involved were too many: fluctuations were too rapid in both supply and demand, and the interests of the parties too diverse to permit a formula which excluded judgement by the people who were actually handling the marketing and distribution of the oil. One result was that the Arab countries' civil servants charged with looking after petroleum affairs became aware of aspects of the oil business that had not previously concerned them. This awareness was demonstrated vividly by a paper presented to an Arab Petroleum Congress by Sheikh

Abdulla Tariki, then in charge of petroleum affairs in Saudi Arabia, in 1960. He accused the major oil companies of having bilked the governments of the Middle East out of three billion dollars in the preceding ten years by manipulating prices. That the oil companies disagreed wholly with his logic and that no government considered his conclusions sound enough to warrant an attempt at recovery of the "loss" is beside the point. The Arab countries had become seriously involved in the price of oil.

➤ *Production Costs*

The cost of production of the oil in the countries around the Persian Gulf has had essentially no effect on prices. In all the Arab countries save Iraq, the fields discovered before and in the ten years after World War II were large, relatively near the sea, and comparatively simple to exploit. Moreover, they were prolific, i.e., the production of oil per individual well was high. To illustrate, in 1974 Saudi Arabia produced from some 700 wells nearly as much oil as the United States got from 500,000 wells.

Iraq's principal production until the late nineteen-sixties came from the fields in the north, especially Kirkuk, 500 miles from the Mediterranean. Whereas Kirkuk oil may have cost some 50 cents per barrel to produce and transport to the Mediterranean, oil at point of export in the Gulf cost some 10 to 35 cents. This depended more or less upon the particular time and country, since cost per barrel decreased markedly with increased volume. These circumstances had two effects on the market prices and the markets which the oil could reach. First, as long as realized prices were a basis for paying taxes, the spread between actual producing cost and selling price was large enough so that the oil could be sold profitably, in many instances, beyond the theoretical "watershed" between the Middle East and the Caribbean oils. This condition probably obtained even after the governments refused to accept actual realizations as a base for calculating taxes and insisted on use of the posted price only. Second, the cost of additional productive capacity in the Gulf states with fields close to export points was much lower than anywhere else in the world. Hence, as world demand grew, these fields were the cheapest and quickest source of additional oil available for almost any market in the world. Moreover, the profits from the crude production provided the capital for the enormous investments in transportation, refining and marketing, the "downstream facilities," necessary to handle the very rapid growth in oil consumption in Europe and Asia.

➤ *Organization of Petroleum Exporting Countries (OPEC)*

The actual posted prices that were in effect from 1950 to 1974 and the government "take" on what came to be known as Arabian light crude are shown in Table III. This particular crude oil, produced in Saudi Arabia, has been adopted by OPEC as the "marker crude" for price purposes. That is, once the price of Arabian light crude has been fixed, all other oils of greater or lesser value, in terms of quality and cost of transport to market, are adjusted to that price. "Government-take" is total government revenue per barrel in royalties and taxes. It varies not only with posted price, but also with cost of production as well as royalty and tax rates. The cost of oil to an offtaker at point of export is the total cost of production plus government take.

By June 1957 the price of Arabian light crude had risen to $2.08 from $1.75 in 1950. This rise reflected in large part the shortages of supply in western Europe resulting from the closure of the Suez Canal and the destruction of the Iraq Petroleum Company's pump stations in Syria during the Suez Arab-Israeli war of October-November 1956. After a reduction to $1.90 in 1959, a further reduction was posted by one company in August 1960, bringing the price of crude down almost to the price in 1950. Not only were there vehe-

TABLE III

1950-1974 SELECTED POSTED PRICES AND GOVERNMENT-TAKE FOR ARABIAN LIGHT CRUDE OIL 34° SPI GRAVITY

	Posted Price	Approximate Government-Take
1950	$ 1.75/bbl.	$ 0.77/bbl.
December 1956	1.93/bbl.	0.82/bbl.
June 1957	2.08/bbl.	0.87/bbl.
February 1959	1.90/bbl.	0.81/bbl.
September 1960	1.80/bbl.	0.75/bbl.
August 1970	1.80/bbl.	0.84/bbl.
June 1, 1971	2.28/bbl.	1.10/bbl.
January 20, 1972	2.48/bbl.	1.20/bbl.
August 1, 1973	3.07/bbl.	1.75/bbl.
October 16, 1973	5.12/bbl.	3.00/bbl.
January 1, 1974	11.65/bbl.	8.30/bbl.
November 1, 1974	11.25/bbl.	10.20/bbl.

ment objections from the producing governments, but there was also a period of confusion, and indications that not all the companies felt the reduction was justified. The price finally settled at $1.80. The immediate reaction of the governments to this change in price was the formation of the Organization of Petroleum Producing Countries (OPEC). Such an organization was probably inevitable, but the time of its formation was certainly triggered by the price cuts of August 1960.

Sheikh Abdulla Tariki, then Director of Petroleum and Mineral Affairs in Saudi Arabia, and the Venezuelan Minister of Mines and Hydrocarbons, Dr. Perez Alfonso, were the moving spirits in convening a meeting of the producing countries in Baghdad in September 1960. On September 14th the Organization of Petroleum Exporting Countries came into being. The founding members were Venezuela, Saudi Arabia, Iran, Kuwait, and Iraq. OPEC has since expanded to include Algeria, Ecuador, Indonesia, Libya, Nigeria, Qatar, and the United Arab Emirates. Gabon is an associate member and Mexico was reported to be applying for "observer status" following the 1974 discoveries in southern Mexico.

The initial resolutions of the Organization stressed the following aims: (1) the need for the unification of the policies of the producing countries; (2) the necessity for stability in prices; (3) the need for a steady income in the producing countries; (4) an efficient, economic, and regular supply of oil to the consuming countries; and (5) a fair return to those who invested in the petroleum industry. Needless to say, the terms "stability," "steady," "efficient," "economic," "regular," and "fair" were not easily susceptible to rigorous definition to the satisfaction of all concerned.

The most obvious initial achievement of OPEC was that the posted price of Arabian light crude did not subsequently fall below the price of September 1960, which was $1.80 per barrel. The companies maintained that setting the price of crude was their prerogative exclusively, as they were responsible for marketing the oil. The governments maintained that no change in the posted price could be made without "consultation" with them. The difference of viewpoint was never put to test.

The formation of OPEC and the establishment of headquarters in Geneva (later moved to Vienna), with a permanent secretariat, gave the producing countries a formal and regular means of communication among themselves on oil matters for the first time. The rotation of the position of secretary-general among the member countries insured that all gained experience in the wider fields of world oil. The secretariat served to gather, correlate, and disseminate information. Thus coordination of policies in a systematic way became possible for the producing countries.

Fairly soon after the formation of OPEC the members tried to get the companies who held concessions to negotiate with an OPEC-designated committee. The companies refused, on the grounds that their concessions came from individual governments and they could negotiate only with representatives of such governments. In either case, the people actually doing the talking were the same whatever hat they wore. Following a paper given at the fourth Arab Petroleum Congress in 1961 by a Saudi accountant, OPEC demanded a change in the accounting for royalty payments. Though discussions began on a company-to-government basis, it was soon apparent that the "expensing of royalty" was a matter that would affect all the concessionaires.

The 50/50 agreement had provided that part of the government 50 percent share of the profits would be paid as royalty and the rest as taxes. The governments now demanded that royalty be treated as a cost, as in the United States, and deducted from profits which then would be subject to a 50 percent tax. (In the United States, however, the royalty was paid to the private landowner and the tax was levied by government authority.) The financial effect would be to increase the "government-take" by half the amount of the royalty or, in most cases, by about $0.11 per barrel. In the end the discussions moved to Teheran (more oil companies were involved in the Iranian Consortium than any other organization in the Gulf), representatives from other OPEC governments joined, and a complex agreement that spread the "expensing of royalties" over several years was hammered out. The formula, as it contained provisions for crude oils of types not produced in Iran, applied to nearly all the OPEC countries with concession arrangements similar to those in the Gulf. It was the first such arrangement.

By the mid-sixties the realized prices had weakened as productive capacity outran demand. Although the governments were being paid on the basis of posted prices, and although the government/company split of earnings was nearer 60/40 than 50/50, the price weakness led OPEC to consider production restrictions. "Production Programming" was the name given to the idea. The idea died aborning for the same reasons it had died several years earlier when Venezuela and Saudi Arabia proposed international prorationing, and a tentative formula had been set forth in a paper at the third Arab Petroleum Congress in 1960. OPEC cited the "conservation" program that had operated in the United States since the nineteen-thirties as a model for what they had in mind. When it became understood that an essential part of the program required limiting Texas' production to the difference between market demand and the total production of the rest of the United States, no one was ready to play the role of Texas. No one had enough money in the bank for the experiment. And it soon became clear that agreement on the factors to be taken into account (including population, non-oil income, per capita GNP, etc.) in order to determine each country's share of total production would be difficult, if not impossible.

Before the end of the nineteen-sixties it was obvious that whatever changes in concession terms were made in one OPEC country would be extended to all who cared to apply them. So the negotiations shifted from a country-by-country basis to an industry vs. OPEC basis, not formally at first, but substantially. When the Libyans forced a rise in the posted prices and a change in tax rates in 1970, posted prices rose at the Mediterranean ports for oil delivered from Iraq and Saudi Arabia. And these postings in turn were reflected in Gulf prices. In February 1971 "The Teheran Agreement" was negotiated under the auspices of OPEC. It was billed as a "Five Year Moratorium" — i.e., a respite from changes by governments — and it was then clear that the governments could negotiate through OPEC while the companies had no choice but to accommodate them.

➤ OAPEC

In 1968 the Organization of Arab Petroleum Exporting Countries (OAPEC — pronounced oh-ay-pek) was formed by Saudi Arabia, Kuwait, and Libya as a sort of Arab OPEC. The announcement of its founding and the subsequent statements of the participants did not shed much light on its raison d'etre, as it was stated specifically that OAPEC was not to be a substitute for or competitor of OPEC. Among the more plausible speculations was that it was a device to keep oil matters out of the politicization and bureaucracy of the Arab League and in the hands of those countries who had the oil. Another was that it would become a vehicle for common Arab investments in petroleum-related projects. In any event it proved to be a most useful instrument for initiating and coordinating the Arab embargo of October 1973. At that time the organization had grown to include all the Arab producers except Oman: that is, Algeria, Bahrain, Egypt, Iraq, Qatar, Syria and the United Arab Emirates, as well as the three founders. Since the 1973-74 rise in oil revenue OAPEC has grown greatly in importance as one of the principal agencies for coordinating and fostering large-scale projects undertaken in common by its members.

➤ Participation

Participation by the governments began to become an element of new concessions as early as the mid-1950's and usually was embodied as a government option in all concessions after 1960. But participation in the form that later became effective was first raised by Sheikh Ahmad Yamani, Saudi Minister of Petroleum, in discussions with Aramco in 1968. Fundamental objectives and forms were vague. Long discussions reached no conclusions. At the beginning, it seemed that Sheikh Ahmad was looking for a share in the downstream activities (refining and marketing) of the shareholders of Aramco. Negotiations dragged on until finally in December 1972 the first "participation" agreement was concluded. Essentially, under this agreement, the government would buy a 25 percent interest in Aramco immediately. It would gradually increase its purchases until in 1982 it would own 51 percent of the company. The rest of the Arab Gulf states followed with similar agreements early in 1973.

Iraq went a different route. In 1958, after the overthrow of the constitutional monarchy, the government of General Qasim engaged in a long series of negotiations with the Iraq Petroleum Company (IPC). When no agreement was reached by 1961 the government promulgated Law 80, voiding all the company's rights to 99.5 percent of the area of its concession, allowing it to retain only those areas in which oil was being actively produced. This cut IPC off from North Rumailah, the northern portion of a large field in southern Iraq then in the process of development. Negotiations continued interminably. In 1971, because of a drop in production from the Kirkuk field, Iraq "nationalized" the field. The French company, Compagnie Française de Pétroles, one of the shareholders in IPC whose share was not "nationalized," tried to negotiate on behalf of its partners. But the negotiations ended with the company only getting a ten-year contract to continue to receive its former share of Kirkuk oil. In October 1973 Iraq did not partake in the general Arab embargo, but it nationalized the remaining American and Dutch interests in the Iraq Petroleum Company elsewhere in the country, thus getting a great deal of participation without agreement.

THE ARAB OIL EMBARGO OF 1973

Most Americans including some politicians, diplomats, and economists who should have known better, were unaware that the Arab oil embargo of 1973 was the third imposed by the Arabs in the course of their resistance to Israel.

The first embargo, imposed during the Suez War of 1956, was against the British and the French as partners in a conspiracy with the Israelis. The Iraq Petroleum Company's pump stations in Syria were destroyed, French and British tankers were not permitted to load at oil terminals in Arab territories, and Aramco was forced to suspend shipments by pipeline to the Bahrain refinery, since Bahrain was regarded as being under British control at the time. Even the IPC pipeline branch through Jordan to Haifa was blown up, although no oil had been transported through it since 1948.

The second embargo was imposed in the course of the Six-Day War in 1967. This time the embargo was placed on all oil shipments to the United States, Great Britain, and West Germany, all of whom were supposed at the time to be aiding Israel.

The first two embargoes were utterly ineffective because

they were not supported by a cut in the production of Arab oil. The Arab states did not have sufficient financial reserves to sustain a loss in revenue for any period long enough to effect their objective and they did not fully understand the flexibility of world oil trade. With no cutback in the amount of oil being produced for export, cargoes destined for embargoed countries were simply lifted from countries not involved in the embargo, such as Iran, and other ships were sent to the Arab countries to replace those thus diverted. Although crude oils are not exactly replaceable, in an emergency a refiner who would like to have a particular Iranian crude could get along with a similar Arabian crude and vice versa.

Even more important to the failure of the 1967 embargo was the fact that the United States imported very little Arab oil, and the shut-in capacity of the United States oil fields were considerable. U. S. "conservation" operated largely through the import quota system, and the Texas Railroad Commission had left available an unused domestic producing capacity. So during the embargo the United States was able to increase its production rapidly, not only to supply its own needs, but also to help the European countries affected. Because imports from the Middle East were almost negligible, the early embargoes had no important effect on U. S. supplies and were largely unnoticed by the American public.

When Iraq, to demonstrate its strong commitment to the Arab cause, urged a continuation of the 1967 embargo months after the war had ended, Saudi Arabia refused to go along unless the embargo were made total; that is, a cessation of exports from all Arab countries. The Saudis argued correctly that unless Arab production were cut drastically, the embargo would continue to be ineffective. They also knew that the treasury of Iraq could not stand the loss of revenue that would follow. The embargo was lifted in November, five months after its imposition. Debates among the Arab countries on the issue showed their awareness of the reasons for its ineffectiveness.

In 1973 the changes that had taken place in six years were not lost on the Arab countries. The OPEC secretariat and the Arab petroleum ministries were perfectly aware that American production had gone to 100 percent of capacity in March 1972 in order to supply American demand. They knew there was little or no spare capacity in the rest of the world and that not only the American, but the OECD estimates as well, were looking to increased Arab production to supply demand. Estimates of oil demand had led to published projections that by the mid-1980's, for example, Saudi Arabia, as the sole producer with reserves adequate for expansion, would have to produce 20 million barrels a day to satisfy world demand. All the Arab states had enough surplus financial reserves to survive a cut in production. The United States was using either at home or supplying military forces abroad some 2.5 million barrels of Arab oil per day.

The 1973 embargo was tailored to meet these circumstances. Not only were direct shipments to the United States embargoed, but shipments were also stopped to the Caribbean Islands, where refineries supply the United States with much of its product imports. Holland was included for two reasons: the Dutch seemed pro-Israeli and the Rotterdam refineries were a source of products exported to the United States. The shipments to the U. S. military, which are not shown as U. S. "imports," ceased and they had to be made up from U. S. sources. Most important, the Arab countries cut their production by somewhat more than the sum total of the Arab oil that went to the United States, whether as crude directly or as products refined at some intermediate point. So if the Japanese, for example, wished to sell some of their reduced supply of oil to the U. S. and burn dollars instead, that was their choice. The embargo was self-enforcing.

➤ *Aftermath of Embargo*

Saudi Arabia and Aramco had signed their "participation" agreement at the end of 1972. The agreement had provided for the supply of small amounts of oil to the Saudi government oil company, officially the General Organization for Petroleum and Mineral Development, better known as Petromin, and not, initially, the full 25 percent to which they would eventually be entitled. The companies were to have time to expand production to take care of their future requirements, including long-term contracts, and gradually to supply Petromin with its full share.

In early 1973 Petromin decided to test the market and put its oil up for auction. The response from independent oil companies at a time when supply was very tight everywhere was most gratifying. Petromin calculated that it had received some 93 percent of the posted price on its sale. This percentage is important as it became enshrined for over a year and a half in calculations of what oil ought to be worth. Enthused by the results of the sales of participation oil, the OPEC countries had a meeting on 16 October 1973, at which they decreed a price of oil unilaterally for the first time. The price was $5.11 for Arabian light crude, posted price that is, for the purpose of calculating royalties and taxes. No one actually had posted it. In early November an auction of a small amount of non-embargoed Tunisian oil (Tunisia as a small producer had not joined the Arab embargo) brought an actual price of $12.64 per barrel. And finally, in early December an auction of Iranian oil brought $17.00 per barrel actual price. So, having learned what an industrial world in desperation was willing to pay for oil, the OPEC meeting of 23 December 1973 set the posted price for Arabian light at $11.60, obtained by deciding the government-take should be $7.00 per barrel, then calculating the posted price that would give this result, given the current royalty and tax rates.

Prices in the following months were confusion confounded. The posted price of $11.60 gave a cost price to the companies in Aramco, for example, of about $7.16 for their "equity oil," that is 75 percent of the total production. For the oil they bought from the Saudi Government's participation share, "buy-back oil," they paid 93 percent of posted prices, since the Government insisted that percentage had been determined as a fair, arms-length price by public auction. Their average costs per barrel were a weighted average of the two kinds of oil.

Early in 1974 Saudi Arabia notified Aramco that they wished to take over 100 percent of the company and that negotiations to that end should be undertaken. As these negotiations went on, Kuwait concluded a 60/40 participation agreement with its concession holders and Qatar followed suit. Aramco then was notified that its oil would be considered for tax purposes as priced equivalent to the Kuwait 60/40 arrangement, retroactive to 1 January 1974, while the negotiations on achieving the 100 percent acquisition continued.

During the first half of 1974, there were two OPEC meetings at which further small increases were agreed on in terms sufficiently ambiguous so that they could be applied differently by the various countries. An OPEC meeting on 13 December announced a single-price system, which had the effect of raising prices another three or four percent. Posted prices were actually reduced, but the royalty and tax rates were raised in such fashion that a concessionaire company still having a 40 percent equity and buying the other 60 percent of its oil from the state would pay approximately $10.20 to the government. (The corresponding government-take before November 1974 would have been $9.68, making this an increase of $0.52.) The increase in government-take, with the cost of production relatively fixed, is the principal determinant of the increase in prices to the consumer. (See Table III.) Though posted prices were about 2¼ times more in November 1974 than a year earlier, government-take had more than tripled. It is true, as claimed by the OPEC countries, that the price of oil to independent buyers had been reduced, as their prices were based on a percentage of the posted price. But what OPEC did not mention is that the proportion of oil in the world market handled by the independent buyer has been much smaller than that handled by the concessionaire companies, to the extent that the total flow has meant a considerably higher average price for the consumer. Prices so chaotically administered must inevitably be brought into a single-price system and this seems to be the trend in most OPEC countries in 1975.

➤ *Aramco Negotiations*

The Aramco negotiations with Saudi Arabia dragged on through 1974 until December, when an announcement was made that an agreement in principle had been reached. It was clear that the government wished an arrangement which would keep the Aramco operating organization intact. The shareholders of Aramco would be paid for their investment in Saudi Arabia; special arrangements would apply to the refinery at Ras Tanura, one of the largest in the world; and the former shareholders would be given guaranteed access to some part of Saudi production and would be asked to carry on further exploration in Saudi Arabia. The acceptance of such arrangements was predictable in view of the fact that all the companies had been seeking to carry on joint ventures with the Saudis in oil- and gas-related projects.

Such principles as the following seem to underlie the new arrangements between Saudi Arabia and Aramco: the government wishes to insure that the operations will be carried on without a break in continuity of management; that the refinery will be operated efficiently and profitably; that Saudi Arabia will retain access to the expertise of the Aramco shareholders; and that the shareholders will have sufficient oil at least for their own marketing needs if not for sale to third parties. It is now perfectly plain, if it had not been earlier, that this pattern of 100 percent ownership will be adopted by all those OPEC countries who feel it suitable to their own peculiar circumstances, and if it is not, they will most certainly try to obtain equal financial benefits.

The acceleration of "participation" to 100 percent ownership as well as the drastic increases in price in 1973-74 were in large part a result of the 1973 Arab-Israeli War. It can be argued that these changes would have come about without the war. But the war clearly demonstrated the fearful power the OPEC countries had in their possession of oil and so accelerated these trends. Without the frantic bidding for the Iranian government oil in December, preceded by the scramble for the Tunisian oil in November, it is most unlikely that the OPEC meeting of 23 December 1973 would even have been called, to say nothing of doubling the posted price set only two and one-half months earlier. Without the graphic demonstration of the world's need for oil, would Saudi Arabia have pressed ahead with the full takeover of Aramco? The Aramco participation agreement of 1972 provided that during a three-year period, Petromin rights to oil produced by Aramco would increase gradually to 25 percent of the total production by virtue of its 25 percent ownership in Aramco. At the same time Aramco shareholders were not obligated to take any oil that Petromin could not sell. As government participation there increased beyond 25 percent, Petromin's share of the oil produced would also increase. But of this oil the shareholders would be obliged to take any that Petromin did not require. This provision was a safety precaution on the part of the government so that Petromin would not be left with oil it was unable to sell. After October 1973 any doubts of Petromin's ability to sell oil were swept away, a drastic change in less than a year.

➤ Revenues

Table IV gives the total revenues from oil received by the OPEC members of the Arab Gulf states for the years selected, not only to illustrate the developments discussed in the text, but to summarize what oil has meant to their economies. The increase in revenues between 1966 and 1972 was the result of production cost decreases coupled with increases in both volume and price. The increase in 1974 is almost wholly the result of the enormous price increases decreed by OPEC in 1973 and 1974.

TABLE IV

PAYMENTS TO GOVERNMENTS AND CRUDE OIL PRODUCTION
$MILLIONS – B/D THOUSANDS

Year	Iraq $	B/D	Kuwait $	B/D	Saudi Arabia $	B/D	Qatar $	B/D	Abu Dhabi $	B/D
1938	7.6	92	0.1	–	0.4	1.4	0.4	–	–	–
1948	10.3	77	13.7	127	31.5	390	0.4	–	–	–
1950	14.8	140	12.4	344	112	548	1	32	–	–
1951	38.5	181	30	560	155	762	3.8	50	–	–
1952	91	389	175	750	211	825	9	69	–	–
1962	266	1009	526	1957	451	1642	56	193	2.8	15
1966	394	1392	707	2485	777	2602	92	289	100	360
1972	575	1466	1657	3283	3107	6012	255	482	551	1203
1974	7500	1900	9300	2550	25000	8500	2000	520	5500	1400

OFFSHORE OIL AND NATURAL GAS

The greatest assemblage of offshore oil fields in the world lies in the Persian Gulf. Over 20 fields, including the largest in the world, the Safaniyah-Khafji field lying partly in Saudi waters and partly in the Neutral Zone, contain some 60 billion barrels of reserves. The Emirates of Sharjah and Dubai obtain all their production of oil from offshore fields. Nearly half that of Qatar comes from two offshore fields. Bahrain gets nearly half of its oil income from its share of the production from the Abu Sa'afah field in Saudi waters. But, as if to emphasize the vagaries of oil distribution, no oil has yet been found in the sea off Kuwait proper, despite the enormous field onshore in Kuwait. Neither of the two states with the shortest shorelines on the Gulf, Iraq and Oman, has any oil fields in its territorial waters.

The Persian Gulf is a very shallow sea, less than 200 meters in depth throughout almost its whole extent. With its shallow waters and relatively calm weather, offshore oil drilling and production have been much easier than in many parts of the world. In addition, the whole of the sea sits upon the kind of continental shelf referred to by President Harry S.

Truman in his proclamation of 1945, in which the United States claimed for its control and usage "the seabed and subsoil of the continental shelf beneath the high seas" contiguous to the United States. A press release accompanying the Truman Proclamation suggested that the continental shelf extended seaward to a depth of about 600 feet of water. The term "continental shelf" was derived from the geographical fact that around the continents the slope of the sea floor seems to break very sharply and become much steeper at water depths averaging about 200 meters. This depth gained legal status in the Geneva Continental Shelf Convention of 1958. Though the Gulf is not technically a continental shelf (but an epeiric sea) it has been treated as if it were, and the legal principles that have been developed since 1945 in respect to the continental shelf have helped define the offshore boundaries of adjacent states contiguous to the Gulf.

Given the number of states involved and the peculiarities of their coastlines, the definition and agreements on boundaries have progressed very well. A few settlements have contributed to the development of techniques in the settlement of boundaries. Saudi Arabia issued a "Royal Pronouncement" in May 1949 claiming jurisdiction similar to that of the Truman Proclamation. All the Arab states save Iraq and Oman issued similar proclamations later that same year, and Iraq made a similar claim in 1958. Iran asserted its claims by a law passed in 1955. The area of potential disputes then included not only those states adjacent to one another but also those across the Gulf from each other, inasmuch as the water between them does not exceed 200 meters in depth. Besides containing the larger islands such as Bahrain and Kharg, the shallow Gulf has numerous shoals that become islets at certain tides. Moreover, the tidelands, especially on the flat shores of the eastern and southern parts of the Gulf, are wide and make the determination of the shoreline subject to great uncertainty. Finally, until all the states had settled on the width of twelve miles for their claimed territorial seas, negotiations between the states were difficult.

The first offshore boundary agreement was concluded by Bahrain and Saudi Arabia in February 1958. Besides various compromises on conflicting claims to shoals and islands, the two parties arrived at a statesmanlike decision on a disputed area which both sides believed likely to contain oil. The whole of the area, a six-sided parcel defined by the latitude and longitude of the corner points, was put under the sovereignty of Saudi Arabia, but it was agreed that the Saudi Government would give the Bahrain Government one-half the proceeds from any oil found within the area. Four years later the Abu Sa'afah field was discovered within the area. At the urging of the Saudi Government it was developed and put into production somewhat before the more easily developed onshore fields within Saudi Arabia, so that Bahrain might enjoy the revenues from its production at an earlier time.

Representatives of Iraq, Kuwait, Saudi Arabia, and Iran met in Geneva in October 1963 to begin discussions on equitable means of settling their respective common boundaries. Numerous bilateral and multilateral discussions have taken place since that time. The first result was an agreement initialed by Saudi Arabia and Iran in December 1965. A dispute over the ownership of two islands about midway between the two countries was resolved by allocating one island to each country and giving each island its own twelve-mile width of territorial sea. As the islands were closer together than 24 miles it was provided that where the territorial seas overlapped, the boundary would be the "median line" between the islands, that is, a line in which all points compromising it are equidistant from the nearest points on the two shores.

Kharg Island lies farther than twelve miles from the Iranian shore and ordinarily would not be considered part of the mainland. But the Iranians claimed that, as the intervening water was so shallow and the island was connected to the mainland by pipelines, it should be considered as mainland in drawing the median line between Iran and Saudi Arabia. This dispute was solved by drawing two median lines in the area affected. One considered Kharg to be an island and the other considered it as part of the mainland. A third median line between the two, called "the half-island effect line," was then taken as the boundary.

However, the initialed agreement was not ratified by Iran. Then oil was discovered on the Iranian side of the line in a concession that had been granted in 1958 by the Iranian Government. The concession had specified the boundary on the Gulf side in precise geographical terms rather than by a phrase indicating that the concession went only so far as Iranian sovereignty extended. Continued exploration of the new oil discovery progressed steadily toward the median line that had been agreed upon. In January 1968, to the surprise of Saudi Arabia and Aramco, preparations began to set a drilling platform on the Saudi side of the line. Saudi Arabia not only protested to the Iranian Government but also arranged for an Aramco mobile drilling platform in the area to move into position after sunset one night between the Iranian platform and the median line. Drilling was underway before sunrise. In the next few days the Iranian Navy seized the Aramco drilling platform, took off most of the crew, and threatened to tow away the platform. After many tense moments, the Iranians released the crew and permitted the platform to move out of the area. Negotiations were resumed in October. The Iranian platform on the Saudi side of the line was abandoned and never used. The boundary line was again defined and a new agreement was ratified by both sides in early 1969.

The new agreement was based on an Aramco suggestion that both sides exchange all the geological and seismic data then available and permit no more geological or seismic work on either side, so that both would have the same degree of ignorance. A joint commission would then decide on the probable extent of the oil field, and a new line would be drawn so as to divide the presumed reserves equally in the area under dispute. The Geneva Convention of 1958 had emphasized the principle of a fair division of resources; therefore it made just as much sense to divide the unknown resources on geological grounds as to divide them on geographical grounds in the conventional way.

Several other boundaries have been settled in the Gulf, but some boundaries still are uncertain. The Iranian seizure in December 1971 of Abu Musa and the Tunb Islands, claimed respectively by Sharjah and Ras al-Khaimah of the United Arab Emirates, did not contribute much to international law. One result was the retaliatory nationalization of British Petroleum's concession in Libya by the Government to demonstrate Arab solidarity. The Iranian seizure took place one day before the British treaty of protection with the two emirates ended, and the Libyan government felt that the British Government should have prevented it. According to an Iranian Government announcement, Iran and the United Arab Emirates on 13 August 1974 signed an agreement defining the boundaries between the two countries along a median line in the Gulf.

At the other end of the Gulf the problems of production from an oil field that extended across underwater boundaries became acute in the early nineteen-sixties. The offshore Saudi Arabian-Neutral Zone boundary had been agreed upon by both the Saudi and Kuwait Governments, after it was found that the Khafji field discovered by the Arabian Oil Company in the Neutral Zone and the Safaniyah field in Saudi Arabian waters were parts of a single oil field. The problem that arose was not only one of working the field in such a manner that neither party obtained more oil than underlay its side of the geographical boundary but also of convincing both governments that this end was being achieved.

Deciding whether or not migration of oil is actually

taking place across a boundary, and in which direction, is not easy. Oil flows through rocks very slowly; you cannot put down a well and see a stream of oil flowing in a certain direction. The determination is, in fact, a complex problem in reservoir engineering, requiring careful measurements and careful records over a fairly long period of time. There is room for disagreement, both as to the effect and the causes of the phenomena revealed by the measurements and records. Once it is determined that migration is taking place, and in which direction, the questions of how best to stop migration, how to retrieve losses, and how to maintain zero migration remain.

After much negotiation, facilitated by the interest of the Saudi Government in both sides of the line, the Arabian Oil Company and Aramco reservoir and production engineers exchanged data through government channels and worked together with government observers to agree on production practices. Among these was an agreement that neither side would drill a well closer than one kilometer to the boundary line. In effect, this was a practical demonstration that such a situation is soluble only if each side lets the other know everything needed for calculation of the behavior of the oil reservoir as a whole.

The one great lesson that comes out of the experience of the Gulf countries in determining offshore boundaries is that such boundaries ought to be fixed before either side knows what resources are involved. After oil, or anything else valuable, is discovered in a disputed area, the settlement becomes more difficult in proportion to the stakes.

➤ *Natural Gas*

The countries about the Gulf have been producing not only great quantities of oil but also very large quantities of natural gas. Most of this gas is "associated gas," that is, it is dissolved in the oil at the temperatures and pressures existing in the oil reservoirs and it is released when the oil is brought to surface temperature and atmospheric pressure. The proportion of gas to oil produced varies widely from field to field. Most of this gas has been "flared" — that is, burned because of the lack of an economic use. At a rate of 16 million barrels of oil per day (about the rate for these countries in 1974) some 3 trillion cubic feet of gas is produced annually with the oil. Some has been used for power generation, refinery fuel, water distillation, fertilizer manufacture, and reinjection into the oil reservoirs to maintain pressure. But at least three-quarters of the total gas has been flared.

As the price of oil has gone up, the economics of gathering and utilizing the associated gas has changed. The energy content of the gas so produced is about one-tenth of that in the barrel of oil with which it is associated. Gathering and handling gas so as to utilize it in beneficial ways is more costly than handling an equivalent amount of energy as oil, unless it can be done on a fairly large scale. There was no industrial demand for gas in the Gulf states, and their warm climate does not provide much of a market for space heating, such as in northern Europe and the United States. But the growth of industry in the Arab countries, especially such high energy consumers as aluminum reduction, will lead to the use of more and more gas. Moreover, the growing demand for gas in the industrialized countries of the world, the rise in the cost of oil everywhere, and the increase in the size of tankers have made plants in the Gulf for the liquefaction of natural gas (LNG) or its conversion into methanol, economically viable. And in due time OPEC will undoubtedly be concerned with the pricing of LNG in export trade.

The gas reserves of these countries have been estimated at more than 150 trillion cubic feet, more than half the reserves of the United States. Most of the gas so estimated is associated gas. Because of the great surplus of associated gas produced with the oil, there has been no need or incentive to explore for and develop unassociated gas, except in Bahrain where the aluminum reduction plant uses non-associated gas. Once a market develops for more gas than can be supplied economically by the associated gas now being flared, exploration for non-associated gas will undoubtedly discover very large new reserves. Some flared gas, as in offshore fields, may always be too expensive to gather and transmit to a central plant for liquefaction or other uses.

CONSIDERATIONS IN MAKING ENERGY POLICY

The preceding analysis has covered briefly the historical experience as well as most of the physical elements that will influence the determination of energy policy in the seven Arab states that border the Persian Gulf. Some broad energy policies will be peculiar to one or only a few of them. No one who is not a member of their government, of course, can be certain about all the elements that ultimately will go into the making of their decisions. But a knowledge of what their leaders and their expert advisers have said and of the factors that most of these governments will have to consider may help to understand their actions or, at least, to anticipate the general lines on which their polcies may develop.

➤ Reserves

The first consideration in energy policy for a state dependent, as all these are, on the production of oil for the greater part of their gross national product must be a consideration of its reserves: their size, their rate of depletion, their rate of accretion, and their quality. Table V shows approximately how each of the countries stood at the end of 1974.

In this table there are two elements of uncertainty. The first is the estimate of reserves. These are estimates of the amount of oil that can be produced under present technology at present prices. The estimates do not try to prophesy advances in technology, change in prices, and the discovery of extensions to existing fields or the discovery of new fields. The second is the rate of production. Here, the experience of the United States is illustrative. In 1946 U. S. reserves were estimated at 21 billion barrels. In the succeeding twenty years, 45 billion barrels were produced and the estimate of remaining reserves had *increased* to 32 billion barrels. In other words, 56 billion barrels had been found in those twenty years and, more remarkable, most of these barrels had resulted from improvements in the technology of recovery from fields. Since 1966, however, U. S. reserves in the lower 48 states, excluding the discovery of Prudhoe Bay in 1968, have declined steadily as annual production has exceeded additions to reserves.

In large part, the discovery of additional reserves in the Arab states of the Persian Gulf will be a function of the area to be explored. Saudi Arabia and Iraq, obviously, have a much greater opportunity for the discovery of new fields than Kuwait, Bahrain, or Qatar. Equally those countries with the greatest reserves have much more to gain from advances in technology that assure recovery of a higher percentage of the oil in place in the earth. In the United States the average percentage of recovery of original oil in place in the reservoir rocks is about 30 percent, ranging from 10 percent to about 60 percent, depending on many factors, but chiefly the character of the oil and the rocks in which it is held.

In making guesses, educated perhaps but still guesses, about future discoveries of oil and technological improvements, the experience of the United States is not necessarily

TABLE V

RESERVES AS OF DECEMBER 31, 1973
YEARS TO EXHAUSTION
AT 1974 RATE OF PRODUCTION

	Proved Reserves Billions of Barrels	1974 Production Millions Barrels Per Day	Years to Exhaustion
Iraq	35	1.90	50
Kuwait	72.75	2.60	77
Saudi Arabia	104	8.50	34
Bahrain	0.34	0.07	13*
Qatar	6.0	0.55	30
United Arab Emirates:			
Abu Dhabi	30	1.50	55
Dubai	2.4	0.25	26
Sharjah	1.0	0.10	27
Oman	6.0	0.35	47

*Bahrain also receives one-half of the Saudi Government income from the Abu Sa'afah field with reserves of 6+ billion.

NOTE: *This table is useful only if it is firmly held in mind that oil fields, like old soldiers, never die, they only fade away. Production of oil will go on for many years at rates much below those postulated. In 1973 the Brea Olinda field in the Los Angeles basin discovered in 1884 was still producing 10,000 barrels per day from 700 wells, an average of less than 15 BPD each.*

directly applicable to the Persian Gulf countries. The fields of the Middle East were developed initially at a level of technology far higher than in the United States. They were developed later, so more advanced technology was available initially, and without the legal and bureaucratic obstacles that inhibited the prompt application of technical knowledge in the United States. Consequently, the opportunities for improvement of initial estimates are not as great. On the other hand, the Middle East has not been as extensively explored as the United States, and there is considerable likelihood of the discovery of many small fields, if not many more giants. All these factors must be weighed by a state in deciding upon the rate at which its oil resources should be depleted.

➤ Income

A second consideration of energy policy is the level of income to be derived from oil, which obviously depends directly on the level of production and the price per barrel. But the desirable level of income needed to achieve the broader objectives of a government must also take into consideration factors such as the size of the population, the available natural resources to be developed, estimates as to future value of oil, and the effects of competition from other sources of energy. One estimate that must be a prerequisite to all others in making policy is that of the income considered to be the minimum the state will require for current expenditures and those capital projects believed to be necessary for the common welfare. Such an estimate by government would be indispensable should the members of OPEC decide that a revival of "production programming" (limiting production to maintain prices) is necessary in some form to maintain a desirable price level. If income is likely to outrun current expenditures, estimates of the most profitable, stable, and dependable investments must be made, all of which in turn will affect decisions on the levels of production at given prices.

If production and prices are such that a surplus of income beyond current requirements is generated, the determination of what to do with it will involve at least: (1) an examination of developable natural resources for which oil revenues will supply the capital; (2) an estimate of manpower required and available for such development; (3) an estimate of which investments abroad may be more desirable than those at home; (4) an estimate of optimum rate of development and whether manpower or management capabilities are deficient; and (5) an estimate of how these deficiencies can be overcome.

Possibly the most difficult and preoccupying decisions that confront energy policymakers in these countries are those involving comparison of the value of present and future income. Is it really better to take all the income that can be gotten today and rely on compound interest for future needs rather than to postpone income and adjust to an uncertain future? Is the buying power of oil likely to improve or deteriorate? What competitive forms of energy are likely to develop? When? And what will their effect be on oil demand? What will be the principal uses of oil twenty, thirty, or fifty years from now? How much confidence can be placed in which foreign investments? What moral or political obligations or considerations relative to the economy of the world should bear on the determination of the levels of production? Obviously, definitive answers to such questions are impossible. However, some kind of strategy for weighing the risks and making estimates is necessary, even though it may not be formalized and is done more by instinct than by computer.

➤ Social and Political Considerations

Decisions about production levels and income in the last analysis must always depend upon social and political considerations. If the country has a small population and a large income from energy production, whether oil or gas, it has several alternatives. It can put the surplus money into investments abroad. It can try to industrialize the country at a rapid rate by bringing in the technicians, experts, and craftsmen and artisans necessary to erect the plants required. It can invest in downstream operations abroad, e.g. refineries, not only for the purpose of putting its surplus income to work but also to provide a controlled training place for its nationals as they become able to absorb such training. Such a choice may be made to avoid disturbing the fabric of local culture by too rapid industrialization. It can decide to invest in relatively small plants within the country, which would introduce the process of industrialization at a rate that can be absorbed without importing an undue number of foreigners. There are combinations of approaches that can be followed simultaneously, geared to the speed and progress of training and education of the local population. At the same time, if the income is sufficient and as education spreads, a good many social services will be demanded, such as hospitals, schools, and municipal works (power plants, water and sewer systems, etc.) whether or not cadres of local craftsmen and skilled technicians are available to support such institutions. One of the problems long apparent in such countries is that the excellent opportunities for personal advancement in the fields of finance and commerce siphon some of the best talent in the country from industrial pursuits.

Above all, political reasons must dictate much of any state's energy policy. The United Arab Emirates, for example, is a loose confederation in which each member handles its own domestic affairs. What should be the relationship between those members who have oil and those who do not? What can be expected if those who have resources keep the income all to themselves? Should there be a larger (e.g., Bahrain, Qatar) or tighter union? What should be the relationships between functions carried on by both the Union and the individual states (e.g., defense)? What should be the relationships of the various states of OAPEC? Which matters will they handle in OPEC and which in OAPEC? And always, until the conflict is settled, the Arab-Israeli issue will surely be in mind as a factor to be considered by most of these states in almost all major policy decisions.

➤ Common Policies

Statements and declarations on specific aspects of energy policy have been fairly numerous and explicit, but no government in the area has set forth a definitive statement of its total policy. Nevertheless, from written and oral material and from an examination of past and present actions, a fair statement of their current policies can be constructed. Some policies, moreover, seem common to all the Arab countries along the Persian Gulf.

The two principal concerns of the policymakers in all the countries are "industrialization" and "conservation." The first not only includes the building of industrial complexes but also the modernization of agriculture and the provision of the infrastructure for an industrial society that will support itself without oil. The second has not only to do with the prevention of waste but includes, above all, the husbanding of hydrocarbon resources in such a fashion as to obtain optimum conditions of life for generations to come.

The instrument for industrialization in these Gulf countires is money, lots of it. And the instrument which will safeguard the flow of money is OPEC. Because OPEC has been so helpful to its members, they will continue to support it, no matter how much the members may quarrel among themselves. OPEC has been the means by which the governments' take from a barrel of oil was raised eight-fold in the space of two years. As producing capacity grows and the rate of consumption fails to keep pace, the organization will be the means by which production will be adjusted to the market. So the Arab states of the Gulf will continue to support OPEC and, although they may stray from the fold occasionally, they will not eliminate it.

Conservation has also been served by OPEC. Although each state makes its own decisions on production levels, the coordination through OPEC of such decisons, which may affect both price and conservation, with other producing countries has been a most valuable service to the members.

The OPEC members in this group of countries have had great leverage on OPEC policies. In 1974 they generated a bit more than half of the surplus funds of the OPEC countries: that is, over $30 billion of the total of some $60 billion, looking for investment outside the OPEC countries. At the same time the Arab countries surrounding the Gulf had only one-tenth of the total population of the OPEC group, which roughly indicates how much more they can afford to cut back production to sustain prices than the other members of the cartel. Conversely, they could also increase production enough to bring about lower prices should they choose to do so. Saudi Arabia is well able to play the part in OPEC that Texas played for nearly 40 years in stabilizing U. S. prices.

OAPEC has rapidly been developing into the principal agency for coordinating industrial projects in which all the Arab states can participate to their mutual advantage. It may well bring more unity to the Arab states than the Arab league and Israel together have been able to do. All the OAPEC states have contributed to the Arab Shipbuilding and Repair Yard (ASRY) in Bahrain to handle supertankers. All have contributed to the Arab Fund for Economic and Social Development (AFESD), whose chief function seems to be the making of very soft loans to the poorer Arab countries to help pay for oil. These loans have been free of payment of principal and interest for ten years and thereafter repaid at very low rates of interest. Such loans can produce an effective price for oil of about $2.00 per barrel. Other organizations created by OAPEC have been the Arab Petroleum Investments Company (APIC) for financing oil- and gas-related projects mainly in, but not limited to, Arab countries; the Arab Company for Petroleum Services; and the Arab Maritime Petroleum Transport Company (AMPTC) which has six supertankers building and has sent trainees to Alexandria, England, and Scandinavia. Thus far Arab countries of all political hues seem to be comfortable in OAPEC and ready to support its projects wholeheartedly, an indication of an organization likely to be durable as well as one that will provide for cooperative industrialization.

The only purely political matter impinging on oil policy and on which all the Arab states of the Gulf agree is their common policy with all the other Arab countries toward Israel. As none of them is a "front line" country, their chief, direct contribution to the struggle with Israel has been money, and this is likely to be so in the future. Indirectly, their contribution has been their readiness to embargo oil exports to countries they believed could be instrumental in containing Israeli expansionism. Given the financial reserves they now possess, they will undoubtedly use the same tactics in the future should the occasion arise. It is true that Iraq did not join in the 1973 embargo, but only because it thought the presumed supporters of Israel could be hurt more in other ways. Except for Israel, there does not seem to be any other political matter on which these countries are in general agreement.

The Arab states of the Gulf have acknowledged the importance of consumers, but beyond the acknowledgement that someone buys the oil, no consensus is discernible on how to treat the buyers. Much effort has been put into justifying the present prices of oil on the grounds that it has long been underpriced, that commodities purchased from the industrial countries are overpriced, and that the market makes the price now that the hold of the international oil companies has been broken. Nevertheless, any dialogue with consumers is a moot question, and OAPEC has seemed to lean toward starting discussions with the European Economic Community. But in the end, most likely, the consumers will be handled through OPEC decisions which, it must be noted, do not take effect until ratified by the individual members.

Other matters have been of common concern to all or most of the Arab countries on the Gulf, but the manner of dealing with them may differ markedly from country to country, with the exception of inflation. To prevent the erosion of the Arab purchasing power of oil and gas revenues, due to rising prices in the industrialized world, OPEC will be the most likely agent. Other policies with respect to access to technology, marketing of crude and products, participation in downstream operations abroad, investments, and concessions will vary with the individual state.

POLICIES OF THE SEVEN GULF COUNTRIES

As shown in Table V, Iraq has enough reserves to produce at current rates well into the 21st century. Reserves of this magnitude should be able to sustain a far higher rate of production with no loss of ultimate recovery. The United States is producing four times as much from reserves of similar size. Additionally, the government of Iraq is justifiably expecting to discover substantial new reserves as comparatively little exploration of the country has been carried on since 1960, when the Iraq Petroleum Company was forced to cease work. Consequently, the question of conservation for Iraq involves decisions as to how much more money they need than the sum provided by present production, how much they wish to spend for more production facilities, and whether they should increase production capability when the OPEC countries already have several million barrels per day of producing capacity in excess of demand. No public pronouncement by Iraqi officials had addressed these questions in 1974. It would seem that available manpower utilizing present income may be so occupied with building the infrastructure as fast as possible, and with the training of more Iraqis for higher industrial capabilities, that the government will make no overt decisons on these questions until present undertakings are further along, and meantime develop the known oil fields slowly but steadily.

A cataloging of some of the international agreements and the projects contracted for in only the last six months of 1974 will give an idea of the pace of industrialization in Iraq. At least seven "protocols" or agreements have been made with seven countries for economic and technical or scientific cooperation. These are: the Soviet Union, Italy, the German Democratic Republic (East Germany), Yugoslavia, Japan, India, and Syria. Japan is to extend $1 billion credit and France $500 million, presumbably to be repaid in oil or gas exports. Yugoslavia is to participate in projects totaling some $3 billion. India has received a loan of $110 million to be repaid, after five years grace, in five years at 2.5% interest. Four cement plants at a total cost of half a billion dollars are to be built by Danish, Japanese, Russian and French companies, one each. A Swiss company is to build a 190-megawatt power plant. French companies are building an aluminum smelter for $100 million, and a sponge-iron reduction plant and steel complex that will cost about $500 million when completed. A joint company with Egypt, capitalized at $350 million, is to produce tractors, trucks, and agricultural machinery. A new technical university costing $88 million with a capacity for an eventual enrollment of 16,000 students is to be built in Baghdad. A new pipeline from the northern fields in Iraq is to be constructed jointly with the Turkish government to carry crude oil from Iraq's northern fields to a Turkish port on the Mediterranean, both for Turkish consumption and for export; the cost estimate is $700 million.

The industrialization projects in Iraq have been notable for the diversity of the nationalities involved and for the mixture of kinds of projects to be undertaken. Especially notable has been the protocol with Syria. The two governments have long been most antagonistic, yet a November 1974 agreement provided for an Iraqi free trade zone in Syria on the Mediterranean, a railroad to the Syrian town of Deir al Zor, whence, presumably, the Syrians would link up with Aleppo, providing a railroad link from the port of Latakia, bypassing the Suez Canal for Iraqi merchandise imports from the West; a joint electric power network; and arrangements for supplying Syrian cotton to Iraq and for a joint textile industry. For the 1975-79 period the government projection was that domestic investments would exceed $17 billion. This seems low, since internal spending for 1974 was estimated at some $6.5 billion out of revenues of $7.5 billion.

As for general policy, significant statements were made at the Second International Oil Seminar in Baghdad in November 1974. Some of the rhetoric may be ascribed to the tone of the gathering. It was sponsored by the "National Council for Peace and Solidarity in Iraq" in cooperation with the "World Peace Council" and the "Afro-Asian Solidarity Organization." The Iraqi Minister of Oil and Minerals called on the Arab oil-producing countries to use their monetary surpluses to free the economies of the underdeveloped countries from the monetary fluctuations resulting from their links with the economies of the capitalist countries. He urged the oil producers to assist the developing countries by extending soft loans and establishing economic relations to help them with their industrial development. The Secretary General of Iraq's "Follow-Up Committee for Oil Affairs and Implementation of Agreements" states: "We aim at liquidating the monopolistic organizations and setting up direct producer-consumer relations, not only as regards oil but also for the transfer of modern technology from the advanced countries to the developing states."

Dr. Sa'adoon Hammadi, then Minister of Oil and Minerals, in a statement published at the end of the Second International Oil Seminar in 1974, made the following points:

Inflation, the monetary crisis, unemployment and reduced production levels are not attributable to the increase in oil prices but are due to the inherent rising contradictions in the capitalist system, the escalating monopolistic activities of multinational corporations, and the large return in interest — amounting to billions of dollars — accruing to the major international banks; the balance of payments problems... oil prices, since they had reached crisis level prior to the oil price increase... the basic problem (in the U. S.) is related to huge military expenditures abroad, the transfer of capital outside the U. S. by the multinationals... and the devaluation of the dollar...; at the same time it is true that a number of capitalist developed countries are facing urgent balance of payments problems because of the sharp increases in the prices of raw materials, including oil;... the principles of cooperation between the oil exporting countries and the oil importing countries are a matter of great importance. Such cooperation may take the form of barter deals...; plans for industrial cooperation with division of labor; and special deferred payment arrangements... [for] developing countries... unable to adjust their balance of payments in the short term because of the rising costs of oil and foodstuffs, the oil exporting countries could provide... soft loans and other financial assistance...; the oil exporting countries could also make arrangements with the socialist states for the importation of technical equipment and expertise under special credit arrangements; such arrangements would help ease the balance of payments problems of the socialist states.

➤ *Kuwait*

The Kuwait government's policies toward its energy resources have been spelled out in various speechs by the Foreign Minister and the Minister of Finance and Oil, and by the Crown Prince in presenting the Ruler's State-of-the-Nation message in October 1974.

General oil policy since August 1974 has been the responsibility of the Supreme Petroleum Council within the

Council of Ministers. The president of the Council of Ministers is chairman of the six-man council, which includes the ministers of Finance, Oil, Foreign Affairs, and Trade and Industry as well as a minister of State for Council of Ministers' Affairs. The Supreme Petroleum Council formulates general oil policy "within the framework of the state's economic and social development philosophy" with particular attention to the conservation of oil resources, the development of oil-based industries to ensure optimum utilization of oil resources with a maximum of return and the development of a fully integrated national oil industry. Oil policies have also been the subject of frequent animated debates in the Kuwait parliament.

The most noteworthy aspect of Kuwait's policy has been the emphasis on the conservation of resources. After the Kuwait Oil Company had relinquished most of the area it formerly held under concession, retaining essentially only those areas with active producing oil fields, the government let out the relinquished areas to new concessionaires who then re-explored. No new fields were discovered. The offshore waters of Kuwait, exhaustively explored by the Shell company, have yet to produce any oil. Consequently, the government has come to the conclusion that most of the oil likely to be found in Kuwait's territory has already been discovered. In January 1972 Kuwait was producing oil at an annual rate of about 3775 million barrels a day (MBD), including 275 MBD from its share of the Neutral Zone. In the following month a proposal was made in Parliament to limit Kuwait's production to 3 million barrels per day. The proposal was adopted by the government in April of that year. In the debate on the 1974-75 budget a parliamentary committee proposed that the production ceiling should be cut by 50 percent, but the government opposed this further cut, although since then Kuwait production has been lowered, both to meet market demands and to maintain prices, according to the Minister of Oil and Finance.

By virtue of its reserves, which are the largest in the world after Saudi Arabia and the Soviet Union, and its relatively large production for a small population and area, Kuwait's revenues have long been greater than its current needs. Consequently, it has been able to promote industrialization more than other nations in the area by way of several government-owned projects, such as desalination plants, a refinery, a fertilizer plant, and a tanker fleet. The ample revenues from oil over a considerable period of time had also resulted in the development of both expertise and institutions for investment abroad that are probably unmatched in the Gulf. Finally, the close relationship between oil and revenues was recognized by placing responsibility for both oil and finance in a single ministry until January 1975.

As explained by Kuwait's Adviser on Financial Affairs, Khalid Abu al Sa'ud, oil revenues have been divided into three categories: funds to be spent in one year; funds to be spent in one to five years; and funds to be saved for long periods for use by future generations. The first category has been invested until recently in sterling and dollars only, since these were the only currencies able to provide the markets and institutions that could absorb the money, pay an acceptable rate of interest, and permit withdrawal at short notice. The second category required recourse to markets in the industrial states for financing guaranteed projects that would repay the capital and interest at maturity. In the past, the third category could be invested in real estate, securities, and commercial and industrial projects in Arab, European, and U. S. markets with little difficulty, including the building up of a portfolio of a small number of shares in many companies for protection against loss. But the sheer size of present revenues requires means to convert these into tangible assets which the conventional markets may not provide. Thought is being given to the creation of an Arab financial market, which, for success, will require the same conditions as exist in

Britain and the United States: namely, short-term credit instruments, such as treasury bonds; a willingness of the market to absorb any amount of sterling or dollars; the availability of an organized market like a stock exchange; and the existence of financial legislation to protect the investor.

In a revealing response to a question on the oppositon of some Europeans to Arab investment in European industries, the Adviser replied that such opposition was political and not economic. If the accumulated funds are not invested in long-term industrial projects by equity shareholding, they will remain in short-term liquid form, which would tend to destabilize European economies. These funds represent the value of oil extracted from the ground and they should be invested in productive projects to compensate for the rapid depletion of the resource. The producers must either stop production or invest their capital in "real" assets, "the most significant of which are stocks." As Khalid Abu al Sa'ud said, "The motive for holding these stocks is not to control the economies of industrial nations but to assist those countries that are suffering from a lack of capital."

Among the most important financial organizations in Kuwait are the Kuwait Central Bank, the Kuwait Industrial Bank, the Kuwait Fund for Arab Economic Development, the Kuwait International Investment Company, the Kuwait-Egyptian Investment Company, and the newest organization, the Kuwaiti Financial Center SAK. These organizations made loans or participated in bond issues to finance a very diverse list of clients in the last six months of 1974, which illustrates the scope of their activities. Loans were made to the Republic of Ireland, the Philippines, Hungary, and the city of Marseilles. Yugoslavian state bonds in the amount of $105 million were purchased. In order to obtain 14 percent of the shares of Daimler-Benz, $403 million was paid. In addition, Kuwait financial institutions underwrote or participated in bond issues of many municipalities, such as Quebec, Copenhagen, Bergen, and Marseilles, as well as the government of Brazil.

In 1974 a new entity, the Kuwait Oil, Gas and Energy Corporation (KOGEC), was formed to take charge of all the government's interests in oil and gas operations, projects, and related activities, both inside Kuwait and outside. These activities include Kuwait's interest in the Kuwait Oil Company, the Kuwait share in the various projects sponsored by OAPEC as well as the Kuwait National Petroleum Company, the Kuwait Gas Utilization Project, the Kuwait Fertilizer Company, the Petrochemical Industries Company, the Kuwait Maritime Shipping Company, and the Kuwait Foreign Trading, Contracting and Investment Company. KOGEC is also responsible for marketing government crude oil, and its board of directors is composed of members from the private sector as well as from the government.

Despite an educational system that provides free schooling for all from kindergarten through the university, Kuwait seems to have neglected the kind of training necessary for a nation that looks to an industrial future. Only in late 1974 was the decision made to add a petroleum faculty to Kuwait University. The first students will enter in the 1976-77 academic year.

In early 1975, the details of the policy Kuwait intends to follow toward the major concessionaire, the Kuwait Oil Company, were not known. But the general policy and its trend seemed clear enough. One of the guidelines of the Supreme Petroleum Council requires it to pursue the development of a fully-integrated national oil company. Such an oil company would not be incompatible with the existence of a concessionaire working side by side with the national oil company. But given the political history of Kuwait, it is unlikely that the government will resist for long a takeover of the Kuwait Oil Company so that Kuwait, like neighboring Saudi Arabia, can claim 100 percent ownership and control of its oil. In the debates in parliament on the occasion of assuming 60 percent ownership in the Kuwait Oil Company in 1974, the government defended vigorously its decision not to take a larger percentage of ownership. Judging by those debates, if the government feels compelled to buy out the Kuwait Oil Company completely, it will probably, like Saudi Arabia, do so in such a way as to insure access to the technology of its former concessionaires and their expertise for continuing to operate the industry as efficiently as in the past.

➤ *Saudi Arabia*

The energy policy of Saudi Arabia is of more importance to the world than the policies of all the other Arab Gulf states put together. This importance derives not only from its great production and its possession of the most reserves, but also from the character of its officials, the location and size of the country, and its preeminent position in the Islamic world because of its holy cities of Mecca and Medina.

Saudi Arabia will, in general, conform to the policy lines set forth earlier in this study with respect to OPEC, OAPEC, and Israel. Development of the details of a Saudi policy on conservation, however, is more complex than for most of the other nations. As noted in Table V, Saudi proved reserves of 104 billion barrels have a life of 34 years at present rates of production. But Aramco has published an estimate of "possible reserves" of 173 billion barrels (including the "proved reserves"), which would give a life of 56 years to exhaustion. The probability that the "possible" reserves will be found to actually exist is very high. In addition, Saudi Arabia has some 450,000 square miles of land underlain by sedimentary rocks which have by no means been as intensively explored as the prospective oil-bearing land in the other states. And the chances for discovering wholly new fields in such a large area are relatively good. Another factor, mentioned earlier in this paper, becomes operative when considering reserves; that is the probability of increased recovery from the oil-in-place in the presently-known reservoirs because of improvements in technology. The greater the amount of oil originally in place, other factors being equal, the more oil will be recovered. If it is assumed that the present proved reserves have been calculated on the U.S. average recovery factor of 30 percent (which is not unreasonable, given the various types of crude oils and reservoirs in Saudi Arabia), the original oil-in-place would be somewhat more than 300 billion barrels. A ten percent increase in ultimate recovery would provide 30 billion barrels more oil and extend the life of known fields some ten years. In other words, the probability of Saudi Arabia finding reserves far greater than its present proved reserves is very great, both by means of further exploration and by the improvement of recovery of the oil-in-place in the rocks of the known fields. Nevertheless, prudent government officials must necessarily be conservative in calculations vitally affecting the well-being of their country.

With respect to the industrialization of the economy, the Saudi government is well underway. The Central Planning Organization, having estimated that thirty to forty years will be required "to create a new income base" to replace revenues from oil, contemplates spending $60 billion by 1980 on development projects. Negotiations have been undertaken by Petromin for a sponge-iron and steel complex which would use surplus gas for the direct reduction of Brazilian iron ore brought to a new port on the Gulf in combination carriers. These ships would haul oil to the Western Hemisphere on their return journey. Moreover, a large methanol plant in conjunction with the sponge-iron plant would furnish at least part of the hydrogen required for the sponge-iron production. At the same port, Jubail, a very large refinery and petrochemical plant is also being considered. These installations together with the port facilities, now non-existent, and the infrastructure necessary to support them, would require an investment upwards of $2 billion.

Other large oil-related facilities are in the planning stage in Saudi Arabia, including a 750-mile pipeline across the peninsula to a port of the Red Sea, where another sizable refinery would be built. This project would require another billion dollars or more. And there are hosts of smaller projects in progress or for which contracts have been let. Most notably, all the shareholders of Aramco have been discussing the establishment of joint enterprises in oil-related projects with Petromin.

The training of the indigenous people to manage industrial development in Saudi Arabia seems to be much more advanced than in the other Arab countries of the Gulf. The College (now University) of Petroleum and Minerals established at Dharan in 1964 is a first-class institution operated under the direction of the Ministry of Petroleum. The Board of Trustees is composed of prominent educators of diverse nationalities, including men of stature from universities such as the Massachusetts Institute of Technology and the American University of Beirut. Two other Saudi universities have been established in Riyadh and Jiddah, but the College of Petroleum and Minerals has advanced to the stage at which it can cooperate with American technical institutions – as an example, in providing facilities for research on solar energy. Nevertheless, it is apparent that one of the most critical problems facing Saudi Arabia is the lack of sufficient manpower to accomplish the government's goals in the desired time span. The lack of craftsmen and technicians is likely to be more troublesome than a shortage of engineers and managers. As yet, no articulated policy on the importation of foreigners to supply such skills seems to have been formulated.

The manner of the takeover of Aramco demonstrated the Saudi government's concern for continued access to the technology of the developed countries and its desire to have efficient management operation of its industries. The Aramco operating organization is to be held together, essentially, as it existed before the takeover. The Ras Ranura refinery is likely to be operated in conjunction with the Aramco shareholders. The Aramco organizaton, whatever it may be called, is to continue exploration work on behalf of the government. It is also probable that the scope of Aramco activity will be enlarged to allow it, for example, to take over all the bulk generation and distribution of power in the Eastern Province. Such an arrangement will greatly facilitate the creation of the large new industrial projects by relieving them of the burden of providing their own power. The new projects are to be joint enterprises with contributions of foreign capital so that the foreign partners have a direct financial interest in providing whatever expertise is necessary to make them viable commercial enterprises.

Saudi policy toward the consuming countries and the price of oil has been less than clear. In the OPEC meeting of December 1973 that doubled the posted price of October 1973, Saudi Arabia was said to have opposed proposals for an even higher price. The posted price of $11.65 for Arabian light crude was believed to have been a compromise between the Saudi position and those who wanted higher prices. In subsequent OPEC meetings in the first half of 1974 the Saudis continued to oppose suggestions for further price raises on the grounds that the world economy was indivisible and that the price of oil was so high already as to threaten the economic health of the world. But at mid-year they cancelled plans for an auction of government oil that had been billed as one in which they would accept whatever prices were bid, unlike the Kuwait auction in which the oil was withdrawn from sale when the prices offered were lower than expected. Then, in November 1974 at a special meeting of OPEC members from the Gulf, the Saudis were the leaders in a new pricing system. The posted price of Arabian light was dropped by forty cents per barrel, but both taxation and royalty rates were raised. Depending on how much government oil the Aramco owners bought from the government in addition to their "equity" oil, the average cost of their oil went up some fifty cents a barrel. The actual price to an independent oil company buying from the government company was reduced thirty-seven cents a barrel.

Since the concession-holders were buying far more oil for their own uses than the independent companies, the average price to consumers for the total stream was raised. It is believed that part of the reason for this action was to put pressure on the Aramco shareholding companies to speed up negotiations. If this is true Saudi Arabia may try to lower prices once again after the Aramco agreement has been concluded. In public statements Saudi spokesmen have repeatedly said that Saudi Arabia would not cut production.

The combination of a growth in producing capacity with little or no growth in demand for oil since 1973 had brought about an excess of producing capacity in the OPEC countries of several million barrels a day by the end of 1974. If this condition persists, or the gap between productive capacity and demand grows even greater due to worldwide industrial slowdown and further conservation measures in the consuming countries, Saudi production may begin to put pressure on prices. Production in some of the OPEC countries dropped markedly in 1974. Using the last full month of 1973 before the embargo, September, as a point of comparison, six of the OPEC countries produced about 3.2 million barrels a day less in September 1974 than in 1973; the other six produced a little over half a million barrels more in September 1974 than in 1973, of which nearly one-half was from Saudi Arabia.

Unlike Kuwait, Saudi Arabia has separate "Supreme Councils" drawn from the Council of Ministers, one for petroleum and one for investment. Both are chaired by the Amir Fahd bin Abdul Aziz, First Vice-President of the Council of Ministers. Prior to the establishment of these two supreme councils, the whole of the Council of Ministers had passed on policy matters presented by the Minister of Petroleum and on investment by the Governor of the Saudi Monetary Agency. In 1975, it seems that these two councils, with several of the ministers as members of both councils, have been doing the detail work on proposals, screening them before submission to the whole council – and effectively determining policy, subject only to the King's consent.

The Saudi policies on oil and gas have been fairly well indicated both by speeches abroad and the presentation of papers to various international conferences and by usage and practice, if not by official proclamation. For example, the policy for handling the investment of some $18 to $19 billion dollars in surplus revenues for 1974 may have been formulated, but it certainly has not been defined in any public proclamation. The outlines of policy can be seen in contributions to the International Monetary Fund, the World Bank, the Islamic Development Bank, the Arab agencies that are making very soft loans to some of the less developed countries to cover oil purchases, and to U.N. agencies. The large loan to Japan for one billion dollars is significant. But as yet there are no indications that firm decisions by the government have been made as to the priorities, preferred methods of investment, and procedures to handle sums which are so much larger than any accumulated in similar circumstances in the past. These enormous revenues constitute a problem for which neither Saudi Arabia nor any other country has had precedent experience.

➤ *Bahrain*

Bahrain's energy policy primarily consists of expending a great deal of time and thought to make the most of the revenues from oil and gas. The production from the one and only onshore field, named Awali, will soon begin to decrease. Exploration of Bahrain's offshore areas has been unsuccessful in finding oil. Fortunately, the boundary settlement with

Saudi Arabia has given Bahrain a one-half interest in the Abu Sa'afah offshore field which, at the present rate of production, has sufficient reserves to last for over a century. And, as noted earlier, Bahrain has developed non-associated gas in the Awali onshore oil field to supply fuel to an aluminum reduction plant.

More than a decade ago Bahrain set up a commission charged with developing new industries that would be viable after Bahrain's oil was depleted. The discovery of Abu Sa'afah in 1963 eased the country's financial worries and the pipeline connection to Saudi Arabia for supplying oil to the Bahrain refinery assured a source of energy beyond the life of the Awali field. In addition to the aluminum plant, there are smaller industries in Bahrain, but all of them will be overshadowed by the OAPEC-sponsored Arab Shipbuilding and Repair Yard. Stage one of this giant project, to be completed in the first half of 1977, will be a drydock capable of accommodating vessels up to 500,000 dead weight tons, employing over 1000 workers, and intended to concentrate on hull-scraping and repainting services. Stage two, a second drydock, will provide full-fledged maintenance and survey services.

The claims of Iran to Bahrain having been relinquished after a U.N.-sponsored plebiscite, Bahrain is under no special political pressure from abroad. While generally supporting the Arab side of any issue with the non-Arab world, Bahrain will tend to concentrate on its own economy and follow the lead of the OPEC members in oil policy so long as it benefits Bahrain.

► *Qatar*

Qatar has the smallest oil production of the Arab members of OPEC but nevertheless had enough to provide nearly $2 billion of surplus revenue in 1974. Its prospects for further discoveries of oil are not great. The onshore area has been thoroughly explored by two different concessionaires and offshore exploration has been intensive for a number of years. Its reserves at 1974 production rates are such that oil production must begin to decline within the next ten years unless new discoveries are made. The Qatar government, consequently, has been vitally interested in conservation but it has not cut production, as some other OPEC members have, in the face of growing overcapacity. If prices hold at high levels, some modest reductions in production can be expected.

Shell Oil (30 percent) and Qatar have formed a joint venture for undertaking gas projects; the first undertaking has been a plant for recovery of natural gas liquids. Moreover, a French chemical firm has been engaged in a joint venture capitalized at $50 million for petrochemical manufacture, while Gazocean, a French government company, has entered a 50/50 venture for the transport of petrochemicals and gas liquids. Two Japanese firms, each with a 20 percent interest, and Qatar have been engaged in the construction of a $100 million steel mill with a capacity of 300,000 tons per year, to increase to 400,000 tons by 1977. Available manpower, however, is likely to put a sharp limit on indigenous industrial enterprise, both in Qatar and the United Arab Emirates.

Qatar will probably continue to follow the lead of OPEC, adapting concession changes in other Arab countries to what it conceives to be its best interests. It will support the Arab countries directly in conflict with Israel, as its $50 million grant to Egypt for the Suez Canal reconstruction indicates. Moreover, it will contribute what it believes to be its proper share to the projects undertaken by OAPEC and the Arab Economic Conferences. Improvement in education on the other hand has been slow, and generally Qatar has not displayed anything like the vigor of neighboring Bahrain in striving for self-sufficiency while building a modern economy.

► United Arab Emirates (UAE)

Abu Dhabi dominates the United Arab Emirates in matters of oil policy. Its production of oil is much greater than all the rest of the members of the federation put together and, having been concerned with oil much longer than the others, Abu Dhabi has more experienced officials. In reports on UAE activities and Abu Dhabi's own actions, it is sometimes difficult to distinguish between the two. The UAE Minister of Petroleum and Mineral Resources is also the Abu Dhabi Minister of Petroleum and Industry and Chairman of the Abu Dhabi National Oil Company.

Dubai, the most populous state in the UAE, is also the most advanced in terms of finance and commerce. It is a center of trade and well-known for gold smuggling activities. In 1975, oil production rose to some 250 thousand barrels per day. The ninth Arab Petroleum Congress was held in Dubai in 1975. Four of the other states in the United Arab Emirate have yet to find any oil in their onshore or offshore territories, while Sharjah became an oil producer only in 1974.

Abu Dhabi and Dubai dominate the federation politically. The ruler of Abu Dhabi is the President of the Union and the Commander-in-Chief of the Union Defense Force, while the ruler of Dubai is Vice-President and his son is Prime Minister. Abu Dhabi's wealth further enhances its position because of the dependence of the poorer states on its largesse for substantial portions of government income.

After a meeting of the OPEC Gulf countries in Abu Dhabi in November 1974, the UAE Minister of Petroleum, in response to a criticism that the meeting was detrimental to the Organization, issued a statement reaffirming support of the unity of OPEC. He went on to state the UAE determination to back the Arab cause and the "front-line" countries politically, economically, and militarily. He further defended the actions taken on the price of oil (described under the section on Saudi Arabia) as follows:

> We are concerned about the stability of the world economic system and the stability of oil prices. Such stability helps us to determine our income and to draw up our economic plans while at the same time assuring the consumer countries access to oil at a price which will remain stable for the longest possible period. It was this motive that prompted us to freeze the sale price of our oil until the end of next July, which will certainly help the world economy and refute allegations that oil prices are not stable.

Industrialization is being pursued in the UAE, as in the other Arab states, but apparently at a somewhat slower pace. A $255 million drydock and a $60 million cement plant were being built in Dubai in 1974 as well as a large expansion of Port Rashid with new breakwaters, dredging equipment, and 22 new berths. The Abu Dhabi National Oil Company was acquiring three 250,000 d.w.t. tankers and, in a joint venture with a Japanese firm, was building a plastic pipe factory. Finally, the UAE contracted for a steel rolling mill to be built in Abu Dhabi by the Pakistan Engineering Company.

UAE investments abroad illustratively include: a joint investment company with Egypt capitalized at $50 million, with Abu Dhabi furnishing $200 million in credit for industrial and agricultural projects; a loan to Bahrain of $10 million for water desalination; an $80 million assistance fund to Bahrain in Multan, Pakistan, developed through a joint venture between the Abu Dhabi National Oil Company and the West Pakistan Development Corporation, with the oil company supplying 30 percent of the capital for a plant costing over $100 million; and a joint UAE (51 percent)-Dutch tanker firm to purchase four 250,000 d.w.t. tankers at a cost of $152 million. Some of the financial transactions include: participation in a loan to the Swedish Hambros Bank; a $100 million contribution and a $33 million soft loan to develop the Suez Canal Zone; $120 million to the Islamic Development Bank; $7.5 million granted to Jordan; and $10 million to the U.N. Emergency Fund.

It seems that Abu Dhabi has not yet defined a specific investment policy nor does it seem to have yet developed the machinery, bureaucratic and financial, required to handle its surplus revenues capably. With respect to concessions, Abu Dhabi has close relationships with the Saudi Arab petroleum experts and is likely to follow the Saudi example, though with special modifications for its offshore concessions. Neither Dubai nor Sharjah is likely to attempt to take over and run its oil production facilities in the near future. For example, in September 1974 Dubai concluded a new concession agreement of 35 years' duration with an American oil company for an offshore area that had been relinquished by the previous concessionaire. Both Dubai and Sharjah will assuredly try to get a proportion of the revenue approaching that which full ownership would give them.

► Oman

Until the deposition of Sultan Said bin Taimur by his son in 1970, Oman had no secondary schools, no newspaper, and no radio station, and it was ruled with an iron hand. Since then, the new Sultan has been opening up the country, trying to raise the standard of living and education, and fighting a small but costly war on the southwestern border against rebels supported by the People's Democratic Republic of Yemen. In 1975 oil production may be about 350,000 barrels per day, up some 50,000 barrels from 1974 by virtue of new fields coming into production. Intensive exploration has been going on for more than 25 years, and despite the complexity of the geology, the prospects for finding new small fields are relatively good.

Though Oman is one of America's oldest "allies" by

virtue of a treaty of commerce concluded in 1843 when Oman was possibly the most powerful state in the Arabian Peninsula, it has no diplomatic representatives abroad. It has not been a member of the Arab League, nor of OPEC or OAPEC. In oil matters it has followed the developments in the revision of concessionary terms only slowly, after they have been put into effect elsewhere in the Arab countries. In the circumstances, Oman is not likely to try to nationalize its petroleum production for some time but it will not be content unless the revenue from this production approaches that of the members of OPEC. In sum, Oman will be perfectly content to let others lead the way on policy matters and it will be careful not to jeopardize its current income now – or in the future.

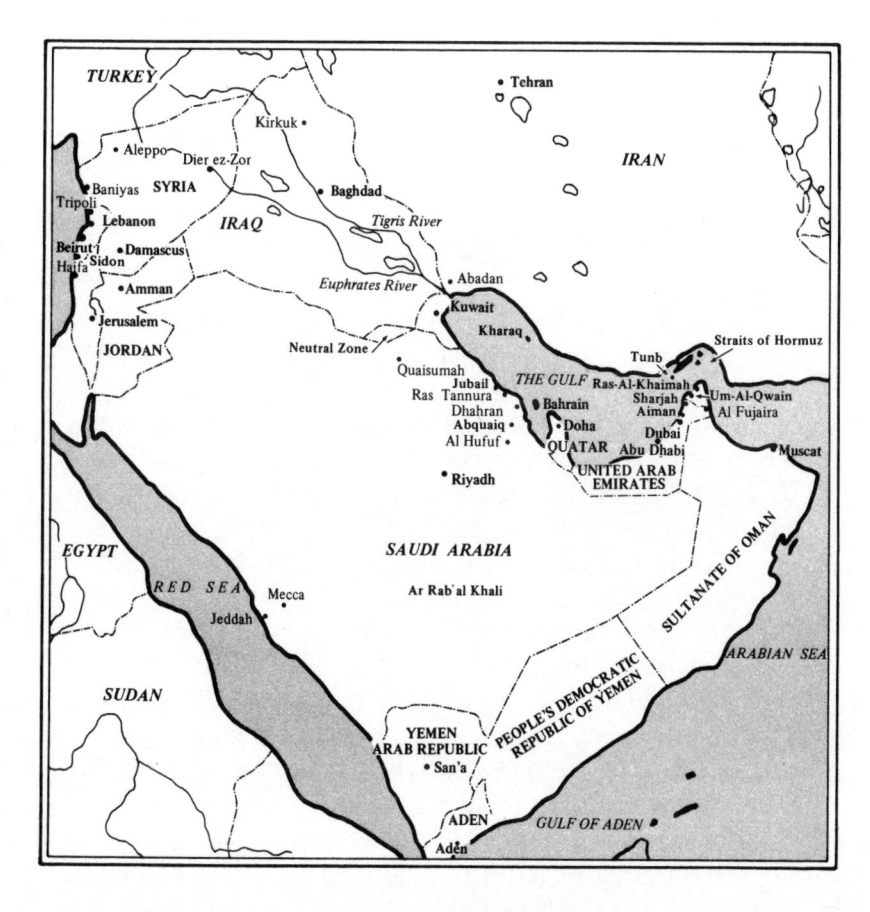

Map of the Gulf Countries

CONCLUSION

Behind the energy policies of the Arab states of the Gulf there always lies the anticipation of the fearful "day when the oil runs out." That day is probably much further away in terms of absolute exhaustion of the wells than most Arabs believe. But it is near enough in practical terms — and in its inevitability — to be always in the back of the mind of the leaders of these governments.

"Conservation" is the process of delaying the inevitable, both to gain time for substitution and to minimize the squandering of wealth before experience in handling it has been acquired. "Industrialization" is seen as the means of building a society and an economy that will survive with the affluence close to the level that has been provided by oil. And "OPEC" is the name for the association of other like nations who have the same resource, the same threat of its ultimate exhaustion.

The process of industrialization is subject to numerous constraints, not the least of which is uneasiness as to the unknown and unpredictable side effects that come from the radical changes so ardently desired. Some of the side effects are already discernible in the Gulf states: domestic inflation, hordes of foreigners, changes in old customs, and sharper ideological cleavages between the young and the old. Others, not yet fully evident, but apparent to any thoughtful Arab, are more important, such as the political and sociological results of the changes accompanying industrialization. And questions have arisen whose answers are anything but clear. What is going to be the effect of the large number of unenfranchised foreigners who in some states outnumber the local population and who have resided in the country for a very long period, but are utterly unassimilated? Can they be governed indefinitely as if they were mere migrant workers? If they are Arabic-speaking and do assimilate, what will be the effect upon the system of government? What sort of indigenous culture will develop? Is it possible to develop an ongoing industrial society in which most of the work is done by foreigners in such a way that it will remain viable when the oil is gone? Will the local population become so dependent that it will never be able to carry on without foreign help? Considerations of questions such as these must inevitably trouble policy makers.

Further indications to trouble the thoughtful man are to be found in Kuwait. The Kuwait Oil Company has long had difficulty in recruiting Kuwaitis for its operations despite the early development of the state educational system. Opportunities for young Kuwaitis to make more money in other ways has diverted them from the long and toilsome process of learning the nuts and bolts of the everyday operations of a complex industry. It has been easier and more profitable to hire foreigners. But citizenship in Kuwait, once so easily gained, is now difficult. Is the industry forever to depend on foreigners to manipulate the valves of enterprise?

Investment policies must in some degree turn on the non-economic decisions of industrialization. A country moving full speed ahead, hampered only by the recruitment of manpower and availability of materials, will put all the money it needs for industrialization into relatively short-term investments as a purely economic decision. But a country moving cautiously for whatever reasons — political, demographic, cultural, or even economic — will put a much larger part of its current surplus of oil revenues into longer term investments. And one like Kuwait, with much of its industrialization connected to oil and reaching a saturation point, will look for very long term investments. As Khalid Abu Sa'ud told a reporter for *Der Spiegel* in 1975 with regard to investment in the German Daimler-Benz firm, the Arabs are not looking for a quick return, but rather "investing" for the next generation, for the next 20 or 25 years. We did not buy these shares in order to speculate."

Investments in the lesser developed countries may be expected as more of the Gulf states reach the economic level of Kuwait. The Arabs may decide to slow industrialization within their own borders even as they become more sophisticated in organizing and handling large industrial enterprises. One combination not yet much developed, but which may become important, is that in which the oil-producing state enters into a three-party arrangement — one of the parties being a developing country (whether by way of government or private organizations is immaterial) and the other party being a multinational company. Here the intent of the oil producer may be not only to put surplus funds to productive work, but also to assist the developing country in need of capital, markets, technology, and foreign exchange to pay for oil.

The oil-producing countries are used to dealing with multinationals; they understand what is meant by providing markets and technology, including management; they are not afraid of multinationals; and they would safeguard their investment by asking that the multinational company also put some of its capital into the enterprise. Such an arrangement may well be very profitable for all concerned and more easy on the nerves of the multinational corporation than the usual two-way arrangement with a developing country.

This study has shown the genesis of OPEC, and it should be clear that it is wrong to describe it, as A. Gary Shilling has done on 10 March 1975 in the *Wall Street Journal*, as "imposed by the Arabs in a period of strong demand, not to quadruple the price, but as a weapon against Israel." It is also wrong to believe that it was conceived to "exercise monopolistic control to raise prices and revenues by limiting production, restricting exports, and dividing up markets" or "to increase their market share by expanding production" — all characteristics ascribed to cartels in general. The founding fathers of OPEC, Perez Alfonso of Venezuela and Abdullah Tariki of Saudi Arabia, were determined to prevent price reduction, not only to get more money for their countries, but also because both of them believed they were dealing with a nonrenewable resource to be husbanded for future generations. And Perez Alfonso also felt strongly that too much money too fast would destroy the moral fiber of Venezuela. Its organization has nothing to do with the Arab-Israeli problem. But it did have to do with the question of the right price for raw materials supplied by single-resource countries to the industrial countries of the world. This is not to argue that OPEC may not do some of the things that cartels have done, but rather that OPEC is not the typical cartel of economic history. Mr. R. Mabro of St. Anthony's College, Oxford, put its objectives very well in a speech delivered at the London School of Oriental and African studies in early 1975: "To increase (rather than maximize) members' revenues when circumstances are favorable and to check a fall in revenue per barrel where circumstances are adverse. OPEC has not been explicitly concerned with the distribution of gains between members .... The wisdom is to accept that significant gains, unequally distributed, are better than no gains at all. ... It is founded on the belief that all members — including the largest producers — would be worse off without OPEC. This belief is both rational and deeply felt."

Unless these characteristics of OPEC are thoroughly understood, efforts to devise ways of dealing with OPEC are likely to be abortive. "Pressure" is likely to be counter-productive. Expectation that quarrels among the members will lead to its early dissolution is unwarranted. Arguments that cohesion will be destroyed because the members are disparate in their reserves and their needs for income are based on the assumption of unlimited cupidity of the members. The very fact of disparity contributes immensely to the stability of the organization, since the reserves of oil are distributed almost in inverse ratio to the population of the OPEC member states. Those with the least immediate need are well able to cut back the most in a period of declining demand.

Disputes, of course, will continue to arise within OPEC. Largely they will occur over the important details of the price of oil. For some two years, 1973-75, prices could be set in a rather gross and imperfect way because demand was sufficient to overcome disparities in relative prices, and most important, because the offtaking companies had sufficient profit leeway to absorb aberrations in the market value of the various crude oils. But with demand down because of a decline in consumption, due to conservation measures compounded by a worldwide economic recession, marginal prices became most important. Abu Dhabi's low-sulphur high-gravity crude became overpriced in 1975. Tapline closed down because the $2.00 differential between Arabian light crude in the Gulf and the same oil at Sidon in the Eastern Mediterranean became too great. Moreover, changes in the market — that is, in the demand for various qualities in the oils and in the costs of tanker transportation — revealed the OPEC-decreed prices to be out of joint. These incongruities will continue unless the members find some easier way to adjust within general guidelines. And such guidelines are likely to be set only by mutual consent and understanding, not by rigid prescriptions embodied in formal resolutions.

Many new refinery projects are planned within the Gulf states. The pricing of refined products, however, will present many more formidable problems for OPEC. Products are much more sensitive to the demands of the marketplace, varying with weather, political decrees, the state of the economies of the consumers, technological changes, and the costs of transportation and further processing. Furthermore, the base production of some of the states will be in products largely unregulated by OPEC, with the balance handled by some agreement on crude prices. Thus competition on products may flourish, yet be non-existent on crude, except for tanker rates which have been about as stable as ocean waves and which greatly influence costs to the ultimate consumer.

Whatever happens, the consumer states would do well to have a multiplicity of buyers of crude and products. The simplistic notion that a single agency such as an American government institution, through its purchasing power, can drive down the price of crude by calling for sealed bids from OPEC members is hardly worth discussing, except that it has been proposed. Such a transparent device, in which all the sealed bids would perforce be made public in the acceptance process and could easily be subverted by even a loosely organized association, is obviously no way to go about creating competition amongst OPEC members. It is far better for the consumer that a hundred buyers, whose business is privately held, should make their own arrangements. They can be far more flexible and ingenious than any government agency imaginable. Undoubtedly some of these private enterprises may make "windfall" profits, but at a cost far less to the consuming public than a clumsy bureaucratic behemoth.

In the end no two of the Arab states will be exactly alike in their policies. Their individual needs will determine their decisions. But their judgements will continue to be based on the knowledge that their oil is an exhaustible resource and that the leaders of today have an obligation to their people and their heirs of tomorrow.

BIBLIOGRAPHICAL NOTE

To keep abreast of current developments in the Arab countries' oil affairs, two periodicals are indispensable: *Middle East Economic Survey*, a weekly review of news and views on Middle East oil, published by The Middle East Research and Publishing Center, P. O. Box 1224, Beirut, Lebanon; and *Petroleum Intelligence Weekly*, for oil executives around the world, a weekly published at 48 West 48th Street, New York, New York 10036.

For further background on the Arab countries, one of the best short books is Joseph J. Malone, *The Arab Lands of Western Asia*, Prentice-Hall, Englewood Cliffs, New Jersey. *The International Petroleum Encyclopedia*, published annually by the Petroleum Publishing Company, P. O. Box 260, Tulsa, Oklahoma 74101, has not only excellent maps but a review of the previous year's developments in each of the Arab countries (as well as the rest of the world) and tables of reserves, production, and fields for both gas and oil.

One of the best, and most interesting accounts of the development of the industry to 1962 is J. E. Hartshorn's *Politics and World Oil Economics*, Praeger, New York, 1967. A much less technical description is *The Kingdom of Oil* by Ray Vickers, a correspondent for the Wall Street Journal, Scribner's, New York, 1974. *Middle Eastern Oil and the Western World* by S. H. Schurr and P. T. Homan, Elsevier, New York, 1971 is an excellent account of the history of oil developments in the Middle East, though the projections of the future have been largely vitiated by events unforeseen. See also Stephen H. Longrigg, *Oil in the Middle East*, 3rd ed., Oxford University Press, New York, 1968, a thorough history of Middle Eastern oil by one who participated personally in its development.

Venezuela
Aníbal R. Martínez

Critical Contemporary Issues

"Energy policy," beyond the usual popular references to the exploitation of petroleum, was not a common phrase in Venezuela until 1973. The word "energy" gained currency as part of the reform program offered to the electors by the Acción Democrática party and the political manifesto of Carlos Andrés Pérez who was elected as President in March 1974.

Like other countries of the world, Venezuela has witnessed a spectacular rise in the production, consumption, and price of petroleum products. And, as elsewhere, a thorough re-examination of the ways and means of managing very valuable, but exhaustible resources for the long-term benefit of the nation is underway. However, for a country that was for some time the largest exporter of petroleum in the world, an examination of energy policy is complex and often confusing. Statistics, analyses, and graphs, as well as previous policy, have sometimes been seriously distorted. Substantial petroleum exports are essential to the continuing development of the country, but there will need to be an accommodation between producing profits for both internal investment and balance of payment requirements and the maintenance of a sound policy of long-term resource allocation.

Venezuela ranks fifth in the world in total oil output, and 92% of its production in 1974 was exported — thus making it the third largest exporter after Saudi Arabia and Iran. In 1974 the production of crude petroleum in Venezuela was 154 million tons, which was 12% less than in 1973. Reductions in the oil extraction rates were imposed by the Federal Executive on the private concessionaire companies from April 1974 onwards. Attention was also focused upon better use of the associated natural gas, so much so that by the end of the year, the waste of gas by burning or venting to the atmosphere had been reduced by two-thirds. Thus, some 23 million cubic meters of gas per day are being saved for the future use of the nation.

While no comprehensive energy policy has yet been reached, important separate decisions by the government indicate policy directions. For example, in 1974 a project for cryogenically liquefied gas plants was cancelled. Moreover, the Ministry of Mines and Hydrocarbons sternly informed the State electricity distribution company that no gas would be supplied nor would it become available for an installation at Punta Moron in the central region, which had been planned to generate on completion 800 megawatts of power. At the same time, engineering work proceeded on schedule on the third stage of the hydroelectric Guri system, which was expected to produce 10 million kilowatts of power by 1988.

The use of energy in Venezuela has been conditioned, as in other countries of the world, by the characteristics of the existing resources and by the political-economic plans that evolve from private choices and government regulation. The success of any energy policy, of course, will depend largely on the effectiveness, efficiency, and authority of the government and its several agencies. Presently the public organizations governing energy tend to be diverse and independent, a situation which has many parallels in other countries.

Two ministries have handled matters pertaining to energy, the Ministry of Mines and Hydrocarbons and the Ministry for Development. The Office of Planning has also been involved in energy matters. Mines and Hydrocarbons have had responsibility for petroleum, natural gas, coal, prospecting for radioactive minerals, evaluation of the ultra-heavy Orinoco Tar Belt, and the autonomous Corporación Venezolana del Petróleo (CVP), the State oil company. The Ministry for Development has supervised electricity generation and distribution through a public corporation and regulated a number of privately owned power companies. The Planning Ministry has directed the National Commission for Nuclear Affairs and coordinated the work of other State organs. In addition, the National Research Council (CONICIT) and the Guayana Development Corporation, whose wholly-owned subsidiary EDELCA generates all hydroelectricity in Guri at the Caroní river, have been attached to the office of the President of the Republic, while a totally ineffective National Energy Council has been formed. Exploitation of coal deposits, moreover, has been entrusted to regional development corporations, although a National Coal Council exists. Finally, some research in the field of petroleum has been done at various universities, in the National Research Institute (IVIC), and at the Venezuelan Institute for Petroleum and Petrochemical Research (INVEPET), which was established in 1974.

A proposal to create a Ministry of Energy as an executive organ of the federal administration, to be entrusted with the coordination, supervision, and direction of all the various institutes, corporations, and companies just enumerated was made by the author of this study, and was adopted by the Presidential Commission on Nationalization of the Oil Industry in November 1974. At the same time the formulation of a national energy policy became a matter of national concern. Both the Ninth Venezuelan Engineering Congress and the Third Petroleum Congress debated the issue in day-long sessions. Books have been published presenting individual views on the subject and scientific and technical societies have contributed ideas and observations. Beginning in January 1975 a working group has met under the auspices of CONICIT and, for the first time, highly placed representatives of all fields of energy seemed to be working in unison.

In 1975 Venezuela was in the final stages of the process of acquiring full control of the petroleum industry. Concessions that had been granted for 40 years in 1943-45 and 1956-57, plus three service contracts that had been negotiated in 1971 by CVP, the State oil company, were all being terminated. On Christmas Eve, 1974, a 36-man presidential commission had submitted a 525-page report on the process of nationalization of the industry. Besides recommending precisely the procedures for the actual take-over of the plants and the operations of the concessionaires, the document contained the draft of an organic law which reserved to the State the entire industry and commerce of hydrocarbons. Subsequently, on 11 March 1975 the Minister of Mines and Hydrocarbons introduced in the National Congress a draft Reserve Law prepared by the Federal Executive. Debated, amended, and approved by the Venezuelan Congress, the bill ordering the nationalization of the petroleum industry was signed into law by the President on 29 August 1975.

Under this law, the Venezuelan government will run the oil industry by substituting after 1 January 1976 the State holding company, CVP, for the parent corporations of the foreign-owned enterprises. An association with private enterprises would be possible for some areas of operation, but such associations would be temporary and made only under certain conditions. Acknowledging Anglo-Saxon legal tenets, the Venezuelan Supreme Court could rule on expropriation procedures if no agreement had been reached on the compensation to be paid to the concessionaires. But the amount of this compensation would be calculated on the basis of the undepreciated book value of assets. It is the only item subject to litigation. The new law, moreover, spelled out exactly what would be subtracted from the payout total: first of all, the amounts earned by the employees in the companies' social benefit programs, such as retirement benefits, severance payments, and so forth; then, any amount owed to the government, such as the value of oil drained beyond the physical limits of the leases.

The most fundamental aspect of the nationalization program will be the creation of a Venezuelan holding company as the management-decision center for the industry, instead of the head-offices of the foreign multinational corporations. The actual operating units, for a start, may be the same organizations currently looking for, producing, refining, or selling Venezuelan crude oil. The government does not wish any discontinuity of operations at any time during the nationalization process, for two critical problems for Venezuela are well recognized. One is the need to sell to an international market as long as Venezuela continues in the role of exporter of large volumes of crude petroleum; the other is the need to assure technological support for the complex production and distribution processes of the industry in the post-nationalization period. Although in-depth surveys and very detailed studies have been conducted on both problems, full responsibility for solution will rest with the Venezuelan holding company. Hopefully, arrangements to maintain established channels and mechanisms for the dynamic industry will be devised.

The State oil company, CVP, which was established in 1960, has barely entered the field of international marketing, although it has some experience with petroleum prospecting. Its role after nationalization of the concessionaires has not really been determined. Some believe CVP is an example of what might be done, others believe it demonstrates how bureaucracy can impair commercial efficiency. A likely course may be the use of the CVP expertise that has been acquired in certain areas as the nucleus of an operating company under the guidance of the holding corporation.

Whatever the final corporate or organizational details of the nationalization program, it should fit within the bounds of a national Venezuelan energy policy. In the past, attention had been fixed only on the prices for petroleum in the international market. Fluctuations were measured in cents or dollars. Gains or losses depended entirely on the world prices for oil and gas, which were beyond the control of Venezuela. For almost two decades, however, the leaders of Venezuela's government have been part of a world-wide change in attitude toward the petroleum industry: first, the world price structure of petroleum has become a fundamental element of national policy; and, second, the producing countries have recognized the need to conserve their physical resources. There is a "new era" in the energy policy of Venezuela, part of which can be seen in the Federal Executive's orders to reduce oil production, cancel gas-liquefying export-plants, and alter programs for electrical energy generation. Plans for changes in the pattern of refining products are advancing. And for the first time the government is considering a comprehensive approach, with central responsibility, for all aspects of energy policy in the nation.

Historical Development of Energy Uses

Before the discovery of Venezuela by Columbus, the Indians had used petroleum, which could be found on the surface of water or seeping out of the land, for glueing the walls and thatched roofs of their habitations, caulking boats, curing wounds, or even catching game in the sticky expanses of black tars converted into traps by the tropical sun. The Indian word *mene* is still used to designate the oil seeps. The Spanish conquerors quickly learned about petroleum. The first reference to Venezuelan oil in literature is in Book XIX of the monumental *General and Natural History of the Indies* by Gonzalo Fernández de Oviedo y Valdez, published in Seville in September 1535. The first documented "export" of Venezuelan oil is dated 30 April 1539, for on that day a "barrel" of petroleum was sent to the Queen of Spain to alleviate the gout of her son, Emperor Charles V.

Historically the labor of animals and slaves supplemented the burning of wood or charcoal for primitive heat and power needs. Water mills, crude contraptions with extremely low efficiency, were used along the arid coastal plains of the Caribbean. Coal mining developed near population centers, most probably in Coro, then south of Caracas, later in the foothills of the Perijá range, west of Maracaibo, and in the neighbourhood of San Cristóbal. Both the demand and consumption of energy were certainly very low well into the second half of the 19th century. Venezuela had not developed much. There was no important mining or processing of minerals, nor any great industry for a rather small, mainly agrarian population.

European naturalists visiting Venezuela, starting with Baron von Humboldt in 1799, meticulously reported the asphalt and hot springs found in the northern territories. The first geological report and map on central and eastern Venezuela was published in 1850 in the *Journal of the German Geological Society* by Hermann Karsten. The first concession for the exploitation of asphalt was granted in 1864, less than six months after the first mining code was enacted, and the first oil concession was granted in 1865 by the Governor of Zulia State to an American citizen, to seek, drill for, and gain petroleum, naphtha, "or whatever is the name of the oil which exists in the ground." The rights to the oil concession, however, expired within the year. In 1876 a Venezuelan general and engineer submitted to the local government a detailed, accurate report on the coal deposits of Maracaibo and its surrounding areas.

Asphalt exploitation proceeded in the west of Venezuela, mainly in Inciarte, and in the east, deposits were taken from the marvellous Guanoco pitch lake, whence it was exported for paving the streets of major cities, both in the United States and in Europe. Electric illumination was first introduced in Maracaibo in 1890 and some years later in Caracas.

The first commercial petroleum operations were carried out in 1878 in La Alquitrana, a remote coffee-plantation on the fringes of a sedimentary basin that later became the mainstay of the petroleum industry. A small company was formed by local merchants and peasants, and it was called Petrolia. Shallow holes were dug with pick and shovel; then, as the oil seeped into the wells, blankets were thrown in and became inpregnated; the oil was then wrung out of the blankets, as the Indians had done, and put in buckets for transportation to a teapot-like still with a capacity of 2,000 liters per day. One of the partners in the Petrolia venture travelled to the United States and brought back to Venezuela a percussion drilling rig. After a nightmarish trip to the site, the bit broke as it was spudding in the first boring. Nevertheless, by 1890 Petrolia had completed ten wells, one of them to a depth of 86 meters. Various refined products were sold locally in 2-liter bottles, while some were exported to Colombia. In many respects Petrolia, which continued its operations until 1934, was an early integrated company.

In the 20th century mining in Venezuela shifted gradually from the asphalts to the liquid bitumens. The mining law of 1905 was the basis for very large concessions, which eventually became stupendous leases for the exploitation of petroleum. The first systematic search for oil took place between 1911 and 1915, and the first true commercial finds came in 1913 and 1914. The discovery of the largest oilfield in Venezuela and still the third largest in the world occurred in the Bolívar Coastal field, which had been virtually unnoticed until 14 December 1922, when the La Rosa well blew out. In nine days of wild, uncontrolled flow, that well gushed out a torrent of oil equal to one-fourth of all the oil produced up to then in Venezuela. Within weeks the country was converted into a great oil producer as exploration parties flocked to Venezuela, and companies were incorporated in haste to begin "operations."

From the beginning of Venezuela's modern oil industry, output had been almost exclusively for export. Internal consumption was for the most part for the producing operations themselves, particularly for power to drill and transport the crude oils. By the end of 1926 petroleum had become the first export commodity of Venezuela, when nearly 4 million tons were sent abroad at a value of $60 million. In 1929 offshore operations in the Maracaibo lake first introduced the use of wooden and concrete foundations for wells that were drilled under 15 meters of water. When the Mexican expropriation of the oil leases of the United States and Great Britain in 1938 interrupted some of the flow of petroleum to the international market, the demand for Venezuelan crude increased. By 1938 about 90% of the Venezuelan export trade was petroleum products. During World War II Venezuelan oil production mounted to help fuel the war effort of the Allies and in the 1950's Venezuela was the second largest (after the United States) producer of crude petroleum in the world. In fact, until 1969 Venezuela was the third largest (after the United States and the Soviet Union) producer of crude oil in the world.

Obviously petroleum has dominated the sources of energy available to Venezuela, but natural gas provided the generation of three-fourths of the electricity used in the country between 1957 and 1967 — and still provides about half the total. The generation of electricity by water power started in a significant way in 1963 and by 1973 was accounting for about 8% of domestic energy consumption. Coal has never been mined extensively and from 1962 onwards it was imported for the steel industry.

Further details about the current potentials and the uses of Venezuelan energy sources follow. But ultimately energy policy is going to be determined by political goals and means, which already have an historical record. The Technical Office of Hydrocarbons was established in the Ministry of Development as early as 1930. Venezuelan policy toward foreign concessions, contrary to the Mexican expropriations in 1938, was to seek larger and more equitable payments from the industry through taxes and revisions of the agreements themselves. By 1948, however, a policy of "no more concessions" had been approved by the National Congress during a review of a report of the Permanent Commission for Development. Implementation of that resolve, however, had to wait until

1958 when the Acción Democrática party came to power. The renegotiations of the existing concessions, moreover, inexorably led to a larger sharing of income by the Venezuelan government so that by the early 1960's about one-half of all the gross profits of the companies was going to the national treasury and, in addition, the companies were providing the Venezuelan workers with special benefits in health care, housing, and training for technical and managerial posts. More policy changes were to come. The State oil company, Corporación Venezolana del Petróleo (CVP), was created in 1960 and in that year Venezuela joined four of the largest oil exporters in the world to sign the protocol establishing the Organization of Petroleum Exporting Countries (OPEC).

The Energy Resources of Venezuela

The energy resources of Venezuela are significant by any measure. The following survey is a quantitative appraisal of resources, not a review of the geology of the petroleum deposits nor a study of the state of the art in the exploitation of geothermal or eolic energy.

With respect to crude oil and natural gas, the term "resources" by definition refers to the ultimate volumes to be recovered from the total quantities contained in place in the reservoirs. It is an amount related only to the physical occurrence of the resource, independent of any other consideration, such as economics. The volume of recoverable hydrocarbons is only geologically meaningful insofar as it represents the substances contained in or among sedimentary rocks.

Hydrocarbon resources are the sum total of four different volumes: production, proved reserves, supplementary reserves, and undiscovered reserves. *Production* is the amount brought up to the surface and not returned or lost; *proved reserves* are the quantities estimated to be recoverable from the reservoirs by primary production mechanisms in areas reasonably defined due to previous drilling; *supplementary reserves* refer mainly to crude oil and by definition are the additional volumes that could be gained following the application of various secondary recovery methods of production;

undiscovered reserves are the estimated hydrocarbons that could be found in presently unexplored portions of the sedimentary areas, based upon separate studies of the geology of each basin, and supplemented by thorough analyses of the relationships between the genesis and occurrence of hydrocarbons and the type, architecture, and geological history of the basins.

There are important deposits of non-conventional (shale and tar sands) hydrocarbons in Venezuela. Largest of these is the tar sands belt in the southern limit of the Maturín basin in Eastern Venezuela, but no important occurrences of bituminous shales are known. The estimates of coal reserves are the result of volumetric computations following detailed geological surveys. As with petroleum, proved reserves refer to quantities measured, while the term "inferred" or "probable reserves" is used to designate the volumes expected to occur on the basis of studies of sedimentary rock and sand patterns, geological history, and geologic structures. It should be noted that unless the precise methods used in the calculation of coal reserves are known, it would be incorrect to attempt to compare sets of data from different countries. The two fundamental criteria for estimates of coal are the minimum thickness of the seams and their depth below the surface. On the other hand, the reserves of radioactive minerals have been computed on the basis of the valuation of ores in terms of currency per unit of weight. Different grades of radioactive materials have usually been estimated volumetrically once the cost is stated: for instance, $26 per kilogram equals one million tons of proved reserves. In the case of measuring the potential of hydraulic resources, units of power are used. Water power output is a rate of production measurable in units of work. The "installed capacity" to use hydraulic energy grows with time, usually as an exponential function, but there is a finite maximum rate of work when all available power has been developed.

Crude Petroleum in the Traditional Basins

Four inland geological basins are the traditional sources of crude petroleum in Venezuela. The Maracaibo basin is by far the most important oil region of the country. It has contributed three-fourths of the production, contains 80% of the proved reserves, and probably accounts for at least 70% of the undiscovered reserves. An extraordinary and unparalleled value in the Maracaibo basin is the occurrence of the Bolívar Coastal field. This is the third largest oilfield in the world, and after more than 50 years of draining, new pools and producing areas have been discovered: for instance, the development of deep reservoirs in fractured Cretaceous limestone was underway at the end of 1974.

The second geological basin of petroliferous interest is the Maturín basin. Oilfields there are of more limited size, but numerous oil-bearing sands in the stratigraphic section add considerable reserves. Together the Maracaibo and Maturín basins support most of the Venezuelan oil industry, for both the Barinas and Falcón basins have so far proved to be of minor importance.

The magnitude of oil in the traditional basins has been estimated on the basis of the four component volumes of the resources. Figures for 1973 have been used because for 1974 the Ministry of Mines and Hydrocarbons unfortunately introduced an economic element into the estimation of proved reserves: on the basis of quadrupled prices, the quantity added to proven volumes shot up 34%. It can, of course, be expected that better values for petroleum will allow the exploitation of hitherto unattractive deposits and marginal fields; however, in the long run of development there will hardly be a significant change in total volume.

The production of petroleum in the traditional basins from inception to 1973 was 4,776 million cubic meters (30 billion barrels). For a decade, output fluttered around 200 million cubic meters (1.26 billion barrels) per year. Production during the 1961-1973 period equalled the volume obtained from 1917 to 1960.

Proved reserves surpassed 2,000 million cubic meters (12.6 billion barrels) in 1958. Since then there have been both gains and losses depending upon the balance between discoveries or other additions and withdrawals. From 2,742 million cubic meters (17.3 billion barrels) in 1965, the reserves slipped to 2,217 million cubic meters (13.9 billion barrels) in 1973. It is noteworthy that between 1953 and 1958, the quantity of proven reserves was 1,994 million cubic meters (12.5 billion barrels), which was three-fourths of the oil discovered up to then. Furthermore, comparing the amount of all oil found in the traditional basins over 55 years, 30% of the total was discovered during the golden '53-'58 period.

The supplementary reserves can be calculated from the volume of proved reserves by means of a coefficient which is based upon a comprehensive reservoir engineering study. The present value of the coefficient of supplementary reserves is 0.45. At the end of 1973, the volume of supplementary reserves of conventional oil in the traditional basins was 998 million cubic meters (6.3 billion barrels).

Estimates of the undiscovered reserves undoubtedly constitute the most difficult and controversial problem in a serious study of petroleum resources. If the limitations of expertise in this area are clearly understood and if all the geological facts can be gathered, the results may be reasonable and useful, even if not quite accurate.

Venezuelan geologists unanimously agreed that the most favorable area for oil exploration was the so-called "South Lake Maracaibo." A system of service contracts with the oil companies, rather than concessions, had been developed over many years, and agreements were signed by CVP and three private companies for the exploration and development of

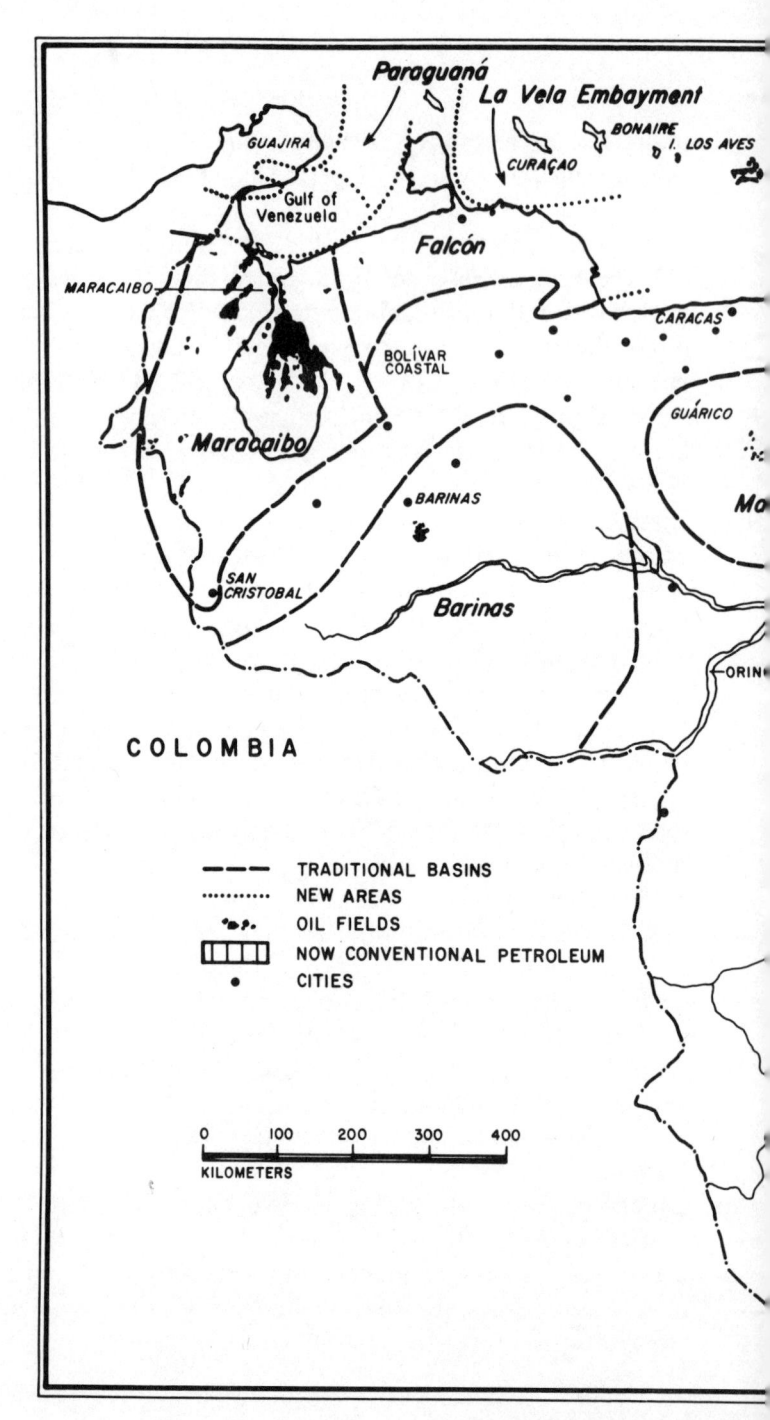

Map 1. Sedimentary basins (

onal & new areas) and "tar belt"

five 30,000 hectare blocks. At the end of 30 months of drilling, 14 dry holes had been completed. Unsuspected geological conditions in the subsurface showed the area to be mostly barren. Final wildcat wells, however, discovered three accumulations that may require either additional drilling or prolonged production testing to prove commercial.

In spite of the South Lake Maracaibo failure, there are many areas in the traditional basins, such as the tectonic saddle of Táchira, the Perijá foothills, Western Guárico, deep formations in the Falcón basin, and stratigraphic traps in Barinas, which should be adequately explored. At the request of officials of the Technical Bureau of Hydrocarbons in the Ministry of Mines and Hydrocarbons, a considerable number of new pool wildcat and outpost wells have been drilled since 1972 and a rather high proportion of them have been successfully completed, indicating that the extent of petroleum exploration in the traditional basins has been less than previously believed. The undiscovered reserves of crude oil in the traditional basins as of 31 December 1973 were 3,049 million cubic meters (19.2 billion barrels).

The total of the four volumes comprising the resources of petroleum in Venezuela is 11,040 million cubic meters (69,440 million barrels). The various parameters in million cubic meters have changed over the years since 1961 as follows:

	1961	1968	1973
Production	2,374	3,758	4,776
Proved reserves	2,684	2,492	2,217
Supplementary reserves	1,342	1,120	998
Undiscovered reserves	4,640	3,670	3,049
Resources	11,040	11,040	11,040

If discovered oil reserves are defined as production plus proved reserves, it can be observed that discovered oil reserves were 46% of the total resources in 1961 and had increased to 63% of the total in 1973.

Natural Gas in the Traditional Basins

Estimates of the reserves of natural gas can be made in the same way as estimates of petroleum. In the case of gas there will be no supplementary reserves because the conservation and enhancement of ultimate production is attained by a stringent use of the best field practices and technological methods available. It should be stressed, however, that the degree of reliability for natural gas data in Venezuela is many times lower than for crude petroleum.

The cumulative production of natural gas to 1973 was 961,000 million cubic meters (34 trillion cubic feet), of which 45% had been reinjected to the petroleum reservoirs. The volume of gas flared during the 1962-74 period alone was 204,200 million cubic meters (7.2 trillion cubic feet); however, for 1974 the waste was scarcely 9,862 million cubic meters (348 billion cubic feet), almost 40% less than the average loss of the twelve years 1962-73.

The proved reserves of natural gas were 1,072,575 million cubic meters (37.9 trillion cubic feet) as of 31 December 1973. The actual rate of increase of proved reserves has shown very wide fluctuations: from 1965 to 1968 the reserves declined by 118,000 million cubic meters, but 1969 showed an increased volume of 173,000 million cubic meters in reserve. Again in 1970 and 1971 there were small declines, but 1972 brought an increase of 76,000 million cubic meters to the total proved reserves. Some 42% of the proved reserves of natural gas occurs in the Maturín basin and one-third in the Maracaibo basin.

An estimate of undiscovered gas reserves in the traditional areas must necessarily be based on an evaluation of undiscovered crude petroleum, omitting any free gas likely to

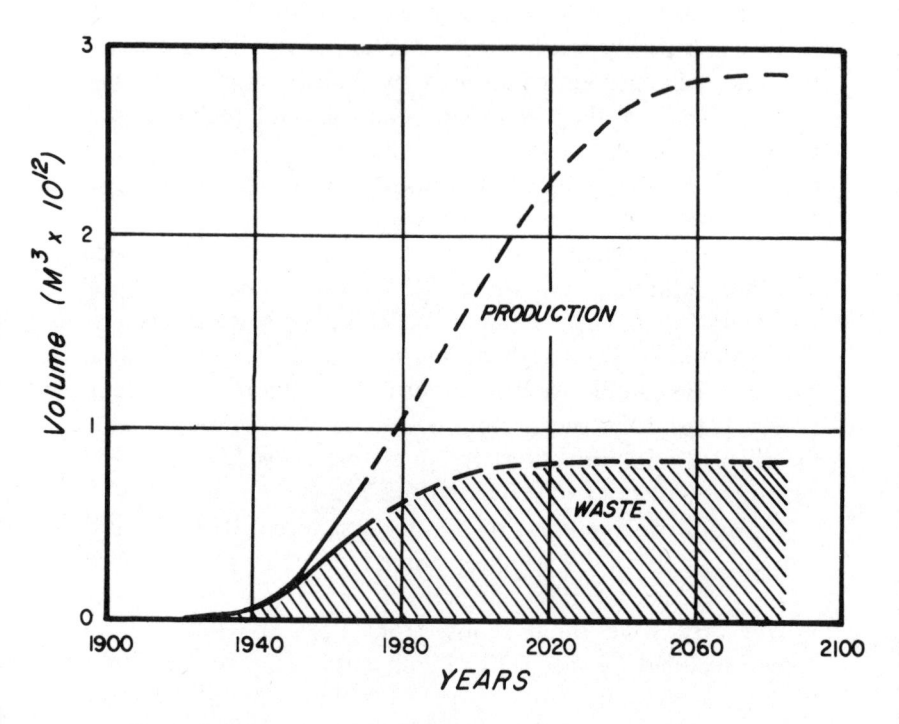

Figure 1. Wasted resources of natural gas in the traditional basins

be found by exploration. Natural gas associated with petroleum reservoirs has been estimated at 372,425 million cubic meters (13.2 trillion cubic feet), of which 165,000 million are in the Maracaibo basin and 187,000 million in the Maturín basin. Free gas is probably more abundant in the latter basin, perhaps 240,000 million cubic meters compared to 220,000 million in Maracaibo, to give a total of 460,000 million cubic meters (16.2 trillion cubic feet). Total undiscovered natural gas in the traditional basins is thus 832,425 million cubic meters (29.4 trillion cubic feet). The most favorable areas are in the western and central regions of the Maturín basin — Guárico and Anzoátegui states, the South Lake Maracaibo area and the northern flank of the Falcon basin.

The magnitude of the natural gas resources in Venezuela has been calculated by adding the three volumes of production, proved reserves, and undiscovered reserves. The total amounts to 2,886,000 million cubic meters (101.1 trillion cubic feet). Notwithstanding increasingly effective programs to limit the waste of natural gas, it is estimated that some 30% of the resources will be irremediably lost.

Changes in the three parameters that make up the natural gas resources for 1968 and 1973 are shown below:

	1968	1973
Production	725,000	961,000
Proved reserves	753,000	1,072,575
Undiscovered reserves	1,388,000	832,425
Resources (million cubic meters)	2,866,000	2,866,000

Hydrocarbon Resources in New Areas

The new areas all lie within the continental shelf and slope of the Caribbean Sea and the Atlantic Ocean off the Orinoco delta. The submerged Venezuelan continent to the continental rise covers an estimated surface of a half-million square kilometers (193,000 square miles). It forms in the Caribbean a huge "L" recumbent against the northern coast of the country, encompassing the string of smaller Antilles — minus the Dutch possessions — pointing northwards in the Aves swell.

It is impossible to give a rational approximation of the hydrocarbon resources in a completely new area, for variability in the occurrence of oil or gas in the sedimentary basins is measurable by a factor of 100, and any estimate could be off ten times on the lower or higher side. To apply to an estimate a certain factor, like the "cubek" or "cubem," that is, the volume of hydrocarbons per unit volume of sediments, would be worse than useless. The genesis and migration of hydrocarbons must proceed, in time and space, in conjunction with the transformation of sterile rock formations into enclosures capable of nurturing the rich petroleum or gas deposits that provide rewards for the explorer. Data through drilling is the only dependable way for getting secure knowledge.

The experience of CVP in the La Vela Embayment basin is noteworthy. The Embayment covers at least 3,000 square kilometers (1,160 square meters) and it was surveyed by seismic methods in 1968. Indications were up to 5,000 meters (16,400 feet) of sediments to the east, while a prominent north-south fault at the western margin subparallel to the coast could influence oil occurrence greatly in a section of Miocene age no more than 2,800 meters thick (9,200 feet). A series of north-south structural axes within the basin were also identified as possible favorable sites for hydrocarbon accumulation.

The first wildcat well in the new areas for hydrocarbons exploration spudded in on 18 July 1972. Exploration drilling in the embayment ended 10 September 1974. A total of 13 wildcats were sunk, of which five were completed as discov-

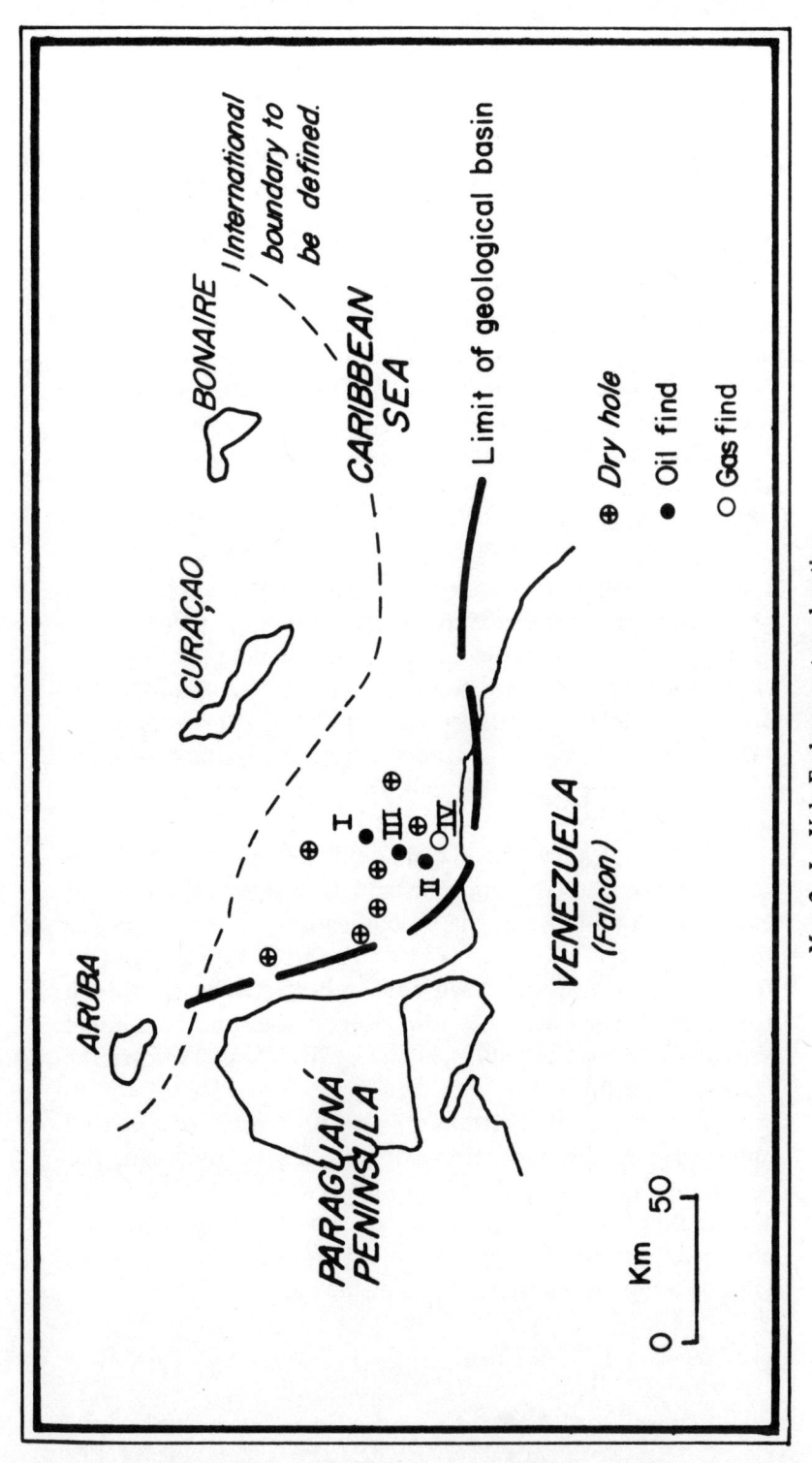

Map 2. La Vela Embayment exploration

eries of three oil fields and one gas field. CVP estimated that between 20 and 85 million cubic meters (125 and 530 million barrels) of reserves of crude petroleum were found, as well as 28,330 million cubic meters (1 billion cubic feet) of associated natural gas, 8,500 million cubic meters of free gas (300 billion cubic feet), and an undisclosed volume of other liquid hydrocarbons. At least 20 appraisal wells and 15 new field wildcats will be needed to complete the evaluation of the areas likely to produce as well as the rest of the basin.

The Gulf of Venezuela basin is separated from the Maracaibo basin by a prominent east-west fault. It is divided into two areas of considerable interest to petroleum prospecting, namely, the Calabozo Platform to the west and the Lagarto Syncline to the east. There seems to be a good possibility of occurrence of mother-rocks, perhaps Cretaceous shales, and of recipient-rocks ranging in age from upper Cretaceous to Miocene. Seismic surveys have shown that many prominent structures are present in the subsurface; furthermore, stratigraphic traps of Bolivar Coastal type combined with Eocene faulting and truncation of Oligocene beds may exist.

Three holes have been drilled inland along the southeast shore of the Guajira peninsula and four new field wildcats have been completed in the Falcón shores, at depths ranging from 3,500 to 4,500 meters (11,480 and 14,700 feet), but no traces of hydrocarbons have been reported. The Northwest Paraguaná basin might be intimately related to the Gulf of Venezuela basin, but only exploratory drilling will resolve the issue in the future.

Subsidence of portions of the pre-Cretaceous coastal ranges caused the formation of the Cariaco-Tuy basin. Excepting the Eocene of Margarita island, which is highly folded and faulted, gentle dips and near horizontal position are noticeable in the Cretaceous and younger sediments. The rock outcrops along the margins of the basin seem to indicate that there are neither source rocks nor likely reservoir rocks. Very faint hydrocarbon impregnation has been reported at various places in the Tuy river valley; by contrast, historical references in the non-technical literature with respect to seeps in Margarita or Cubagua islands have never been substantiated. Two shallow wildcats drilled in the nineteen-forties in the northwest shore of Cubagua were completely dry. Some holes, down to 198 meters, were completed as part of the deep-sea drilling JOIDES project in a location 25 kilometers (16 miles) southeast of Tortuga Island in waters 900 meters deep (2,950 feet). The sediments that were penetrated consisted of Pleistocene calcareous clays with high organic content, bearing some methane.

The platform north of the Paria peninsula is cut by a very deep but rather narrow sedimentary trench which I call the Margarita basin. It continues eastward between Grenada and Tobago. Thickness of the sedimentary section may surpass 10,000 meters (32,810 feet), and the low seismic velocities indicate that the stratigraphy is composed mainly of clastic rocks.

Enumerated among the new areas of the continental shelves of Venezuela is the eastern continuation of the Maturín basin, adjacent to the Orinoco delta. The main objective of the exploration here should be the porous and permeable sands of the Oficina formation or equivalents. Moreover, Miocene and even Pliocene beds might be of great interest, if one recalls the paleo-environment related to the delta of a mighty river. Traps in east-west trending anticlines or against normal east-west faults downthrown to the north are a good possibility.

The Aves swell is a chain of submarine ridges subparallel to the arc of the Leeward Islands, extending northwards for 400 kilometers (250 miles) from north-northeast of Margarita Island to Las Aves Island. Two JOIDES holes have been completed in the prominence; one is located 190 kilometers

(120 miles) north of Margarita in water depth of 1,218 meters (4,000 feet) and recovered at the bottom very fossiliferous sand with some thick beds of volcanic material; the other, located 250 kilometers (150 miles) north of Margarita, found Recent and Pliocene sands and clays.

Other Sources of Petroleum

Within the Maturín basin there is a long but narrow east-west "belt" of petroleum saturated in the loose, lowermost sands of the Oficina formation. No uncertainties of exploration are involved in evaluating this immense accumulation. The problem is the definition of the petrophysics and the availability of new technology for the extraction and processing of the bitumens.

The first well drilled (Canoa No. 1) through the "tar belt" in 1935 went unnoticed in spite of the fact that it yielded up to 20 cubic meters (125 barrels) per day of heavier-than-water petroleum. In the next 20 years, some 30 holes demonstrated unequivocally the presence of nonconventional oil immediately north of the Orinoco river from Tucupita to Calabozo, a distance of 600 kilometers (375 miles).

The objective of these borings was not the ultra-heavy hydrocarbons. The belt has been a separate oil — or energy — province only since the last years of the nineteen-sixties. By the end of 1968 the area had been pierced in 58 places, but geological data was barely useful because the drilling or well-completion techniques had been primitive. Incomplete records were the rule, and the distribution of the data-source points exceedingly wide. For instance, in the 100 kilometers (63 miles) between the Canoa No. 1 and another well, Hato Viejo No. 1, there was no other point from which data could be gathered. Information from thousands of wells immediately north of the belt, however, has been a helpful indicator of the stratigraphic and structural composition of the area.

On the basis of all available evidence, a preliminary geological report with an evaluation of potential reserves of the belt was submitted to the Mexican World Petroleum Congress of 1967. Four zones of fundamental interest were detected within the 32,000 square kilometers (12,355 square miles) of the area called Gorrín-Machete, Altamira-Iguana-Suata, Hamaca-Santa Clara, and Cerro Negro. The volumes of non-conventional hydrocarbons *in situ* were estimated as follows:

	Million Cubic Meters	Billions of Barrels
Gorrín-Machete	21,000	135.5
Altamira-Iguana-Suata	44,000	258.6
Hamaca-Santa Clara	12,000	80.0
Cerro Negro	18,000	110.9
Total	92,000	582.0

The cumulative production of non-conventional petroleum of the Orinoco belt has been estimated by the author at 5 million cubic meters (32 million barrels). Proved reserves of non-conventional oil will be very small until all geological queries have been satisfactorily answered. It is probable that hydrocarbons in the belt amount to 100 million cubic meters (630 million barrels), but it would be futile to discuss resources computed by applying a recovery factor to the very preliminary geological report and evaluation data.

Coal

All coal deposits in Venezuela are found north of a line formed by the Andes and the coastal ranges in Paleocene, Eocene and Miocene formations. The names "First," "Second," and "Third Coal Horizon," now in disuse, were used in the first book on Venezuelan geology to designate the series of coal-bearing rocks. Although the geographical distribution of coal is widespread in Venezuela, the main deposits are located at Naricual near Barcelona, the Perijá foothills in Zulia, and the Lobatera area north of San Cristóbal. Exploitation of coal resources has been slight, and cumulative coal production from 1940 to 1974 was only 900,000 tons. It is estimated that no more than one million tons have been mined in Venezuela since 1500.

There are up to 15 mineable beds in Naricual, with an individual thickness of no more than 90 centimeters (35 inches), although they might reach 2.5 meters (8 feet). The coal is shining black with good combustibility, and its volatile components have caused some disasters in the past. The seams are contained in the geological formation Naricual of Oligo-Miocene age, first called "Naricual Coal Measures." The maximum production was 30,000 metric tons in 1921. When the workings were suspended in 1963, the coal being extracted totalled 12,000 tons per year. The proved reserves are 46 million tons, and inferred reserves, particularly in the southern foothills of the Coastal Ranges – Taguay, Guárico – could be about 500 million tons, located to depths of 500 meters (1,650 feet) and in layers of more than 25 centimeters (10 inches) thick.

The Lobatera deposits have supplied almost all Venezuelan needs during recent years. Coal layers are part of the Los Cuervos formation of the Paleocene-Eocene age. There are 8 to 10 seams with maximum thickness of 2.5 meters (8 feet). Average production from 1962-1974 was 38,300 tons per year, but output increased sharply from 39,900 tons in 1972 to 49,700 in 1973 then 57,100 in 1974. Recent prospecting has increased volumetric estimates of the proved reserves to some 20 million tons, while the probable reserves in neighbouring areas could reach 2,000 million tons.

The most important coal deposits in Venezuela lie in the foothills of the Perijá mountain range, notably in the

Manuelote syncline, due west of Maracaibo. Outcrops in the western flank of the structure cover 150 square kilometers (58 square miles). The coal beds are found in the Marcelina Paleocene formation, a lateral equivalent of the Los Cuervos formation. Seams reach 12 meters (39 feet) in thickness in the locality of Santa Rosa and there are 15 beds between 2 and 7 meters (7 and 23 feet) thick. The average total thickness in the Guasare area is 3.3 meters (11 feet). The coal is black, hard, and brittle, with conchoidal fracture and a high luster; it could be described in places as anthracite, with a low ash content. Another section of thick coal beds in the subsurface of the Alturitas field, 120 kilometers (75 miles) to the south, has been correlated with the Marcelina formation.

Field work in a systematic manner in the Manuelote syncline started in 1969. Reserves down to 150 meters (500 feet) have been estimated at 173 million tons for beds thicker than 0.5 meters (20 inches) and at 780 million tons to a depth of 500 meters (1,650 feet). Considering the lateral extent of the geological sequence, the absence of facies changes, and the geographical distribution of the Marcelina formation, it can be estimated that the volume of additional reserves susceptible to mining along the Perijá foothills might reach 10,000 million tons.

In summary, the resources of producible coal in Venezuela down to 150 meters and in seams of more than 25 centimeters (10 feet) in thickness have been estimated at 12,800 million tons.

Hydraulic Resources

The hydrographic basin of the Orinoco River covers four-fifths of the surface of Venezuela. Of particular interest for water power resources are the Orinoco tributaries on the right bank and the Andean rivers which flow to the Apure, a left-bank tributary of the Orinoco. Of secondary importance

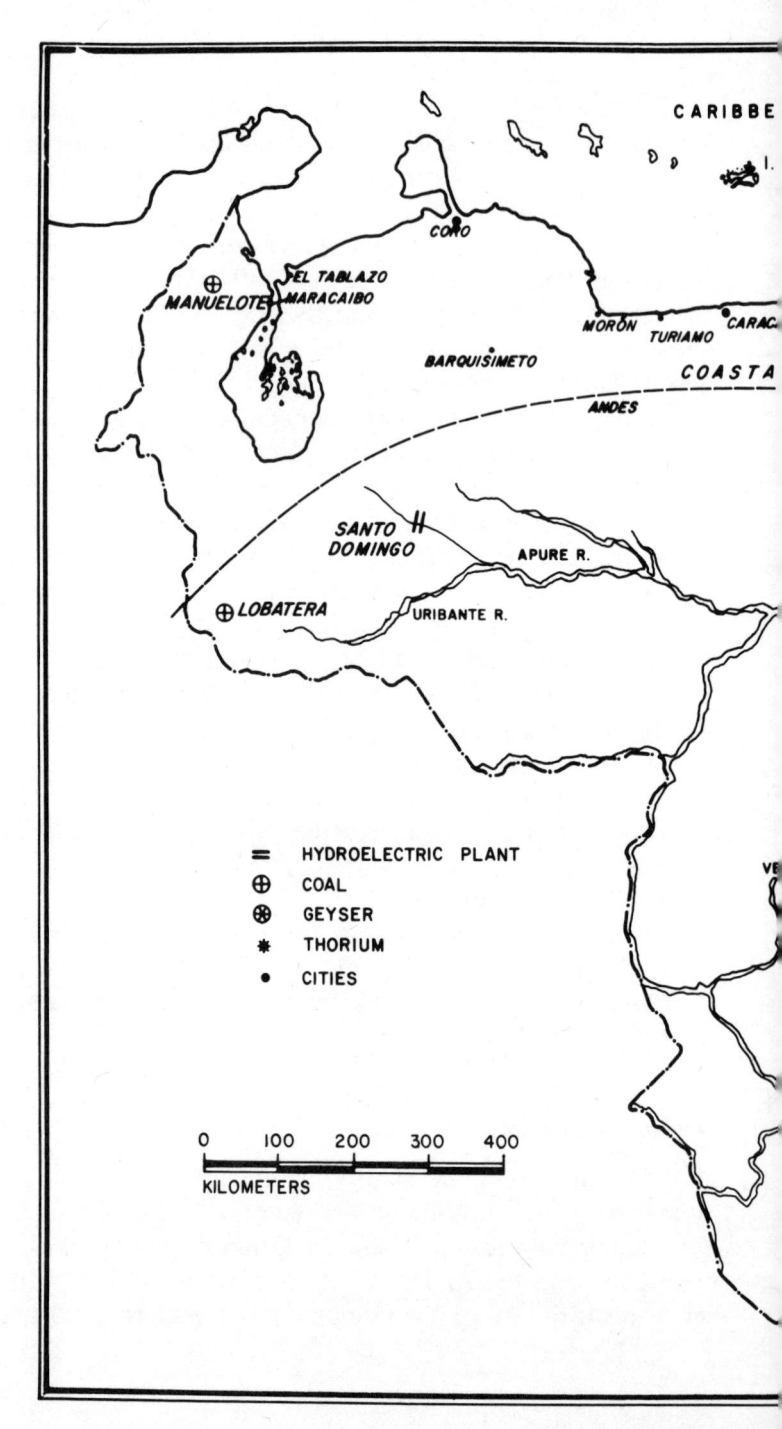

Map 3. Energy resou

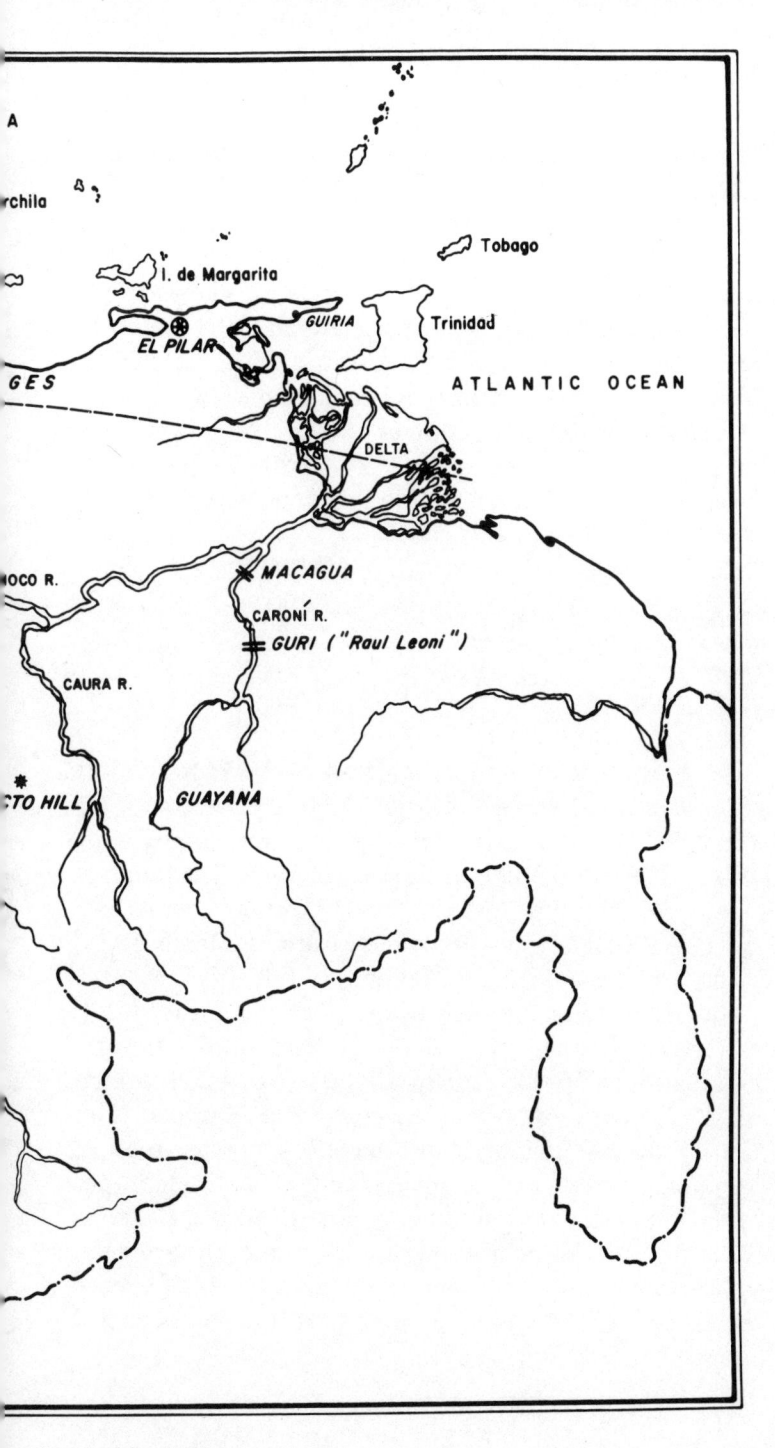

er than hydrocarbons

for hydraulic power are the rivers of the Maracaibo lake basin that originate in the Perijá ranges.

The first published estimate of the hydraulic power reserves for Venezuela was 15,049 megawatts. This is equal to 16.5 kilowatts per square kilometer (42.7 kilowatts per square mile). The most recent estimate of total potential hydraulic power was 21,000 megawatts, which is slightly higher than the average reported for South America.

Outstanding among all sources of hydraulic power is the Caroní River, with a total of at least 10,500 megawatts of potential capacity estimated for the following locations:

	Megawatts
Guri	6,000
Caruachí	1,500
Río Claro	1,100
Lower Rapids	1,900

The mean annual volume of flow of the Caroní River from 1949 to 1972 was 4,910 cubic meters per second (2.3 million cubic feet per minute), ranging from 3,567 (1.7 million) in 1964 to 6,540 (3.1 million) in 1949. The minimal flow rate for any one month was 193 cubic meters per second (91 thousand feet per minute) during March 1964, while the largest was 17,031 (8 million) in July 1957.

The Caura River, another tributary of the Orinoco 200 kilometers (125 miles) west and upstream of the Caroní, drains a basin of 50,000 square kilometers (19,300 square miles). The volume of water delivered to the Orinoco is an average of 82,000 million cubic meters per year, that is, 1,500 cubic meters per second (706,000 cubic feet per minute). The estimated hydraulic power of the Caura is 2,500 megawatts. Some 500 megawatts of power have been estimated for the Ventuari River; the estimated rate of energy for the Uribante River running down from the Andes is 800 megawatts; 240 for the Santo Domingo, and between 200 and 300 for the Capazón River. The force of the rivers flowing out of the Perijá range has not been studied in detail.

The exploitation of water power in Venezuela started in the nineteen-fifties. A Commission for the Study of Electrification of the Caroní was established in 1953 within the Ministry of Development. Construction of the first hydroelectric plant at Macagua was started in 1956 and operations commenced in 1959 with the delivery of 55 megawatts of power. The plant now has a maximum power generation of 370 megawatts. The biggest project undertaken was the Guri dam and its associated generating units. The first unit started producing hydroelectricity (175 megawatts) in 1968, and by the end of 1974 five of the ten generating units were completed and in operation, delivering a total power of 965 megawatts. At Santo Domingo a plant has been in operation since 1974, and delivers a maximum of 240 megawatts of power.

The total installed capacity for hydroelectric generation in Venezuela was 1,855 megawatts at the end of 1974, supplying about 9% of the total energy demand in the country. The production of hydroelectricity has increased fourteenfold from 1962 to 1974. Preliminary data show that the State company in charge of the development of hydraulic power resources in the Caroní River generated 7,285 million kilowatt-hours in 1974, or almost half of the electricity produced in Venezuela.

Geothermal Energy

Surface geothermal energy resources are found in Venezuela in the usual locations of folded young mountain belts, and numerous manifestations of such structures extend in the wide arc of the Andes with its continuation in the northern coastal ranges. Tectonism occurred from the Middle Cretaceous to Paleocene or even Eocene times, and thermal gradient increases could have been the cause for the rock metamorphism associated with the mountain-building process.

Hot springs are relatively abundant in Venezuela, with nearly 60 localities reported in the literature. Water temperature may be as low as 40°C (104°F), but the mode is 60°C (140°F). At Las Trincheras and Batatal, the temperature goes as high as 90°C (194°F). There is a geyser at El Pilar, near Carúpano, in the Paria peninsula, and abnormal bottom-hole temperatures have been recorded in many wells drilled for oil exploration, which is an indication of deep crustal geothermal energy locations. However, with the scant data on hand it is not possible to evaluate, even in a tentative manner, the geothermal resources of Venezuela.

Nuclear Energy Resources

Uranium and thorium are found in miniscule concentrations in granites and diorites associated with isostatic masses. Recent aereal surveys have shown many zones of somewhat significant radioactivity, in particular in the remote regions of the Pacaraima and Maigualida ranges of the Guayana massif. Minerals are embedded in Precambrian rocks between 1.7 and 2.0 million years old. A small curiously-shaped physiographic feature called Cerro Impacto has been the only site observed by surface geology, and there laterites along the spine of the hill show concentrations of 0.2 and 0.4 thorium. The Geological Office in the Ministry of Mines and Hydrocarbons is programming a methodical study of attractive spots, not only in the Guayana region, but also in or near the batoliths of the Andean mountains.

Solar Energy

Venezuela is a country in the tropics with one million square kilometers (386,100 square miles) of area and a maximum average daily sunlight of about 11 hours. The author has estimated that 1.2×10^{12} megawatts of solar power fall upon Venezuelan territory. In the coastal plains of Falcón, the energy from the sun absorbed at ground level is 0.4 megawatts per square kilometer. Assuming an efficiency of 10% in the conversion to electrical power, it would require a panel, shaped as a square, of 1.38 meters on each side (4.5 feet by 4.5 feet) to light a 100-watt bulb. A square solar panel 6 kilometers on each side (3.75 x 3.75 miles) might provide the elctricity consumed by the metropolitan area of Caracas, inhabited by 2 million people.

Wind Energy

Trade winds blow predominantly from the northeast of Venezuela, but are seasonal along certain areas of the northern coastal plains. The average velocity is 15 kilometers per hour (9 miles per hour); however, in the meterological station at Coro and La Orchila Island the averages for June and July increase to 27 kilometers per hour (17 miles per hour). During 1971 the average wind velocity at El Tablazo, on the east side of the Maracaibo lake mouth, was measured at 23 kilometers per hour (14 miles per hour). Winds from the northeast and the east blow strongly, sweeping the arid Paraguaná peninsula with velocities of up to 35 kilometers per hour (22 miles per hour). Obstructed by the Andes, the trade winds change direction or lose their force. Over the plains belt of Central Venezuela, the dominant wind direction is still from the northeast, but velocities are reduced. Wind speeds in Barquisimeto average 15 kilometers per hour (9 miles per hour), with a maximum of 18 kilometers per hour (11 miles per hour) during August. In the Guayana plateau, winds blow from the southeast quarter, along the intertropical front of northern South America, with an average wind velocity of 8 kilometers per hour (5 miles per hour).

A system of 10 windmills with aerodynamic blades

some 3 meters (10 feet) long could generate 9.7 megawatts power all year round, and in theory, up to 24,000 megawatts of wind power is available in the northern coastal areas. Considering present technology, however, wind power utilization seems unlikely in the near future.

Tidal Energy Resources

There are more than 2,800 kilometers (some 1,800 miles) of shoreline in the Caribbean and the Atlantic, but very few places seem to be of interest for tidal energy generation. The difference between high and low tide in Amuay is 1.15 meters (4 feet), but median amplitude is only 0.38 meters (1 foot and one-quarter). At the port of Güiria in the Paria gulf, amplitude of tides is 1.41 meters (4 feet 7 inches), but spring tides, that is, when the sun and the moon are in conjunction or opposition, increase to 1.56 meters (5 feet 1 inch). The Turiamo Bay in Central Venezuela measures 6 by 3 kilometers (3.75 x 1.9 miles), hardly enough to sustain a tidal power plant.

The hydrographic regime of the Orinoco River and the Maracaibo lake might prove of importance for tidal energy resources. Although the amplitude of the spring tides in the Orinoco is only 1.25 meters (4 feet) at Puerto de Hierro, and 2.04 meters (7 feet) at "Milla 32" in the dredged shipping channel, the volume of water flow is estimated at 16,000 cubic meters per second (7.5 million cubic feet per minute). El Tablazo Bay, which connects the lake and gulf of Venezuela, has 374 square kilometers of surface (145 square miles), a shipping channel 36 kilometers long (22.5 miles) and 11 meters deep (36 feet), and facilitates the entrance and discharge of large volumes of water according to the tides.

The Production and Consumption of Energy in Venezuela

In absolute quantities the production of energy in Venezuela is high, and its internal consumption is one of the largest per capita in South America or among all the underdeveloped nations of the world.

Great confusion exists with respect to the terms currently employed in describing or evaluating energy, which further complicates any discussion of energy policy. The petroleum engineer thinks in barrels of crude petroleum or cubic feet of natural gas, but the manager of an electrical plant talks of kilowatt-hours; a heating expert will naturally refer to British Thermal Units (BTU's), while those converted to the metric system will propose consideration of gram-calories. For the purpose of this study, the *ton of petroleum equivalent* (TPE) will be used. It is defined as the calorific value of 1,000 kilograms of Venezuelan crude oil of specific gravity 0.904 grams per cubic centimeter (25.0° API). The calorific value of the TPE in metric units of heat is 10,694,900 kilocalories, that is, 42,459,000 BTU's. When expressed in metric units of mechanical power, the TPE equals 12,830 kilowatt-hours. In a conventional steam power plant, one barrel of Venezuelan crude petroleum would provide 550 kilowatt-hours. One TPE of such oil equals the volume of 1.11 cubic meters.

In the case of Venezuela, a comparison of energy resources by conversion to thermal values is not misleading, because the large order of magnitude of energy production or consumption of energy materials makes irrelevant any discounting of their non-energy uses or process beneficiation. Other energy resources can be converted to TPE in accordance with their respective heat values. Average Venezuelan natural gas has a calorific value of 10,230 kilocalories per cubic meter, that is, 1,150 BTU's per cubic foot. Crude oil and natural gas have close calorific values by weight, although the heat content by volume is very different. Coal from Naricual has a caloric value of 7,000 kilocalories per kilogram (61,200 BTU's per pound), while Guasare coal has 6,200 (54,200). One TPE, then, equals 1.53 tons of Naricual coal or 1.72 tons of Guasare coal. To express the calorific value of one TPE in units of hydroelectricity, a reduction factor must be considered in order to reflect the efficiencies of the Guri plants in converting kinetic water energy into electricity. Here one TPE equals 3,330 kilowatt-hours and conversely 1,000 kilowatt-hours equal 0.30 TPE.

Gasoline of average specific gravity 0.750 grams per cubic centimeter (57.2° API) has a calorific value of 11.41 million kilocalories per ton (5.4 million BTU's per barrel), therefore, 0.94 cubic meters of gasoline equals 1.0 TPE. Conversion factors for other petroleum products are as follows:

	Specific gravity (gr./cm^3)	API°	M^3 per TPE
Kerosene, turbo-fuel	0.820	41.1	0.97
Diesel, gas oil	0.845	36.0	0.98
Fuel oil	0.960	15.9	1.02

Refinery gas has a calorific value of 10.41 million kilocalories per ton, so 0.97 cubic meters equal 1 TPE. Considering the average yield of the principal products obtained in the refinery operations in Venezuela for the 1963-1973 period (that is, 63.6% heavy fuel oil, 15.3% diesel oil and gas oil and 13.3% gasolines), the weighted factor for conversion of petroleum products to TPE is 1.00.

Production

The production of energy in Venezuela increased very rapidly from 1940 to 1954, doubling between 1940 and 1946, then doubling again from 1946 to 1954. However, the rate of growth fell from 1957 onward. From 1960 to 1974, the production curve was practically flat. Energy production surpassed 100 million TPE in 1951 and reached 200 million TPE in 1964. The largest volume obtained was almost 220 million TPE in 1970, but in 1974 the TPE was only 185 million. Production by five-year periods was as follows:

	Production (millions of TPE)
1950-1954	540
1955-1959	779
1960-1964	925
1965-1969	1,047
1970-1974	1,023

The total energy production for 1900 to 1949 was approximately 900 million TPE. Thus, the amount of energy produced during the last decade in Venezuela was equal to all the energy produced for the first half of the century.

The production of energy in Venezuela has been dominated by the rate of withdrawal of crude petroleum from the traditional basins, particularly since the 1940's. The contribution of oil to the total energy production has always been higher than 84%, amounting to about 89% from 1960 to 1966, and about 86% in 1973 and 1974. The production of

TABLE I

VENEZUELA: PRODUCTION OF ENERGY
(Thousand tons of petroleum equivalent)

	Liquid Hydrocarbons	Natural Gas	Coal	Charcoal, Wood	Hydraulic	Total
1920	90	18				110
1925	2700	500				3200
1930	19600	3300				23000
1935	21400	3800				25200
1940	25800	4100				30000
1945	46000	7800				53800
1948	70316	12642	11	16	11	82996
1949	68878	12694	15	12	11	81610
1950	78161	14176	11	11	14	92372
1951	89348	17156	18	8	14	106543
1952	94943	18394	16	6	12	113373
1953	92532	17355	19	9	12	109926
1954	99390	18776	21	10	13	118208
1955	113372	19268	20	11	15	132965
1956	129530	21797	20	12	16	151374
1957	146159	23658	22	11	13	169863
1958	136533	23860	24	8	11	157631
1959	145654	20944	22	7	8	166635
1960	150084	19459	23	9	8	169582
1961	153696	19055	20	7	7	172785
1962	168263	21435	18	11	52	189779
1963	170675	20026	27	11	286	191026
1964	179426	21182	24	9	318	200959
1965	183788	21849	19	10	359	206026
1966	177780	21540	22	10	360	199713
1967	186986	24489	22	20	431	211948
1968	190645	23982	20	19	752	215419

	Liquid Hydrocarbons	Natural Gas	Coal	Charcoal, Wood	Hydraulic	Total
1969	189451	24617	21	17	873	214979
1970	196225	22077	26	15	1138	219482
1971	188280	26752	28	16	1504	216580
1972	171645	24098	26	19	1689	197476
1973	179555	26117	32	23	1730	207457
1974	158758	24528	37	23	2047	185393

Source: Ministry of Mines and Hydrocarbons: *PODE* 1973 for years 1963-1973; *PODE* 1963 for years 1948-1962. Year 1974, from First Message of the President to National Congress on 12 March 1975. Estimates of the author for 1920, 1925, 1930, 1935, 1940, and 1945.

liquid hydrocarbons peaked at 196 million TPE during 1970. It was reduced to less than 160 million TPE in 1974 and is expected to amount to some 145 million TPE during 1975. Average petroleum production during the last 15 years has been 176.4 million TPE, with a maximum deviation of 20 million TPE. There has been no growth in the rate of production, which can be shown by a curve drawn on a logarithmic scale.

Production of energy from natural gas doubled from 12.6 million TPE in 1948 to 24.5 million TPE in 1967. Since then, production has hovered between 24 and 26 million TPE. Natural gas had contributed up to 16% of the total energy production in Venezuela from 1950 to 1954, but dropped to about 11% in 1974. Coal production in Venezuela has always been one-hundredth to five-hundredths of one percent of the total energy output. From 1953 to 1969 it amounted to some 20,000 TPE per year, increasing to

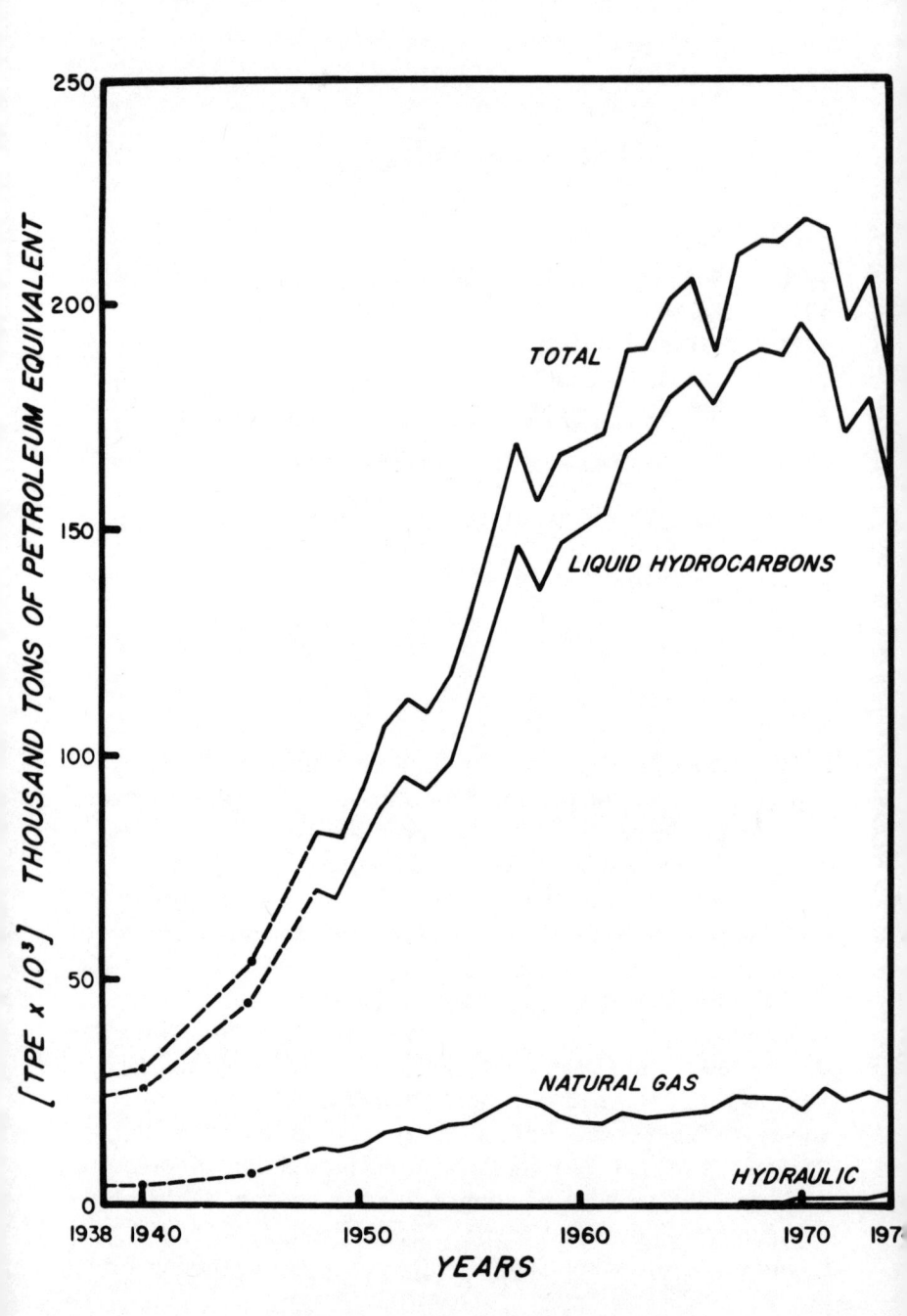

Figure 2. Venezuela: Production of energy

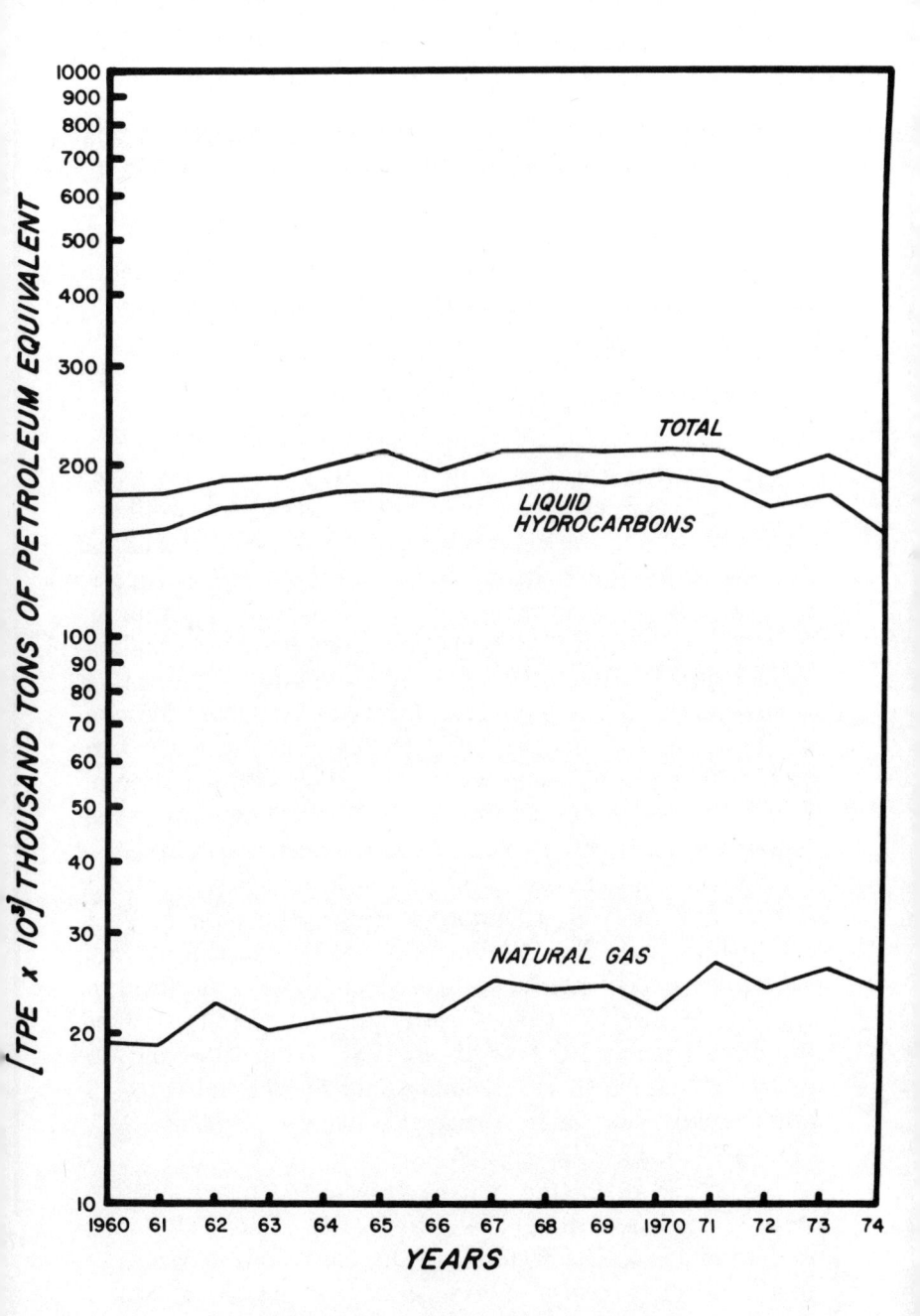

Figure 3. Venezuela: Production of energy

37,000 TPE in 1974. Energy obtained from charcoal and wood has also been insignificant, estimated at 23,000 TPE in both 1973 and 1974. The contribution of hydraulic energy to Venezuelan energy had also been measured in the hundredths of one percent until 1962. However, the figure almost reached 1% in 1974 when 2 million TPE were produced by water power.

Consumption

In recent years the growth of energy consumption in Venezuela has been spectacular, but it was very low until the beginning of the present century. Perhaps some 25 million TPE was the total energy consumed from the European discovery of the country in 1498 to 1900. Energy consumption from 1900 to 1950 may have amounted to 85 million TPE. However, from 1948 to 1962 consumption grew at an annual rate of 0.5 million TPE; from 1962 to 1969 the rate increased to 0.75 million TPE per year; and from 1969 to 1974, the rate of growth was 1.25 million TPE per annum. The 1948 energy consumption first doubled in eight years, doubled again in ten years, and again in nine years. In gross figures, the consumption of energy in Venezuela surpassed 5 million TPE in 1954, 10 million in 1963, 20 million in 1973, and amounted to 22.3 million TPE in 1974. Moreover, only 3% of the energy produced in Venezuela was consumed in the country itself in 1948. Consumption increased to 4% of the production in 1952, to 5% in 1958, 6% in 1964, and 7% in 1970. The percentage of domestic consumption has grown quite rapidly since then, rising to 8% in 1971, 9% in 1972, 10% in 1973, and 12% in 1974.

The use of energy derived from crude petroleum has steadily increased since 1948, from 1.6 million TPE to 9 million in 1974. The doubling of this consumption of energy first took eight years, then doubled again in fifteen years.

However, as a percentage of the total energy consumed in Venezuela, petroleum has continuously decreased from 66% in 1950 to 40% in 1970. From 1958 on, energy from oil dropped to second among the energy materials consumed with natural gas taking first place.

Natural gas started its rapid ascent in 1950 as a provider of energy for the domestic market. A sustained rate of increase of some 340,000 TPE per year to 1969 became even higher during the following five years, increasing by a half-million TPE each year. The gross production of natural gas increased from some 30 million TPE in the early nineteen-sixties to 47 million in 1973; the volumes reinjected to the oil reservoir augmented proportionately, from 15 million TPE to 29 million in 1974 (47% of gross production). The volume of gas flared reached 18 million TPE at the time of the peak in crude petroleum production, but it was brought down forcefully to half the waste in 1974 (9.4 million TPE). Quantities used by the oil industry for their own operations have increased steadily to nearly 6 million TPE in 1974. The amount of natural gas transformed in products is less than 2 million TPE per year.

Energy from coal, charcoal, and wood contributed very little to the total consumption. The steel industry has required the import of 100 to 200 thousand TPE per year of metallurgical coal since 1962, and the Naricual coal mines were closed in 1963.

Hydraulic energy, which provided about 120,000 TPE in 1961 rose to almost 2,000,000 TPE in the mid-1970's. From 3% of the total energy consumed during the period 1963-1967, the share of hydraulic energy grew to 8% in 1974.

Production and Consumption of Electrical Energy

The production of electrical energy in Venezuela was

TABLE II

VENEZUELA: CONSUMPTION OF ENERGY
(Thousand tons of petroleum equivalent)

	Liquid Hydrocarbons	Natural Gas	Coal	Charcoal, Wood	Hydraulic	Total
1948	1600	1089	12	16	11	2728
1949	1942	1020	15	12	11	3000
1950	2057	1046	10	11	14	3137
1951	2265	1348	17	8	14	3652
1952	2505	1644	17	6	12	4184
1953	2566	2031	19	9	12	4636
1954	2917	2193	21	10	13	5153
1955	3194	2574	20	11	15	5813
1956	3491	2803	21	12	16	6343
1957	3832	3393	23	11	13	7271
1958	3766	3679	24	8	11	7489
1959	4040	3925	22	7	8	8002
1960	3760	4313	23	9	8	8113
1961	3767	4591	28	7	7	8400
1962	3803	4854	101	11	52	8821
1963	4547	5300	119	11	256	10234
1964	4808	5831	142	9	286	11077
1965	5152	6177	151	10	323	11813
1966	5437	6477	123	10	324	12372
1967	5566	7095	160	20	388	13229
1968	6012	7325	265	19	677	14298
1969	6130	7539	217	17	786	14690
1970	6471	8494	248	15	1026	16252
1971	6924	8849	179	16	1354	17322
1972	7751	8998	229	19	1520	18518

	Liquid Hydrocarbons	Natural Gas	Coal	Charcoal, Wood	Hydraulic	Total
1973	8546	10679	235	23	1557	21041
1974	8950	11216	250	21	1842	22279

Source: Ministry of Mines and Hydrocarbons: *PODE* 1973 for years 1963-1973; *PODE* 1963 for years 1948-1962. Year 1974, from First Message of the President to National Congress on 12 March 1975.

less than 100,000 TPE in 1950, but by 1962 it had surpassed one million TPE. Consumption doubled in five years and doubled again in eight years to 4 million TPE in 1974. While electricity generation quadrupled from 1962 to 1974, the number of subscribers doubled. The generation of electricity in thermal plants was 98.2% in 1961, but since then, hydroelectricity has rapidly increased its share of the total to 26% in 1968 and 50% in 1974.

Electrical energy consumption has been increasing exponentially as shown by a curve plotted on semilogarithmic paper. From less than one million TPE in 1962, the amount for 1974 was 3.5 million TPE. Per capita energy consumption increased rather quickly from 0.11 TPE per year in 1962 to 0.19 in 1968, then to 0.29 TPE per year in 1974.

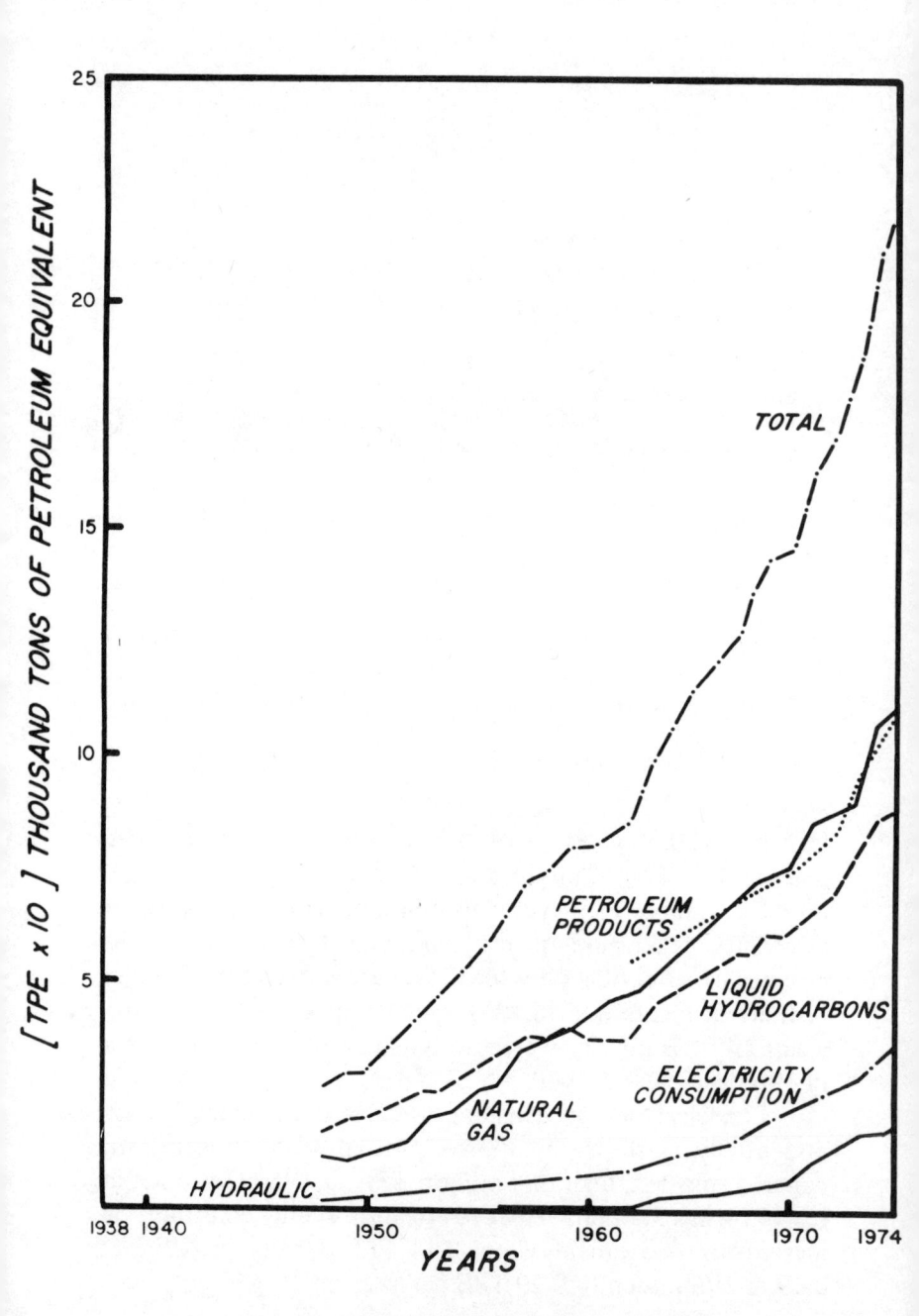

Figure 4: Venezuela: Consumption of energy

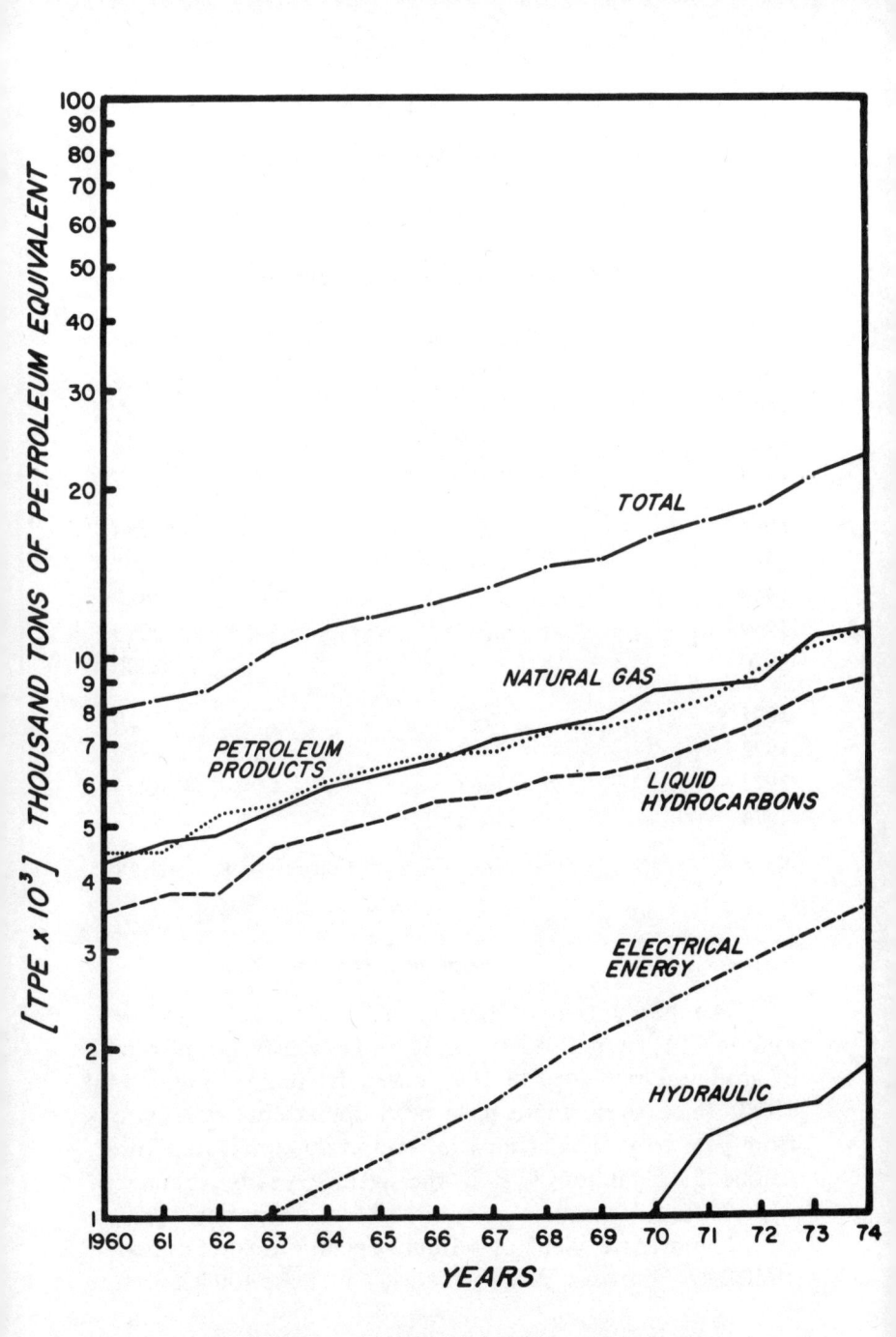

Figure 5. Venezuela: Consumption of energy

TABLE III

VENEZUELA: PRODUCTION AND CONSUMPTION OF ELECTRICITY
(Thousand tons of petroleum equivalent)

	Production	*Consumption*
1962	1037	876
1963	1240	1027
1964	1387	1150
1965	1547	1267
1966	1720	1443
1967	2183	1597
1968	2243	1887
1969	2627	2050
1970	2760	2300
1971	2927	2550
1972	3307	2870
1973	3663	3203
1974	4077	3537

Source: Message of the President to National Congress on 12 March 1975.

Production, Exports, and Consumption of Petroleum Products

The production of petroleum products averaged 58.7 million TPE from 1960-1974. The steady increase in volume of crude oil processed by the Venezuelan refineries ended by 1967; since then, there have been appreciable fluctuations from year to year, and most of the production is for export. About 52.1 million TPE is the average yearly volume of exports from Venezuela — that is, 89% of the production.

The average yield of refining operations for the period 1960-1974 shows a slow but steady increase for heavy fuel

TABLE IV

VENEZUELA: PRODUCTION, EXPORTS AND CONSUMPTION OF PETROLEUM PRODUCTS
(Thousand tons of petroleum equivalent)

	Production	Exports	Consumption
1960	45928	40003	4553
1961	48177	42156	4521
1962	53234	46283	5380
1963	54505	48232	5677
1964	57207	50120	5989
1965	61441	53405	6325
1966	61351	53270	6643
1967	60901	54067	6800
1968	62162	53146	7299
1969	60450	54218	7419
1970	67568	60027	7819
1971	65135	56165	8348
1972	59009	54230	9404
1973	67928	59542	10392
1974	56036	56200	10990

Source: Ministry of Mines and Hydrocarbons: *PODE* for years 1960 to 1973. Year 1974, from First Message of the President to National Congress on 12 March 1975.

oil, from 56% to 64% of the total, a production of between 33 and 38 million TPE yearly. The production of gasolines and naphtha has also been augmented from about 7 million TPE per year in the early sixties to some 9 million TPE per year in the seventies. In consequence, diesel oil and gas oil production has decreased gradually from 11 million TPE per year in 1963 and 1964 to less than 7 million TPE in 1974.

Means and Ends in Formulating Policy

A sound energy policy for Venezuela is obviously of critical importance to the country, yet the resolution of such policy faces extraordinary difficulties. The word for "policy" in the Spanish language *(política)* is also used to mean "politics," that is, the noisy contest of parties for power, in appeals of the political parties or politicians, the partisan campaigns and elections of candidates, and so forth. For a sound energy policy, the first consideration is the insulation, as far as practicable, of "politics" from rational and long-term considerations of national "policy."

While scientists and technicians must respect the role of the politician in translating popular demand into legislation, the politician must also heed the advice and counsel of the scientist and technician on the effectiveness and costs of any policy.

If policy is regarded as the principles that guide any measure or course of action, the government must be constantly alert to see that both the means and ends are involved in the implementation of those principles. The means for the formulation of an energy policy for Venezuela could be identified as the resources themselves. The ends tend to be those national objectives designed by the government under programs for economic development and social evolution.

Means for an Energy Policy

Hydrocarbons in the traditional basins and new areas, whether petroleum or other types, and coal deposits make up the non-renewable energy resources of Venezuela. Hydraulic, geothermal, nuclear, solar, eolic, and tidal sources of energy are generally renewable.

Summarizing the earlier sections of this study, the resources of petroleum in the traditional basins amount to 9,946 million TPE, of which 2,082 millions had been produced by the end of the 1974; about 2,896 million TPE have been proved or can be recovered; and about 2,746 millions are to be found. Resources of natural gas were 2,730 million TPE, but 915 million have already been produced or lost. The proved reserves of gas amount to about 1,022 million TPE and undiscovered quantities in the traditional basins are estimated at 793 million.

The proved reserves of petroleum from tars and other sources in the Orinoco Belt might be 80 million TPE, although production has yet to reach one million TPE. Both estimates in no way detract from the preliminary geological evaluation indicating the occurrence of 75,000 million TPE of bitumens in the subsurface. The stratigraphic holes completed to the end of 1974, as has been pointed out in the beginning of the geological evaluation of the immense deposit, are indications that the volume of hydrocarbons *in situ* might well be greater than the first estimate.

Coal reserves, qualified by the critical parameters of 25 centimeters minimum seam thickness and 150 meters minimum for depth, amount to 8,000 million TPE.

Hydraulic energy resources are equal to 21,000 megawatts of power, of which less than 10% has been developed. There are about 5,000 megawatts capacity under construction, with the target date for various plants to enter into operation between 1976 and 1978. Hydroelectrical energy used in 1974 was 7,285 million kilowatt-hours, that is, 4 million TPE.

Solar energy, considered unavailable at the present time, could produce 1,200,000,000,000 megawatts power. Wind energy in the coastal areas, also unavailable, is estimated at 24,000 megawatts. Geothermal resources await investigation. Minerals used as fuel in first-generation uranium and thorium-consuming nuclear plants have been found in the Guayana region, but might occur in other areas of igneous rocks in the Andean mountain belt, although only one site has actually

TABLE V

ENERGY RESOURCES OF VENEZUELA

Non-renewable

		mill. TPE
Petroleum in traditional basins	11,040 mill. m^3	9,946
Natural gas	2,866,000 mill. m^3	2,730
New areas	?	
Non-conventional petroleum	?	
Coal	12,800 mill. ton	8,000

Renewable

	Power	*Work Used*	*mill. TPE*
Hydraulic	21,000 MW	15 mill. MW-h	4
Geothermal	?		
Nuclear	?		
Solar	1,200,000,000,000 MW	inaccessible ?	
Wind (coastal areas)	24,000 MW	inaccessible ?	
Tidal	?		

been surveyed. It seems farfetched to expect any large plant utilizing tidal energy; however, no detailed studies have been made on the subject.

State of the Economy

At no other time had the economic well-being of Venezuela depended so heavily on the exportation of petroleum as at the beginning of 1975. One TPE had brought to the national treasury $6.39 during most of the nineteen-sixties; by 1973, however, the revenues had almost tripled ($17.71 per TPE), and in 1974 the sale of one TPE on the international market brought an income of $57.83 to the government, a ninefold increase over the income from the nineteen-sixties.

The royalty receipts had been some $600 million per year between 1963 and 1969. The larger volume of production in 1970, 1971, and 1972 augmented the "exploitation tax," as it is called in the Hydrocarbons Law, to $650 million per year. In November 1973 the values of the Texas crudes that were used as a basis for calculation of the royalty were increased by 182%, and the full force of this higher reference price brought royalty payments in 1974 up to $2,100 million. The income tax, however, has been for many years the main instrument for obtaining government income from the oil industry operations. Payments have increased continuously from $500 million in 1963 to $1,058 million in 1971, then to $2,219 million in 1973 and to some $7,000 million in 1974. In January 1975 the income tax rate to concessionaires was increased to 70% of net gains, which raised the government income tax from $57.83 per TPE to $60.22 per TPE.

The total government petroleum income, which includes royalty, income tax, and a number of very small payments for other taxes, was $1,100 million per year in the

1963-1966 period and $1,250 million from 1967 to 1969. It grew to $1,715 in year 1971 and to $1,956 in 1972, then leaped to $3,180 million in 1973 and $9,183 million in 1974.

An inventory of properties, plants, and equipment of concessionaire companies as of 31 December 1973 shows the total investment at acquisition cost of $4.9 million, of which $3.7 million had been depreciated, thus leaving a book value of $1.2 million — precisely the amount proposed by the Presidential Commission on Nationalization and by the Federal Executive as compensation for the impending take-over of the properties. Creole, an Exxon subsidiary, accounted for 48% of the total investments; and the subsidiary of Dutch-Shell accounted for 26%.

The production of oil has permitted the Venezuelan gross national product to grow an average of 5.3% per year between 1969 and 1974 at constant 1968 prices. Prices were controlled for a number of years, but the economic policies set in operation during 1974 caused the wholesale price index to escalate from 127 to 148, with 1968 as the base (100) year. In 1975 it was expected that the rate of inflation would be reduced. Due to the petroleum industry, the treasury reserves, which had ranged from $100 to $170 million from 1962 to 1972, increased to $442 million in 1973 and $1,095 million in 1974. In consequence, the monetary reserves of Venezuela were the tenth highest in the world. The contribution of petroleum and petroleum products to Venezuelan exports by value, which has always been very large, reached 94% in 1974.

The estimated population of Venezuela on 30 June 1974, was 11.6 million. The birth rate decreased from 43.4 per thousand in 1962 to 35.5 in 1974; however, the mortality rate also fell from 7.0 per thousand in 1962 to 6.1 in 1974, so that population growth rate is still very high. The strain on the education system has been tremendous as three million children have recently been added to the classrooms.

TABLE VI

VENEZUELA: GOVERNMENT PETROLEUM INCOME
(Millions of $)

	Royalty	Income Tax	Total	$/TPE
1963	560	500	1,078	6.34
1964	589	519	1,120	6.24
1965	583	528	1,122	6.10
1966	575	514	1,099	6.18
1967	605	625	1,241	6.64
1968	617	626	1,253	6.57
1969	619	625	1,256	6.63
1970	653	743	1,409	7.18
1971	645	1,058	1,715	9.11
1972	650	1,293	1,956	11.40
1973	951	2,219	3,180	17.71
1974	(2,100)	(7,000)	9,183	57.83

(Estimated) Other taxes not shown.

Source: Ministry of Mines and Hydrocarbons, *PODE* 1973; Message of the President to National Congress on 12 March 1975.

To strengthen technical and professional education, an ambitious plan to train abroad 10,000 people in critical areas of need was launched in 1974 at a cost of $120 million. While the health programs in the country are fairly satisfactory, the problems of underemployment of labor, inadequate housing, and pockets of poverty among luxurious developments are evident. The distribution of Venezuela's petroleum wealth has been very imperfect and has not yet benefitted a large part of the population.

An investment fund was established in April 1974 to withdraw from international circulation half of the highly-increased petroleum income in order to prevent an inflated economy and wasteful consumption. The initial contribution to the Fund was $3,095 million. Fiduciary loans by Venezuela to the InterAmerican Development Bank and other regional credit organisms such as the Andean Development Corporation, totalling $600 million, will be handled by the Fund, while commitments will be made to bilateral or multilateral programs for development. Another important 1974 contribution was $540 million for the special fund of the International Monetary Fund to aid developing countries. Two other funds for internal loans in the agricultural and industrial sectors were also established in 1974 with an initial capital of $475 million in each.

Objectives of an Energy Policy

The energy policy of Venezuela will, of course, depend upon the national economic objectives as well as the resources available. The idea of a balanced, autonomous development of the country was enunciated 40 years ago in the slogan "sow the petroleum," but until now such a course of action has been just a beautiful phrase. Little has been done to change the pre-eminence of oil in the whole life of the country, for the apparent — rather than the real — character of the accumulated or forthcoming riches has obscured future needs and delayed constructive action.

The fourth 4-year plan for the nation ended in 1973 and no new short-range program has since been published. The contrast between reality and the idealistic goals which had pervaded previous programs at last seems to have sobered the nation's planners and made them avoid another long, ethereal exercise in hopes or wishful thinking. The principal source for what may be taken as an overview of economic, social, and political planning in Venezuela in 1975 can be taken from the First Message of the President of the Republic to the National Congress on March 12th. Four areas seem to be the main targets for immediate and vigorous action to start widening the economic base of the country: namely, siderurgy, petrochemistry, mining, and agriculture.

The State steel company SIDOR started operations in July 1962 some 12 years after two subsidiaries of multinational corporations had begun large-scale mining of iron ores in Guayana. The production of SIDOR has approached, but never reached, one million tons per year. A program for expanding the plants has been geared to a production of 5 million tons by 1978 and 15 million tons per year by 1985. The regional development corporation in Zulia and the Andes has pretentious plans for additional siderurgical plants near Maracaibo and San Cristóbal respectively.

Petrochemicals have been a dismal item of development in Venezuela. A multitude of factors have contributed to the continuous postponement of truly productive operations. The total output of the State petrochemical institute (IVP) in 1974 was a little over half a million tons, of which 50% came from fertilizers and another 120,000 tons from phosphatic rocks. IVP's subsidiary Nitroven sold 236,000 tons of urea and 55,000 tons of ammonia in 1974. Two large plants for chloro-soda and olefins are nearing mechanical completion at the El Tablazo complex near Maracaibo. To regain two lost decades, the National Petrochemical Council, established in 1974, has been hard at work devising a five-year plan of action. It is expected that an organization similar to that of the nationalized oil industry — that is, a holding company to control and supervise the operating and technological support subsidiaries — will be proposed. Exports could be significant, but they would have to stay within the bounds imposed by the regional commercial association of the Andean Pact.

Mining had been a limited activity in Venezuela until

iron ore extraction started in 1950. All efforts by the government have been directed to the exportation and sale of more than 90% of the production abroad, following the example of the petroleum industry. By the end of 1974 the accumulated extraction of iron was 354 million tons. The production of aluminum is expected to increase to 400,000 tons per year by 1977. Both gold and diamond mining are to be improved with a better organization of the industry, while the promising deposit of nickel at Loma de Hierro is scheduled for development by a mixed-capital corporation.

Agricultural improvement programs are to be initiated in several regions: in the south, for example, plans for the control of floods will go beyond the present research stage and allow the actual irrigation of half a million hectares (1.2 million acres), while a national program of ponds for the collection of rain water will start in numerous sites. The government has also promised to give particular attention to housing, road construction, the development of medium-sized and small industries, education, and railroad expansion.

The guidelines set by the government on matters relating to energy resources have only been of a general nature, and they have been expressed in confusing terminology. The outline of a national energy policy will, of course, serve as framework for a national policy on petroleum, the most valuable resource of Venezuela today. In any case, Venezuela will need to program the use by the country and for the country of all her energy resources: hydraulic, coal, oil, and gas; to determine the reserves of liquid and gaseous hydrocarbons; and to set bounds to encourage the development and treatment of hydrocarbon resources other than oil and gas, particularly the conditions for exploration and exploitation in the Orinoco Petroliferous Belt.

Messages of the President to the National Congress have stressed the need to regulate the usage of petroleum as part of a sound conservation policy and to reduce by compulsion

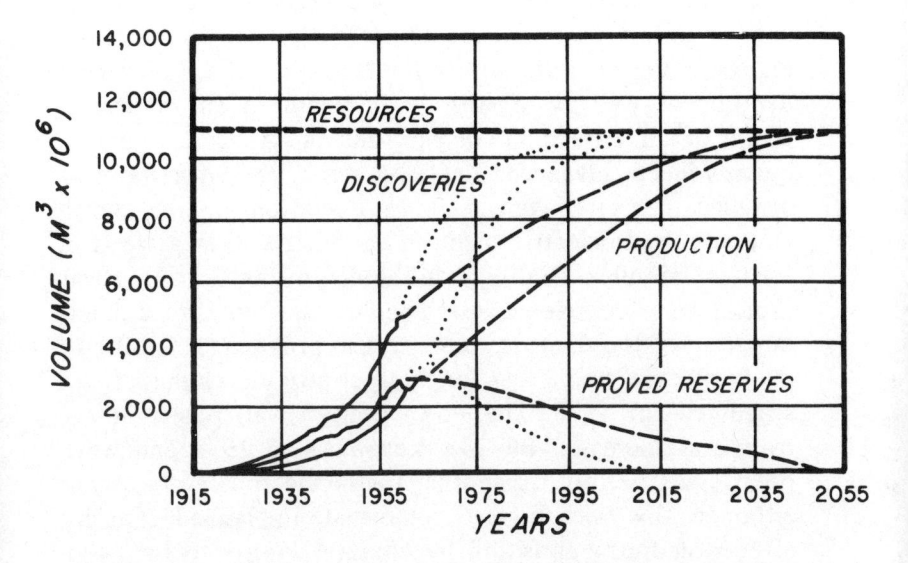

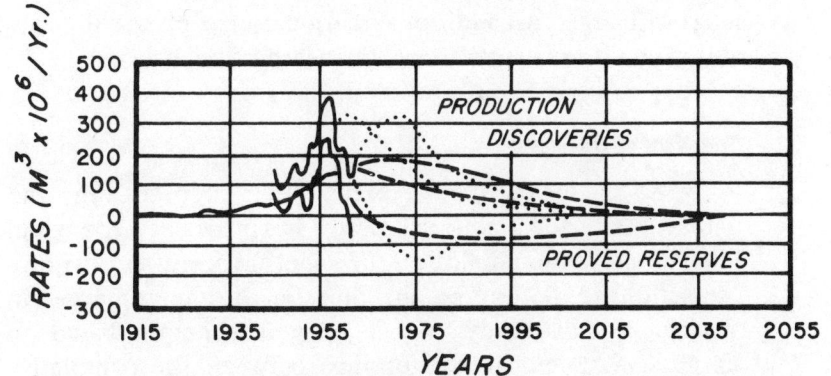

Figure 6. Conditioned evolution of conventional petroleum resources in the traditional basins

the production of oil and gas. Bold plans for exploration and research in the Orinoco belt have been of particular interest to the government, and energy resources other than oil products or gas are preferred for domestic electricity generation. Plans for the exploitation of the Naricual and Guasare coal deposits as well as for the development of the hydraulic power of some rivers in Guayana and the Andes have consequently been advanced. In 1974 alone, 180 megawatts of installed capacity were put in operation in the Santo Domingo hydroelectric plant and another 440 megawatts in the Guri complex. Hydrographic studies of the Uribante River project were completed and a geological survey for a determination of the dam site there was in progress. A feasibility study of the Caura River for hydroelectric development was scheduled for 1975. Thermoelectricity (coal) power, moreover, was increased by 243 megawatts in 1974 and work progressed speedily on another thermoelectric central plant, although this was reduced somewhat in planned capacity after strenuous opposition by conservationists to two 400-megawatt units. An additional thermoelectric plant will probably be built at Guanta to use the nearby Naricual coal.

Non-Renewable Resources

The evolution of the exploitation of petroleum and natural gas in the traditional basins has progressed enough in time to allow the application of scientific measures of future projection to determine the duration of the resources in Venezuela. This study uses an integral technique based on simple mathematical relationships between the cumulative production, the proved reserves, and the cumulative discoveries, with their time derivatives, the rate of production, the rate of increase of proved reserves, and the rate of discoveries. The logistic curves obtained represent the theoretical evolution of the natural hydrocarbon system. A more realis-

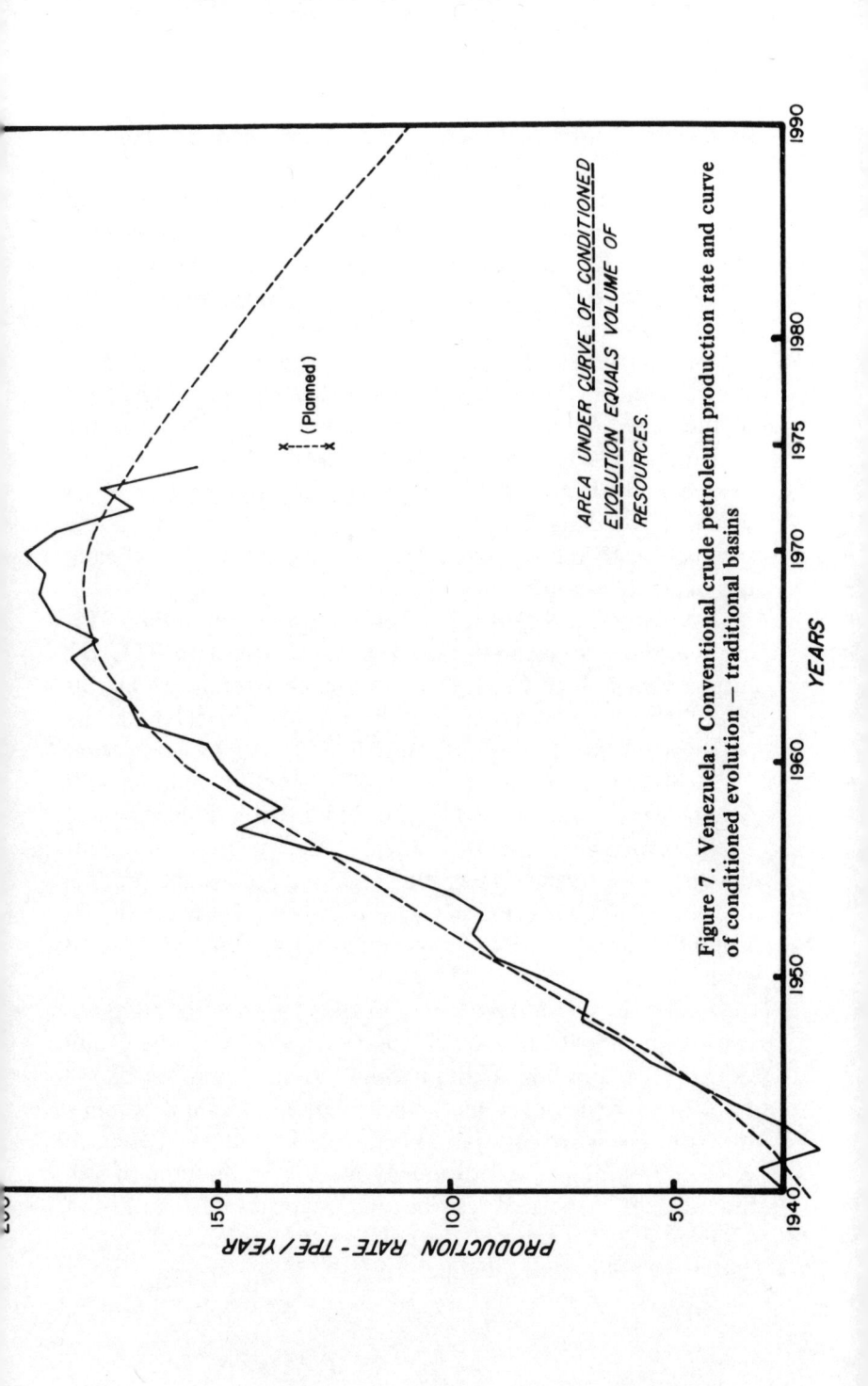

Figure 7. Venezuela: Conventional crude petroleum production rate and curve of conditioned evolution — traditional basins

tic development could be produced if one were to take into consideration the various limitations that influence future behaviour, such as government regulations which relate to known national objectives or the feasibility of reaching goals beyond the capacities of existing plant and equipment.

The rate of production curve circumscribes an area which represents the volume of the resources, and the rate of production slowly declines after passing a maximum, if there is no increment in the magnitude of the resources. The peak in the curve for the rate of production of petroleum in the traditional basins occurs in 1969 at 200 million cubic meters per year (180 million TPE per year; 1.3 billion barrels per year). The actual data shows that from 1965 to 1973 the production of oil was above the normal capacity for efficient use of the reservoirs.

A reduction in the rate of production to 90 million TPE per year would mean the saving of 125 million TPE for future years. Were the rate of production stabilized at this level, the curve of actual output would intersect with the curve of resource growth during 1994. In the 15-year period 1980-94, an additional volume of some 260 million TPE would have been preserved. The 315 million TPE set aside could supplement the theoretical deficit in production for the following two decades, thus assuring a constant production of 90 million TPE per year of conventional petroleum from the traditional basins for some 40 years from 1980 to year 2020.

Gas can be produced only in association with the recovery of crude petroleum. The curves for depicting the evolution of the duration of the natural gas extracted out of the traditional basins of Venezuela cannot be a simple summation of associated or free gas potentials, but must depend upon development conditioned by the production of oil. Should non-associated gas become significant in terms of total outputs, of course, the evolution curves for both hydrocarbons would show a distinct variance.

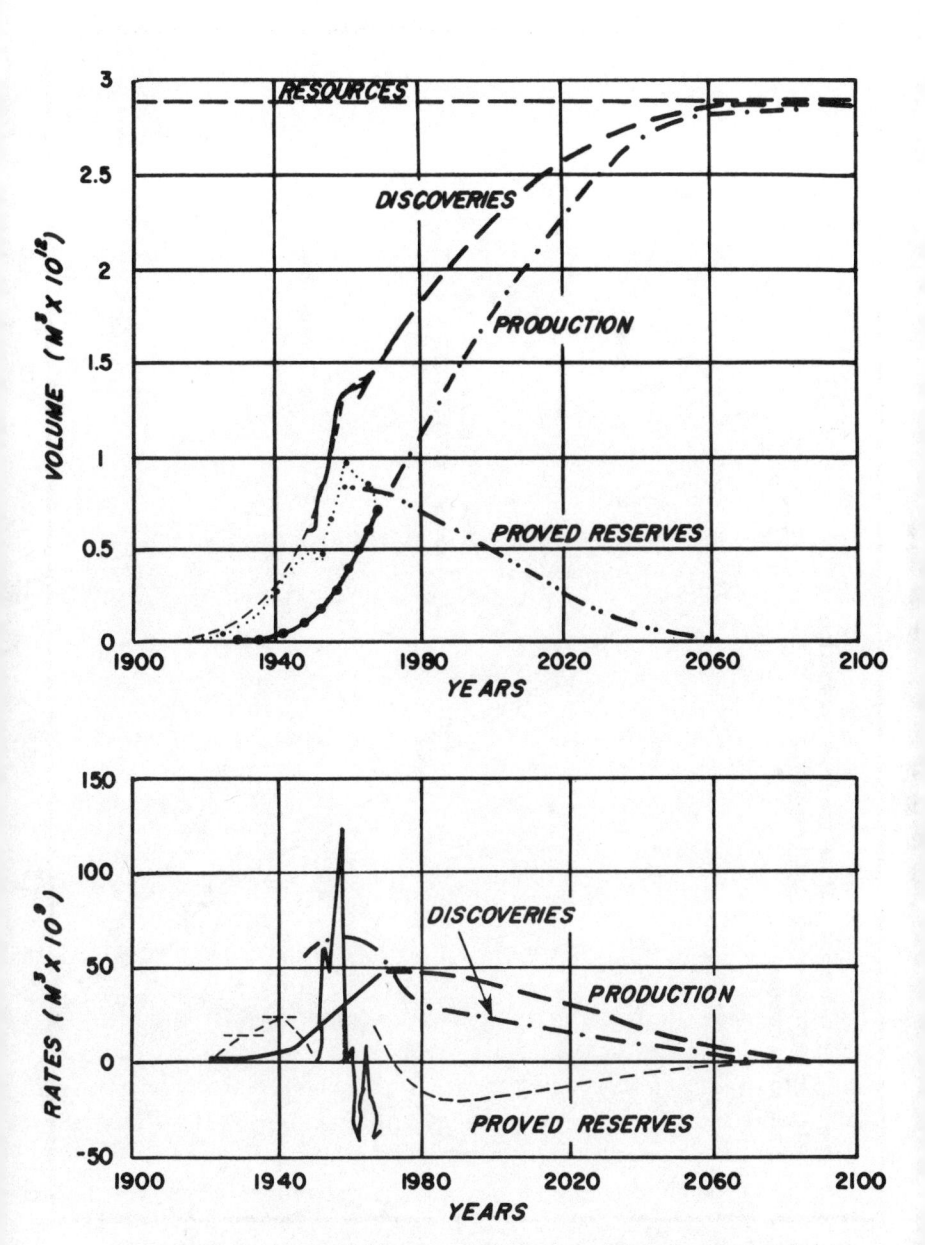

Figure 8. Conditioned evolution of natural gas resources in the traditional basins

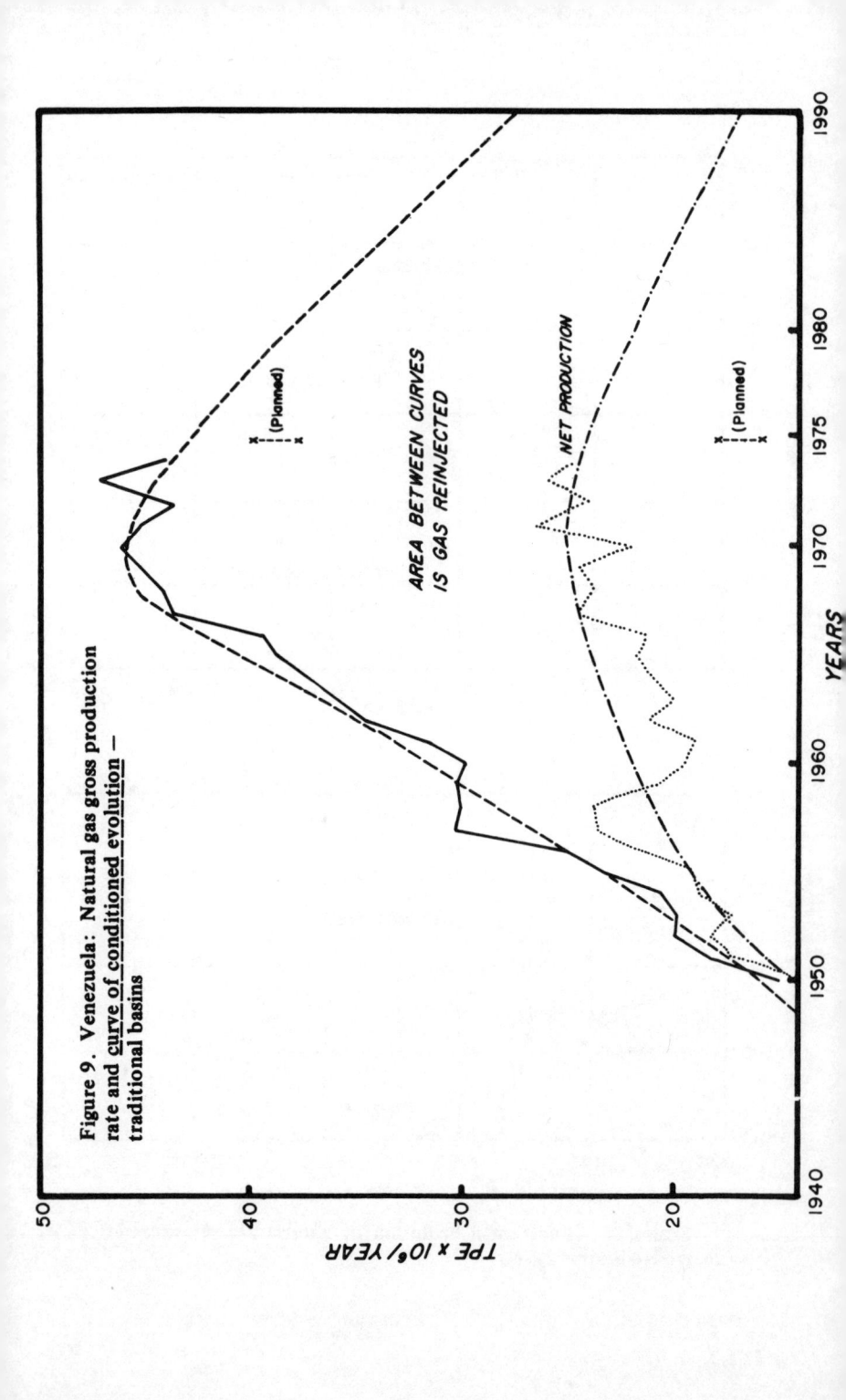

Figure 9. Venezuela: Natural gas gross production rate and curve of conditioned evolution — traditional basins

The maximum theoretical rate of gross production in the conditioned evolution occurred in 1969 at 46 million TPE. The curve is noticeably skewed, as the impact of conservation measures is expected to influence the down-slope evolution. The curve of net production shows not so steep a growth, as it is composed of a rather stable element — the amount of gas used — and the quantity flared or vented to the atmosphere. The area between the curves of gross and net production measures the volume of natural gas reinjected to the oil reservoirs.

Recommendations for a Venezuelan Energy Policy

Consideration of the resources of petroleum in the traditional basins must be first in formulating any energy policy for Venezuela. At 1974 prices the country can afford a substantial reduction in the volume of crude oil allocated for export.

Production should be reduced gradually so that by 1980 it would be 90 million TPE per year (in the metric system, 100 million cubic meters per year; 629 million barrels per year, or 1.7 million barrels per day). Since the volume of internal consumption is estimated at 10 million TPE per year for 1980, the quantity left for export would be 80 million TPE.

Next, there is the problem of the differential depletion of the crude oil proved reserves by gravity ranges. Petroleum of more than 0.923 grams per cubic centimeter gravity (22° API) constitutes 44 percent of the total reserves or 874 million TPE (6.1 billion barrels). Crude oil of medium gravity — 0.923 to 0.823 (30° API) — makes up about 35% of the reserves or 701 million TPE (4.9 billion barrels). The lighter crudes of gravity over 0.873 comprise about 2.1% of the total or 422 million TPE (2.9 billion barrels). It should be noted that the percentages of production by gravity ranges have not followed the percentages of reserves. More than half of the production has consisted of medium gravity

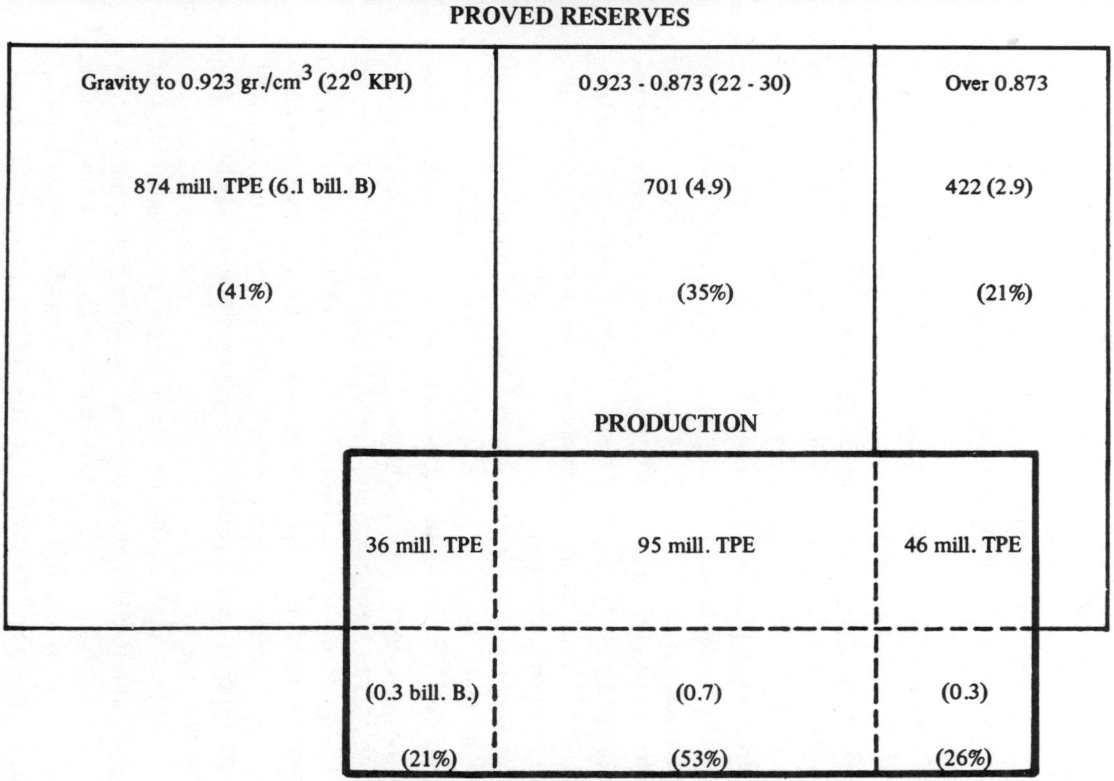

PROVED RESERVES

Gravity to 0.923 gr./cm^3 (22° KPI)	0.923 - 0.873 (22 - 30)	Over 0.873
874 mill. TPE (6.1 bill. B)	701 (4.9)	422 (2.9)
(41%)	(35%)	(21%)

PRODUCTION

36 mill. TPE	95 mill. TPE	46 mill. TPE
(0.3 bill. B.)	(0.7)	(0.3)
(21%)	(53%)	(26%)

Figure 10. Venezuela: Depletion of proved reserves by petroleum gravity ranges
(Source: Report of the Presidential Mission on Nationalization.)

crude oil and more than one-quarter of it has been light crudes. On the other hand, the production of the heavy oils has only been about one-fifth of the total. In other words, the rate of withdrawal of medium gravity petroleum has been three times higher than that of heavy oil, and the corresponding rate for lighter crudes has been two and one-half higher.

Since there is a disproportionate production of the various gravity ranges of crude petroleum with respect to their proved reserves, there should be suitable adjustments in the total output as it is being reduced. Such adjustments can be made by regulating domestic comsumption, international marketing, and refinery operations.

First, domestic consumption of energy in Venezuela, as indicated earlier, has been increasing at a very high rate, but it has depended upon only a few resources. Expensive petroleum and natural gas have been utilized to generate electricity, and high octane gasoline has been spent mainly for personal transportation.

Second, the offshore market for Venezuelan crudes and products has been limited, notwithstanding the many destinations reported by outgoing tankers. In fact, three-fourths of all exports have been going directly to or from island refineries in the Caribbean and the Atlantic to North America. The enforcement of an overall policy to reduce the volume of exports could also serve the purpose of changing its composition in at least two ways: substituting heavy for medium and light crudes, and exporting a larger share of "white" distillates.

Third, much could be done in the refining process of petroleum itself. The metal and sulphur content of Venezuelan crudes, as well as tars, has usually been considered a hindrance to the industry. On the contrary, proper treating could produce invaluable benefits for the product. Research on demetalization and desulfurization of Venezuelan ultra-heavy and very heavy oils should be of particular importance to the government in giving technological support to the industry. Moreover, new refinery processes at the present time can obtain higher proportions of gasoline, naphthas, and other light distillates. Very heavy residuums could be allotted primarily to electricity generation instead of diesel oil or gas oil. Asphaltenes can be processed for metal and metalloid extraction. It is noteworthy that Venezuelan heavy crude oils can advantageously produce heavy naphthas which, once converted into reformed gasoline, could be utilized as prime feedstock for production of the aromatics like benzene, toluene, and xilene.

It hardly seems advisable to increase refining capacity, which at the end of 1974 was in the order of 247,300 cubic meters per day (1.6 million barrels per day), or 83.4 million tons per year. Decreases in the production rate of oil should lead to a thorough study of refinery operations in Venezuela, with a view towards elimination of some of the smaller plants and increasing industry sophistication in the refining of diverse products. Total refining capacity of the country might be stabilized at about 60 million tons per year (1.2 million barrels per day).

One of the sensitive areas of operation for the nationalized industry will be the refining complex that is composed of the two refineries on the Paraguaná peninsula at Cardón and Amuay in Venezuela, and the two refineries that are located in the Dutch Antilles in Curaçao and Aruba.

Natural Gas

Natural gas produced in association with oil in the traditional Venezuelan basins should no longer be utilized to increase the capacity of thermoelectrical plants after 1975, nor should natural gas be used for international marketing in its liquefied form. By 1980 natural gas should not provide more than half the energy consumed in the country as it did after 1959. It should be noted that the volume of natural gas used in 1973 alone by the petrochemical industry was but 0.3 million TPE!

Although the gas-to-oil ratio (GOR) normally increases with time as production advances, there has been a noticeable and disquieting rise in the ratio. From 199 cubic meters of gas per cubic meter of petroleum (1,117 cubic feet per barrel) in 1963, the ratio reached 268 cubic meters per cubic meter (1,503 cubic feet per barrel) in 1974. The rate of growth of the gas-oil ratio, 4 cubic meters per cubic meter per year (22 cubic feet per barrel per year) during the period from 1960 to 1971, quadrupled to 15 cubic meters per cubic meter per year (84 cubic feet per barrel per year) for the period 1972-74. This rate of growth should slacken as a response to the associated gas conservation measures implemented since April 1974 and respond to the reductions in the production of petroleum from the traditional basins.

A geological evaluation of the non-associated national gas should also be undertaken, with the Maturín and Maracaibo basins as the principal targets of study, as well as the deep formations of the Falcón basin as a secondary objective, and the Barinas basin with a lower priority. After 1985 it might be helpful to start an exploratory drilling program to find free natural gas in the traditional basins. It must be remembered that the steel, aluminum, and other mineral industries in Guayana, Zulia, and the Andes will require after 1980 important volumes of natural gas for their industrial uses, although in 1974 they only used 0.7 million TPE. In any event, a national pricing policy for natural gas will contribute effectively to a clearer definition of the markets and the alternative production needs.

New Areas for Resources

To proceed judiciously with the exploration of the new

areas, all boundary problems between Venezuela and adjacent states will need to be resolved. There should be no undivided waters on the continental platform and its slope. In this respect, it should be stressed that the 1958 Geneva Convention on the Continental Shelf was not a mandate requiring adjacent states to use the so-called equidistance principle for the delimitation of shelf areas, nor has international custom subsequent to the Convention made such a method a rule of law or a legal obligation.

The delimitation of undivided submarine waters with neighbouring states will be essential to permit appropriate exploration programs. In the extreme east, there is one problem inherited from the United Kingdom where the boundary with Guyana is temporarily "frozen." In the extreme west protracted negotiations have been held with Colombia. The Netherlands has requested discussions on the Aruba to Bonaire boundaries. While the Venezuela-United Kingdom international agreement of 1942, which partitioned the Gulf of Paria, was the first of its kind, it unfortunately did not dispose of many questions, and now there must be an accord between Venezuela and Trinidad-Tobago to regulate the continuation of the boundary lines. Another area for delimitation lies between Grenada and Venezuela. One legal theory has been advanced that in the case of an inward curving or recessed coastline, the State might create a coastal front or façade, which in essence will be a new baseline for delimitation in the form of a straight line joining the ends. It has also been suggested that the Federal Executive declare as internal waters that portion of the Caribbean Sea enclosed between the Venezuelan insular dependencies of the Lesser Antilles and the northern coast.

All the new areas of the submerged Venezuelan continent have been explored by geophysical methods. Apart from the La Vela Embayment basin, an initial effort of exploration drilling as indicated by the interpretation of the seismic and other surveys would require the completion of

315 wildcats in all areas of the Caribbean and Atlantic shelves. This would provide one control point for about every 400 square kilometers (155 square miles) of new basin. It is estimated that six rigs working continuously during five years might complete the program once locations had been chosen and auxiliary facilities readied. An exhaustive evaluation of the region would require further testing of the prospective areas, with an initial effort of at least one well down to the basement or 7,000 meters (22,965 feet), whichever is less deep, per each 10 square kilometers (4 square miles), say, 1,000 wells. The cost of such exploration would probably amount to about $18,000 million in 1972 currency values.

Until there is exploratory drilling and discoveries of hydrocarbon accumulations, and a determination of the petrophysics and fluid characteristics, it is hardly possible to prescribe the best courses for policy. One alternative for the future, of course, would be the substitution of production of petroleum from the new areas for the petroleum now taken from the traditional basins.

Tar Sands

Geophysical surveys have been completed in three-fourths of the Orinoco belt with its tar sands. Of a total of 12,350 kilometers (7,720 miles) to be surveyed, 9,500 kilometers (5,940 miles) had been finished by year-end 1974 in the eastern and central areas. Following three years of seismic work, 16 stratigraphic holes were drilled in the area northwest of Ciudad Bolívar during 1973. In 1974, 31 holes were completed in the eastern end of the belt, so that the extent of the Cerro Negro and Hamaca-Santa Clara areas could be outlined in some detail. It was found that the saturation of non-conventional oil extended southward closer to the left bank of the Orinoco than originally estimated. The overall thickness of net oil sands in Hamaca was found to be con-

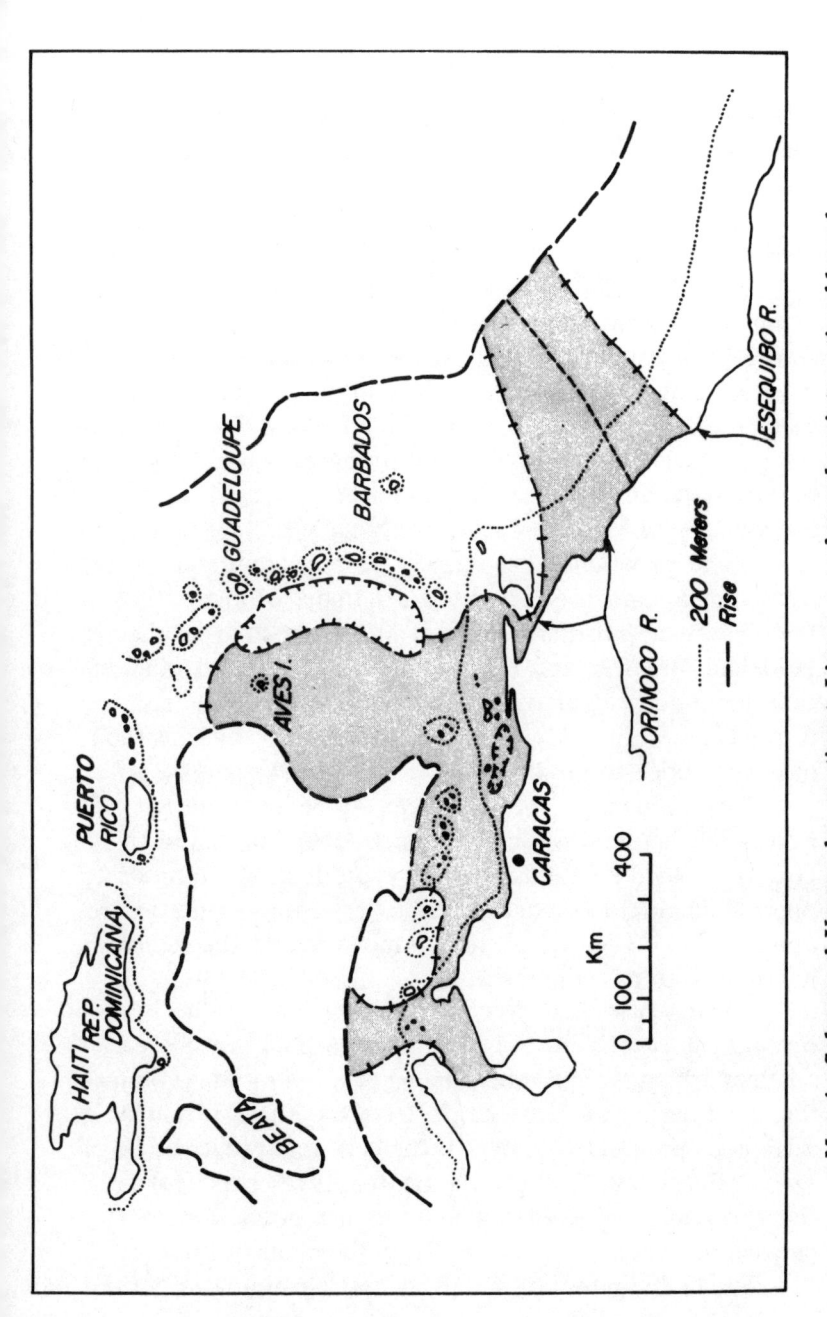

Map 4. Submerged Venezuelan continent. Lines +++ show where international boundaries have to be negotiated.

siderably larger than anticipated and the gravity of the hydrocarbons lighter than foreseen, 1.00 grams per cubic centimeter or very near 1.00 (10° API).

The stratigraphic holes program, which calls for the completion of 60 locations during 1975, should be speeded up. By early 1975 two wells had been drilled, cased, and completed, using funds of the Research Institute, in order to start a program of field testing of various primary production methods and to begin the investigation of secondary recovery techniques. It was the decision of the Federal Executive that the geological and petrophysical information obtained should be processed and analysed by laboratories and other units of the Ministry of Mines and Hydrocarbons.

Some experience has already been accumulated on the development and production of a number of giant fields in the undefined northern limit of the Orinoco belt, that is, Morichal, Melones, and Jobo-Pilón, where an overlaying section of conventional oil-bearing sands and an underlaying distinct series of beds saturated with "belt" hydrocarbons have been open to production.

Certain parameters will have to be determined with exactitude in the Orinoco belt, such as the minimum thickness of individual sands, to allow production methods to operate adequately and to permit the critical saturation required for the very viscous oil to move out of the reservoirs rather than to the connate water.

In any case, the eventual development of the hydrocarbons in the Orinoco belt should not be considered in schemes which would entail the exportation of large volumes for the international market. Of course, there would be a certain geopolitical advantage if the belt were proven to be of extraordinary value to the nation for its reserves. However, the recommended policy would be the extraction of this petroleum only for utilization within the country itself.

The high content of metals such as vanadium, nickel and

chromium, and of sulphur in the belt hydrocarbons should be analysed and considered in conjunction with the occurrence of another long and rich belt across the Orinoco river in the Guayana province. Estimates of the reserves of iron ores in the eastern and central portions of this belt have been in the order of 1,850 million tons, of which some 400 million tons lie near San Isidro, 260 million tons at María Luisa, and 230 million tons at Los Barrancos. The national reserves of María Luisa have lower grade ores, but they still reach almost 55% in metal content. The largest iron deposit in Guayana today is at Cerro Bolívar, exploited since 1954, with 300 million tons of remaining reserves. The combination of the occurrence of geographically close belts of such minerals and hydrocarbons offers an excellent opportunity to the country. Venezuela could then become a producer of high stress steels and finished products.

The cost of developing a daily capacity of production of synthetic crude and other materials in the Orinoco belt, however, is very high and can increase in an unpredictable way. The latest estimate indicates that to obtain one cubic meter of capacity will require an investment of $57,100 ($9,085 per barrel). An industrial plant with 10,000 cubic meters per day capacity (62,900 barrels per day) would thus cost some $570 million. Finally, it is possible that fields of conventional petroleum of heavy gravity could be found within an extension of the Orinoco belt, for geologically similar producing areas have been exploited successfully since the early nineteen-sixties in a number of elongated, east-west traps against regional faults trending parallel to the axis of the basin.

Coal

To use the coal deposits of Venezuela as an alternative for electric generation in setting national energy policy will require the quantification of all inferred reserves, bearing in mind that 1,400 tons of Guasare bituminous coal could provide a thermoelectric plant with 4.5 million kilowatt-hours of work daily.

It may be assumed that coal will contribute effectively to the energy consumption of the country only after the mid-nineteen-eighties. It is possible that native coal could be processed to furnish metallurgical coke to the steel industry in such a way that gases of low calorific content could be utilized in electricity generation. Venezuelan coals are unusually rich in vanadium and sulphur. Such coal, often looked upon as handicapped, might be of great importance for the development of carbochemistry in the country.

Hydraulic Resources

The modest energy obtained so far from hydraulic re-

TABLE VII

VENEZUELA: ELECTRICITY GENERATION
(By 5-year periods, 1975-2000)
(Thousand tons of petroleum equivalent)

	Hydroelectricity	Other	Total
1975-1979	31	15	46
1980-1984	61	19	80
1985-1989	97	24	122
1990-1994	146	36	182
1995-1999	226	56	282
(2000)	56	14	70

Source: Tellería (1975); author's estimates, 1995-1999 and 2000.

sources in Venezuela makes them a key factor in the formulation of an integral energy policy. The objective should be to obtain about 80% of the demand for electricity from water power by the year 1980. Thermoelectric plants in operation or advanced planning (Central region) should be able to generate the balance of electricity demand. In terms of energy, the hydraulic resources of the Caroní River alone are equal to 85 million megawatt-hours; those of rivers in the Andes, 20 million megawatt-hours; and another 20 million megawatt-hours can be obtained from the Caura River. The total energy available and usable will probably exceed 150 million megawatt-hours. It is therefore feasible to expect that from 1980 to the end of the century, hydraulic energy resources could generate adequately all the electricity required by the country.

Nuclear Energy

The discovery of abundant or relatively significant reserves of radioactive minerals would be helpful to Venezuela's energy outlook. Nuclear plants using thorium as a fuel are of the high-termperature, gas-cooled type. A shift to uranium would only require a different reactor. The construction of second-generation nuclear plants, that is, the breeder reactors, would mean that Venezuela would be completely dependent on those countries which could provide the enriched uranium. Technological capability in Venezuela to handle other nuclear power plants such as fusion plants, lies beyond present or near-term capabilities of the nation. Nevertheless, the future lies with nuclear energy and its importance over time is bound to grow. At present Venezuela does not have the technological capacity for entering the nuclear energy field. It would be highly advisable that Venezuela's energy policy include efforts to acquire ample and precise knowledge about all forms of atomic power.

Other Resources

Geothermal, solar, and eolic resources of energy should be the subject of detailed evaluation in Venezuela as soon as possible. At the same time, it would be necessary and particularly useful for Venezuelans to keep abreast and informed of the state of the art as a wealth of data and experience is collected around the world, and as more experimental plants begin to enter the commercial stage. Finally, although hydrogen is not an energy resource, it might very well be an important energy agent in the future, and could provide the necessary link between primary sources and expanding consumption. A hydrogen energy system would not entail any loss of Venezuelan self-sufficiency, which is an important policy consideration, but would certainly require mastery of the technology for production, transportation, storage, and usage of this abundant element of nature.

Observations and Conclusions

Venezuela is a country rich in energy resources and, like many other countries, it has been wasteful. An ever-greater use of electricity has been encouraged and a virtually unlimited utilization of gasoline has been stimulated. Perhaps about 30% of all the electricity consumed in Venezuela and 20% of the fuels burned could be regarded as wasteful. The cost of gasoline in the domestic market has been very low, with the price of 78-octane gasoline fixed by government regulation since 1945 at B^S 0.10 per liter or $0.09 per gallon. Natural gas has been sold internally at values unrelated to its real worth. It could be said that Venezuela has pursued in recent years a program for promotion of the waste of energy.

The loudest voices condemning this situation were heard in the Commission on Energy in the First National Congress of Science and Technology held in Caracas early in July 1975. The Commission recommended that natural gas should be valued at levels corresponding to the actual substitution price of other forms of energy-producing substances and that there should be an immediate reorganization of the internal market in order to slow or stop the acceleration in the consumption of energy. This would require a restriction in gasoline consumption and perhaps more realistic prices. It was recommended that government agencies start discussions with public authorities and private institutions immediately on ways of achieving substantial savings of energy.

In April 1974 the Venezuelan government had already ordered a reduction of petroleum production from the traditional basins of the country. Output for 1975 has been estimated at 145 million TPE, but may be as low as 130 million TPE. Production in 1976 is not expected to exceed 120 million TPE and that figure has been used for national budgeting purposes. The maximum efficient rate of petroleum production, according to the Technical Office of the Ministry of Mines and Hydrocarbons, would be 180 million TPE per year. Although it would be possible to decrease the rate of extraction to even lower levels, international commitments and a consideration of economic-social conditions within Venezuela have deterred the government from taking extreme measures. For years to come, it is anticipated that significant volumes of crude petroleum will continue to be exported by Venezuela to the international markets.

Substitution of the production of light and medium crudes by heavy oil, even by "tar belt" non-conventional petroleum, has not gone beyond the talking stage in the government. This objective would be associated with a change in refinery patterns, so that the average yield of processing operations would be modified to obtain fewer residual and heavy derivates and more light distillates. At the same time, the new refinery model would permit the internal market to be served adequately with the products required.

The government seems interested in the promotion of extractive operations in a string of fields of very heavy conventional petroleum that occur close to or within the northern fringes of the bituminous belt in the Maturín basin. At a meeting of the Organization of Latin American State oil companies, an official of the Ministry of Mines and Hydrocarbons announced that those reservoirs, improperly included in the Tar Belt, could be producing 16 million TPE in the year 1981 and 26 million TPE during 1985. In this connection, a refinery with an 8 million ton per year capacity has been planned for a site near Puerto Ordaz.

Moreover, in July 1975 the First National Congress of Science and Technology recommended with respect to the non-conventional Orinoco Petroliferous Belt that, first, an immediate and intensive effort be undertaken by all capable Venezuelan sectors to complete the geological evaluation, determine the extraction mechanisms, and test processing systems for possible use. This monumental task would be undertaken by Venezuelans, with limited foreign assistance, and might require 15 years to complete. Second, at that future date, with an exact knowledge of the geopolitical worth of the accumulation, the government would be able to decide how to proceed into the future. It should be mentioned that, at current prices, the development of one cubic meter of daily capacity of the non-conventional petroleum will require the investment of B^{S}225,000 ($8,360 per barrel per day); in other words, to have in operation a modest plant processing 22,260 cubic meters per day (140,000 barrels per day) might require an investment of B^{S}5,000 million ($1.2 billion).

Apart from the reduction of oil output, in no other aspect of the petroleum industry has government policy been more firmly or clearly expressed than in the regulation of natural gas. Areas of high production of associated gas have been carefully identified and ordered to be shut-in. Notwithstanding all efforts over the years to conserve valuable hydrocarbons, the volume of gas flared or vented into the atmosphere during the first quarter of 1974 amounted to 38 million cubic meters a day (1.1 million cubic feet) or about 27% of the gross production. This useless expenditure of gas had been reduced by 60% by the first quarter of 1975, that is, 15 million cubic meters per day (425,000 cubic feet) flared or vented, or about 13% of the total production. It should be noted that the volume of natural gas conserved by injection into reservoirs changed only slightly from 63 million cubic meters (1.8 million cubic feet) in the first quarter of 1974 to 60 million cubic meters (1.7 million cubic feet) in the first quarter of 1975.

The Ministry of Mines and Hydrocarbons has taken a strong position against making natural gas available to new projects for the generation of electricity. For example, the addition of 800 megawatts of capacity in the Central region of Venezuela by 1980 in thermal plants will be made possible by burning residual fuels, not natural gas. Moreover, work underway will increase the power available from the Guri or Raul Leoni dam to 6,970 megawatts by 1978. The Caroní River thus will be able to provide 85×10^{12} kilowatt-hours of work to the national interconnected grid. While this program seems ambitious enough to many people directly involved with energy matters, others who promote the rapid development of many rivers find it parsimonious, and would prefer accelerating the use of power from the Caura River.

Concurrent with this exploitation of hydroelectric energy, Venezuelan development corporations have promoted radical changes in industry and agriculture on a regional scale. One town, which today has 150,000 inhabitants, was started from scratch at the confluence of the Caroní and Orinoco Rivers, where its convenient location provided work in the steel industry and adequate facilities. State development of the corporations has promoted agricultural projects, including the planting of millions of pine trees, and advanced both farming and fishing. Other hydroelectric projects, like that of the Caura River, suggest additional large-scale industrial and agricultural developments throughout Venezuela.

In the past, the low prices assigned to hydroelectric power generation have acted as a kind of subsidy for certain heavy industries, particularly in Guayana. Following the nationalization of the iron industry on 1 January 1975, the heavy industry mixed companies that had been constituted for aluminum processing and production had to rearrange their corporate structure so that 80% of the capital would be Venezuelan. This will probably be a model for all future joint ventures, and it clearly places a greater responsibility on the Venezuelan government for their efficient operation with higher priced energy.

Under present plans in Venezuela the exploitation of coal will be handled by several regional corporations; many regard this as a negative proposal, for diversification of standards and methods of exploitation could result in a loss of efficiency, with no possibility of integrating policies in this field. Meanwhile, geological prospecting for radioactive minerals continues at a good pace and will probably cover all the most promising territory by 1980. The abundance of monetary reserves due to the overseas marketing of Venezuelan crude oil and products has stimulated a constant temptation to acquire nuclear plants for the generation of electricity. Such plants would most likely be the high-temperature, gas-cooled type, which would use as fuel the minerals already found in the Impacto area of southeast Venezuela.

The increase of capacity to generate electricity and the per capita consumption of electricity have been used as indices to indicate national progress and, of course, have benefited company growth. People have been encouraged to use and abuse electricity. Similarly, there is an ambition, stemming from pride, in many developing countries to install nuclear power plants, but the entrance of Venezuela into the field of nuclear-generated electricity would mean a great dependence upon those developed countries capable of furnishing the technology. When the time comes for the construction of breeder reactors or even passing on to fusion power directly, that reliance upon external sources would be further increased. Timid advances, therefore, have already been made to acquire and substitute energy-generating technologies which could be both beneficial to the country and less dependent upon foreign sources. Solar energy has been the subject of study by a task force set up in the State electricity distribution company CADAFE, while universities and individuals have been analyzing hydrogen as an energy agent, assessing the production and handling of this element within the Venezuelan economic system with local technology.

In the final analysis the economy of Venezuela will depend for some time to come upon its petroleum resources. In the first half of 1975 the discussion of the law which reserved to the State all the operations in the industry and commerce of hydrocarbons has proceeded with a noisy debate of an intensely political nature. Controversy centered around the clause in the new law that allowed the Federal Executive to form associations in the industry with private companies. Some areas mentioned for possible operation by mixed companies have been the transportation by tanker of crude petroleum or products; participation in refineries, preferably in the countries to which substantial amounts of Venezuelan crudes are exported or where new technologies are in an advanced state of research; petroleum extraction or refining in countries of the Andean Pact, the Latin American Free Trade Association, or OPEC; and the commercial exploitation of very heavy petroleums with the view of substituting production of lighter crudes in the traditional basins, and the refining of heavy crudes, including demetalization and desulphuration in Venezuelan operations. The large multinational oil corporations expect that although many structural changes in the Venezuelan oil industry will be made as a result of the nationalization process in progress in 1975, there will still be some role for them in providing services, technical support, and other assistance to the nationalized industry.

In sum, much valuable time has been lost in developing and enforcing an integral national energy policy in Venezuela. The short-term prospect is that decisions will be taken and programs will be developed in a haphazard manner, as in the past. The recent reorganization of the National Energy Council was a simple shake-up of membership, softening rather than sharpening its voice; and worst of all, the Council remains an advisory group. The only achievement of interest to emerge from the fourth meeting of the Council was the creation of a Coordinating Committee, formed by the managers of the main State enterprises handling energy. The First Congress for Science and Technology in 1975 again urged consideration of establishing an executive organ in the central administration of the Venezuelan government to plan and execute an energy policy, beginning with the creation of a Ministry of Energy, but the prospect is that such a bold step will not be taken this year — or the next.

Selected References

Banco Central de Venezuela. *La economía venezolana en los últimos treinta años.* Caracas, 1971.

Comisión del Plan Nacional de Energía Eléctrica. *Propuesta de Plan.* 8 vol., Caracas, Jan. 1974.

Comisión Presidencial de la Reversión Petrolera. *Informe.* Caracas, Nov. 1974.

Corporación Venezolana del Petróleo. *Annual Reports.* Caracas.

CVG – EDELCA. *Annual Reports,* Caracas.

Martínez, Aníbal R. *Chronology of Venezuelan Oil.* Allen & Unwin, London, 1969.

Martínez, Aníbal R. *Una política energética.* Edreca. ed., Caracas, 1974

Matheus, Alexis. *La electricidad y la energía. El caso de Venezuela.* XXXI Asamb. Fedecamaras, Margarita, Mayo, 1975.

Méndez-Arocha, A. *Bases para una política energética venezolana.* Ed. Banco Central, Caracas, 1975.

Ministerio de Minas e Hidrocarburos. *Léxico estratigráfico de Venezuela.* Ed. Sucre, Caracas, 1970.

Ministerio de Minas e Hidrocarburos. *Petróleo y otros datos estadísticos – 1973.* Caracas, 1974.

Ministerio de Minas e Hidrocarburos. *Memoria – 1973.* Caracas, 1974.

Nogueira, A. et al. *Informe de la primera etapa de estudio de la cuenca carbonífera del Zulia.* Corpozulia, Maracaibo, 1974.

Pérez, Carlos A. *Primer mensaje (del Presidente) al Congreso Nacional.* Caracas, 12 Marzo, 1975.

Pérez-Alfonzo, J. P. *Petróleo y dependencia,* Ed. Sintesis Dosmil, Caracas, 1971.

Tellería, Rodolfo. *Notas sobre el desarrollo futuro de la generación de electricidad en Venezuela.* Revista SVIP, Caracas, Dec. 1974.

Vázquez, Nelson G. *Política Energética.* Revista SVIP, Caracas, Dec. 1974.

Iran
Jahangir Amuzegar

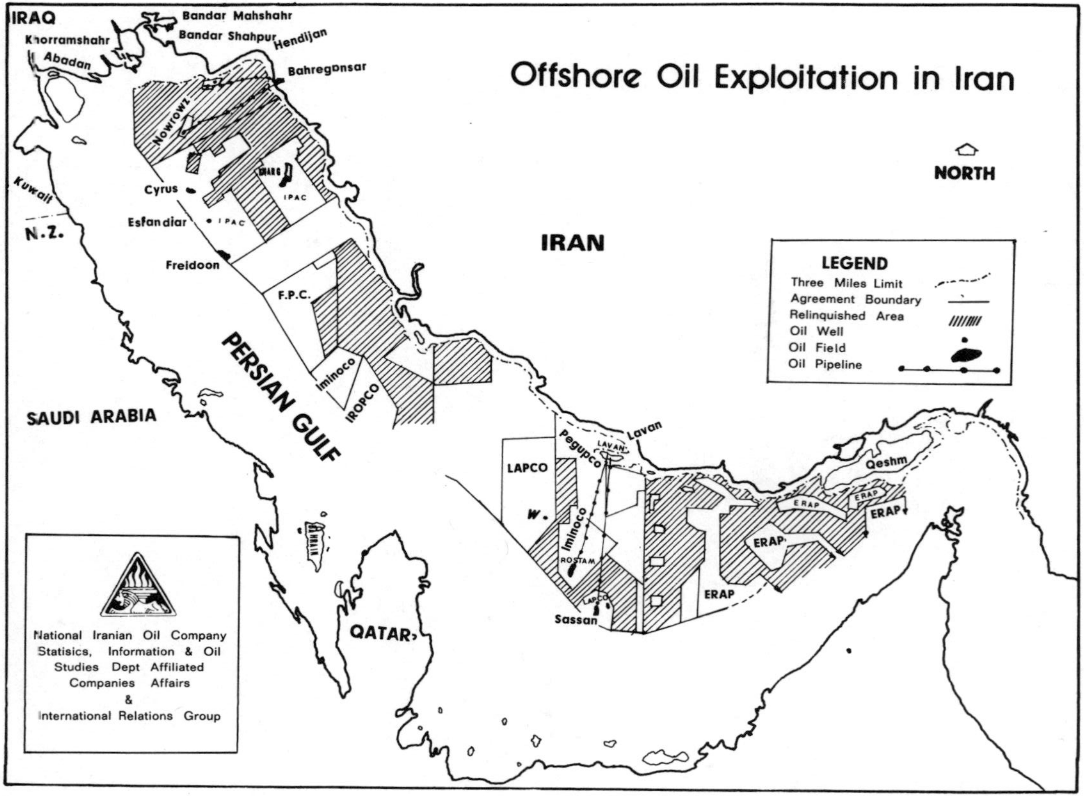
Offshore Oil Exploitation in Iran
NORTH
IRAN
LEGEND
Three Miles Limit
Agreement Boundary
Relinquished Area
Oil Well
Oil Field
Oil Pipeline
IRAQ
Khorramshahr
Abadan
Bandar Mahshahr
Bandar Shahpur
Hendijan
Bahregansar
Nowrowz
Cyrus
Esfandiar
IPAC
Freidoon
F.P.C.
Iminoco
IROPCO
Kuwait
N.Z.
SAUDI ARABIA
PERSIAN GULF
QATAR
LAPCO
Pegupco
LAVAN
Lavan
ROSTAM
Sassan
ERAP
Qeshm
National Iranian Oil Company
Statisics, Information & Oil
Studies Dept Affiliated
Companies Affairs
&
International Relations Group

INTRODUCTION

Iran's present energy policy, as enunciated by the Shahanshah and enacted by the Iranian parliament, is a broad-based national commitment to use different sources of energy in the direction of efficient exploitation and prudent conservation. This basic national objective corresponds to a new theory which is growing in popularity among experts on energy policy around the world. It suggests a rational separation between the sources and the uses of energy for a single purpose (e.g., gas, oil, wood, coal, sun, electric power, and geothermal water — all for heating or air conditioning). According to this theory, it would be far more efficient and intelligent to divide the various energy sources among alternative uses: nuclear fission and coal for steam-electric generation and hence lighting, certain transportation, and mechanical motors; natural gas and other non-fossil fuels — both conventional and exotic — for heating, air conditioning, and other residential or industrial purposes; and petroleum as a raw material base for nutritional, medicinal, petrochemical products, and certain forms of transport not amenable to other forms of energy.

Energy policy based upon such theory would be designed to avoid the irretrievably wasteful energy uses in the world today, and, by avoiding familiar past mistakes, set the stage for fulfilling the needs of the future.

To reach such a sophisticated orientation to energy problems and future policy, Iran has come a long way since 1908, when oil was first discovered. It is only against the backdrop of Iran's historical development that the present policy and its ramifications for the next decades can best be understood and appreciated. To this end, the historical development of individual policies with regard to oil, gas, electricity, and nuclear energy will be discussed in Part One of this study. The establishment of a national energy policy in Iran will be examined in Part Two, and Part Three will conclude with a description of agencies and organizations charged with the establishment and implementation of contemporary energy policy.

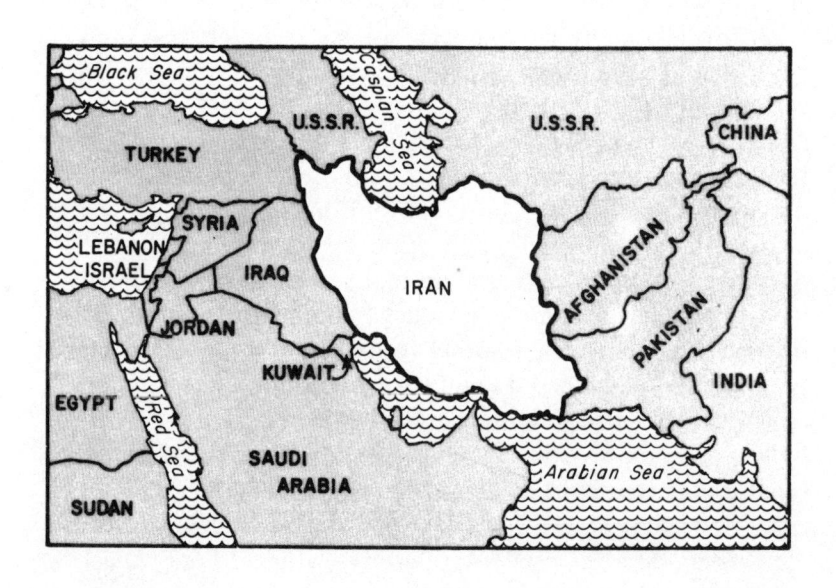

The Development of Individual Fuel Policies

Until the beginning of the post-World War II period when the Iranian government began to embark upon serious national planning, Iran's "energy policy" was focused mainly on oil and was largely unplanned. Even in the early five-year development plans after World War II, scant attention was paid to energy prospects and limitations as a single focus of policy considerations. The emergence of individual fuel policies in recent years marks a turning point.

Historically, before oil was discovered in commercial quantities and profitably exploited in Iran in 1908, the energy needs (heating and lighting) of the country were met largely by firewood, charcoal, and animal manure, and by imports of kerosene from Russia. Up to the mid-1890's, when the Russians maintained an export excise tax on refined products equal to their own domestic sales tax, crude oil was shipped in from Baku and crudely refined in the Caspian port of Enzelli (now Pahlavi) for sale inside Iran. After 1895, the Russian policy of increasing the domestic value-added of the exports led to the abolition of the excise tax, and a shift was immediately made in favor of exporting refined petroleum. As a result, a number of small refining establishments in Enzelli which were no longer able to compete with large Baku refineries were closed, and Iran became an exclusive market for Russian oil for several decades. The importation of refined kerosene and other oil products from Russia to Iran continued until the late 1920's, when the Soviet Union's increasing internal demand and the Anglo-Persian Oil Company's expanding sales network within the country made such trade unprofitable.

Up to the second quarter of the present century, Iran's on-going "energy policy" thus consisted chiefly of meeting relatively modest domestic consumption requirements for lighting, heating, and cooking partly through the use of local non-oil materials, while replacing imported kerosene with domestic production. With the advent of deliberate state industrialization early in the 1920's, oil and oil derivatives began to be used increasingly for energy. Internal oil consumption rose from a mere 3,000 metric tons in 1917 to 30,000 m/t in 1927.[1]

As a percentage of total production, however, local consumption always remained small — between three to four per cent. The aim of the authorities up to the time of nationalization in 1951 was: (a) to encourage increasing production and exports by the Anglo-Iranian Oil Company, and (b) to increase tax and royalty receipts from the foreign concessionnaires in order to meet domestic foreign exchange needs. In the period between the two world wars, also, the government policy was to encourage other foreign interests (particularly American) to invest in Iran's oil fields. The basic objective during this entire period was to use expanded oil revenues to finance Iran's development and defense needs.

During a brief period between 1944 and 1954, there was a turnabout in Government policy. Foreign oil concessions were banned, and national priority was placed on self-reliance in domestic oil development, living, if necessary, with an "oilless" economy. This short-lived policy was fundamentally altered after 1953. With regained strength and greater national self confidence, Iran opened the doors again to cooperation with Western interests under the banner of "positive nationalism." While maintaining the principle of oil nationalization (and keeping the ban on further oil concessions "in the old sense"), the Government expressed its willingness to enter into cooperative agreements with foreign oil groups: (a) to act as its "agents" or its "partners"; (b) to conduct detailed explorations and prospecting on the Government's behalf; and (c) to accept Iran's participation in international oil ventures both financially and managerially.[2]

It was also in the late 1950's that a more extensive oil policy encompassing not only petroleum production and export but also oil transportation (through national tanker fleet and pipelines), and downstream operations, as well as research and development, conservation, and oil substitution programs, became the focus of national policy. Yet a coordinated and comprehensive "energy policy" came into being only with the Fifth Development Plan (1973-1978). In the two previous plans, broad objectives and specific targets had been established for oil, gas, and electric power separately. But there was no overall "energy policy." As we shall see below, however, with new developments in the world oil supply and demand, the policy horizon was both broadened and better canvassed in the Fifth Plan. Parallel with this new detailed and comprehensive policy, the Government proceeded to establish a new Ministry of Energy to provide overall coordination among various agencies in charge of oil, gas, electric power, and nuclear energy.

In the following sections, the development of each fuel policy in Iran will be discussed separately.

PETROLEUM

The history of the development of Iran's oil policy can be divided into four distinctive periods: 1872-1950, 1951-

1953, 1954-1973, and the post-1973 period.

Foreign Oil Concessions and the Struggle for Economic Independence (1872-1950)

Oil and power politics have been so intricately linked in the last hundred years of Iranian history that it is necessary to review oil policy developments against the background of the Big Powers' rivalry for politico-economic influence in Iran. This rivalry has been particularly pronounced in the case of Britain and Russia, with the United States first playing the role of an interested bystander, and more recently as an active participant.

OIL DISCOVERY AND BRITISH ADVENTURES

Although according to legend, oil seepages or natural gas fueled the eternal flames of Zoroastrian fire-temples in northwestern Iran long before Christ was born, the modern saga of Iranian petroleum finds is fairly recent.[3] It goes back to a little-noticed prospecting expedition early in the 19th century by an adventurous English geologist named W. K. Loftus, who pinpointed certain areas of potential reserves in Iran. No serious interest was shown in the matter until much later, when a 70-year broad-based concession was obtained from Nassereddin Shah in 1872 by Julius de Reuter in exchange for £40,000 for the exclusive prospecting and exploitation of minerals (including oil) throughout Iran.[4] Reuter's concession was cancelled a year later under strong Czarist pressures,[5] also because of unfavorable Iranian public opinion, and because work had not begun as required. Several years later, in 1889, under continued British prodding, a second limited concession for petroleum exploration was granted to Reuter — this time for a period of sixty years. The exclusive mineral rights acquired by Reuter's were to be vested in the Persian Bank Mining Rights Corporation (later reorganized as the

Imperial Bank of Persia). No oil was found in the few wells drilled by the concessionaires, and the mining rights were renounced in 1890.[6] However, the bank itself became operational.[7]

Following a report published by a French archeologist, Jacques de Morgan, in 1892, a fresh try for obtaining limited exploration rights was successfully made by a British subject named W. K. D'Arcy. A new concession, covering more than 75 per cent of Iran's total area (but excluding the sensitive five northern provinces close to Russia) was signed by Mozaffaredin Shah on 28 May 1901. In exchange for £20,000 cash and 20,000 paid-up shares of £1 each in the First Exploitation Company paid to Iran, D'Arcy received for sixty years the exclusive rights to explore, extract, lay pipes, and export petroleum in an area of about 480,000 square miles in the southern half of Iran. In addition, Iran was to receive 16 per cent of the Company's annual net profits as royalty, and to obtain all the company's assets at the expiration of the concession.

After some unsuccessful drilling in northwestern Iran during 1902-4, the operations were later moved to the Southwest, where Loftus had indicated good prospects. But having spent a large chunk of his private fortune in the venture during 1902-1905, D'Arcy joined Lord Strathcona and the Burmah Oil Company in 1905 to form a Glasgow-based Concessions Syndicate. The Syndicate's early setbacks in their two wells east of Ahwaz forced D'Arcy and his partners to try their luck at a third site, Masjed-Sulaiman, as a last-ditch effort before their funds were totally exhausted.

The first three wells "spudded in " in early 1908, putting Masjed-Sulaiman on the world oil map, and at the eleventh hour this oil strike rescued the Syndicate from imminent financial bankruptcy. On 14 April 1909 the Concessions Syndicate was dissolved and the Anglo-Persian Oil Company (APOC) was formed, with an initial capital of £2 million. D'Arcy and some Burmah Oil directors were given seats on the board of the new company, whose prospectus was first shown to and approved by the British Admiralty, and whose chairman was handpicked by British authorities. A small portion of the total shares was sold in the market.

Soon afterwards, a 140-mile-long, 400,000 tons-a-year capacity pipeline was constructed from Masjed-Sulaiman to Abadan on the Shatt-al-Arab, and a 120,000-tons-a-year refinery with storage tanks was built at Abadan. The first shipment of some 2200 tons of crude oil was made in August, 1912. For the whole year, oil exports reached 43,000 tons.

The turning point in APOC's checkered history, however, came when on 20 May 1914 the Company, the Admiralty, and the Treasury signed an agreement under which the Treasury, by subscribing to 2 million ordinary new shares at £2 (thus providing a capitalization of £4 million), and paying £200,000 for the entire debenture and preferred stocks of the Company, obtained a majority of voting rights plus a veto power over Company affairs. On the same day the Admiralty, which had long sought to change its fuel base from coal to oil, signed a 20-year contract with the Company for six million tons of oil fuel at a fixed price of 30/per ton f.o.b. Persian Gulf ports, with a provision for price reduction if the Company's profits exceeded ten per cent.

The D'Arcy concession, in retrospect, reflects simultaneously the credulity and weakness of an ailing and financially desperate monarch on the Iranian side, and the well-calculated intentions of a group of profiteers on the other. The shah was evidently under the impression that Iran was getting ten per cent of the Company's ownership in accepting the 20,000 shares of the First Exploration Company, plus 16 per cent of its annual profits. The concessionaires, on the other hand, in the best common-law tradition of *caveat grantor* refrained from equating the 20,000 shares with any percentage ownership of the prospective company (thus enabling them to capitalize the venture in such a way as to give Iran an insignificant share). They also surreptitiously inserted the qualifying adjective "net" before the word "profit" in the agreement (thus later enabling APOC to deduct, *inter alia,* income taxes paid to the British government for *gross* profits, and leaving a paltry base for Iran's 16 per cent share).[8]

The patently exploitative nature of the D'Arcy agreement, which gave Iran an average of 17 cents per barrel of exported crude compared to APOC's own enormous profits, as well as the artificially low price of the oil sold to the British Navy by a company controlled by the British government, sowed the seeds of discontent in Iranian public opinion and government circles.[9]

Iran's complaints about the method of profit calculation and the Company's counterclaims regarding damages to oil pipelines during World War II were subsequently submitted to arbitration in 1920, but the Majles refused to ratify the amended agreement proposed. An uneasy and tension-packed truce continued between the Iranian government and the Company throughout the 1920's, and a showdown finally occurred in the early 1930's.

During the Great Depression, APOC's royalty payments to Iran had dropped from £1.4 million in 1929 to £307 thousand in 1931, which the public attributed to the Company's bad faith. The time thus became ripe for the expression of long-held grievances against APOC's alleged detrimental machinations. On 27 November 1932, Reza Shah, the father of modern Iran, unilaterally cancelled the D'Arcy concession at the risk of Britain's overt intervention. After a series of official protests and naval maneuvers by the British government, an appeal to the Permanent Court of International Justice, and the submission of the dispute to the League of Nations, a new agreement was signed in May, 1933.[10]

Under this agreement: (1) the Concession's area was reduced to only 100,000 square miles, and the Company's monopoly on pipeline construction and control was abolished;

(2) the old 16 per cent formula was replaced by (a) a flat *royalty* rate of four shillings to be paid to the Iranian Government for every ton of oil sold in Iran or exported, (b) a *tax* of 6 pence to one shilling for each ton of oil exported, and (c) a payment to the Iranian government of 20 per cent of the annual declared dividends on ordinary shares in excess of £671,250; and (3) Iran's original right to acquire the Company's assets free of charge upon the expiration of the new agreement in 1993 was reaffirmed. The agreement further provided that: (1) Iran's total annual oil income should, under no circumstances, be less than £750,000 in royalties and no less than £225-300 thousand in taxes;[11] (2) domestic needs for oil and oil products should be supplied by the Company at prices prevailing in the Gulf of Mexico minus a discount; and (3) the Company should pledge to (a) use the most modern techniques of oil production, (b) replace its foreign personnel gradually with domestic employees, and (c) train Iranian nationals for high-level positions. APOC was renamed the Anglo-Iranian Oil Company (AIOC).

The 1932-33 oil dispute marked the auspicious beginning of Iran's independent oil policy which resulted ultimately in the nationalization of oil in 1951 and a complete takeover of the oil industry's operation and management in 1973.

RUSSIAN INTERESTS AND DESIGNS

For both political and financial reasons Russia, from the 1870's onward, had a keen interest in obtaining a foothold in Iran's oil and gas exploration and production.[12] By all indications, her early oil interests in Iran were not so much directed at exploitation and production as they were focused on a profitable sales outlet with a transit line to the vast Asian oil markets. Unlike the British, who lacked indigenous oil resources, felt imprudently dependent on American oil supplies, and wished to develop their own, Russia was self-sufficient in oil. Indeed the Baku oil industrialists had a large quantity of petroleum available for export, so they were not only uninterested in finding new sources of supply in Iran but also fearful of any Iranian oil production that might lead to competition in the Indian and other Asian markets.

Iran itself was of great importance to Russian petroleum interests, not so much as an export market (absorbing only slightly more than two per cent of Russian oil exports), but as a gateway to India, Indochina, Australia, and the Pacific Ocean. As early as 1884, the Palashkovskii project for the construction of a kerosene pipeline from the Caspian Sea to the Persian Gulf made the rounds in Russian political and business circles as a plan for diverting Russian oil export trade from the troublesome Red Sea straits to the relatively tranquil strait of Hormoz at the tip of the Oman sea. Palashkovskii's proposal was rejected by a special Russian committee on grounds of questionable profitability and political risks. But the Czarist Government was notably disturbed by the sixth point in the D'Arcy concession, which provided for a pipeline to be built by the concessionaire, and which required the Iranian Government not to give anyone else the right to construct oil pipelines through Iran to the Persian Gulf. Saint Petersburg suddenly became interested in obtaining a concession from Iran for building a kerosene pipeline and instructed its political and commercial representatives in Tehran in 1901 to negotiate such a concession in the name of the Tehran-based Russo-Persian Discount and Loan Bank.

Having obtained foreign legal opinions regarding its sovereign right to grant a pipeline concession to the Russians, and under a new serious financial crisis (despite a fresh loan of 22.5 million rubles from the Russo-Persian Bank), the Iranian Government showed readiness to grant Russia the concession in exchange for a new loan. However, the British strongly protested both in Tehran and in Saint Petersburg, invoking the D'Arcy agreement. Despite the Russian promise to accept any legal responsibility for possible violations of the

British concession, the Iranian Government finally withdrew from the negotiations and the Russians refrained from pursuing the pipeline matter.

In 1916 an oil concession was given to Akakiy Khoshtaria, a Russian subject, for exploration in Iran's five northern provinces. World War I precluded any serious effort by him in that area, and in 1920 AIOC purchased the concession, forming a North Persian Oil Company and giving the British a monopoly position over the whole of Iran. This move was opposed not only by the Soviet Union, but also by a number of American oil companies as newcomers to the scene. The Iranian Government under Reza Shah rejected the validity of Khoshtaria's concession on the ground that it was never ratified by the Majles according to the Constitution. In 1921, under a new Irano-Soviet Treaty, all concessions and obligations previously obtained by Czarist Russia were renounced, and the Iranian Government used this agreement as a *prima facie* abrogation of Khoshtaria's concession.

Curiously enough, in the face of growing American interest in oil exploration in the northern provinces, and Iran's sympathetic consideration of these overtures in the 1920's, the Soviet Union began to show renewed interest in this matter. Getting hold of a minor and obscure concession given to an Iranian subject by Nasseredin Shah in 1878, the Soviet Union bought itself a 65 per cent interest in a newly set-up "Iranian" company called Kavir Khurian for exploration in a small area in Semnan province, northeast of Tehran. During the occupation of northern Iran by the Soviet Union during World War II, Soviet geologists carried out a series of test drillings near Semnan with no results. The company continued to maintain a token presence in Iran until 1956 when the Soviet Union renounced its rights.

The real oil "imbroglio" occurred toward the end of World War II. In September 1944 a high-level Soviet mission arrived in Tehran for the purpose of negotiating an oil concession while negotiations were underway between Iran and some American oil companies, and while the British Standard Vacuum Oil Company representatives were seeking a concession in southeastern Iran. The Soviet Union's surprise move led the Iranian government to cancel its talks with the Americans and decide to reject all offers for concessions from all foreign interests. In December, 1944 the Majles passed a law prohibiting, under severe penalties, any government official from entering into any negotiation aimed at granting oil concessions to foreigners.

In 1946 the U.S.S.R. renewed its pressure to obtain a comprehensive oil concession in the northern part of Iran, and virtually made its evacuation of Iran's occupied territories in the North conditional upon such a concession. An agreement was negotiated in Moscow shortly thereafter by Ahmad Ghavam, the Iranian Prime Minister. But the 15th Majles in 1947, under strong popular pressure, refused to ratify the oil accord. A new law passed by the Majles then charged the Government (1) to explore oil resources with its own capital and its own direction without foreign partnership, participation, or assistance; (2) to negotiate with the Soviet Union the sale of oil; and (3) to obtain better terms and higher shares of profit from AIOC.

Russia refrained from pursuing the matter further. Meanwhile the U.S.S.R.'s real intentions in seeking oil concessions in Iran's northern provinces during the 1940's became the subject of endless speculations, rumors, and interpretations in the West. Some Western analysts argued that the Soviet Union's real motive was not to obtain commercial interests for itself, but to pre-empt any Anglo-American concessions along its borders. Others held that the prospect of Russia becoming a net oil importer by the 1990's dictated such far-sighted overtures. In any event, it is worth noting that some American analysts in the early 1950's considered U.S. oil intentions in Iran in exactly the same vein, i.e., as a move to block Russia's southbound economic penetration, rather than American's own need for Iranian oil.

AMERICAN INTERESTS AND OVERTURES

As part of its desire for an independent oil policy, viz., to exploit northern oil resources as a countervailing force to the British oil monopoly in the South, the Iranian government in the early 1920's had tried to attract foreign oil interests from "disinterested" countries (namely, neither Britain nor Russia). Two successive overtures were made to American Standard Oil and Sinclair Oil.

The new policy, initiated by Reza Shah, met stiff opposition from both the British and the Soviets. The British, invoking the terms of the D'Arcy Agreement which allegedly gave APOC a monopoly of transporting oil across its concession area, effectively nullified an authorization by the Majles in 1921 to grant American Standard Oil a 50-year concession in exchange for 50 per cent of all crude oil produced. When Standard Oil agreed to share its fortune in northern Iran with AIOC in a joint company, the Soviet government opposed granting any concession to "foreign capitalists" in the North. So the deal was called off.

At the same time, Sinclair had itself obtained a concession from the Soviets for the sale of Russian oil and had tried to seek an overland route to the Black Sea through the Baku-Batum pipeline. But the Soviet Union refused to grant transit permission. A bill authorizing the grant of a concession by Iran to Sinclair in 1923 was never implemented, and finally, believing itself harassed by hostile elements, Sinclair abandoned its efforts in Iran.

In 1937, the Majles again voted to grant an oil concession to the Seaboard Oil Company of Delaware to set up the Amiranian Oil Company for oil exploitation in the northern province of Khorasan, and approved another concession to its affiliate, the Iranian Pipeline Company, for the transportation of oil across Iranian territory (AIOC's original pipeline monopoly had been abrogated by the 1933 Agreement). But after a year of feasibility study and market analysis, the company chose to renounce its concessions for commercial reasons.

American interest in Iranian petroleum was not revived until after oil nationalization in 1951. Following a flurry of diplomatic maneuvers by the State Department in the 21 months after nationalization, a group of American oil companies, backed by the World Bank, contacted the Iranian government in December 1952 with a proposal to settle AIOC's total claims on their own, to form a new Irano-American company with Iran's own National Oil Company, and to deal with AIOC as a long-term purchaser of crude from the joint company. The proposal was opposed by the British and became inoperative.

In April 1953, the Cities Service Company and two other independent American companies were reported to be willing to form a purchasing combine to ship Iranian oil for a period of six months, at a reported discount of 50 per cent from the Persian Gulf price. Little more was heard of this deal during the subsequent turbulent political developments that summer.

After the overthrow of the Mossadegh government in August, 1953, the United States officially approached Iran with a proposal for the establishment of a consortium of major oil companies to take over AIOC's former functions, presumably within the context of the Nationalization Act. Shortly before Christmas, 1953 the five major American oil giants (Gulf, Exxon, Socal, Mobil, and Texaco) reached an agreement with AIOC, Shell, and the Compagnie Francaise de Petroles to share Iranian oil exploitation, refining, and exports under a new agreement to be negotiated with Iran. America's stake in Iran's oil industry was thus firmly established for the first time.[13]

Oil Nationalization and Its Aftermath (1951-1953)

The terms of the 1933 Agreement, in retrospect, proved as undesirable for the Iranian Government as the D'Arcy concession. The annual oil revenues reached a maximum of only £4 million in 1944, giving the Government an average of $.23 per barrel of oil produced and exported. Badly in need of foreign exchange to finance its ambitious development plan, and particularly impressed by Venezuela's new 50-50 profit-sharing agreement, the Government sought to renegotiate the 1933 Agreement.

In the spring of 1949 Iran formally demanded increased revenues from AIOC. The negotiations that followed produced the Supplementary Gass-Golshaian Agreement of July, 1949. This complicated document raised Iran's share of oil income from royalties and taxes considerably above the 1933 Agreement, in return for the reaffirmation by the Iranian Government of AIOC's existing concession. But it fell short of the 50-50 principle demanded by Iran and was considered by a Majles' Special Oil Committee as not satisfactorily safeguarding "Iranian rights and interests."

AIOC's uncompromising attitude, its shortsighted approach, and its irrational fear of the inevitable spread of the 50-50 principle to the Company's other holdings in the Middle East, not only proved fatal to its own survival but also precipitated a chain of ugly events culminating in a complete impasse.

The Iranian demand for 50-50 profit-sharing and the Government's other requests (e.g., training of more Iranians, equal-opportunity employment of local personnel in management, equal treatment by the Company of the Iranian and British Navy purchases) were, in the opinion of many objective analysts, justified. But AIOC refused to accept them until early 1951 when it was too late, for by that time the fervor of nationalization had become politically irresistible.[14]

On 15 March 1951 the Majles passed a "Single Article"

bill, nationalizing the Iranian oil industry. The Senate confirmed the action on 20 March. A more detailed bill, establishing the National Iranian Oil Company[15] and charging it with the sole responsibility for the exploration, extraction, refining, and sale of oil, gas, and related products, was passed by both houses of parliament in April and was signed by the Shahanshah in May, 1951. AIOC's facilities were seized shortly afterwards, and eviction was completed in October, 1951.

The nationalization act was obviously motivated not only by a desire on the part of the Iranian Government to obtain its fair and rightful return from an extremely profitable national resource; it was also meant to terminate once and for all foreign private influence over its economic sovereignty, i.e., to get rid of AIOC's multifaceted local politico-economic machinations. These aspirations for economic independence and full control over domestic resources were, at the time, largely and regrettably belittled by the Western press. And, more tragically, they were ignored by Iran's wartime allies.

AIOC still stubbornly refused to accept the nationalization law and began a series of collusive politico-commercial maneuvers with other major oil companies and their sympathetic governments to (a) impose an almost universal shipping boycott of Iranian oil; (b) block certain Iranian financial assets abroad; (c) place an embargo on parts and equipment needed to maintain Iranian oil facilities as well as on "scarce" Iranian imports; and (d) take legal action against independent buyers and shippers of Iranian oil. An alleged breach of an international obligation by Iran was subsequently brought by Britain before the Permanent Court of International Justice in the Hague in June, 1951, and before the United Nations Security Council in September of the same year. The Security Council in October, 1951 adjourned its discussion of the British "complaint" until there was a ruling on the issue by the International Court, but the Court held in July, 1952 that it had no jurisdiction to entertain the United Kingdom's "application" since the issue involved a national concession, not a public international agreement.

During the period subsequent to nationalization, despite generous discounts and guarantees offered to potential oil buyers, Iran did not succeed in striking any sizable deal. Thus oil operations were cut to a minimum, and oil income was down to a trickle. Of the more than $240 million projected oil revenues for the $650 million first Seven-Year Plan (1948-1955), less than $20 million was realized from this source in 1952 and 1953, some of which came through oil sales to "freelance blockade-runners" in Italy and Japan.

In any event, between the oil nationalization in March, 1951 and the Consortium Agreement in September, 1954, Iran's national oil policy was aimed at (1) making the nationalization law the sole possible basis of negotiation for the resolution of the Anglo-Iranian oil dispute and avoiding any foreign monopoly on Iranian soil; (2) operating the oil industry by hiring non-British technicians and luring away the former Company's customers; (3) restructuring oil operations and activities as a national (rather than multinational) concern and serving domestic petroleum needs with the help of national technicians and native management; (4) reworking the development plan, within the confines of a self-reliant "oil-less" economy, in such a way that an austerity budget could sustain the government on existing revenues; (5) earmarking potential oil incomes to be used only for increased capital formation in the future; and (6) fighting for an independent inroad into the world oil market.[16]

Toward Total Independence in Oil Policy (1954-1973)

The bitter and frustrating 1951-1954 oil dispute was prolonged by two unfortunate miscalculations. The National Front, headed by Prime Minister Mossadegh (and its members in the Majles and the Cabinet) underestimated the political and commercial influence of the major oil companies over their respective governments, the timidity of Western private oil buyers, and the difficulties of transporting oil by non-cartel tankers. They simply believed that the West could not do without Iranian oil. The Company (and its supporting governments), in turn, assumed that Iranians would not be able to run the oil industry without foreign technicians and management, and that the Iranian economy could not long withstand the sharp cut in oil revenues. Both these assumptions proved illusory. The major oil companies managed to make up totally the fall in Iranian oil exports by raising oil exports from Iraq and Kuwait. And the Iranians ran their oil industry (i.e., production and refining) much better than anticipated. The awakening came in 1953 after damage had been done to both sides. The 1954 Agreement was a last-ditch compromise.

Due to the great significance of the various aspects of Iran's oil policy in the post-1954 period, this section will discuss policies on organization and management, price and production, and environmental considerations in separate details.

ORGANIZATION AND MANAGEMENT POLICY

The long, bitter, and ruinous dispute between the Iranian Government and the former AIOC was finally settled in October, 1954. By all accounts, the post-nationalization settlement of Iran's oil crisis was neither the best deal Iran had hoped for, nor perhaps the best it had been previously offered. It was a compromise accepted by the Iranian Government under economic duress. From the very start of the post-nationalization era, the Shahanshah was determined to restore the balance gradually, but surely. As we shall see below, concerted and intensified efforts were directed toward (1) improving the terms of the compromise agreement, (2) making inroads into the world petroleum market, and (3) eventually taking over the entire ownership and management responsibility from foreign companies.

The Consortium As Agent of NIOC

Under the new and unavoidably complex 1954 Agreement, an international consortium of eight major oil companies and a number of independents obtained a 25-year concession, with three five-year renewal options, to extract and refine oil in southwestern Iran.[17]

Under this 1954 Agreement, AIOC, renamed British Petroleum, accepted the principle of nationalization in exchange for £25 million in compensation from Iran. AIOC relinquished its oil rights in Iran to the new Consortium by receiving 40 per cent of the Consortium's shares plus a prior claim of $1 billion on its income over a ten-year period.[18] The Consortium members, agreeing to carry out exploration, production, refining, and transport in the Agreement Area on behalf of NIOC, formed two companies of British registry — Iranian Oil Participants, Ltd. and Iranian Oil Services, Ltd. Oil Participants. Ltd., in turn, formed two subsidiaries, one for oil exploration and production, and the other for oil refining, registered under the laws of both the Netherlands and Iran.[19] These two companies, known as the Iranian Oil Operating Companies, were given the right to "explore, produce and refine crude oil and natural gas" in an area of about 100,000 square miles of land bordering the eastern shores of the Persian Gulf, plus three miles offshore from the coast in Iran's territorial waters. Each participant established a "trading company" under Iranian laws to buy oil from the Consortium — legally from NIOC — at a cost-plus fee, and to sell it in the world markets on behalf of its parent company. All non-oil activities of the former AIOC (i.e., internal distribution, services, etc.) were taken over by NIOC.

NIOC had the right to purchase as much oil from the Operating Companies as it needed for distribution and consumption in Iran at cost-plus fees. In addition, it was also entitled to take 12.5% of crude oil output for export under its own control, or to sell it back to the Operating Companies at the prevailing posted price. Since the late 1960's, NIOC was also allowed to export crude oil beyond its own 12.5% to markets not traditionally supplied by the major oil companies (i.e., Eastern Europe) through barter deals.

Under the Consortium agreement, NIOC was the *owner* and the foreign companies were the operators of the Iranian oil industry. This ownership right plus the new 50-50 profit-sharing arrangement raised Iran's per-barrel revenue to about four times as much as the pre-nationalization level. The "profit-sharing" arrangement with the Consortium was substantially modified after January, 1964 and will be discussed later.

Direct Entry Into World Markets

An important first step toward the establishment of a clear and comprehensive oil policy by Iran came with the passage of the 1957 oil law. Under this law the exclusive rights for the exploration, production, and sale of oil and gas outside the 100,000 square mile Consortium Agreement Area were given to NIOC. These rights could be exercised independently or through joint ventures with other oil companies. Thus NIOC had the right to conclude new oil agreements in two essential ways: (1) through Consortium-type contracts under which exploration and production rights to Iran's oil resources could be ceded to foreign operating companies in return for a 50% tax on the operator's profits; or (2) through joint ventures whereby each partner was entitled to the company's profits in relation to its share, and each party was expected to pay appropriate corporate taxes to the Iranian Government. The 1957 oil law thus opened new vistas for NIOC's operations, not only in the onshore areas outside the Consortium Area, but also on the continental shelf.

The implementation of the new law required a prior determination of the claims by the riparian states to offshore oil resources of the Persian Gulf. The Continental Shelf Convention, worked out by the Geneva Conference on the Law of the Sea in 1958, had given every coastal state sovereign rights over the natural resources found in its continental shelf beyond the limits of territorial waters but adjacent to its coasts. The "shelf" itself was viewed as submerged land less than 200 meters beneath the sea or beyond that depth where the superjacent waters admitted exploitation. Although Iran's neighbors to the south did not question the reasonableness and validity of this doctrine, its actual application proved difficult, because the entire Persian Gulf was shallow enough to be considered continental shelf on both sides and for the neighboring states. In such cases, the Convention on the Continental Shelf prescribes (except for special circumstances) the principle of "equidistance," that is, dividing the "shelf" between the states by a middle line equally distant from the nearest points on each state's shorelines from which its territorial sea is measured.

Two special circumstances made the application of the Convention principles awkward. The first problem involved the question of "baselines" from which the territorial sea and the continental shelf were to be measured. Most troublesome in this respect was the position of islands adjacent to the mainland about which the Convention was silent. The Iranian Government, for instance, considered Kharg Island, some 25 miles off the Iranian coast, as part of its coastline and as a base for measuring its continental shelf. Saudi Arabia considered 25 miles too long a distance from the mainland for the purpose of oil concessions. The second problem was that of the width of the territorial sea. Iran, Iraq, and Saudi Arabia, for example, all had laws defining their territorial seas as extending 12 miles seaward, but the sheikdoms have adopted a distance of only three or six miles from their shores.

It was thus necessary for Iran to settle the question of boundary lines and the division of the continental shelf amicably and equitably with other Persian Gulf states. The urgency of such an "equitable solution" arose when Iran, in the late 1950's and early 1960's, opened a large offshore area in the Persian Gulf to international bids. Kuwait and Saudi Arabia protested on the ground that some of *their* territories had been included in the Iranian tender.

Iran initiated negotiations with both governments in order to reach a mutually satisfactory solution. In 1965 an agreement was reached with Kuwait to discuss the scope of each state's exclusive rights, and a protocol was signed to that effect. But a protest was lodged by Iraq which considered the Kuwait-Iranian understanding a violation of *its* offshore area. Since many of Iraq's objections were closely related to its lingering dispute with Iran on the Shatt-al-Arab boundary, the settlement of that issue in the spring of 1975 has at last opened the way for a tripartite agreement among the riparian states at the head of the Persian Gulf.

With Saudi Arabia, Iran initialed an agreement in December of 1965, but it was not ratified due to fresh evidence of its inequity for Iran. A subsequent *entente* was reached in November, 1968 whereby Kharg Island was given a "half-weight" status (something between considering the island as a demarcation base line and not considering it at all), and two disputed islands in the Gulf were divided between Iran and Saudi Arabia. The Iran-Saudi Agreement was thus based on the principle of "equitable distribution" rather than the strict geographical criterion of "equidistance."

Agreements were also reached by Iran with Qatar in September, 1969, Bahrain in 1970, and Abu Dhabi in 1971 for the division of the continental shelf.[20] These agreements (1) recognize the limit of the territorial sea as 12 miles from the low watermark on shore; (2) use the principle of a shore-to-shore median line as the dividing boundary; (3) use, in the case of islands under sovereignties, the median line between them to establish the limits of the territorial waters; and (4) prohibit the drilling of wells for 500 meters on either side of the demarcation lines, except to obtain technicial information, and then only subject to mutual consent.

* Joint Ventures

While the provisions of the 1957 Oil Law provided NIOC with a new authorization to enter into the world petroleum market, the Third and Fourth Development Plans set the stage for the establishment and implementation of a new formal oil policy. According to the Third Plan (1963-1968), the objectives of Iran's oil policy (in addition to meeting domestic requirements) were (a) increased production from the Consortium's area; (b) new joint ventures to increase production from other fields; (c) direct access to foreign markets; and (d) utilization of previously wasted by-products. The Fourth Plan (1968-72), while reiterating the general objectives of the Third, emphasized (a) direct oil exploration by NIOC in the areas relinquished by the Consortium and more crude exported directly by the Company; (b) better balance in production of oil products for domestic consumption; (c) extension of the internal distribution network, including construction of new regional refineries; and (d) obtaining access to international marketing and transportation directly or in cooperation with oil interests.

The first two joint-venture agreements were signed in 1957 with Agip Mineraria (a subsidiary of the Italian State Oil Corporation, ENI), and in 1958 with the Pan American Petroleum Corporation (an affiliate of Standard Oil of Indiana). These agreements provided for a 50-50 participation between NIOC and its foreign partners and resulted effectively in a 75-25 division of the net profits in favor of the Iranian government. The main advantages of these ventures in comparison with the Consortium's arrangement were NIOC's full participation in the joint-venture's decision-making process and its full control over the disposal of its own 50% share of the crude output. [21]

Furthermore, foreign partners were required to spend at least a minimum amount for exploration and drilling in order to discover and produce oil, and to cede back to NIOC the area where no commercial-quantity oil was discovered. NIOC was to share, on an equal footing, the operational responsibility for the joint ventures in case of success, but it had no financial obligations in case of failure to find oil.

After a series of geophysical and seismic testings by NIOC offshore in the Persian Gulf, some 80,000 Km^2 of promising oil reserve potentials were opened to international bids. Six successful bidders paid NIOC an initial sum of $195 million, and six new agreements (DOPCO, IROPCO, IMINOCO, LAPCO, FPC, and PEGUPCO) were signed in 1965.[22] These agreements provided for the same 50-50 shares of ownership, and 75-25 profit-sharing as before. Yet the new arrangements contained several new features even more advantageous than the previous schemes. For example: foreign partners were now required (a) to export and sell NIOC's 50% share of crude at the "half-way" price (or an agreed formula) if the latter could not find profitable markets abroad; (b) to underwrite, against NIOC's future incomes, the latter's "investment share" for extraction and production once oil was discovered, to be recouped later from future sales of crude; and (c) to extend NIOC's partnership to include "downstream" operations.

Three other joint-venture agreements were signed in 1970 with a Japanese group, the Amarada-Hess, and Mobil Oil. In addition to giving NIOC a $47 million initial bonus plus another $26 million at the time of production, the new agreements contained several other new provisions in NIOC's favor: e.g., (a) the duration and renewal options were shorter than the previous joint ventures; (b) domestic oil needs had priority over exports; (c) the "stated payment" was larger; (d) only 50% of the cost of exploration was to be recovered from future sales of oil by foreign partners; and (e) all litigation and arbitration were for the first time subject to Iranian laws.

* Service-Type Contracts

In its continued efforts toward more independent direct undertakings and operations, NIOC embarked on a new and different contractual arrangement in the mid-1960's. Determined to make a first-hand assessment of Iran's oil reserves, including their scope, location, and other geological characteristics, but lacking sufficient capital funds for such vast and very expensive explorations, NIOC concluded a new type of agreement with the French State Company, ERAP, in 1966. Unlike the previous "agency" arrangements with the Consortium, and the joint ventures with SIRIP, IPAC, and others, the new agreement treated the foreign party merely as a "service contractor." Thus, the ERAP group agreed to finance for NIOC's account all activities connected with geological surveys, exploration, extraction and transportation under an interest-free loan to be paid back within 15 years after the discovery of oil in commercial quantities. According to this agreement, 50% of the discovered reserves had to be ceded to NIOC for its own exclusive account. The rest could be (a) bought by ERAP at cost plus a 2% fee plus the 50% income tax on actual sales price for a period of 25 years, or (b) sold in world markets for NIOC's account at prevailing prices minus a 2% tax-free commission for ERAP. Two other similar "service-type" agreements on even more advantageous terms were later signed in 1969 with a consortium of European (French, Italian, Belgian, Spanish, and Austrian) partners – AREPI – and the American Continental Oil Company – CONOCO. Under this type of agreement, NIOC as the sole owner-operator was to guarantee the foreign contractor long-term sales of a portion of crude output, upon commercial oil discovery.

In July and August of 1974, following the passage of a new oil law amending that of 1957, and after NIOC's invitation for international bidding with participation by some 80 oil companies and groups, six new service-type agreements were signed with Deminx, CFP, Ultramar, AGIP, and Ashland. Some $49.75 million as a cash "bonus" was received by NIOC, and another $17 million was due to be paid at the start of production. In these new agreements, unlike the previous ones, the foreign "contractors" have no purchase options for a specific period. In fact, as soon as oil is discovered in commercial quantities, the exploration agreements are terminated, and new arrangements will be made for the sale to the former contractors of up to 50% of output at market price minus a discount of 3% to 5% for a period of 15 years. Assuming the market price of oil at $10 a barrel, contractor-buyers under the new agreements will have to pay a minimum of $9.50 to NIOC. Previous agreements would have allowed them to pay only about $7.00. Among further new advantages of the new agreements, mention ought to be made of: (a) a shorter maximum exploration period (5 years instead of 12); (b) non-renewability of the agreement after the expiration date if no oil is found; (c) obligation by the contractors to spend a specific sum ($167 million) on exploration against penalty of forfeiture to NIOC; and (d) ownership by NIOC of all contractors' assets engaged in exploration.

The Final Takeover

Iran's ultimate goal in its relation with the Consortium was the full takeover of operation and management of the oil industry as soon as possible, and no later than the expiration of the first phase of the 1954 Agreement. The approach, however, was cautiously calculated and made gradual in order to give NIOC adequate experience, and to give the Consortium the full benefits of its Agreement. To this ultimate end, an amendment to the original Consortium Agreement was worked out after a series of lengthy negotiations in 1966, under which some 25% of the Consortium area not yet utilized by the

Operating Companies was returned to NIOC. The nearly 65,000 Km^2 thus "freed" were then opened to international bidding and "leased" to a number of foreign companies under different schemes, as indicated previously.

At the beginning of 1973, and on the eve of the new and vastly larger Fifth Development Plan (1973/1978), Iran had already come to the conclusion that the Consortium's production and price policies could not safeguard the country's best interests. For this reason, the Government was not prepared to extend the companies' mandate beyond 1979. The Consortium was given two options: First, to continue operations for six more years under the 1954 Agreement on condition that (a) Iran's income from each barrel of oil should be equal to that obtained by any other Middle East oil producer, and (b) Iran's daily crude output should reach 8 million barrels. In that case, the member companies would be given no preferential treatment over other potential buyers of oil from NIOC after 1979. The second option was to replace the 1954 Agreement with a new accord under which NIOC would immediately be given full control over the Consortium's operations in return for a long-term sales agreement for secure delivery of crude at a good discount to the member companies. After a series of top level negotiations under royal direction and supervision, the companies chose the second option. The 1933 and 1954 Agreements were then annulled on 30 July 1973 by a special act of the Iranian Parliament. The legal ownership and sovereignty of the oil industry's reserves, assets, and facilities by Iran, sanctioned by the 1951 Nationalization Act, was supplemented by giving NIOC full and absolute control over Iran's oil industry. The abrogation of these agreements, therefore, meant the end of "concessionary" relationships between Iran and foreign oil interests. It also meant complete ownership, operation, and control of the Iranian oil and gas industry by the Iranian Government with respect to reserves, production, investment, and price policies. Finally, it reasserted Iran's exclusive jurisdiction over new oil agreements and contractual arrangements.

After the cancellation of the previous agreements, a new 20-year Sale and Purchase Agreement was reached between Iran and the Consortium. Under the terms of the 1973 Agreement, the former Iranian Oil Operating Companies were replaced by the Iranian Oil Service Company (IOSCO), a private, non-profit corporation formed in Iran to carry out petroleum activities assigned to it by NIOC. These activities presently consist of oil exploration and production. Refining is under NIOC's direct management. The former Consortium's trading companies are the same as before with the same functions. That is, they purchase crude petroleum from NIOC at the wellhead and export it directly or deliver it to the Abadan Refinery for processing.[23] NIOC is solely responsible for all investment expenditure to maintain and expand oil exploitation, including disbursements for IOSCO's operations. But now the trading companies as a group have the obligation to advance to NIOC 40 per cent of the estimated $1 billion financing for such capital outlays (including secondary recovery facilities) over the first five years of the Agreement, the period of major capital expansion. The advances are prepayment for future crude oil purchases from NIOC and will be offset against future crude oil deliveries in equal installments over a ten-year period. Sixty per cent of the capital investment is provided by NIOC.

Under the terms of the Sale and Purchase Agreement, payments by the trading companies are made to both NIOC and the Iranian Government. Since 21 March 1973, the payment made to NIOC by the trading companies for each barrel of crude oil delivered f.o.b. tanker at the Persian Gulf for export, or to the Abadan Refinery for processing, has included four elements: (1) the "stated payment," i.e., the royalty; (2) the operating cost (including depreciation); (3) an interest payment on investment by NIOC, i.e., the 60 per cent of capital expenditure provided by the Company in the new Agreement's first five years in order to increase the oil wells' productivity; and (4) a "balancing margin" to give Iran the same financial benefits received by other Persian Gulf producers as a result of their "participation" agreements. Another source of revenue to NIOC is the value of the stated quantity of its "entitlement" from crude oil produced in the Agreement Area, which is exported on the Company's own account. The trading companies further pay an income tax to the Iranian Treasury on their "net revenues," defined as the applicable posted price, times the volume of petroleum bought by the trading company from NIOC, less payments made to NIOC for the given quantity of oil.[24]

SUPPLY AND PRICE POLICY

Throughout the life of the D'Arcy concession and long after the oil nationalization, up until October, 1973, the basic managerial decisions regarding oil production and prices were made by the foreign concessionaires and the Consortium. Oil prices were determined unilaterally by the major oil companies. Up to 1950, Iran's annual oil revenues were largely based on a flat per-barrel payment and only marginally on part of AIOC's declared dividends. Thus the Company's price policy had been of secondary significance to Iran. But under the 1954 Agreement whereby government revenues became directly dependent on the so-called "posted price" in the Persian Gulf — on which the Government's 50% share was calculated — the pricing policy gained crucial importance.

Production and Export Policy

In 1950 Iran was the world's fourth largest and the Middle East's leading oil producer, with 28 million annual metric tons of crude. In the aftermath of the nationalization crisis, Iran lost this position to Iraq and Kuwait, and did not regain it until 1969. Total production in 1955 was only about 16 million tons. Thus, during the decade and a half following the resumption of oil output in 1954, the cardinal elements of Iran's oil policy were: (1) to recover the leading position it enjoyed before nationalization by pressuring the Consortium to raise the amount of oil produced in its territory; (2) to gain the greatest possible economic benefits from petroleum export; and (3) to achieve these two goals without cut-throat price competition. The rationale of this realistic, pragmatic, and virtually *apolitical* approach is not difficult to ascertain.

Post-war economic planning in Iran was based mainly on the projected proceeds of exports at given prices, and drastic declines in these revenues resulting from lower posted prices played havoc with such plans. Having witnessed its First seven-year Plan (1948-1955) brought virtually to a standstill after oil nationalization and the drying up of oil revenues, the Government could not withstand further cuts in its projected income. Consequently, as the Consortium, under the pretext of world oil glut, gradually began to lower the Persian Gulf's posted price from $2.17 in 1947 to $1.78 in 1959, Iranian planners were correspondingly deprived of their projected investment outlays.

Powerless to do much about stabilizing oil prices under the Consortium Agreement, the Iranian Government had no other alternative in the meantime than to press for greater production and more offtake from its wells, in order to obtain sufficient revenues to pay for the planned volume of capital-goods imports at rising prices. All through the 1950's and 1960's there were perennial disputes between the Iranian Government and the Consortium. Iran emphasized its huge development needs, its wise use of oil incomes, its large and growing population, its past production record, and its defense requirements for safeguarding regional stability, and it ceaselessly pressed for an increase in oil production. The Consortium, on the other hand, referring to "the free play of economic forces" (i.e., relatively lower costs of Kuwait and Saudi Arabian crude), and citing the Arab countries' desire to retain their relative offtake levels, refused to comply.[25]

Independently of the Consortium, NIOC itself tried to increase production in the areas under its own control or under joint ventures. Diplomatic efforts were also made in the United States with a view to obtaining an "oil quota" for NIOC in exchange for increased purchases of American goods. Various discounts were offered foreign independent buyers. In short, Iran's oil production policy during the 1950's and 1960's was to increase oil offtakes and exports in order to offset the adverse effects of posted-price declines and market discounts on the Government's oil revenues. The pressure on the Consortium particularly mounted with the advent of the Fourth Development Plan (1968-1972), which called for a 18.4% annual increase in crude petroleum. But the oil output, particularly in 1968/69, fell considerably short of the Plan target. In a number of speeches and interviews, the Shahanshah attacked the Consortium's unilateral production decision which he thought gave inadequate heed to Iran's need for financing its socio-economic objectives.

In its postwar oil *export* policy, Iran consistently followed the principle of "oil as business, not politics." This business-like, apolitical attitude, in turn, was reflected in two realistic decisions regarding the country's oil supply and export. First, the Government steadfastly refrained from any direct involvement in the final destination of its oil exports once the tankers left Iranian ports. Basing its argument on the fact that the Consortium, as the rightful owner of oil on board, could ship it anywhere it wished and that Iran had no legal control over such shipments, the Government refused to interfere with the concessionaire's (or buyers') decision to supply oil to any importing country. The second manifestation of Iran's pragmatic oil export policy was the Government's refusal to participate in any embargo, blacklist or boycott of its own against other countries for political considerations. Thus, twice in the last ten years Iran refrained from taking part in the Arab oil embargoes against certain Western countries during the 1967, and again in the 1973, Arab-Israeli wars. Yet while rejecting the use of oil as a "political weapon" in peacetime, Iran respected the rights of its neighboring Arab countries and did not take advantage of the situation for special gain.

At the present time NIOC allocates roughly about ten per cent of its annual crude entitlement for refining in five refineries (Abadan, Tehran, Shiraz, Kermanshah and Masjed-Sulaiman, with a total 825,000 b/d capacity) for the home market as well as for export. [26] NIOC also has equity interests in two overseas refineries: one, a 13 per cent interest in the 50,000 b/d throughput capacity Madras Refinery in India, fed by crude from the offshore oil field of Darius at Kharg Island; and the other, a 17.5 per cent interest in the 50,000 b/d South African Refinery, supplied by NIOC's crude share in the Lavan Petroleum Company (LAPCO) operating the Sassan offshore field.

The remaining crude is exported by NIOC itself, by its partners in joint ventures, and through the former Consortium trading companies from several deepwater terminals in the Persian Gulf. The largest port, on Kharg Island, is capable of accommodating tankers of up to 500,000 dwt. NIOC's direct crude exports have mainly been sent to its joint-venture foreign refineries, its barter trade partners (Romania and Yugoslavia), and lately to Japanese and U.S. independent oil interests. Some bilateral oil-for-goods arrangements have also been made recently.

NIOC's direct exports, together with four of its joint-venture partners, amount to about 15 per cent of total exported crude, although these exports are expected to grow in coming years. There were in 1975 four joint ventures with successful commercial production and export activities: (1)

The Societe Irano-Italienne des Petroles (SIRIP), formed in 1957 with the Italian AGIP group on a 50-50 basis and subject to Iranian taxes, has three offshore fields in production and three inland fields under development. SIRIP produces 75,000 b/d and expects to reach 100,000 b/d in the near future; (2) the Iran-Pan American Company (IPAC), formed in 1958, also on a 50-50 share basis, with Pan American Petroleum Corporation. IPAC has been producing 130,000 b/d from two fields offshore from Kharg Island (supplying the Madras Refinery), and is expected to produce another 300,000 b/d from two other offshore fields by 1977; (3) the Lavan Petroleum Company (LAPCO), formed in 1965, on a 50-50 share basis with four American firms, had two commercial fields in 1975 producing 195,000 b/d and a 1977 potential of another 45,000 b/d; and (4) the Iranian-Marine International Oil Company (IMINOCO), also formed in 1965 on a 50-50 share basis with Italian, American, and Indian interests, had two offshore fields and was producing 65,000 b/d in 1975. Seven other joint ventures and six service contracts have been signed since 1965, but most of them are still in the exploration stage.[27]

The bulk of Iran's crude exports are in the hands of the private Oil Service Company, registered in Iran, and composed of the former Consortium's trading companies as follows: British Petroleum, 40 per cent; Shell, 14 per cent; Gulf, Mobil, Standard of California, Exxon, and Texaco, each 7 per cent; Compagnie Francaise des Petroles, 6 per cent; and six independent American companies, a total of 5 per cent.

According to the 1973 Agreement, NIOC, after allowing each year for Iran's domestic consumption needs and a "stated quantity" of oil for its own export, notifies the Consortium members of the remaining quantity of crude oil for sale to them for export. The "stated quantity" started with 200,000 b/d in 1973 and will increase annually until it reaches 1.5 million b/d in 1981. Thereafter the same proportion of "stated quantity" oil to total 1981 exports will be maintained. NIOC, in turn, will process for the trading companies up to 300,000 b/d at Abadan Refinery for a period of 20 years. The price payable to NIOC by the Consortium is calculated in such a way as to make total financial benefits and advantages available to Iran at all times no less favorable than those available to other countries in the Persian Gulf.[28] The Service Company presently has 20 fields and a 1977 capacity of 7.2 million b/d production.

Table I.1 (page 38) shows Iran's oil production and utilization in recent years.

Price Policy and Financial Arrangements

Toward the end of the 1950's it became evident that an increase in Iran's oil revenues from larger annual oil production could be attained only at the cost of (1) constant and debilitating arguments with the Consortium; (2) an unhealthy rivalry with oil producing neighbors who wished to maintain their own relative production levels; and (3) possibly the permanent loss of some reserves as a result of their too rapid exploitation. The alternative seemed to be control over oil prices as well as improvements in the terms of taxes and royalty payments.

When in both 1959 and 1960 the posted prices of oil in the Persian Gulf were lowered from $2.04 a barrel (API 34°) to $1.78 by the major oil companies, Iran and four other oil producing countries — Iraq, Kuwait, Saudi Arabia and Venezuela — formed the Organization of Petroleum Exporting Countries (OPEC). The initial purpose of OPEC was a collective defense against the decisions by the major oil companies that affected the internal socio-economic development plans of the OPEC states and their control over the price of their depletable assets. After 1960, OPEC resisted any decrease in posted prices, which were the basis for calculating royalties and taxes, although crude oil sales were made at discounts.

TABLE I.1

IRAN'S OIL PRODUCTION AND UTILIZATION IN SELECTED YEARS

(000' metric tons)

	1947	1951	1953	1957	1963	1967	1973	1974
Production[a]								
IOOC/OSCO	20,895[b]	17,400	2,200[c]	35,315	71,719	127,043	286,771	294,629
Affiliated Cos.	---	---	---	35,052	70,666	120,683	263,817	271,167
NIOC (Naft Shah)	---	---	---	---	742	5,925	22,135	22,566
	---	---	---	263	311	435	819	896
Exports[a]								
Crude	17,800	14,200	900	19,012	53,756	105,001	258,246	262,704
Refined	2,490	2,100	---	12,519	13,761	13,918	13,465	13,670
Domestic Consumption[a,d]	605	1,100	1,300	2,144	4,015	6,565	12,950	14,780

a) Figures do not add up due to losses and oil industry uses.
b) AIOC
c) NIOC
d) Excluding LPG

Source: National Iranian Oil Company

OPEC's first step in the direction of improving the terms of the concession was to get the major oil companies to agree to reduce their fictitious "sales and marketing" expenses (deductible from gross revenues before taxes) from two cents a barrel to half a cent. The second and more important move was to separate royalty payments from tax liabilities. In the 1954 Agreement, the customary 12.5% oil royalty ("stated payments") to the owner (NIOC) was part of Iran's 50% share: that is, one-eighth of the posted price which was due to NIOC as "stated payment" was deducted from the 50% income tax paid to the Government in such a way as to give Iran (i.e., NIOC and the Treasury) a total oil revenue equal to 50% of the operating company's net profits. This practice, which was contrary to the customary treatment of oil royalties in the United States and elsewhere, was unanimously denounced in two OPEC resolutions and finally ended after the first amendment to the 1954 Agreement in 1966. Thereafter, the "stated payment" to NIOC was to be treated as part of costs, thus effectively raising Iran's share to 56.25% of net profits.

Further negotiations with the companies culminated in November, 1970 with an increase in the income tax rate on the Consortium's net profits to 55% from the original 50% and an increase of $.09 in the posted price of Iran's heavy crude. The new accord raised the Government's average "take" per barrel of oil to $.96 from $.87, yielding an extra annual oil revenue of $120 million. But early in 1970 Iranian light crude was still sold at about $1.30-.40 per barrel, an average discount of 25 per cent off the posted price.

In early 1971 further discussions with the major oil companies by OPEC members led to a successful change in pricing. Following OPEC's resolution #120 in Caracas late in 1970, the member countries met with the major oil companies in Tehran and concluded an agreement on 14 February 1971. Under this agreement, which was closely guided by the Shahanshah of Iran, (a) the posted price of Iranian heavy and light crude was raised from $1.72-.79 to $2.12-.17; (b) provision was made for an annual increase up to 1975 of 2-1/2 per cent plus $.05 a barrel in the Persian Gulf posted price in order to mitigate the impact of Western inflation; and (c) both the price discounts previously granted to the oil companies and the one-half cent "marketing" allowance were abolished. Under the 1971 Tehran Agreement, the major oil companies thus accepted the principle of "collective bargaining" in determining posted prices as well as an "escalator clause" for parity adjustments. As a result of the Tehran Agreement the average Iranian government "take" per barrel of oil exceeded $1.30 by June 1971, yielding an extra annual revenue of $500 million.

In January 1972 a supplementary agreement with the oil companies was reached in Geneva, under which the producing governments were to be compensated every three months for decreases in the value of the U.S. dollar in terms of nine currencies in world money markets. A second Geneva Agreement in June, 1973 modified the previous accord by increasing the frequency of depreciation adjustments to every month instead of every three months, and by measuring the dollar value against eleven instead of nine currencies. As a consequence of these adjustments, the posted prices of Iranian oil rose to $2.82-.86 a barrel by June, 1973, and $2.95-.99 by October.

During the early months of 1973, moreover, a phenomenon occurred when the actual *market* price of crude oil in the Persian Gulf, which for some 20 years had been about 60 per cent of the posted price, began to rise and finally surpassed it. As a result, Iran and the other OPEC members pressed for a revision of the Tehran Agreement in order to adjust posted prices to changes in actual market conditions. Following a series of protracted and frustrating negotiations with the major oil companies, the Persian Gulf members of OPEC, now six in number, decided at their Kuwait meeting to announce unilaterally new posted prices for crude oil, effective 16 October 1973. Iran's light and crude prices were thus posted at $5.341 and $4.991 respectively, raising the government's "take" to about $3.20,[29] from about $.96 in 1970 and about $1.78 on 1 October 1973. Under the Kuwait declaration, future crude prices were no longer subject to bilateral negotiations, but would be set by the oil exporters in accordance with market conditions. On 1 November and 1 December 1973 posted prices were revised in accordance with the terms of the Geneva II Agreement.

In the wake of the 1973 Yom Kippur war and the Arab oil embargo against certain Western countries, some dramatic new developments occurred in the world supply and demand for crude oil. NIOC successfully auctioned 300,000 b/d of its Consortium entitlement as well as 170,000 b/d of its joint-venture crude oil at $17 a barrel in December, 1973 for delivery in January-June 1974. Meanwhile, a comparative-costs study by a group of OPEC experts of alternative sources of energy showed that the minimum cost per barrel of oil extracted from shale, tar sands, and coal liquefaction amounted to no less than $8. Thus, in OPEC's December, 1973 meeting in Tehran, the posted price of Arabian light crude, chosen as the marker or reference crude, was raised to $11.65 per barrel, which ensured about $7 a barrel as the producing government's average "take." The new posted prices for Iranian light and heavy crudes were fixed at $11.875 and $11.635 respectively, representing an increase of 360 per cent over their January, 1973 levels.

In a Quito (Ecuador) meeting of OPEC in June, 1974, the royalties paid by foreign concessionaires were raised to 14.5 per cent from 12.5 per cent. In the Vienna meeting of September, 1974, the freeze on the posted price established in January continued, but the stated payment rate was increased to 16.67 per cent, effective October 1, "to compensate for inflation in the industrialized countries." Furthermore, an additional tax of 10.75 per cent was levied by Iran, effective 1 October 1974, to maintain tax rate parity with other OPEC members. Accordingly, the weighted average of state income per barrel from both "equity" and "participation" oil for Middle East producers, which under the 1973 Agreement had been *ipso facto* applicable to Iran, rose from $9.41 to $9.74.[30]

Subsequently, Iran took the lead in proposing a single tax-paid price for oil instead of the traditional practice of fictitious posted prices. Iran's proposal was accepted at the December, 1974 Ministerial meeting of OPEC in Vienna and will become fully effective when 100 per cent control of their oil industries has been achieved by all producing countries. The new single price is to be based on the government "take." On the basis of 60 per cent participation and 40 per cent equity for Saudi Arabia and other Arab oil producers, this price was set at $10.46 (including production cost and company profits) yielding a net government "take" of $10.12 for the benchmark Saudi Arabian light crude. This price was to remain fixed until October, 1975.[31]

Since Iran owns 100 per cent of its oil, and there is no distinction between "equity" and "participation" oil, the market prices of Iranian crudes are based on this average government "take" for marker crude, with adjustments for freight differentials and other physical characteristics. This has resulted in a barrel price of $10.67 and an average government take of $10.32.

Iran has also proposed that after October, 1975 the single oil price be adjusted periodically to an index of 20 to 30 major imported manufactured goods and commodities. The Iranian proposal was given official sanction in the Solemn Declarations of the Heads of State of OPEC in their summit meeting in Algiers in March, 1975 stating that "the price of petroleum must be maintained by linking it to certain objective criteria, including the price of manufactured goods, the rate of inflation, and the terms of transfer of goods and technology." The communique further declared OPEC's readiness to negotiate the conditions for the stabilization of oil prices with the consuming countries. In a partial move toward this goal, the OPEC Ministerial meeting in Libreville (Gabon) in June, 1975 decided to switch the pricing of oil from U.S. dollars to the International Monetary Fund's Special Drawing Rights, starting 1 October 1975.

Table I.2 (page 44) shows the per barrel posted price of Iranian light (34° API) crude, and total government oil revenues in selected years.

ENVIRONMENTAL CONSIDERATIONS

In addition to its indirect contribution to the greening of Iran through the provision of ample and cheap oil and gas supplies, which has resulted in reducing the use of wood and charcoal and increasing the supply of fertilizers for major agricultural rehabilitation, NIOC has a broad pollution control program. The Company's Research Center helps oil industry planners in the choice of optimum locations for installations, design of smokestacks, and waste disposal methods. Air, soil, and water in the vicinity of all oil and petrochemical facilities (e.g., oil wells, processing plants, tank farms, and marine terminals) are regularly monitored to make sure that oil operations do not have adverse ecological effects. All tankers must follow stringent regulations for loading and waste disposal. At the Abadan refinery, a new anti-pollution project to recycle spent sulfuric acid and freshen the air is now in operation. To the extent possible, natural gas is also being used to replace kerosene and gas oil. In short, the Company has been using its privileged public position to serve the people and protect the environment to the best of its ability.

TABLE I.2

OIL POSTED PRICE AND IRANIAN GOVERNMENT REVENUE

(In U.S. dollars)

	Posted Price (per barrel)	Average Gov't Take (per barrel)	Total Gov't Oil Revenue[a] ($ millions)
1960			285.0
September	1.78	.79	
1967			751.6
January	1.79	.87	
1970			1,143.5
November	1.79	.96	
1971			1,995.0
February	2.17	1.245	
June	2.27	1.308	
1972			2,399.0
January	2.467	1.354	
1973			4,851.1
January	2.579	1.49	
1 October	2.995	1.78	
16 October	5.341	3.20	
1974			20,400.0
January	11.875	9.26	
November	11.875	10.32	
1975			17,000.0[b]
January	11.475	10.32	

a) Year ending 21 March of the following year (e.g., for 1960, 21 March 1960 - 21 March 1961).
b) Projected.

Source: Bank Markazi Iran.

ELECTRIC POWER

Electricity was introduced in Iran only about fifty years ago.[32] And for nearly four-fifths of the time since then, electric power was considered a luxury, used almost totally for households, street lighting, and commerce, benefiting only a privileged class of people in a small part of the country. In 1940, the total power generation in Iran was less than 50 megawatts (MW). Except for a few municipal plants in large cities, the electric power industry was privately owned and operated on a very small scale. At the start of the Third Plan (1963-68), when the Ministry of Water and Power was established, there were 33 power companies in Tehran alone, with separate production units and distribution systems, lacking any effective organization or coherent policy.

Indicative of the increasing attention paid to the role of electric energy in the country's overall energy balance has been the ever-increasing allocation of development funds to the industry. Thus, while total projected fixed capital investment in the Second Plan was only 4 billion Rials (Rls.), the Third Plan's share was Rls. 16 billion; and the Fourth, Rls. 57 billion. The pinnacle of such investment, however, is to be reached in the Fifth Plan (1973-1978) with an allocation of Rls. 310 billion (nearly $4.5 billion), of which Rls. 17 billion is to go into rural electrification. Public power capacity more than doubled during the Third Plan, from 440 MW to 894 MW. Similarly, the work force in the industry, which consisted of only 7,200 people at the end of the Third Plan, reached over 18,000 at the end of the Fourth, and is expected to surpass 44,000 by the end of the Fifth.

In 1966, a ten-year plan for electricity, including the development of a national grid system, was drawn up. A broad official "power policy," however, was established for the first time in the Fourth Plan which called, *inter alia,* for (a) the expansion of the electricity industry to meet industrial, agricultural, commercial, urban, and household needs through the establishment of a national power grid; (b) improvement in planning, engineering, and management of the industry with a view to reducing unit costs and providing for internal financing of future expansion; and (c) the establishment of a "national energy council" to coordinate separate policies for the use of different energy sources by the Ministries of Water and Power, Housing and Urban Development, and Agriculture, as well as NIOC. In the meantime, water resources were nationalized to prevent their wasteful use.

Implementing these basic policies, the Ministry of Water and Power (MWP) increased installed power capacity during the Fourth Plan (1968-1972) from 894 MW to 2,094 MW, and total installed capacity (i.e., MWP, municipalities, and private) from 1,560 MW to 3,335 MW — an increase of 16.6 per cent a year. Electricity rates were restructured to meet the twin goals of equity and efficiency — lowering the average cost per KW for different uses from Rls. 4 — 7 in 1962 to Rls. 1 — 2.8 in 1972. As a result, energy generation increased at an average annual rate of over 18 per cent; and per capita, the use of electricity nearly doubled. At the same time, the share of the MWP in energy generation increased from 45 per cent in 1967 to 72 per cent in 1972. This trend is expected to continue until only a very small part of national electricity generation will be supplied by industrial facilities outside the Ministry of Energy systems.

At the start of the Fifth Plan in 1973, there were 804 MW of hydroelectric power from seven irrigation dams in the country compared to 1290 MW from steam, gas, and diesel units belonging to the Ministry of Energy, and 1260 MW of such units in the hands of municipalities and private industrial plants. Although a new 1000 MW of additional hydropower is under construction, and another 8,000 MW is under study, the share of hydroelectricity in the national power system is rather modest. It is expected to remain so in the near future, due to the scant supply of water and limited hydroelectric sites in Iran.

Government price policy for the use of electric power since the middle of the 1960's has been directed toward establishing a uniform structure of rates for the entire nation in order to: encourage increased industrial and commercial uses; extend rural electrification; cover part of the initial expenses of production, transmission, and distribution through the users' own financial participation; lower overhead costs through reduced rates for increased consumption; and formulate different rates in such a way as to ensure a 6 per cent net return on invested capital. Thus separate tariffs have been designed for households, small commercial establishments, large public use, industrial units, and farms. Some small charges for street lighting have also been added to each user's monthly bill.[33]

Table II.1 (page 48) shows Iran's actual and projected electric power generation and consumption in recent years.

Of the total publicly generated electricity in 1974, 58.6 per cent was by steam power, 30.7 per cent by hydropower, and 10.7 per cent by gas and diesel turbine units. The industrial sector consumed about 52 per cent of the publicly generated energy; commercial enterprise, 20 per cent; households, 18 per cent; street lighting, 6 per cent, agriculture and others, 4 per cent. Among the 11 power regions, Tehran ranked first in consumption with about 40 per cent of the total, followed by Khuzestan, 21.5 per cent, and so on down to the southeastern provinces, 1.1 per cent.

NATURAL GAS

Iran's gas potential is still the subject of extensive speculation. Present unofficial estimates range from 270 to 395 trillion cubic feet, making Iran's natural gas reserves second

TABLE II.1

NATIONAL ELECTRIC POWER GENERATION
(GWH)

Year	Hydro	Steam	Gas	Diesel	Nuclear	Others	Total
1967	658	732	56	396	--	2,291	4,133
1972	3,528	2,513	265	564	--	2,683	9,553
1973	2,842	5,374	541	567	--	2,769	12,093
1974	3,421	6,545	688	511	--	2,840	14,005
1977 (P)	7,218	13,323	6,500	900	--	2,964	30,905
1982 (P)	11,437	40,425	3,600	500	26,402	3,272	85,636

Columns Hydro–Nuclear are under "Ministry of Energy Systems".

Source: Ministry of Energy

only to the Soviet Union's, and about one-seventh of the world total. With indicators of even up to 600 trillion cubic feet of reserves in known structures, Iran will not only be able to meet its domestic gas needs but will also have sufficient quantities for export. The current proven reserve estimates are believed to consist of 35 trillion cf. of gas associated with oil, 205 trillion cf. of gas in domes, and 155 trillion cf. in non-oil-associated fields. Of the latter, some 14-1/2 trillion cf. exist in Sarakhs near Mashad in northeastern Iran now under utilization; 14 trillion cf. are believed to exist in Qeshm Island, and 46 trillion cf. in Kangan near Bushehr, with both locations being explored.

Despite such enormous reserves, the shift to natural gas from fuel oil, kerosene, and diesel oil has only recently become a matter of national policy. Up until the early 1960's, almost all the associated gas in the Khuzestan oil fields, run by the Consortium, was flared.[34] The first use of gas was initiated by the Consortium after 1954, through the transmission of 1.5 mcf/d from the Agha Jari oil field to Abadan for use in the refinery itself. Liquefied gas was introduced in Iran in 1955. The first pipeline to move gas from the flare stacks of Khuzestan to more distant urban centers was constructed in 1963 from Gach Saran to Shiraz. Domestic distribution and the use of gas in the northern part of the country, which long had been the Government's objective and hope, had to be postponed because of heavy initial capital outlay and the small size of the market. The major breakthrough came in 1966, when a 12-year agreement was reached with the USSR under which Iran was to supply natural gas to the Soviet Union in return for Soviet aid in the construction of the Esfahan steel mill and the Arak machine tool plant. Under this agreement, six billion cubic meters of gas are to be exported to Russia during the first year after completion of the pipeline, and gradually increased to ten billion c/m by the fifth year.

An integrated national gas policy was conceived in 1967,

when the National Iranian Gas Company (NIGC) was formed as a fully-owned subsidiary of NIOC. While the immediate scope of the new company's activities encompassed "production, processing, transmission, distribution, domestic utilization, and export" of natural gas, its long-term objective was "to substitute gas for oil as a fuel in Iran to the maximum possible extent."

In pursuing its principal functions, NIGC has thus far (1) finished the 1106-km. Iranian Gas Trunkline (IGAT), Bid Boland to Astara, in 1970, through which some 19 billion cubic meters of associated gas per year could be gathered from Khuzestan oil fields and transmitted to several major Iranian cities as well as to the Soviet Union; (2) built 676 km. of spur lines to supply natural gas eventually to the cities of Tehran, Ghom, Kashan, Esfahan, and Shiraz, among others; (3) provided the city of Ahwaz near the southern oilfields with a 16-inch 10-km. pipeline directly from the fields, and made provision for a further 220-km. extension to other parts of Khuzestan and a link with IGAT; (4) supplied gas to the city of Mashad in northeastern Iran via a 16-inch 120-km. transmission line from the Sarakhs gas field, and made provision for a later 880-km. link to the Caspian littoral; (5) laid the groundwork for the eventual transmission of gas from Qeshm Island in the Persian Gulf to Bandar Abbas for power generation, for a 2-million ton direct reduction steel mill, and for other uses in Iran's southern region; (6) established facilities for domestic production and distribution of liquefied petroleum gas; and (7) supplied natural gas to Iran's petrochemical industry.[35]

The NIGC has also moved rapidly to gain a major foothold in the world gas market. Major projects reported in this export drive consist of: (1) a trilateral 25-year deal among Iran, USSR, and West Germany, involving the delivery beginning in 1981 of some 13 billion cubic meters of gas a year to the Soviet Union through a 1500-kilometer, 25-billion-cubic-meter capacity gas pipeline (paralleling IGAT); the USSR, in turn, agreeing to deliver an equivalent amount of gas from its own Siberian gas fields to West Germany through Czechoslovakia; (2) a $5 billion LNG (liquefied natural gas) joint venture company — Kalingas — owned by NIGC (50 per cent) and a group of American, Japanese and Norwegian participants, to liquefy 1200 million cfd of gas (or 700 million tons of LNG) by 1976 for export from the Kangan gas field south of Bushehr; (3) a two-billion cfd, $6 billion initial project for gas liquefaction — rising to three billion cfd — between NIGC (50 per cent) and a consortium of American and Belgian interests for LNG export to Europe and the United States; and (4) another methanol-LNG project for export.[36]

Under the 1973 Agreement with the former Consortium, NIOC has acquired the sole ownership rights to all associated gas in the Agreement Area for domestic use (fuel consumption, feedstock for the petrochemical industry, reinjection into oil wells, etc.) as well as for export by pipeline. In projects involving liquefied natural gas export through the Persian Gulf, former Consortium members may become NIOC's partners, or purchase their share of gas output from NIOC at market prices.

Table III.1 (page 52) shows natural gas production, utilization, and revenues in recent years. As can be seen from this table, output has been growing at an annual rate of about 14 per cent a year since 1960. Since 1970 and the deliveries of gas to the Soviet Union, the flared/production ratio has declined. As a result, natural gas has become the second most important source of export earnings for Iran, and a significant contributor to GDP (gross domestic product).

OIL SUBSTITUTES

Iran's orientation toward new sources of energy to replace oil as fuel long preceded the 1973 oil price rise. In the summer of 1971, during an interview with a foreign journalist,

TABLE III.1

NATURAL GAS PRODUCTION, UTILIZATION AND REVENUE

	Production (billions of cubic feet)		Utilization (billions of cubic feet)			Exchange Receipts ($ millions)
	Consortium	NIOC & Affiliates	Flared	Exports	Domestic Use	
1960	263	2	162	--	103	--
1962	322	4	219	--	107	--
1967	707	47	613	--	141	--
1970	1,014	84	663	20	415	7
1973	1,571	127	997	246	455	86
1974	1,639	128	983	321	463	185

Source: NIOC and Bank Markazi Iran.

the Shahanshah said that although it might take several decades before oil could be replaced by nuclear and solar energy, Iran was busy training its talented youth in the intricacies of these energy alternatives.

After the oil price developments in 1973-74, Iran took the lead among oil producing countries to "show the world," so to speak, that it was actually advantageous for a nation with enormous oil reserves to develop alternative sources of energy, particularly nuclear.[37] In March, 1974 the government received a mandate, or *farman,* from the Shahanshah to establish the Atomic Energy Organization of Iran (AEOI). Subsequently, a bill was passed by the Iranian Parliament to specify AEIO's functions and responsibilities, ranging from raw materials exploration and exploitation to the production and use of atomic power and scientific research. Following the passage of the bill, the Organization was placed directly under Royal auspices.

AEOI's main tasks are: (1) to set up an extensive education and training program at home and abroad for the development of needed cadres of atomic scientists and technical experts in various fields of nuclear industry; (2) to initiate and expand research and development in nuclear sciences, and the experimentation required to reach national atomic objectives; (3) to install atomic reactors with a 23,000-MW capacity by 1992 for electricity generation, and large-scale water desalination plants to meet the needs of the arid Southern regions; (4) to procure atomic fuel, particularly enriched uranium, for domestic requirements; (5) to make use of nuclear technology in medicine, agriculture, and industry; and (6) to initiate and develop safety standards and environmental protection regulations to prevent potential hazards.

To these ends, several accords were reached with the French Atomic Energy Commission and other French interests late in 1974, under which (1) a Nuclear Research Center is to be established by 1980 near Esfahan with French technical assistance which will (a) combine Iran's existing atomic research institutes; (b) carry out studies on the application of nuclear technology in the Iranian economy; and (c) serve as the scientific arm of the country's atomic organization; (2) a technical cadre is to be trained by the French Power Authority to supply skilled manpower to operate Iran's future atomic reactors; (3) France is to sell to Iran two 900-MW atomic reactors to become operational in 1982-1983 (with three more to be made available later); and (4) Iran is to obtain 10% to 15% of the shares of Eurodif (the European company with the most advanced gas diffusion process for producing enriched uranium) and about 10% of its output at cost. The two reactors are part of a total of 24 units to be installed during the next 20 years. These reactors will be placed mostly in sparsely populated areas along the Persian Gulf and the Caspian Sea where water is available and possible hazards to people minimal.

An agreement was also signed in November, 1974 for the purchase of two 1200-MW atomic reactors from West Germany's Kraftwerke Union, to go into production by 1980-1981 for water desalination on the Persian Gulf coasts. Another agreement concluded with the United States in March, 1975 provided for the sale to Iran of six atomic power plants totalling 8000-MW capacity, with associated water desalination plants, to start operation in the early 1980's. According to this agreement, the U.S. Atomic Energy Commission has undertaken to provide each plant with some 737,000 pounds of uranium fuel as its initial load. This will involve a sale of over 4.2 million pounds of enriched uranium from the United States over a 20-year period. The agreement also called for cooperation in the civilian uses of atomic energy, i.e., an exchange of information on the application of nuclear power to peaceful purposes. As a signatory to the Non-Proliferation Treaty, Iran will be able to reprocess its spent nuclear fuel at home.

The impetus for the diversified nature of these purchase/service agreements is evidently a determination by the Iranian Government (a) to avoid dependence on any one country for the manufacture of the plants and the sale of uranium; and (b) to use various nuclear technologies, especially those independent of foreign nuclear fuels. AEOI is also currently exploring for uranium in Iran and actively encouraging Iranian atomic energy experts living and working abroad to return home.[38]

In the field of geothermal exploration and development, Iran's effective program began with a request by the Government to the United Nations for technical advice. A preliminary appraisal of the country's geothermal potential was made available in a U.N. report in December, 1974 in which a number of high-temperature springs were identified, and three specific high priority locations were designated for further investigation. Following this report, an agreement was signed in March, 1975 between Iran's Ministry of Energy and the Italian National Electric Energy Agency (ENEL), to (1) undertake geothermal resources development studies, and (2) pinpoint, in a designated part of Iran, both the potential sites and their capabilities for generating electric energy or other uses. The contract will be carried out in two phases. The first phase will consist of reconnaissance studies in the specific regions and recommendations for further work. Phase two will be devoted to making feasibility studies for the development of the sites selected by the Ministry. Both phases will have to be completed in not more than four years.

An initially modest budget has also been allocated for the purpose of research studies and purchase of equipment in the field of solar energy development in Iran.

National Energy Policy: The 1970's and Beyond

Compared with many other industrialized countries suffering from a shortage of domestic energy resources, Iran is fortuitously endowed with large reserves of gas and oil as well as a modest supply of hydroelectric power and coal.[39] Thus, while the task of providing needed energy for its economic development in the next few decades may not cause any grave concern to Iran's economic planners, the problem of a proper allocation and efficient use of these energy resources is foremost in their minds.

At present about 71 per cent of the total energy generated in Iran is derived from petroleum, 18 per cent from natural gas, 5 per cent from hydroelectricity, and the rest from coal and non-commercial sources. At the same time, nearly 95 per cent of the country's energy production is exported in the form of oil, oil products, and natural gas. The consumption of oil products and natural gas has been rising steadily in the last decade, from less than 4-1/2 million tons in 1964 to nearly 15 million in 1974. Given the salutary effects of Iran's social welfare and income redistribution policies on raising the national standard of living (and the aggregate demand for energy) in the coming years, the Iranian authorities have predicted a rising annual need for energy supplies at rates closely approximating the GDP — about 15 per cent a year.

Despite its considerable wealth in fossil fuels (more than

66 billion barrels of proven oil reserves), Iran fears that one of the Fifth Plan's bottlenecks will be the inadequacy of the supply of oil products for some large-scale projects in the electricity, transport, and industrial sectors. Iran presently produces over 10 per cent of total world crude oil, nearly 20 per cent of OPEC's total crude output, and more than 26 per cent of the Middle East's total output. Iran ranks as the world's fourth largest producer (after the USSR, USA, and Saudi Arabia), and the second largest exporter (after Saudi Arabia). At 1975 production rates, however, Iran's proven oil reserves may not last more than 30 years.

To close the gap between energy needs and energy supplies in present and future plans, the Government keenly feels the need to develop and use other sources of energy in lieu of oil and gas. Thus, both the Fifth Plan and a 20-year, long-term perspective for national economic development have devoted a good deal of attention to future individual fuel policies as well as to an integrated national energy policy.

PETROLEUM

The overall guidelines and policy objectives for the Iranian oil industry in the Fifth Development Plan (1973-1978) and beyond are, *inter alia,* (1) to meet total domestic consumption needs for oil and oil products, which are expected to rise nearly 18 per cent a year, from about 22,000 b/d in 1973 to 480,000 b/d in 1978, by (a) expanding the productive capacity of existing refineries in Abadan, Tehran, Kermanshah and Shiraz, and building three new refineries in Tabriz, Esfahan and Ahwaz; and (b) laying a total of 27,000 kilometer-inches of new product pipelines; (2) to strike a balance between production and consumption of oil products by the maximum possible substitution of natural gas for middle distillates;

(3) to seek regular markets for crude oil and oil products in major consumption centers outside Iran by (a) oil exploration and production in the North Sea and Greenland; (b) participation in refining and distribution in the United States, Europe, Africa, and Asia; (c) making use of international pipeline projects in consuming countries; and (d) expanding the capacity of Iran's tanker fleet and participating in joint ventures in oil transportation with other countries; (4) to maximize the utilization of crude oil and gas in the domestic production of petrochemicals with a higher value-added for export to world markets; (5) to conserve national oil and gas reserves through efficient exploitation and optimum development; (6) to expand and speed up exploration programs throughout the country and on the continental shelf in order to increase proven reserves; (7) to increase crude oil exports in a prudent manner at prices which would be commensurate with the production costs of other sources of energy, and would allow for the effects of foreign inflation and currency devaluation; and (8) to conduct basic environmental research, and to take specific measures for combating air and water pollution.

To these ends, NIOC has a $7.5 billion five-year investment program for the expansion of oil, gas, and petrochemical facilities beginning in 1976. The program reportedly aims at raising the oil production capacity from the average 5.6 million b/d in 1974 to 7.2 million b/d in 1978, and increasing gas utilization from the present capacity of 5 billion cfd to 30 billion cfd. NIOC's strategy has also been geared to a considerable expansion of refining capacity, from the existing 825,000 b/d to nearly 1.5 million b/d. This program includes the expansion of the Abadan export-refinery — the world's largest — to 600,000 b/d.

In line with the new objectives, NIOC has moved toward a greater vertical integration of the national oil industry: *upstream* into "service-type" exploration and prospecting, and *downstream* into oil refining, transportation, marketing, and retailing. Such an integration is believed to be not only in the best national financial interests by eliminating the unneeded "middlemen," but it is also considered an integral part of a broader national policy aimed at (a) oil conservation (especially through efficient exploitation and secondary recovery), and (b) environmental protection.

Toward these objectives, NIOC has been increasing its "service-type" agreements with foreign interests to strengthen its own upstream operations. In the area of forward integration, NIOC has set up a marine transportation subsidiary, the National Iranian Tanker Company, which in 1975 had a tanker capacity of some 680,000 tons dwt, including two 230,000-ton supertankers, Azarpad and Kharg. INTC also signed an agreement in April, 1975 with the British Petroleum Corporation to form a jointly-managed oil tanker fleet. In the downstream area (in addition to the Madras and South African refineries), an agreement has reportedly been reached with Senegal for the formation of a 50-50 joint venture under which a 60,000 b/d refinery will be built to supply a chain of gas stations.

Finally, Iran's present oil policy, until the day when alternate sources of energy can replace petroleum as a fuel, is to produce a sufficient quantity for its own use and a reasonable amount for export to those countries dependent on oil for their economic well-being and prosperity. Table IV.1 (page 60) shows past and projected oil production and utilization. From an estimated 66 billion/barrels, production from the Khuzestan oil fields is expected to reach 42.6 b/b, of which 29.4 b/b will be sold to the former Consortium partners; 6 b/b will be consumed domestically (1.6 b/b for petrochemicals); and 7.2 b/b will be exported directly by NIOC. Another 4 b/b is expected to be produced from other Iranian oil fields and offshore activities.

TABLE IV.1

OIL PRODUCTION AND UTILIZATION IN SELECTED YEARS

(Million cubic meters)

	1967	1972	1977	1982
Crude Production	151	292	472	524
Crude Export	125	262	432	422
Domestic Consumption*	10	13	28	57
Petrochemicals	--	--	5	15
Refined Export	16	17	7	30

*Excluding LPG, but including loss and oil industry uses.

Source: For 1967-1972, NIOC; for 1977-1982, unpublished, unofficial projections.

POWER

In the Fifth Plan, the annual generation of electric energy by public sector is expected to grow at an annual rate of 35 per cent (from 6,870 to 31,000 MKWH). Installed capacity will increase from 2,094 MW to 7,500 MW. The national grid will account for nearly 90 per cent of electric generation, and the remainder will be supplied by private industrial enterprises for their own consumption. Nearly 70 per cent of electric generation will be thermal, 25 per cent hydroelectric, and the remainder gas and diesel units. Per capita generation of electric energy will grow at an annual rate of 27.5 per cent (from 307 KWH to 943 KWH).

The establishment and development of electricity facilities and power distribution are to take place within the frame-

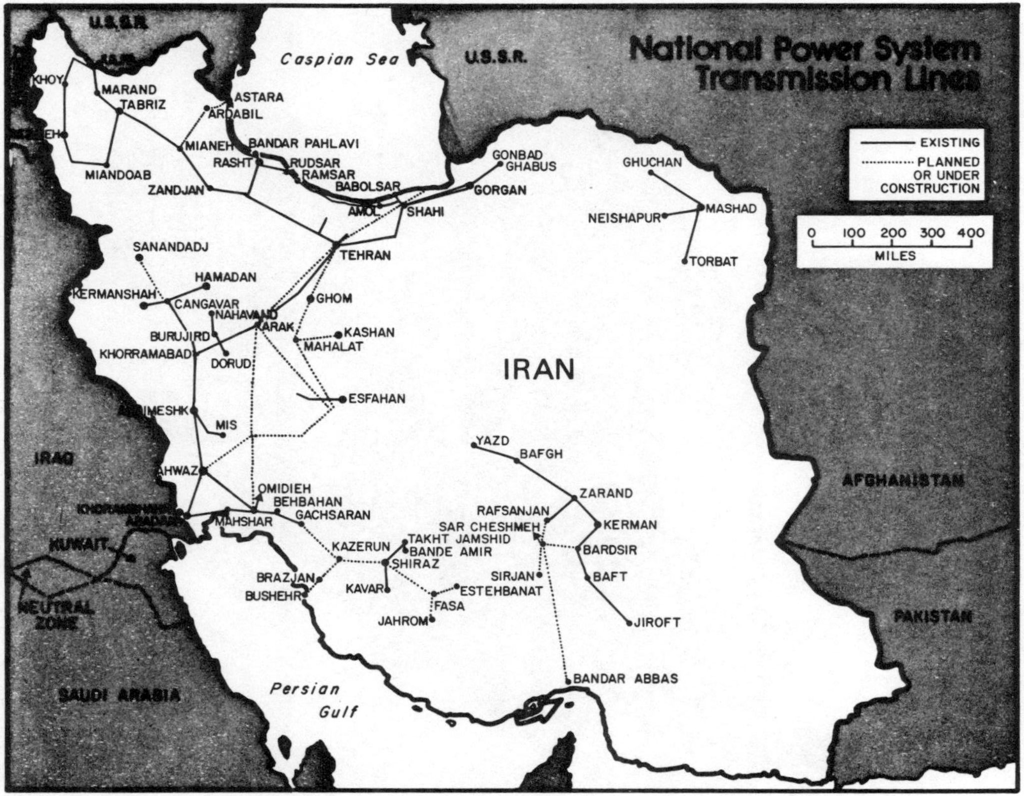
National Power System Transmission Lines
EXISTING
PLANNED OR UNDER CONSTRUCTION
0 100 200 300 400
MILES
U.S.S.R.
Caspian Sea
U.S.S.R.
KHOY
MARAND
TABRIZ
ASTARA
ARDABIL
MIANEH
BANDAR PAHLAVI
RASHT
RUDSAR
RAMSAR
MIANDOAB
ZANDJAN
BABOLSAR
AMOL
SHAHI
GONBAD GHABUS
GORGAN
GHUCHAN
MASHAD
NEISHAPUR
TORBAT
TEHRAN
SANANDADJ
HAMADAN
KERMANSHAH
CANGAVAR
NAHAVAND
GHOM
ARAK
KASHAN
MAHALAT
BURUJIRD
KHORRAMABAD
DORUD
IRAN
ESFAHAN
MIS
IRAQ
AHWAZ
YAZD
BAFGH
ZARAND
AFGHANISTAN
OMIDIEH
BEHBAHAN
GACHSARAN
MAHSHAR
RAFSANJAN
SAR CHESHMEH
KERMAN
KAZERUN
TAKHT JAMSHID
BANDE AMIR
BARDSIR
KUWAIT
SHIRAZ
SIRJAN
BAFT
BRAZJAN
BUSHEHR
KAVAR
ESTEHBANAT
FASA
NEUTRAL ZONE
JAHROM
JIROFT
PAKISTAN
BANDAR ABBAS
SAUDI ARABIA
Persian Gulf

Iranian Gas Trunkline

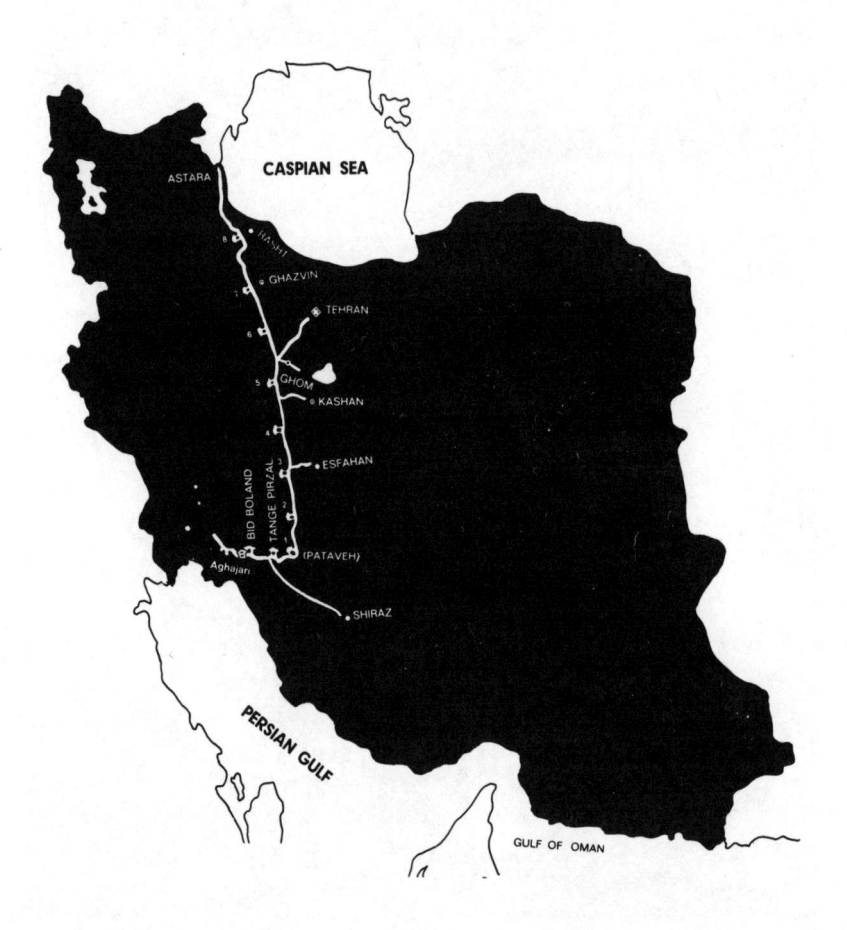

work of an energy master-plan and in coordination with the development of the supply of other forms of energy, particularly nuclear energy. In order to minimize air pollution in urban areas and to economize on fuel for power generation, efforts will be made to establish power-generating facilities close to oil refineries and natural gas fields.

The power transmission network will be expanded and all centers of generation and consumption will be linked. The total length of power transmission lines will be increased from about 3,000 kilometers to nearly 9,200 kilometers. The present power distribution networks will be improved to ensure maximum reliability and minimize voltage fluctuations, and to make sure that they are capable of handling all urban demands.

In the Fifth Plan, electricity rates will be fixed for various categories of consumer on the basis of actual cost and the addition of a reasonable profit, so that the entire development costs of the electricity industry may be obtained from the industry's internal resources over a long-term period. Investment in about 1200 rural electricity facilities, however, will be made from government funds in view of high costs and the non-profit nature of such investments, and as part of a long-term program to raise rural living standards.

Tables IV.2 and IV.3 (page 63) show actual and projected generating capacity of the Ministry of Energy systems, and energy sales during the 1972-1992 period.

NATURAL GAS

Iran's natural gas policies and objectives in the Fifth Plan are to (1) make greater use of Iran's natural gas in the production of petrochemicals; (2) supply a major part of the country's primary energy requirements; (3) expand gas exports; and (4) increase output/capital ratio in the gas industry.

Within these broad objectives, appropriate attempts are to be made to (a) expand, as much as possible, natural gas pipelines and distribution networks; (b) encourage household and commercial consumption of natural gas by regulating consumer prices and facilitating link-ups with gas mains; (c) set gas rates in relation to oil products for both home consumption and export; and (d) ensure adequacy and dependability of supply to gas users, with strict adherence to safety considerations in gas-delivery facilities.

Under these specific policy objectives and guidelines, NIGC is to continue the second phase of the Iran Gas Trunkline project; construct a second gas pipeline to meet the requirements of power plants, petrochemical units, and direct reduction steel complexes and other consumers along the route; develop gas resources in Qeshm Island and construct a gas pipeline from Qeshm to the Bandar Abbas steel mill and Sarcheshmeh copper mine; develop Kangan gas resources; and establish an integrated gas system in Khuzestan.

By the end of the Plan period, these projects are expected to increase the share of natural gas in Iran's energy use from 18 per cent to nearly 24 per cent. Total consumption should reach about 9 billion cf. per year. Over a longer period, natural gas as a fuel source is to replace oil and be in turn replaced by nuclear energy. Priorities will then have to be given to (a) the use of gas in petrochemicals; (b) its replacement of coal in the direct-conversion steel industry; (c) its reinjection into oil wells to increase second-recovery possibilities (variously estimated between 10-60 billion barrels in Khuzestan oil fields); and (d) its export. Table IV.4 (page 64) shows estimated gas utilization in the next few years.

As can be seen in this table, gas consumption (as fuel in household and commercial uses, electric generation, and oil field utilization) of 290 million cubic feet a day in 1972 is expected to reach 2500 mcf/d by 1982 and 6900 mcf/d in

TABLE IV.2
PROJECTED SOURCES AND USES OF PUBLIC POWER: 1972-1992
(Megawatts)

Year	Steam	Gas	Diesel	Hydro	Nuclear	Total
1972	746	172	372	804	–	2,094
1977	2,649	2,357	665	1,804	–	7,475
1982	11,070	2,300	600	5,034	3,400	22,404
1987	17,900	4,000	300	9,800	8,000	40,000
1992	24,000	6,000	–	20,000	20,000	70,000*

*Total installed capacity by public and private sources is expected to be 72,000 MW.

Source: Ministry of Energy

TABLE IV.3
ENERGY SALES BY THE MINISTRY OF ENERGY SYSTEMS
(GWH)

Year	Residential	Commercial	Industrial	Agricultural	Street Lighting	Total
1967	473	324	504	33	127	1,416
1972	1,218	1,296	2,745	141	323	5,723
1977 (P)	3,354	5,474	14,605	748	687	24,868
1982 (P)	10,292	14,771	39,868	1,965	1,109	68,005

Source: Ministry of Energy

1992. Petrochemical and steel needs should also rise from 100 mcf/d in 1972 to 3000 mcf/d and 6100 mcf/d in 1982 and 1992. Coupled with projected requirements for export through pipelines and in liquid form during this period, one may safely assume that while the Fifth Plan demand for gas can be met chiefly from "associated" gas, full use of non-associated gas (in Sarakhs, Qeshm and Kangan) will have to be made toward the end of the Sixth Plan. Future plans will require stepped-up exploration and discovery of new sources, or further inroads into the enormous gas domes.[40]

TABLE IV.4

ESTIMATED DOMESTIC GAS USE AND EXPORT IN SELECTED YEARS

(Million cubic feet daily)

	1962	1967	1972	1977	1982	1987	1992
Household, Commercial, etc.	2	4.2	49.1	465	607	1550	2262
Petrochemicals*	2.6	8	8.5	103	205	350	350
Steel	--	--	5.1	103	509	546	546
Export	--	--	790	1000	5500	5500	5500
Flared & Losses	600	1680	2300	2000	n.a.	n.a.	n.a.

n.a. Not available
*Allocated gas by NIGC only

Source: National Iranian Gas Company

Institutional Arrangements

The responsibility for the establishment and implementation of Iran's national energy policy is shared by three principal public agencies — the Ministry of Energy, the National Iranian Oil Company (and its subsidiaries), and the Atomic Energy Organization — under the supreme leadership and guidance of the Shahanshah, with the participation of the Council of Ministers in specific cases.

THE MINISTRY OF ENERGY

The present institutional arrangements for the administration of national energy resources have evolved over the past decade or so. In 1963 the Iran Electric Authority was established as an autonomous agency to carry out the national power development program and regulate small private plants, municipally-owned utilities, and private industry units. In 1964 the IEA was given ministerial status with wider authority and broad responsibilities. The power sector was largely nationalized in 1965 to facilitate the consolidation of low-efficiency private and municipal plants into large-scale generating and distribution facilities.

In 1969 the Iranian Power Generation and Transmission

Company (TAVANIR) was formed to put the entire electric supply system under a single administration. TAVANIR is now responsible for the generation and transmission of power in the public sector. In addition to TAVANIR, eleven regional electric companies are responsible for the distribution of electric power throughout the country. The construction of irrigation dams and hydroelectric stations, as well as the management and supply of hydropower, are the responsibility of five regional water authorities (in Khuzestan, Tehran, Azerbaijan, Esfahan and Shomal) under the Ministry of Energy.

The Ministry of Energy, established by law in March, 1974 as one of the Government's regular ministries represented in the Council of Ministers, is a successor to the former Ministry of Water and Power. Under the reorganization, the new Ministry is now responsible for setting up the overall national energy policy (Article 1, c). The Ministry has the duty of ensuring an optimum use of national energy and water resources. To this end, it is expected to conduct studies of, and research on, different sources of energy; to draw up short-run and long-term plans for the exploitation of energy resources; to estimate the amount of energy which can be produced annually; to assess the amount of energy needed in the different sectors of the economy; and to coordinate the consumption of all uses of energy (Article 1, a). The Ministry also coordinates the functions of any institutions involved in producing, exploiting, transporting, and distributing energy in the country (Article 1, d). Furthermore, it is charged by law to supervise the use of all energy sources, determine and approve the manner in which they are to be used, and the rates at which they should be sold in local markets (Article 1, 3).

Among a dozen or more other specific functions assigned to the Ministry, mention ought to be made of its responsibility to communicate and exchange scientific, technical, industrial, and commercial information and cooperation in the field of energy with foreign countries and institutions; to devise and implement necessary projects for the establishment of power plants, transmission and distribution networks, and desalination facilities; to carry out necessary research on water-related problems and to use modern, scientific, and technical methods in utilizing water more efficiently; to provide and implement training programs to furnish energy industries with necessary manpower; and even to manufacture equipment and machinery required by water and power industries (Articles 1, h, i, n, o, p).

THE NATIONAL IRANIAN OIL COMPANY

The National Iranian Oil Company, under the provisions of the new Petroleum Act of August, 1974, is a public corporation exercising ownership rights over all oil and gas reserves in Iran. It has responsibility for the exploration, development, production, exploitation, and distribution of petroleum throughout Iran and its continental shelf.

Article 8 of the Ministry of Energy Act places jurisdiction over oil, gas, and related products in the hands of NIOC and its subsidiaries to be carried out in accordance with the Petroleum Act. The Company informs the Ministry of its production, refining, and distribution plans for oil and gas, and the Ministry coordinates the plans with those for other sources of energy. Some activities of NIOC require prior approval of the Council of Ministers.

According to the Petroleum Act of 1974 and a companion law on the internal organization and functions of NIOC, the Company has the right, among other responsibilities, to refine and process oil, natural gas, and other natural hydrocarbons; to supply, transport, distribute, export, and sell oil in both domestic and foreign markets; to participate in activities of the petrochemical and gas industries; and to pursue those development projects which are deemed necessary for the expansion of the oil industry.

Under the provisions of these laws, NIOC is responsible for establishing policies with respect to the sale, distribution, and export of oil and oil products. The domestic price policy for gasoline, kerosene, gas oil, and fuel oil must be submitted to the Council of Ministers for its approval. But prices of other oil products and natural gas can be determined by the Company independently. Iran's international price policy and other cooperative arrangements with the Organization of Petroleum Exporting Countries are conducted by a Cabinet minister under the direct guidance of the Shahanshah.

As an integrated commercial enterprise with almost exclusive power over all phases of oil industry operations, NIOC is, in effect, in charge of gas and oil policies. These, in turn, significantly influence not only policies related to other sources of energy, but also national fiscal and development policies, as well as environmental objectives. Basically the Company operates in three different ways: (1) by independently producing, selling, or exporting oil and oil products; (2) by joint ventures with foreign oil companies on the basis of prearranged profit-sharing plans; and (3) by "service contracts" under which foreign oil interests perform specific activities on behalf of the Company under certain incentives.

NIOC's administration is in the hands of (1) the Board of Shareholders; (2) the Board of Directors; (3) the General Managing Director; and (4) the High Board of Inspection. Since the entire Rls. 100 billion capital of the Company belongs to the Iranian Government, the *ex officio* Shareholders' Board consists of the Prime Minister, the Minister of Energy, and five other ministers in charge of economic affairs, who are responsible for the formulation of Company policies, the approval of annual regular and investment budgets, and the submission of proposals to the Council of Ministers for changes in capitalization or administration.

The Board of Directors is composed of: (a) the Managing Director, who is also the Chairman; (b) nine other directors, one of whom is the managing director of Iran's Petrochemical Company and another the managing director of the National Iranian Gas Company; and (c) five alternate directors who substitute for the principals in their absence. The Managing Director is nominated by the Board of Shareholders, approved by the Council of Ministers, and appointed by Royal decree for a renewable six-year term. The directors are nominated by the Managing Director for a renewable three-year term and receive Royal appointments. Their responsibilities include the formulation of corporate activities and operations (e.g., production, sale, export, and price policies), independently or with the approval of the Government according to the Articles; preparation of annual budgets; establishment of, and changes in, Company by-laws; conclusion of joint-venture or service agreements in accordance with the Petroleum Act of 1974; and the establishment or liquidation of subsidiaries.

The Managing Director and Chairman of the Board of Directors is the highest official of the Company. He is responsible for day-to-day operation and he represents NIOC before all other organizations and agencies at home and abroad. He is also the Chairman of the Board of all NIOC subsidiaries.

Finally, the High Board of Inspection consists of five individuals with expertise in accounting, finance, and oil industry managment who are appointed for a renewable two-year term by the Board of Shareholders. The responsibilities of the controllers include internal audits of NIOC accounts, the inspection of corporate books and documents, and the certification of annual income statements and balance-sheets.

THE ATOMIC ENERGY ORGANIZATION

The Atomic Energy Organization of Iran is an autonomous public institution created by an Act of Parliament in 1974. Its main objectives are to construct nuclear power plants and water desalination facilities, produce raw materials needed in nuclear industries, and coordinate and supervise all nuclear-energy-related affairs. The Organization is expected to expand and develop nuclear knowledge and techniques in Iran and set up a scientific foundation for the use of such knowledge and techniques in development plans; conduct studies and research on atomic-related issues; provide technical services required by nuclear industries; carry out exploratory research and surveys to determine the availability of raw material resources, such as nuclear fuel and radioactive materials, needed in nuclear industries; exploit these resources through extraction and purification processes and use them in atomic power plants and other nuclear facilities; set up water desalination facilities to provide for the water requirements of the economy; produce and distribute radio-isotopes and other required nuclear materials and equipment; and to represent Iran in the International Atomic Energy Agency.

The Atomic Energy Organization has an Atomic Energy Council and an Atomic Energy Committee. The Council is headed by the Prime Minister, and has nine other ex-officio members, mostly Cabinet ministers, including the Minister of Energy, plus four additional experts who are nominated by the Atomic Energy Committee and appointed by Imperial decree. The Atomic Energy Committee has three members: the Minister of Energy, who is the Chief of the Committee, the Minister of Economic Affairs and Finance, and the Minister of State – Chief of the Plan and Budget Organization.

The Council is responsible for establishing national policies and plans related to nuclear science and technology, including safety regulations, environmental protection, and cooperation with other countries in the atomic energy field. The Committee sets forth executive policies and supervises the management of the Organization. The Chief of the Atomic Energy Organization is in charge of day-to-day operations and also acts as secretary of the Council and the Committee. He is nominated by the Prime Minister, appointed by Imperial decree, and participates in the meetings of the Committee without vote.

TABLE IV.5

IRAN'S ENERGY SOURCES IN SELECTED YEARS
(Trillion Kilocalories)

	2nd Plan 1962	3rd 1967	4th 1972	5th 1977	6th 1982	7th 1987	8th 1992
Petroleum	38.4 (60.4)	65.8 (72.3)	119.2 (72.7)	239.3 (66.4)	424.0 (55.8)	629.0 (51.0)	748.0 (39.2)
Natural Gas	9.9 (15.5)	12.9 (14.1)	28.1 (16.9)	98.0 (27.0)	243.0 (32.0)	431.0 (35.0)	668.0 (35.0)
Coal	1.4 (2.2)	1.7 (1.8)	2.5 (1.5)	-- --	-- --	-- --	-- --
Hydroelectricity	0.3 (0.7)	2.4 (2.6)	9.5 (5.7)	19.7 (5.4)	27.8 (3.7)	55.0 (4.4)	110.0 (5.7)
Non-commercial (Charcoal, Wood, etc.)	13.5 (21.2)	8.5 (9.2)	5.3 (3.2)	4.5 (1.2)	-- --	-- --	-- --
Nuclear power	-- --	-- --	-- --	-- --	65 (8.5)	116.0 (9.6)	382.0 (20.1)
Total	63.5 (100)	91.3 (100)	164.6 (100)	361.5 (100)	759.8 (100)	1231.0 (100)	1908.0 (100)

Source: Figures supplied by the National Iranian Oil Company, Ministry of Energy, and the Plan and Budget Organization for 1962-1977. Unpublished, unofficial projections for 1977-1992.

The Future Energy Policy of Iran

As the preceding sections have shown, Iran is determined to pursue a sophisticated energy policy at home and destined to play a major role in the world energy drama. The long-term energy policy adopted under the Fifth Plan has been designed to meet the growing domestic demand for energy, fulfill export commitments for the delivery of oil and gas, and make increasingly efficient use of national energy resources.

The future energy policy of Iran will aim at: (1) a maximum possible reduction in the use of petroleum as energy fuel; an increase in its utilization as a raw material base for petrochemicals; and an extension of the life of oil reserves; (2) the optimum use of atomic energy for electricity generation in order to meet a major part of domestic energy requirements; (3) the maximum use of hydropower and river flows as a supplemental source of electricity; (4) the maximum use of natural gas as a substitute for other fuels (particularly middle distillates) in commercial and residential uses; (5) a limited use of coal as an energy fuel, and its maximum employment in present and potential steel production; (6) the effective use and improvement of modern energy technologies to increase productivity of energy generation, and the efficiency of energy consumption; and finally, (7) basic research and development of economically feasible alternative new sources of energy.

Under these broad guidelines, priority is to be given to electric energy, the annual rate of growth of which is expected to exceed all other sources. Electric power will increase its installed capacity from 3,350 MW in 1972 to nearly 72,000 MW in 1992. Within the power sector, the utmost attention will be paid to the full development of the nation's hydroelectric potential in an attempt to raise installed capacity from a mere 800 MW in 1972 to 10,000 MW in 1992. Nuclear power is to become a reality with plants capable of a 4,000 MW average capacity by the Seventh Plan (1982-1987). It is expected to expand thereafter and provide about 20,000 MW of energy, or 20 per cent of total national energy production and 30 per cent of electric energy by 1992. The share of natural gas consumption will increase from 24 per cent in the Fifth Plan to 35 per cent in the Seventh, and will maintain this ratio from then on. The use of oil and oil products will gradually diminish as the shares of gas and nuclear power increase, in such a way that, at the end of the Seventh Plan, petroleum's share will fall to an average of 44 per cent of total national energy, compared to a 70 per cent average in the Fifth Plan. Table IV.5 (page 72) shows actual and projected components of Iran's energy supplies from the Second Plan to the Eighth Plan.

Given continued enlightened domestic leadership, necessary solidarity and cohesion among OPEC members, an adequate expansion and improvement of the technical cadres, and sufficient coordination among responsible agencies, there is every reason to expect that Iran will succeed in implementing its broad-based and progressive energy policy in the years to come.

NOTES

1. Later, domestic consumption rose to 153,000 m/t in 1937 and more than 603,000 m/t in 1947.

2. See HIM Mohammed Reza Shah Pahlavi, *Mission for My Country* (London: Hutchinson, 1960), Ch. 12.

3. For a fuller historical study of early oil developments in Iran see L.P. Elwell-Sutton, *Persian Oil: A Study in Power Politics* (London: Lawrence and Wishart, 1955); Charles Issawi (ed.), *The Economic History of Iran 1800-1914* (Chicago: University of Chicago Press, 1971); and Benjamin Shwadran, *The Middle East, Oil and the Great Powers* (New York, 1955).

4. Technically, at least, the *first* oil concession was granted by Nasseredin Shah to a British subject in 1866 as part of a general concession to build a railroad in Iran with the right to exploit minerals (including oil) within four miles on both sides of the tracks.

5. As far back as the early 1880's, Russian oil industrialists were intent on beating their American rivals in the Asian markets (i.e., India, Indochina and Australia) through the construction of a kerosene pipeline across Iran between the Caspian Sea and the Persian Gulf. They thus considered Reuter's unlimited concession as an obstacle to their project.

6. Between 1872 and 1890 two other minor concessions for mineral explorations were granted to an Iranian and a Dutch national, neither of which came to fruition.

7. The Imperial Bank finally closed in 1952, following the oil nationalization.

8. For the text of the D'Arcy agreement see J.C. Hurewitz, *Diplomacy*

in the Near and Middle East (Princeton: Van Nostrand, 1956), pp. 249-51.

9. Total revenues received by Iran from 1911 to 1920 amounted to less than £1.8 million.

10. For the text of the "1933 Agreement" see J.C. Hurewitz, *op. cit.*

11. The minimum annual guarantee was raised to £4 million in 1944.

12. For a fuller account of Russian interests in Iranian oil, see George Lenczowski, *Russia and the West in Iran, 1918-1948* (Ithaca: Cornell University Press, 1949).

13. For a background of American oil interests in Iran, including a weak attempt by the Standard Vacuum Oil Company in 1944, see *The International Petroleum Cartel* (U.S. Select Committee on Small Business, 82nd Congress, 2nd Session, 1952).

14. Among the significant developments in the Middle East oil industry, Aramco had signed a 50-50 profit-sharing agreement with Saudi Arabia in January, 1951.

15. NIOC actually took over the Iran Oil Company, which was established in 1949 along with the creation of the Plan Organization as a public corporation to explore and prospect for oil.

16. For a full account of Iran's oil nationalization, see Alan W. Ford, *The Anglo-Iranian Oil Dispute 1951-1952* (Berkeley, the University of California Press, 1954). For the events leading to nationalization and its aftermath, see Lenczowski and Elwell-Sutton, *op. cit.* See also "Iran Presents Its Case for Nationalization," *The Oil Forum,* March, 1952).

17. The shares in the Consortium in 1973 were as follows: The British Petroleum Company Ltd., 40%; Royal Dutch Shell Group, 14%; Gulf Oil Corporation, Socony Mobil Oil Company, Standard Oil Company (New Jersey), Standard Oil Company (California), and the Texas Company, each 7%; Compagnie Francaise des Petroles, 6%; and the Iricon Agency Ltd., consisting of seven smaller American "independents" — Amoco, Arco, Continental, Getty, Signal, Standard Oil of Ohio, and Tidewater — together, 5%.

18. For the text of the new agreement and ownership shares of the Consortium, see *Platt's Oilgram News Service,* 5 October 1954.

19. *Iraanse Aardolie Exploratie en Productie Maatschappij, N.V.,* and *Iraanse Aardolie Raffinage Maatschappij, N.V.*

20. For details of these negotiations and their references, see S. Chubin and S. Zabih, *The Foreign Relations of Iran* (Berkeley: The University of California Press, 1974), Ch. IX.

21. The IPAC agreement also contained a $25 million prepaid "bonus" to NIOC.

22. For details, see *Petroleum Industry in Iran* (Tehran: NIOC [1975]).

23. The purchase price follows OPEC's basic price for Arabian light 34° API, adjusted for specific Iranian light and heavy characteristics. See below.

24. As a public corporation, NIOC transfers to the Government of Iran 98% of the royalty and balancing margin payments, as well as proceeds from its own export. It also pays the Government annually a tax on its profits and a portion of its net income as dividends.

25. For numerous source references to this policy and their analysis, see Chubin and Zabih, *op. cit.*, Ch. IX.

26. The domestic refining capacity is to be expanded to 1,100,000 b/d by 1977 with completion of Tabriz and Esfahan refineries. The second Tehran Refinery with a capacity of 100,000 b/d (5.8 million cubic meters a year) was inaugurated in March, 1975.

27. For the list and details see *Petroleum Industry in Iran*.

28. For the full provisions of the new accord, see *Sale and Purchase Agreement* (Tehran: NIOC, 31 July 1973).

29. NIOC set the f.o.b. market price of its own entitlement of crude from the Consortium Area at $3.62-.70 in October, 1973, and at $3.66-.85 during November.

30. These new changes set the royalty at 16.67 per cent, and the income tax rate at 65.75 per cent.

31. In November, 1974, Saudi Arabia, Qatar, and Abu Dhabi lowered the posted price for their oil to $11.25 from $11.65, but raised the royalty rate to 20 per cent and income tax rate to 85 per cent, thus raising the government's "take" to $10.12. This decision, taken outside OPEC's framework, was later sanctioned by the Organization.

32. The first plant was built in 1908 by the then Anglo-Persian Oil Company, and the first major unit outside the oilfields was a 6 MW plant installed in Tehran in 1934.

33. For further details see *Electric Power Industry in Iran, 1973* (Tehran: Ministry of Water and Power, 1974).

34. By one Iranian estimate, about 200×10^9 cubic meters of gas have been flared from the beginning of the oil industry in Iran until 1971. Even in 1974, of the 4.4 billion cubic feet of associated gas produced daily, only a little more than 2 billion cfd was utilized (including some

880 million cfd export to the Soviet Union), and the rest was flared.

35. For further details of these agreements see *Petroleum Industry in Iran* (Tehran: NIOC [1975]).

36. For details of gas projects and programs, see *Petroleum Industry in Iran*, and Charles Snow, "Iran: Gas on the Move," *Middle East Economic Survey*, 7 February 1975.

37. By one Westerner's account, Iran is inching toward nuclear energy because it pays to burn cheaper materials (uranium) and sell the more expensive one (oil). According to this account, uranium cost 22 cents per million BTU's and oil $2.20.

38. For further details, see the Iran Atomic Energy Organization *Annual Report* (in Persian) (Tehran: IAO, 1975).

39. Coal is reserved for industrial use, and particularly for Iran's growing steel industry. Only one small electic plant is expected to use the coal rejected from the steel industry in the future. Coal consumption is expected to increase from 300,000 metric tons in 1967 to 2.5 million m/t in 1977 and 4 million m/t in 1982.

40. The reinjection needs of the Khuzestan fields are privately estimated to range between 8 and 13 billion cfd. With available associated gas expected to be about 2 billion cfd by 1980, the balance will have to be made up from the pure natural gas fields. A modest inroad has already been made into the Naft Sefid dome in order to deliver 300 million cfd to the Haft Kel oil field.

THE EDITOR

Gerard J. Mangone is H. Rodney Sharp Professor of International Law and Organization in the graduate professional College of Marine Studies, and is Director of the Center for the Study of Marine Policy. He has been Coordinator of Ocean Studies, Woodrow Wilson International Center for Scholars; Executive Director of the President's Comission on the United Nations; Consultant to the State Department, White House, and United Nations; Faculty member or Visiting Professor at ten universities; Dean and Provost; author, co-author, or editor of twenty books on world affairs.

CONTRIBUTING AUTHORS

LAWSON A. W. HUNTER *(Canada)* — LL.B., University of New Brunswick; LL.M., Harvard University School of Law; and post-doctoral Fellow at Woods Hole Oceanographic Institution. He served in the Department of Justice of Canada and was then appointed to the Department of Consumer and Corporate Affairs.

CHOON-HO PARK *(China)* — B.A. in Political Science, Seoul, Korea and Ph.D. in public international law at Edinburgh University. He was a member of Korean UN Law of the Sea delegation and a Research Fellow in the East Asian Legal Studies Program at Harvard University.

THOMAS C. BARGER *(Persian Gulf)* — B.S., University of North Dakota; mining engineer; expert in governmental relations; linguist; and administrator with a lifetime experience in the Middle East. He was President of the Arabian-American Oil Company in 1959 and Chairman of the Board in 1968.

ANIBAL R. MARTINEZ B.S., Central University, Caracas, Venezuela
(Venezuela) and M.S. in geology and petroleum engineering, Stanford University. He worked for Creole Petroleum and the Organization of Petroleum Exporting Companies. In 1974 he became President of the Energy Commission of the Venezuelan National Research Council.

JAHANGIR AMUZEGAR Law and political science degrees from the
(Iran) University of Teheran, M.A. in economics at University of Washington, Ph.D. in economics, University of California; Minister of Finance, Minister of Commerce, and then Ambassador at Large and Chief of the Iranian Economic Mission in Washington.

MAPS AND CHARTS

Canada

Chart | Energy Supply by Energy Source, 1960-1970 | **16**
Chart | Energy Supply by Region, 1960-1970 | **18**
Map | 1973 Supply & Disposition of Crude, N.G.L., and Products | **21**
Map | Supply & Disposition of Natural Gas, 1972 | **22**
Chart | Consumption by Source and Use, 1960-1970 | **23**
Chart | Consumption by Use and Region, 1960-1970 | **24**
Map | Petroleum Basins | **31**
Chart | Projected Demand for Solid Fuels, 1975-2000 | **34**
Chart | Projected Demand for Liquid Fuels, 1975-2000 | **35**
Chart | Projected Demand for Gas Fuels, 1975-2000 | **36**

China

Map | Major Crude Oil Production Centers | **85**
Map | Major Oil Shale and Natural Gas Centers | **86**
Map | Major Refining Centers | **101**
Map | Areas of Coal Deposits | **102**
Map | Seabed Areas with Oil Prospects | **111**
Map | Unilateral Claims and Concession Areas | **112**

Arab States of the Persian Gulf

Map | The Gulf Countries | **197**

Venezuela

Map | *Sedimentary Basins and "Tar Belt"* | **222-223**
Chart | *Wasted Resources of Natural Gas
   in the Traditional Basins* | **226**
Map | *La Vela Embayment Exploration* | **229**
Map | *Energy Resources other than Hydrocarbons* | **236-237**
Charts | *Production of Energy* | **248-249**
Charts | *Consumption of Energy* | **254-255**
Chart | *Conditioned Evolution of Conventional Petroleum
   Resources in the Traditional Basins* | **267**
Chart | *Conventional Crude Petroleum Production Rate;
   Curve of Conditioned Evolution—Traditional Basins* | **269**
Chart | *Conditioned Evolution of Natural Gas Resources
   in the Traditional Basins* | **271**
Chart | *Natural Gas Gross Production Rate and Curve of
   Conditioned Evolution—Traditional Basins* | **272**
Chart | *Depletion of Proved Reserves by Petroleum Gravity
   Ranges* | **275**
Map | *Submerged Venezuelan Continent* | **281**

Iran

Map | *Offshore Oil Exploitation* | **296**
Map | *Iran and Surrounding Countries* | **298**
Map | *National Power System Transmission Lines* | **355**
Map | *Iranian Gas Trunkline* | **356**

Index

Entries with italic folios are maps, charts, or tables

Abadan, 304
Abu Dhabi, 124
 low sulphur crude, 202
 National Oil Company, 193
Abu Musa, 163
Acción Democratica, 207
AEDI. *See* Iran, Atomic Energy Organizations.
Agha Jari oil field, 343
Agip Mineraria, 320
AIOC. *See* Anglo-Iranian Oil Company.
Alberta, 4
 Energy Resources Conservation Board, 10
 heavy oil, 26, 28
 Petroleum Marketing Commission, 17
 Public Utilities Board, 10
 tar sands, 28, 45
Alfonso, Dr. Perez, 145, 201
American Continental Oil Company, 322
American Independent Oil Company, 131
American Standard Oil Company, 310
Amiranian Oil Company, 310
Amuay, 277
Andean Development Corporation, 264
Andrés Pérez, Carlos, 207
Anglo-Persian Oil Company (APOC), 133, 134, 303
APOC. *See* Anglo-Persian Oil Company.

Arab oil embargo (1973), 149, 151ff, 335
 Fund for Economic and Social Development (AFESD) League, 149
 Petroleum Congress (4th), 147; (9th), 193
 Shipbuilding and Repair Yard (ASRY), 174
 states, problems of foreign workers, 199
 see also Persian Gulf
Arab-Israeli war (1956), 144, 149
Arabian-American Oil Company (Aramco), 134, 136, 137
 nationalization of, 155, 187
 negotiations, Saudi Arabia, 156
Arabian Gulf, 123
 light crude oil, 144, 188
 Oil Company, 131
Aramco. *See* Arabian-American Oil Company.
Arctic coastal plain, 30
 fold belt, 30
 stable platform, 30
Aruba, 277
 boundary with Venezuela, 279
Athabasca tar sands, 26, 37
Avalon uplift, 29
Aves swell, 231

Ba'athist, 127
Baffin Island shelf, 29
Bahrain, 124, 190ff
Baku refineries, 299
Barinas basin, 220, 278

379

Baselines, continental shelf measurement, 318
Beaufort Sea-Mackenzie Delta, 32
Bonaire, 279
Borden, Henry, 7
British Columbia, 4, 14
   energy legislation, 14
   Petroleum Corporation, 15
British North America Act, 5
British Petroleum Corporation, 316, 353
   Standard Vacuum Oil Company, 309
   thermal unit (BTU), 243
BTU. *See* British thermal unit.
Burmah Oil Company, 303

CADAFE. *See* Venezuela, state electric distribution company.
Calabozo platform, 230
Canada
   coordination of energy policy, 51
   demand for gas fuels, *36*
   demand for liquid fuels, *30*
   demand for solid fuels, *34*
   energy consumption and supply patterns, 19
   Energy Conservation, Office of, 12
   energy consumption by sectors, *23*
   energy crisis and, 3
   Energy, Mines and Resources, Department of, 9
   energy policy factors, 38
   energy prices, 40
   energy producing provinces, 4
   energy reserves, 27
   Energy Supplies Allocation Board, 11
   energy supply
      production by source, *16*
      production by province, *18*
   environmental issues, 49
   federal agencies, 11

Canada *(cont.)*
   Federal Atomic Energy Control Commission, 10
   federal jurisdiction, 5
   fiscal measures, 43
   Foreign Investment Review Act (1973), 51
   future energy demand, 13
   government framework for energy, 5
   Indian Affairs and Northern Development, Department of, 9
   movement of oil to, 54
   National Energy Board, 7
   natural gas supply and disposition, 22
   offshore drilling, 29
   ownership of energy industry, 50
   Petroleum Administration Act, 12
   petroleum basins, *31*
   provincial energy agencies, 9
   provincial energy companies, 17
   reserves of various energy sources, 26
   self-sufficiency in energy, 44
   structure of energy industry, 48
   supply of eastern provinces, 7
   supply and disposition of petroleum products, *21*
Canadian Arctic, 30
   gas, 11
Cardon, 277
Caroni river, 209, 238, 290
Caura river, 238, 268, 290
Chien Yuan-heng, 84
Chiling oil field, 73, 84, 89
China
   cabinet government organization, 109
   coal
      deposits, *102*
      production, *97*

China *(cont.)*
  data reliability, 66
  electric power output, 98
  energy demand by products, *94*
  energy history, 67, 68
  energy supply by products, *99*
  energy supply structure, *96*
  Five-Year Plan, 68
  gas and oil shale centers, *86*
  gasoline consumption, 93
  "Great Leap Forward", 69, 77
  Itu oil discovery, 73
  military demand for oil, 93
  natural gas production, *98*
  natural resources development policy, 65
  offshore oil deposits, 77
  Oil
    development facilities, *103*
    foreign estimates of, 76, 80
    imports and exports, 104, 107
    production centers, *85*
    production forecast, 64
    production of, 79, 82
    refineries location, 100
    refining capacity, 99
    Refining Centers, 101
    reserves, 75
    relations with Japan and Korea, 109
    rift with Soviet Union, 71
    Seabed boundary disputes, 79
      claims and concessions, *112*
      oil areas, *111*
    Second Peoples Congress (1963), 72
    self-reliance principle, 108, 114
    trade deficit, 108
    shale oil deposits, 77
    production, 91
Chou En-lai, 74, 79, 113
Cities Service Company, 311
Compagnie Française de Pétroles, 150
CONICIT. *See* Venezuela, National Research Council.
Consortium of international oil companies, 134
Continental Shelf Convention (1958), 317
Corporación Venezolana del Petróleo (CVP), 209, 217
Curaçao, 277
CVP. *See* Corporación Venezolana del Petróleo.

D'Arcy
  concession, 132, 304, 307, 310, 312
  William Knox, 131, 303
Dharan, 187
Dubai, 124, 193
Dutch Antiles, 277
Dzungarian Basin, 87

ENI. *See* Agip Mineraria.
Enzelli port, 299

Fahd bin Abdul Azia Amir, 189
Faisal I, 127
Falcón basin, 220, 278
Flemish Cap, 29
France, Iran agreement on atomic reactors, 348
French State Company, 322

Gass-Golshaian Agreement (1949), 312
Ghavam, Ahmad, 309
Guanoco pitch lake, 214
Guasare coal, 244, 268
Guayana Development Corporation, 209
Guyana, boundary with Venezuela, 279
Gulf Oil Canada, Ltd., 48
Guri dam and river, 209, 290

Hammadi, Sa'adoon, 179
Heilungchiang Province, 69
Hormuz, Strait of, 124
Humboldt, Baron von, 214

IGAT. *See* Iranian Gas Trunkline.
Imperial Oil Ltd., 13, 48
Inter-American Development Bank, 264
International Monetary Fund, 264
International Oil Seminar, Second (1974), 179
IOSCO. *See* Iranian Oil Service Co.
Iran
  agreement foreign oil companies (1953), 311
  American interests in, 310ff
  Atomic Energy Organization, 347, 366
  boundary questions in Persian Gulf, 318
  British adventures in, 302
  case before International Court of Justice (1951), 313
  claim to Bahrain, 191
  Consortium Agreement (1954), 314
  electric power, 339ff
  energy, future policy, 351ff
    new sources, 345ff
    production and use, 350
    sales, *359*
    sources (1962-1992), *368*
  environmental considerations, 337
  Fifth Development Plan (1973-1978), 301, 324, 351
  Fourth Development Plan (1968-1972), 328
  fuel policies, 299ff
  gas use and export (1962-1992), *360*
  generation, *342*

Iran *(cont.)*
  geothermal development, 349
  institutional arrangements for energy policy, 361
  Mossadegh government, 311
  natural gas, 341ff
  National Iranian Oil Company, 316ff, 363ff
  nationalization of Anglo-Iranian Oil Co., 316
    see also Oil
  Natural Gas Production, Utilization, Revenue, 346
    under Fifth Plan, 357
  nuclear fuels, 348
  offshore oil exploitation, *296*
    agreements, 319
    dispute with Saudi Arabia, 162
  Russian interests in, 306ff
  Oil
    disputes (1925-1933), 306ff
    independent policy after 1954, 314ff
    joint ventures, 320ff
    law of 1957, 317
    nationalization (1951), 312ff
    operating companies, 316
    Participants Ltd., 316
    posted prices and revenues, *338*
    pricing policies, 336
    production (1967-1982), 354
    production-consumption (1947-1974), *332*
    production and export policy, 326ff
    refineries, 329
    royalties, 305
  petroleum, future policy, 351ff
    history, 301ff
    see also Oil
  public power, *359*
    see also electric power
  Sale and Purchase Agreement

Iran *(cont.)*
    (1973), 325
  service contracts, 322
  supply and pricing policy, 326
  takeover of industry (1973), 323
  Seven Year Plan (1948-1955), 327
Iranian Gas Trunkline (IGAT), 344
Iranian Oil Service Company (IOSCO), 325
Iranian Oil Services, Ltd., 316
Iranian Pipeline Company, 310
Iranian Power Generation and Transmission Company (TAVANIR), 316
Iraq
  aid agreements with other countries, 178
  British mandate, 127
  industrialization of, 178
  people, land, religion, 125ff
  Petroleum Company, 151, 177
  Turkish government and, 128
Islam, advent of, 129
Israel, Arab policy toward, 175
Italy, AGIP of, 330

Japan
  oil strategy, 113
  Russian Siberian resources and, 113
  seabed oil, 110
Jiddah, 187
Jubail, 186

Kavir Khurian, 308
Khafji field, 163
Khalid, King, 128
Khalid, Abu al Sa'ud, 182
Kharg Island, 160, 318
Khoshtaria, Akakiy, 308
Khuzestan oil fields, 343, 353
Kirkuk oil field, 129, 143
  nationalization of, 150

Korea, seabed oil, 110
Kuwait
  Central Bank, 183
  Egyptian Investment Company, 183
  Financial Center SAK, 183
  Fund for Arab Economic Development, 183
  Industrial Bank, 183
  International Investment Company, 183
  investment in Daimler-Benz, 100, 200
  offshore oil, 181
  Oil Company, 199
  Oil, Gas, and Energy Corporation (KOGEC), 184
  oil reserves, 182

Labrado shelf, 29
Lagarto syncline, 230
La Vela embayment, 228, 279
Leoni dam, Raul, 290
Li Chiang, 105, 108
Li Jen-chun, 77
Liquified Petroleum Gas (LPG), 137
Lobatera, 234
Loftus, W. K., 302
Loma de Hierro, 266

Mackenzie delta, 32
  valley, 25
    pipeline, 11
Majles, 305
Maracaibo lake, 215, 242, 278
Margarita island, 230
Masjed-Sulaiman, 303
Maturín basin, 220, 231, 278, 288
mene, 213
Montreal pipeline, 46, 54
Morgan, Jacques de, 303
Mozaffaredin Shah, 303

Naricual coal, 234, 244, 268
Nassereddin Shah, 302, 308
National Iranian Gas Company (NIGC), 344
   Oil Company, 313
   Tanker Company, 353
   see also Iran
Netherlands, boundary questions with Venezuela, 279
Neutral Zone, 130, 163
   see also Persian Gulf
NIGC. *See* National Iranian Gas Company.
NIOC. *See* National Iranian Oil Company.
Nitroven, 265
Nova Scotia energy legislation, 14
   Gasoline Licensing Act, 13
   see also Canada
Nuclear fuels. *See* country or region name.

OAPEC. *See* Organization of Arab Petroleum Exporting Countries.
Offshore oil. *See* region or country name.
Oil
   posted prices, 334
   pricing, international, 140ff
   production costs, 143ff
   quotas, 140
   see also region or country name, field names, company names
Oklahoma crude oil, 133
OPEC. *See* Organization of Petroleum Exporting Countries.
Oman, 124, 195ff
Organization of Arab Petroleum Exporting Countries (OAPEC), 173ff, 180ff, 201ff

Organization of Petroleum Exporting Countries (OPEC)
   founding and formation, 144, 331
   founding fathers, 201
   negotiations with foreign companies, 333
   Quito meeting (1974), 335
   revenues from oil, 157
   Teheran Agreement (1971), 334
Orinoco petroliferous belt, 259, 266, 288, 289
   river, 235, 242, 290
Oviedo y Valdez, Gonzalo Fernández de, 213

Pahlavi port. *See* Enzelli port.
Palashkovskii project, 307
Paraguana peninsula, 277
Paria, Gulf of, 279
   peninsula, 231
Peace river, 28
Peking Petroleum College, 70
Perijá coal deposits, 234
Persia, Imperial Bank of, 302
   Bank Mining Rights Corporation, 302
Persian Gulf
   boundary disputes, 163
   concessions, oil discoveries, and production, *130*
   definition, 123
   history of oil concessions, 131
   islands in, 160
   natural gas, 164ff
   offshore boundary agreements, 161
   offshore oil, 159
   oil pricing, 135
   oil reserves, *169*
   pattern of oil royalties, 133
   physical characteristics, 159
   policies of Arab States, 178

Persian Gulf *(cont.)*
   see also names of Arab States
Petro-Can, 12
Petroleum products, conversion to energy equivalents, 244
   see also oil, natural gas, gasoline
Petromin, 154
Posted prices, 135, 144
   see also oil
Pu Hsuan, 105

Qasim, General, 150
Qatar, 124, 191ff
Qatif oil field, 138

Ras al-Khaimah, 163
Ras Tanura, 156
Reuter, Julius de, 302
Rez Shah, 305
Riyadh, 187
Rumailah, 129
Russian Siberian resources, 113
   see also Soviet Union
Russo-Persian Bank, 307

Safaniyah field, 163
Said bin Taiumr, Sultan, 195
St. Lawrence platform, 29
Sakhalin seabed oil, 113
Santo Domingo hydroelectric plant, 268
Saudi Arabia
   Aramco and, 187
   claim to offshore oil, 160
   offshore dispute with Iran, 162
   oil reserves, 185, 186
   pipeline planning, 187
   policies on oil and gas, 190
   Sa'ud family, 128
   University of Petroleum and Minerals, 187
Scotian basin, 29
Seaboard Oil Company, 310

Sharjah, 124, 163
Shatt-Al-Arab, 304
Shell Oil, 192
Shengli oil fields, 72, 74, 84, 88
Shen Kuo, 67
Shensi, 67
Shih-you, 67
Shi'ites, 127
Siberian timber, 113
SIDOR. *See* Venezuela, state steel company (SIDOR), 265
Sinclair Oil Company, 310
SIRIP. *See* Société Irano-Italienne des Pétroles, 330
Six-Day War (1967), 151
Snow, Edgar, 74
Société Irano-Italienne des Pétroles (SIRIP), 330
South China Sea, 78
Strathcona, Lord, 303
Soviet Union, oil strategy, 113
Suez Canal, closure of, 144
Sungliao basin, 69, 88
Sverdrup basin, 30
Szechwan basin, 87

Taching oil field, 69, 74, 84
Takang oil field, 72, 74, 84, 88
Tapline, 202
"tar belt", 288
Tariki, Abdullah, 143, 145, 201
Tavanir. *See* Iranian Power Generation and Transmission Co.
Teng Hsiao-ping, 105
Texas Railroad Commission, 152
Ton of petroleum equivalent (TPE), 243
TPE. *See* ton of petroleum equivalent.
Trans-Canada Pipeline Company, 42
transfer prices, 136

see also Oil
Trindad, boundary with Venezuela, 279
Trinidad-Tobago, 279
Trucial States, 127
Trudeau, P. E., 38
Truman Proclamation (1945) on offshore oil, 160
Tsaidam basin, 87
Tunb Island, 163
Tunisian oil, 154
Turkish Petroleum Company, 131, 133
Tyumen oil, 113

UAE. See United Arab Emirates.
United Arab Emirates (UAE), 124, 172, 193ff
UN Economic Commission for Asia and the Far East (ECAFE), 73
General Assembly Special Session (1974), 114
United States
Atomic Energy Commission and Iran, 348
oil quotas, 140, 328
oil reserves, 168
oil tankers change in size, 139
Uribanter river, 268

Venezuela
agricultural improvements, 266
asphalt exploitation, 214
boundary with Guyana, Trinidad, Bonaire, Aruba, 279
coal deposit exploitation, 283, 291
Congress for Science and Technology, First (1975), 293
contemporary issues, 207ff
development corporations, 290
economy, state of, 261
energy

Venezuela *(cont.)*
consumption of, *252*
electric, production and consumption, 251ff
geothermal, 239, 286
historical development, 213ff
hydro-electricity production, 239
ministries for, 208
nuclear, 240, 285
policy, means, recommendations, 259, 274ff
production of, *246*
solar, 240, 286
tidal, 242
wind, 241, 286
see also petroleum products
geological evaluation, 289
geothermal energy, 239, 286
hydraulic resources, 235ff, 284
hydrocarbon resources, new areas, 227
see also Energy
hydroelectric power, 290
see also Energy
iron deposits, Guayana, 266, 283
mining laws, early, 215
National Congress of Science and Technology, First (1975), 287, 289
National Energy Council, 209, 293
National Petrochemical Council, 265
National Research Council (CONICIT), 209
National Research Institute (IVIC), 209
natural gas, 270ff
policy, 277
regulation, 289
reserves, 225
wasted resources, *226*
new area resources, 278

Venezuela *(cont.)*
  "no concessions policy" (1948), 216
  nuclear energy, 240, 285
  oil
    early discoveries, 215
    first offshore operations, 215
    income, 263
    output, 207
    production, exports, consumption, 256
    reduction in production, 288
    royalties, 261
    see also petroleum
  petrochemicals and state steel company (SIDOR, 265)
  petroleum, consumption and exports, 256
    income, 263
    production, 256
    production reduction, 288
    reserves, 220
    royalty receipts, 261
    see also Energy *and* Oil
  shale and tar sands, 219, 280

Venezuela *(cont.)*
  state electric distribution company (CADAFE), 292
  steel company (SIDOR), 265
  Petrolia, 214
  population, 262
  Presidential Commission on Naturalization, 209
  Venezuelan Institute for Petroleum and Petrochemical Research (INVEPET), 209

Wabasca, 28
Wang, Yao-ting, 105

Yakut, 113
Yemen, People's Democratic Republic of, 195
Yenchang, 67
Yom Kippur war, 335
Yukon, 5
Yumen oil fields, 87

Zoroastrian fire-temples, 302
Zulia, 214